Early Rome and Latium

Early Rome and Latium

Economy and Society
c.1000 *to* 500 BC

Christopher John Smith

CLARENDON PRESS · OXFORD
1996

Oxford University Press, Walton Street, Oxford OX2 6DP
Oxford New York
Athens Auckland Bangkok Bombay
Calcutta Cape Town Dar es Salaam Delhi
Florence Hong Kong Istanbul Karachi
Kuala Lumpur Madras Madrid Melbourne
Mexico City Nairobi Paris Singapore
Taipei Tokyo Toronto
and associated companies in
Berlin Ibadan

Oxford is a trade mark of Oxford University Press

Published in the United States
by Oxford University Press Inc., New York

© Christopher Smith 1996

All rights reserved. No part of this publication may be reproduced, stored in a retrieval system, or transmitted, in any form or by any means, without the prior permission in writing of Oxford University Press. Within the UK, exceptions are allowed in respect of any fair dealing for the purpose of research or private study, or criticism or review, as permitted under the Copyright, Designs and Patents Act, 1988, or in the case of reprographic reproduction in accordance with the terms of the licences issued by the Copyright Licensing Agency. Enquiries concerning reproduction outside these terms and in other countries should be sent to the Rights Department, Oxford University Press, at the address above

British Library Cataloguing in Publication Data
Data available

Library of Congress Cataloging in Publication Data
Early Rome and Latium: economy and society c. 1000 to 500 BC
Christopher John Smith.
(Oxford classical monographs)
Revision of the author's thesis (D. Phil.—University of Oxford, 1992).
Includes bibliographical references.
1. Rome—History—to 510 BC 2. Lazio (Italy)—History.
3. Excavations (Archaeology)—Italy—Lazio. 4. Lazio (Italy)—
antiquities. I. Title. II. Series.
DG233.2.S63 1995   937'.601—dc20   95-22082
ISBN 0-19-815031-8

1 3 5 7 9 10 8 6 4 2

Typeset by
J&L Composition Ltd, Filey, North Yorkshire
Printed in Great Britain on acid-free paper by
Bookcraft Ltd., Midsomer Norton

ACKNOWLEDGEMENTS

This book is a revision of my D.Phil. thesis, which was submitted to the University of Oxford in 1992. In the course of writing and revising the work I have incurred a number of debts, which it is my pleasure to acknowledge here. I pursued my studies at Keble College, Oxford, and also at the British School at Rome, which I was able to visit thanks to funding from the Craven Committee, Oxford University, the British Academy, and the Hugh Last Fund of the British School itself. I am particularly grateful to Amanda Claridge and Valerie Scott of the British School at Rome for long-standing kindness and assistance. The Bryce Research Fund in History at the University of Oxford awarded me a scholarship in 1991/2 which allowed me to begin the revision of this work.

Various individuals have read and commented on my work. Dr A. W. Lintott and Dr P. S. Derow supervised my research. Professor B. W. Cunliffe, Dr M. E. Curry, Mr N. Purcell, Dr A. Sherratt, Dr S. Sherratt, Dr C. Sourvinou-Inwood, and Ms J. Toms all gave me useful advice at various stages. Dr T. J. Cornell examined my thesis and has been extremely helpful during the process of revision. Professors A. Bedini, A. M. Bietti-Sestieri, L. Quilici and S. Quilici Gigli, and J. T. Meyer all kindly gave me permission to use their work. I remain responsible for any errors.

I am also grateful for all the friends at Oxford, Rome, and more recently in St Andrews who have supported me in many different ways through the past years. The book is dedicated to my parents.

C.J.S.

St Andrews
July 1994

CONTENTS

List of Tables ix
List of Figures ix
List of Maps x
Abbreviations xi
Chronology xii
Introduction 1

PART I Rome and Latium before the Sixth Century

1 Archaeological Prolegomena 9
   Archaeological Theory and Mortuary Evidence 9
   The Economics of Grave Goods 16
   The Chronology of Latin Culture 21
2 The Late Bronze Age and Latial Period I,
   *c.*1200–900 BC 24
   Italy during the Mycenaean Period 24
   Between Bronze Age and Iron Age 29
   Models of Transition 31
   Settlement Patterns and Indications of Habitation 34
   Pottery, Metalwork, and Other Grave Goods 37
   Burial Ritual and Society 40
3 Latial Period II, *c.*900–770 BC 44
   The Transformation of Etruria 44
   Rome and the Alban Hills 49
   The Development of Sites Outside the Alban Hills 54
   Osteria dell'Osa 57
4 Latial Period III, *c.*770–730 BC 72
   Phoenician and Greek Contacts with Campania and
   Etruria 75
   Developments in Latium in Period III 77
   Rome 79
   Osteria dell'Osa 82
5 Latial Period IVA, *c.*730–630 BC 84
   The Archaeological Evidence 86
   Praeneste 93

Contents

6	Latial Period IVB, c.630–580 BC	98
7	Lines of Interpretation	106
	The Identification of Luxury Goods and their Role 106	
	Surplus Production and Subsistence Economies 114	
	The Development of Latin Society 122	

PART II Rome and Latium in the Sixth Century BC

8	Latium: The Archaeological Evidence	129
9	Etruria: The Archaeological Evidence	143
10	Rome: The Archaeological Evidence	150
	Defining the City 151	
	Temples and Sanctuaries 158	
	The Archaic Forum 166	
	The Forum Boarium 179	
	Conclusions 183	
11	Rome and Latium in the Sixth Century	185
	The Organization of Society 185	
	The Legal Organization of Rome and Latium 202	
	The Religious Organizations of Latium 215	
12	General Conclusions	224
Appendix 1. Inscriptions in Latium		233
Appendix 2. Latin Sites		239
List of References		256
Index		283

LIST OF TABLES

1. Burials of males by age and period at Osteria dell'Osa   67
2. Burials of females by age and period at Osteria dell'Osa   68

LIST OF FIGURES

1. Male burials in Period IIA at Osteria dell'Osa   68
2. Female burials in Period IIA at Osteria dell'Osa   69
3. Male burials in Period IIB at Osteria dell'Osa   69
4. Female burials in Period IIB at Osteria dell'Osa   69
5. Male burials in Period III at Osteria dell'Osa   70
6. Female burials in Period III at Osteria dell'Osa   70
7. Male burials in Period IV at Osteria dell'Osa   70
8. Female burials in Period IV at Osteria dell'Osa   71

LIST OF MAPS

1	Archaic Latium	240
2	Ardea	242
3	Lavinium	247
4	Osteria dell'Osa	248
5	Early Rome	250
6	The Roman Forum	251
7	Sixth-century Rome: temples and houses along the Via Sacra	252
8	Satricum: mid-sixth century	254

ABBREVIATIONS

AIONArchStAnt	Annali dell'Istituto Universitario Orientale Archeologia e Storia Antica
AL	*Archeologia Laziale*
Atti 1980	*La formazione della città nel Lazio, Dd'A* 2 (1980)
Atti 1989	*Secondo Congresso Internazionale Etrusco 1985* [1989] (Rome)
CAH iv (2)	*Cambridge Ancient History* vol. iv², eds. Boardman, J., Hammond, N. G. L., Lewis, D. M., Ostwald, M. (Cambridge, 1989)
CAH vii 2(2)	*Cambridge Ancient History* vol. vii.2², eds. Walbank, F. W., Astin, A. E., Frederiksen, M. W., Ogilvie, R. M., Drummond, A. (Cambridge, 1989)
CIL	Corpus Inscriptionum Latinarum
CLP	*Civiltà del Lazio Primitivo* (exhibition catalogue; Rome, 1976)
GRT	*La Grande Roma dei Tarquinii* (exhibition catalogue; Rome, 1990)
TLE	*Thesaurus Linguae Etruscae*, ed. Pallottino, M. (Rome, 1978)

CHRONOLOGY

The following date chart is an approximate guide to the standard chronology, as represented by *Atti* 1980 and *CLP*. All dates should be prefixed with ± 25 YEARS.

Latial period I	1000–900 BC
Latial period IIA	900–830 BC
Latial period IIB	830–770 BC
Latial period III	770–730 BC
Latial period IVA	730–630 BC
Latial period IVB	630–580 BC

Introduction

This book is an attempt by a historian to interpret and analyse the evidence for a particular region across a number of centuries, beginning with a period which can only be understood from its material remains and continuing into a period when the literary record possesses a degree of truth which may be discovered with caution and due scepticism.

One aspect of such a work is that it is a study of the *longue durée*. This book covers over seven centuries of human endeavour and, without wishing to underplay the contribution of individuals within the period, it is necessarily focused on the contribution of such factors as geography, trade systems, and the long-term development of society.

This approach is especially valuable when trying to describe a region. Regional history, once forbidden by the magisterial voice of Finley, has now assumed its rightful place at the centre of studies of the ancient world, laying emphasis as it does on the particularity of experience, and sometimes turning attention away from the major centres to less well-known sites. I have tried in this account to stress the contribution of the Latins outside Rome, and this provides an important counterpoint to the Romans' own self-centred approach.

The major themes of this book include the necessity of setting any particular region in its context as part of a larger system, in this case the trading network of the Mediterranean. What follows is in part an attempt to define where Latium is situated in the grand movements of the first half of the first millennium BC. It is also a case study in the emergence of one state, Rome, or better, in the development of a region to the point at which it can sustain a city-state. The consequences of that development were ultimately the rise of Rome to a position of pre-eminence in the known world, and I believe that this process can only be fully understood against the background of Rome's early history in Latium.

Although far from comprehensive, I hope I have given a working synthesis of the most important archaeological evidence from Latium, much of which has come to light over the past twenty or thirty years as part of the development of Rome and the Campagna. Few regions of Italy are so well represented in the archaeological record in terms of both mortuary and settlement evidence, and this in itself gives value to the exercise.

The book proceeds chronologically. It is divided into two parts, the second being devoted to the sixth century BC when literary evidence and archaeological remains illuminate each other to a greater extent than before, and when one can begin to see the emergence of Rome as the central site in the region. This should not be taken as reinforcing the somewhat artificial divide between prehistory and history; both disciplines require one to use all the available evidence, and the later part makes less sense if read without the long preparation which had gone before. For anyone who wishes to pursue the development of one particular site, there is an account of the major settlements with a bibliography in Appendix 2.

The distinction between prehistory and history cannot be dissociated from the question of the reliability of the written sources about Rome and Latium.[1] Cornell has shown that there is no need to be totally sceptical about the earliest accounts of Roman history, and that it is not necessary at the same time to credit the more clearly fictitious or anachronistic elements. As Wiseman recently demonstrated, the writing of history in Roman times was not a matter of providing the truth but of giving a good account, and various techniques were used to secure the desired result.[2] We may take these into account, but it remains the case that any student of the sixth century BC must be struck by the remarkable agreement in main outline between the literary accounts and the picture which archaeology has produced over the past thirty years or so. Obviously this is to some extent a circular argument, since we are apt to find in the archaeological record that which the literary accounts have encouraged us to look for, but the position is not so inescapably subjective.

[1] The debate is well represented by Cornell and Raaflaub in Raaflaub (ed.) 1986, and by Ogilvie and Drummond in *CAH* vii 2(2).
[2] Wiseman in Gill and Wiseman 1993.

Introduction 3

While I have tried not to base any arguments in Part I on the literary accounts, this is impossible and undesirable for the sixth century. For this period there is a clear and coherent account of Roman expansion (possibly exaggerated); we have names of individual kings and consuls which are not evidently fictitious, and if we accept, as we must in outline, the tradition of the foundation of the Republic, we must assume the beginning of certain institutions and practices clearly attested later (for instance, the consulship, some of the priesthoods and festivals, and some distinction between patricians and plebeians).

If we are tempted to put some faith in the records, we must explain how genuine knowledge about such an early period could be transmitted over some centuries to the first annalistic accounts in the third century BC and after. Cornell has argued that we underestimate the extent to which inscriptions may have survived from the sixth century, to be used by later writers as sources, but then lost. One good example of this is the inscription which Cato the Elder seems to quote (fr. 58P), which represents the sixth century dedication of a grove in Aricia, but which has not survived to our own time.[3]

Myths may also preserve aspects of genuine knowledge, but it is difficult to sort out truth from invention. The Romans' myths about their earliest foundation and the visit of Aeneas, for example, are likely to be as unreliable as Greek myths about the Trojan Wars; perhaps more so, since some of these Greek myths were supported by the sort of visible archaeological evidence that we find at Mycenae or in the tholos tombs, evidence which did not exist in Latium before the eighth century at the earliest. The first reference to Aeneas as founder of Rome comes from the late fifth century Greek writer Hellanicus and is dubious evidence for the self-presentation of the Romans. It is at least arguable that the myth of Aeneas was first imported to Etruria, where a large proportion of Greek and imitation Greek pottery has the iconography of Aeneas and Anchises, and came thence to Rome at a later date, possibly in the fourth century, when Rome also appropriated some of the religious connections of Lavinium.[4]

[3] Cornell 1991. On Aricia see II. 4. 3 below.
[4] Dion. Hal. 1. 72. 2 for Hellanicus; see Perret 1942, Galinsky 1969: 141 ff., Cornell 1975, Dubourdieu 1989 for lengthy treatments of Aeneas and the importance of Lavinium in the story.

4   *Introduction*

It seems impossible that one should be able to distinguish accurately between what is a genuine or 'primitive' myth and myths which are 'secondary', that is, 'the products of antiquarian industry, literary activity, a desire for impressive antecedents, a good nose for suggestive analogies and for what might pass for a credibly antique story, a talent for creating a seductive but illusory pattern of hoarily ancient authenticity, and, lastly, wide reading'.[5]

Whenever there are convergences between literary texts and archaic evidence, it is tempting to put more faith in the tradition, but, as Purcell pointed out, if the Romans did come close with some of their guesses about their past, this means simply that they were capable of the sort of deductive reasoning which Thucydides employs at the beginning of his histories, but which is not always reliable.[6]

There is some indication that, in the sixth century, records were kept which would give names of magistrates and important events of the year.[7] Others have suggested that songs may have been sung celebrating the brave exploits of ancestors, helping to preserve but also to create a past.[8] The evidence most likely to be reliable concerns laws, since the antiquity of the Twelve Tables, though not of the preceding *leges regiae*, seems acceptable; some of the laws of the kings are simply the reasoning of later historians and come to us through the credulous Dionysius of Halicarnassus.[9] For instance, Dionysius attributes to Romulus laws concerning the distinction between patricians and plebeians, the power of the *paterfamilias*, and the punishment of death for women found drunk or adulterous. Some of these provisions may well be inferred from the Twelve Tables, but Romulus himself is an invented founding father, and some of the provisions perhaps suggest a tendentious political pamphlet of a much later time[10]. Other conditions, such as the economic and social conditions of Rome and the advance of literacy, so far as we can

[5] Horsfall in Bremer and Horsfall 1987 ch. 1.   [6] Purcell 1989.
[7] Frier 1979, for an account of the Fasti and some concerns about their reliability.   [8] Zorzetti in Murray (ed.) 1990: 289–307.
[9] On the XII Tables see Watson 1975, Wieacker in *Origines* 1967: 293–362, id. 1988: 287 ff., Magdelain 1990: 1 ff.; Watson 1972 defends the authenticity of the *leges regiae* but cannot put a date to them. Wieacker 1988: 307 ff. assumes that they are a late reconstruction.
[10] Balsdon 1971 for an account of suggested political interpretations.

Introduction 5

judge, tend to indicate that such laws, if genuine, are more likely to be preserved only from the late sixth century, and thus their antiquity cannot be judged. Even the apparently archaic laws of Numa may be the product of later pontifical law, and Momigliano's sober judgement is followed here: 'we shall not therefore use these laws as evidence for the monarchic period, though in doing so we may well miss some interesting facts.'[11] Institutions and religious practices may also preserve the past, though the conservatism of the Romans can be over-rated. The problem remains that we cannot give a 'stratigraphy' of myth, as we can for material remains, and what appears to be early may actually be the deliberate invention of a later period.

All of these considerations make it difficult to be certain of anything, and this is why a serious study of the material record is of such value, for while there is much that archaeology cannot tell us, there is no richer field of discovery available to us for early Rome. We may not find answers to the questions which Livy, Dionysius, and others inspire us to ask, but we can find answers and questions which are more penetrating, valuable, and interesting than the literary record alone can provide.

[11] Momigliano in *CAH* vii (2).

PART I
Rome and Latium before the Sixth Century

I
Archaeological Prolegomena

ARCHAEOLOGICAL THEORY AND MORTUARY EVIDENCE

This introduction is an attempt to give a brief theoretical basis to an analysis of the material culture of Latium in the early first millennium. It is important to be clear about the nature of the evidence from necropoleis and why it is so predominant, and also to have some approach to the study of 'things' as statements about people.

The nature of the archaeological record in early Latium changes over time. For the second millennium BC, there are some traces of habitation in caves and fortified settlements, and route-ways for animal pasturage; gradually it becomes more possible to identify sites through ceramic scatters, which can be put into a rough series. During the Final Bronze Age, in Etruscan sites and in the Rome–Alban Hills complex, the necropolis evidence becomes crucial, and it is largely from this that conclusions have to be drawn.[1]

Burial goods are placed below ground at the moment of deposition, which affords some of them the chance of survival; by contrast, the huts which are represented in the hut-urns are transient, and can only be recognized by their post-holes, which are not datable except by a deduction from context. Furthermore, some burial areas seem to have been regarded as in some sense untouchable even after they had ceased to be used, therefore the existence of burial evidence is often a clue to the existence of a settlement otherwise represented only by a ceramic scatter, and the burial goods offer the best possibilities for seriation.

Consequently, the archaeological focus on necropolis evidence

[1] e.g. Potter 1979: 40 ff.; Barker 1981: 90 ff.

in the early phases of Latin culture is not unnatural; paradoxically, the dead are more 'visible' than the living and to an extent remained so into periods of greater prosperity. It is difficult to say whether burials were more obvious than habitations at that time, though it appears that building over a necropolis was avoided where possible, and it makes sense to regard the necropolis as a privileged part of a settlement's territory.

The necropoleis will inevitably remain important, whatever evidence about habitation new excavations bring to light, because more material is preserved in them than elsewhere. The collections of material from necropoleis allow a concentration on factual detail and chronological order (the concerns of pioneers of nineteenth-century research),[2] and the production of relative and absolute chronologies, though these can never be completely accurate.

A different impetus for the study of necropolis evidence came from the theoretical models for archaeology developed in the 1960s. The 'New Archaeology' of Clarke and Binford, among others, was deeply and directly concerned with the issue of culture. The definition of the culture of early society in Italy is most easily gleaned from burial practices and the evidence from necropoleis, which alone as yet provide sufficient material. Consequently cultures are defined by mortuary practice, and the questions that arise from this use of the evidence are central to the validity of the newer archaeological positions.

Binford addresses this most clearly. It is perhaps a product of what has been described as his positivism[3] that he demands a very close link between the nature of the mortuary practices and the social system that employed them.[4] It is important to stress, however, that mortuary evidence is not qualitatively different

[2] The central works are: Worsaae 1849; Montelius 1885–1910, 1903, 1912; Karo 1898, 1920; Pinza 1905. A summary of the issues can be found in Meyer 1983: 10 ff.
[3] Shanks and Tilley 1987: 43 f.
[4] But cf. O'Shea (1984: 7 f.), quoting Binford (1972: 235), and concluding, 'there is no statement suggesting congruence between the differentiation in the living society and mortuary treatment, nor is a simple one-to-one correspondence between types of mortuary differentiation and social organization suggested. At its most fundamental level, Binford's analysis does establish that, without necessarily specifying the nature of the link, mortuary differentiation does not vary independently of the organization of the society that produced it, but rather that the former is conditioned by the latter.'

from other forms of material evidence, either in its ambiguities or its significance. Burial evidence is simply a form of material culture, and we remain impoverished when we have no control against which to place it.

A recent book by Morris gives another slant to this question. For our purposes, Morris's most important observation is that burial can only tell us about ritual and not directly about society. In other words, we can move to statements about the way in which people approached the issues of burying their dead, but this is a separate issue from that of how the society was structured.[5]

Central to Binford's work is the concept that variability can be examined in such a way as to throw light on social practices;[6] consequently the variations in Etruscan and Latin tombs within and between sites are of crucial importance; this principle is more important to his approach than the identification of a culture. D. Clarke's *Analytical Archaeology*[7] preserves the traditional hierarchy of entities from artefact to assemblage to culture; yet the whole purpose of the book is deeply relevant to the study of necropolis evidence. Clarke believes that the move from artefact to culture is the central one in archaeological logic, and that is precisely the move which, despite all reference to Binford, is made in the use of necropolis evidence, since one's concern cannot simply be with internal social differentiation, but must also embrace variation between neighbouring but clearly distinct cultures, for instance, the Latial and the Etruscan (Villanovan) cultures. Binford's implication that Clarke's work was normative, that is, it worked by grouping things together and thus masked variability, seems unfair.[8]

Hodder[9] points out that Clarke's work, if interpreted to mean that culture as an entity need not be connected to 'entities defined in other sciences such as social anthropology', brings into question the validity of the move from archaeology as a discipline into other disciplines, a move central to Hodder's own position.[10] For Shanks and Tilley too, 'attempting to reduce archaeology to the science of the artefact would entail silence. The attributes

[5] Morris 1992.   [6] Binford 1972: 264 f.   [7] Clarke 1978.
[8] See Chapman in Clarke 1979: 124 ff., defending Clarke against Binford's criticism (Binford 1972: 330–1).   [9] Hodder 1982: 3 f.
[10] This is not so applicable to Clarke's later work, e.g. Clarke 1979: 435–43, 'Towns in the Development of Early Civilization' (originally published in 1976).

ascribed to artefacts are a product of social relations existing both in the past and in the present, amongst dead social actors and the living archaeological community.'[11] Ultimately it is the combination of these two approaches that is the most fruitful.

Since Clarke and Binford revolutionized the study of archaeology, perhaps the most significant contribution has been to cast doubt on the notion of culture as a concept as it became increasingly difficult to make a fit between a group of distinct objects and a distinct ethnic grouping. Culture becomes a key to understanding adaptation and change, and it is a particularly important feature of the areas of intense activity at the interface between people of different geographical or ethnic areas. This view is open to further careful nuances; Hodder stresses the importance of artefacts as symbols and claims that 'material culture patterning is thus a structural transformation of other aspects of life.'[12] (Hodder's views are severely criticized by Binford,[13] who accuses him of leading archaeologists directly to a position of relativism, since the translator of material culture has a free hand in its interpretation.)

The issue of culture and ethnicity is one with obvious implications for Central Italy; but Ridgway, for instance, is anxious to make plain that the terms Proto-Villanovan and Villanovan describe 'certain cultural features' concerned with artefact types and to a lesser degree geographical location, and have nothing to do with a mythical Villanovan people.[14]

Processual archaeology sets out to question the idea that change indicates invasion or immigration by focusing on processes of social and linguistic change. Such an approach contributes to an understanding of the move from incineration to inhumation, for example, and of the development of urban forms, without reference to invasion.

Hodder addresses funerary material throughout *Symbols in Action*; he is explicitly concerned with moving away from Binford's direct correlation of mortuary practice and social differentiation. His ethno-archaeological approach, however, offers little to the prehistorian who does not have the aid of detailed knowledge of social forms and daily life. Hodder's approach

[11] Shanks and Tilley 1987: 244.   [12] Hodder 1982: 210 n. 8.
[13] Binford 1983: 57 f.   [14] Ridgway 1988: 628 f.

Archaeological Prolegomena

requires evidence beyond the archaeological record; where that does not exist, attempting to understand the symbolic nature of a society and its material remains becomes so hazardous as to make statements about either practically worthless.[15]

A particularly useful recent book is O'Shea's *Mortuary Variability: An Archaeological Investigation* (1984), which studies six sites of the late eighteenth and early nineteenth centuries, inhabited by the Pawnee, Omaha, and Arikara tribes of Nebraska and South Dakota. O'Shea sets out the following principles 'as an explicit and logical foundation upon which analysis can be based':[16]

Principle 1: All societies employ some regular procedure or set of procedures for the disposal of the dead.

Principle 2: A mortuary population will exhibit demographic and physical characteristics reflecting those of the living population.

Principle 3: Within a mortuary occurrence, each interment represents the systematic application of a series of prescriptive and proscriptive directives relevant to that individual.

Corollary 3*a*: The nature of the society will pattern and circumscribe the practices for the disposal of the dead.

Corollary 3*b*: The specific treatment accorded an individual in death will be consistent with that individual's social position in life.

Principle 4: Elements combined within a burial context will have been contemporary in the living society at the time of interment (Worsaae's Law).

These principles are largely sound, but there are still some problems. Contrary to Principle 2, a sample of a burial site may not reflect the whole living community. With regard to Corollary 3*b*, we should not underestimate the desire to present an image at death which is not wholly consonant with status in life. As for Principle 4, the date of deposition of an object is not the same as its date of production, and considerable allowance for error must be made.

O'Shea makes other interesting suggestions. He is concerned with explicit study of the factors limiting recovery of the evidence as a means of improving understanding of the original situation. He gives a detailed account of the evidence from the sites and

---

[15] Hodder's approach was central to the 1986 Southampton Conference and the book (Hodder (ed.) 1989) that arose from it. [16] O'Shea 1984: 33 f.

compares the conclusions with the ethnographical accounts of the tribes. The evidence was found to be consistent, but this is obviously not a reliable indication of the value of either. O'Shea discovered that while 'vertical social distinction' (status or rank) could be recognized, 'horizontal' distinctions ('sodalities, individual descent units . . . , task groups, territorial bands and the like' [p.16]) were much harder to detect, and that the precise nuances of the social system were not recoverable from grave goods. This may not be a surprising conclusion but, given the unusual combination of archaeological and ethnographical evidence of reasonable quality, it is an important one.

To move from theoretical issues to Latium itself, although it is true that the necropoleis remain our most extensive evidence for the prehistoric society of the region, they are far from unambiguous indications of the nature of that society. It may be suggested that the early burial rituals represent a social and not an individual response to death, and that they were sufficiently flexible to incorporate and reflect the conditions of society, but it should be made clear at the outset that burial ritual may give only a distorted reflection of society.

In the absence of other significant evidence, at least for the early phases of Latial civilization, the nature of the goods deposited in graves with respect to goods not so deposited, can only be a matter of conjecture. It is important that the use of miniatures in early graves suggests that deposited goods were some sort of proxy for the actual objects. On the other hand, we cannot tell whether these were goods owned by the individual person or communal symbols. The presence of miniature weapons might be an indication of gender. It is true that early societies frequently resorted to raiding as a means of supplementing their own possessions, and it is plausible that this was so for early Latin society, but it is perhaps not to be inferred solely from the presence of miniature weapons in graves.

The classification of prestige goods from burials, to take another example, is often a circular argument; we assume a stratified society from differences in grave-finds and associate the elements of these grave-finds with prestige. Yet quality and value are not the only indices of prestige; age or newness may also give independent value to objects.

Moreover, the archaeological record is unlikely to make clear a distinction between precious objects owned by an individual or his or her family, and buried with him or her, and precious objects owned by the social group and awarded by the group to the individual in death.

We should not forget either that burials may not have been private and local affairs. Many settlements, though distinct, were very close together, like those in the Alban Hills and around Lake Castiglione, and intermarriage even further afield may have helped some burials to become great social events, involving the competitive conspicuous consumption of wealth. Displaying the wealth of a society as a whole before other settlements may have developed into the extravagant display of individual wealth before individuals of other settlements.

The focus of archaeological exploration in Central Italy (and, of course, elsewhere) has thus combined with a major theme of recent archaeological theory to perpetuate the dominance of burial evidence in the area, but the limitation of both the material record and its theoretical analysis are evident. We may now begin to look at the deposition of an object in a burial context as the last link in a chain of human activity starting at least at the point of production; it is in this way that the culture of the dead can tell us most about the activities of the living.[17]

It is clear from the archaeological evidence that the people of early Latium were concerned to find a response to death. Although it is not possible to reconstruct with certainty the nature and the significance of their ritual, it would be impossible to deny that the necropoleis show an evolving system which incorporates the development of social features in the mediation between the dead person, the world of the living, and the world of the dead. By focusing on the nature of things, that is, of the goods which are deposited in the graves, we can move towards an interpretation of a society through its burial culture. We can move from artefact through assemblage to culture; and we can use the variability of that culture as an index to status, local

[17] Other full-scale treatments of burial evidence with comparative essays in Humphreys and King (eds.) 1981; Chapman, Kinnes, and Randsborg (eds.) 1981 (esp. the opening essay by Chapman and Randsborg). Also D'Agostino 1982, 1987, and Bartoloni, Cataldi Dini, and Zevi 1982, both influential treatments of specific sites in Central Italy.

demand and taste, and eventually to the motivations for economic expansion.

It seems possible that, at the beginning of the first millennium BC in Central Italy, the funeral ritual was a social act; it was intended to reaffirm the social order at the same time as expressing grief for the deceased. In other words, leaving aside the question of how far, if at all, the funeral rite and the goods buried with the deceased reflect the conditions of the society, we may at least accept that the practice of burying artefacts must have led to a system of supply and demand, that is, a dynamic within settlements and between settlements existing from the very beginning of our period and perhaps conditioning some of its developments. This section will be a preliminary consideration of the economic aspects of the burial rite.

THE ECONOMICS OF GRAVE GOODS

Any examination of burial goods is a particularly clear instance of the need to take into account all the stages of an exchange system, that is, production, distribution, and consumption. Understanding the whole system is the only way to attain a clearer conception of the social and economic structures and processes involved.

One has to consider the difficult but perhaps not impossible task of tracing the genealogy or cultural biography of objects from their production to their consumption. Goods do not necessarily keep a constant value over time and space; as we shall see, time and space may give an object a disproportionate value compared to its intrinsic worth. Production does not hold the key to the whole system. As Chapman said, 'the deposition of goods has to be studied in relation to production and circulation, as part of a single model, and this model involves the flow of goods through time and space . . . the system will be an economic one, the main aim of which is to ensure the continuous circulation of goods, which are used to establish, reinforce and symbolize networks of social interaction.'[18]

Distribution is also a problematic concept. It has been shown that many archaeologically based distribution patterns could in

---

[18] In Boddington, Garland, and Janaway (eds.) 1987: 207. There are similar remarks in Bradley 1985.

Archaeological Prolegomena 17

fact be generated equally well by a completely random method. This does not mean that the archaeological discoveries are to be discounted, but it brings sharply into focus the extent of the limitations of archaeology, especially in early periods. We have a considerable amount of evidence for Central Italy in the prehistoric period, but even so, we have only a tiny proportion of the whole, and more seriously, our evidence does not indicate the means by which objects moved from place to place, nor the routes they took, whether direct or not. At the point of consumption, an object may well have had a different value from the one it had at the point of production; and as has been noted, the argument about an object's prestige may be circular.

Yet, with the knowledge we have now of typology and seriation in Central Italy, it is possible to describe the genealogy of some of the objects found in Latium. This is particularly true for imported goods, such as those found in the major tombs at Praeneste. Their places of origin can be identified with some accuracy. The remarkable coincidences between these assemblages and those at Caere seem to suggest that the goods entered Italy at one point, whence they were distributed, and one can make a strong argument for this being Caere, since it has the best attested port at this period, and its contacts with imported goods, as indicated by grave goods, were better than those in Latium. The precise manner of the passage from Caere to Praeneste is a further question, which can only be the subject of hypothesis. Nevertheless, it would be hard to believe that at both places, and especially at Praeneste, in a culture less exposed to foreign and exotic imports like these, their status value at the point of deposition was not high. The case of Praeneste is in some ways misleading because it is so unusual, but it is also a very clear instance of what one would like to be able to do with other less clear-cut examples.

It is also interesting to note, though this is a large generalization, that whenever local production catches up with imported models, something else is brought in as a foreign model to be imitated in its turn. The arrival of bucchero ware from Etruria in the seventh century adds a new element to assemblages of local ceramic impasto; local bucchero production begins in the late seventh and sixth centuries, and the new element is Greek pottery. The same processes can be seen at an earlier and a later date, and this indicates that local demand may have been a very important factor in the equation.

It is not only objects which can be imported; the widespread imitation of different pottery types and decorations indicates a further aspect. The development of Latin pottery tends to show steadily increasing confidence, which may tell us something about the development of the status of pottery, or perhaps even of the potter. Slight variations in style within Latium may indeed indicate local production and distribution. It seems unlikely that we could overestimate the complexity of the patterns of interaction at work through the phases of Latin civilization.

An optimistic statement of these issues was made by Hodder,[19] who recommends 'an approach which examines how traded items are involved in internally generated strategies within societies, and which examines how the items are given a local meaning, incorporated via local conceptual schemes into strategies and intents', but unfortunately it is unlikely that we have sufficient evidence to establish conclusions in more than a couple of instances in Central Italy. Nevertheless it is useful to bear in mind the focus on the recipients and their perception and use of objects.

The whole subject of things has been the focus of much interesting anthropological work. Appaduri has some important definitions. He says that 'the commodity situation in the social life of any "thing" [can] be defined as the situation in which its exchangeability (past, present or future) for some other thing is its socially relevant feature', so that at the production and distribution phases, value, the source of which is in exchange, is most important. This also holds true for the consumption stage, unless this involves deposition in a grave, in which case, as Chapman for instance pointed out, the object is removed from circulation. For Appaduri demand, and hence consumption, is 'an aspect of the overall political economy of societies' (which holds even for early societies like Iron Age Latium, if the term 'political' is understood as broadly as was intended), and it is 'a function of a variety of social practices and classifications, rather than a mysterious emanation of human needs, a mechanical response to social manipulation . . . or the narrowing down of a

[19] Hodder 1982: 202 f.

universal and voracious desire for objects to whatever happens to be available'. Demand is thus a focus for the sending and receiving of social messages, and 'luxuries' are 'goods whose principal use is *rhetorical* and *social*, goods that are simply *incarnated signs*' (author's emphasis).[20] As Kopytoff indicates in the same volume, culture is a way of keeping things 'singular' and even 'sacred', and can be contrasted with what he calls 'commoditization', which is the process of making each thing exchangeable for more other things, and making more different things more widely exchangeable. Public and private schemes of valuation, commoditization, and singularization can coexist. These are important considerations for an understanding of the value of imported Greek pottery, and perhaps for miniaturized goods, which tend to be found in burials and votive deposits, and would be of little use in other contexts. Moreover, at the point when burials give way to public building, the value of goods when deposited in graves presumably dropped, which may be of interest if one could surmise that imported Greek pottery, for instance, and imitations of it were becoming more widely available.[21]

In a similar vein, Douglas wrote that 'goods are neutral, their uses are social; they can be used as fences or bridges', and 'the essential function of consumption is its capacity to make sense . . . commodities are good for thinking . . . a nonverbal medium for the human creative faculty.' A last quotation ties together the aspect of the rationality of burial deposition for the individual and the political importance of the act with regard to the society: 'The rational individual must interpret his universe as intelligible, and he needs the services of other people to affirm and stabilize its intelligibility. Goods are a medium for eliciting that consensus.'[22]

The true currency of pre-market societies is often said to be prestige (though prestige is a common concern even in modern capitalist societies); but the means by which exchange systems can create prestige and impose obligations are numerous. The necropoleis themselves, by their position and by the fact that

---

[20] Appaduri in Appaduri (ed.) 1986; quotes at 13, 29, 38. Chapman in Appaduri (ed.) n. 1. [21] Kopytoff in Appaduri (ed.) 1986: 64–91.
[22] Douglas and Isherwood 1979; quotes at 12, 62, 81.

many were spared from being built over in later times, may have conferred a certain prestige on the goods that were chosen to be used at the funeral; clearly many held an important symbolic value as areas closely tied to the settlement but yet distinct from it. From the eighth century the practice of burying babies and children underneath houses rather than in the necropolis as before may be an indication of a selectiveness with regard to those who were entitled to a place, but this is mere conjecture, and we cannot definitely say if this was the beginning of a change in the membership of reserved necropoleis, or if the situation had always been the same; this issue is further discussed in the following chapters.[23]

Objects may also have specific value by association with a certain social rank. It is not necessarily the case that an object is a premonetal form of currency, exchangeable with other objects of a different nature; it is also possible that certain prestigious objects may only be exchanged with similar ones, thus forming closed social classes from settlements which operate in the same system, and this may lead to the upper classes having geographical and limited social mobility.

Geographical distance may also give value to objects, especially if it is obvious. Having links with far-off exotic places is itself prestigious, a factor which had a part to play throughout Rome's history; conquering the furthest reaches of the known world was a sure path to importance at Rome. These links are best shown in the extraordinary and quite unique collection of exotic memorabilia to be found in the great tombs at Praeneste.

Having links with far-off places is perhaps an aspect of another point, that one can exercise power through knowing what other people do not know. One wonders what early stories were brought into Central Italy by the eastern traders who frequented the coast from the eighth century on. Their merchandise may have had an air of the spiritual about it, like something from a mythical past, a spiritual homeland, or even from a place of the dead or the gods.

---

[23] On this subject, the treatment of the Attic evidence by Morris (1987) is very important but has met with some opposition. The evidence in Attica appears to show fluctuations in the numbers of graves that are not attributable solely to population changes. There are damaging criticisms of Morris's approach in Humphreys (1990); cf. ead. 1983 for a number of important essays.

Archaeological Prolegomena

In this context we may note the Homeric lines and scenes on pottery and other artefacts at Pithecusa.

Even where, as in the Tomba Bernardini at Praeneste, the intrinsic value of the objects is so evident that it cannot be ignored, the strategy of deposition may be of at least as much importance as the objects themselves. We have very little understanding of the rules of property in prehistoric Latium, of whether goods could be inherited, or whether their associations with the dead person had to be extinguished to permit his or her easy transition into death, either by deposition of the actual items or by proxy.

Some goods may have been deposited as a means of keeping down their frequency in the society of the living, for an object loses its prestige value if it becomes common. In the context of competitive display, the cycle may become self-destructive, a sort of potlatch. It is interesting therefore that after the major late seventh-century tombs at Praeneste, expenditure moves towards the community, where it might be of greater communal value, and might provide a more permanent reminder of a wealthy person's prestige.

THE CHRONOLOGY OF LATIN CULTURE

If the issues of intention and the relationship between the culture of the living and the culture of the dead are fraught with difficulty, the use of even so large a body of evidence as we have from Latin and Etruscan tombs for the establishment of chronologies is no more straightforward.

As was stated above, early scholars like Worsaae and Montelius saw the possibilities inherent in seriated groups of material, and since then, numerous attempts have been made in this direction. A consensus has been reached for the Latin material, represented by Colonna 1974, *CLP* 1976, and *Atti* 1980.

This consensus represents a careful and cautious advance on the independent but largely compatible systems of Müller-Karpe and Peroni, but it has recently been challenged by Meyer.[24] The value of his work rests perhaps in the indication of how arbitrary the system is; absolute chronology, when given, is based largely

---

[24] Müller-Karpe 1959*a*, 1959*b*; Meyer 1983.

on the association of local objects with Greek or Eastern objects, but the Greek chronology is not firm, and the effects of the cultural lag of types of object or of whole areas cannot be quantified. At best, anachronisms and local differences may be ironed out, but it is also possible that they may be exaggerated.

The position is not hopeless, however; the work of Gjerstad and Gierow,[25] besides demonstrating that early pottery is not susceptible to very fine criteria of art-historical judgement, also led to a lengthy and concentrated effort to set the chronological framework more accurately, so that the present consensus is methodologically quite sophisticated.

Essentially, the chronology most commonly used is roughly fixed at its lower points, from the late eighth century on, by objects like an Egyptian scarab, or imported Greek pottery, or imitations thereof, objects, in other words, whose date we believe we know. Earlier phases are reconstructed occasionally with the help of stratigraphy, and otherwise in the belief that artistic techniques improve over time. The division into phases is based on criteria such as the evident improvement of pottery and metalwork, or a shift from inhumation to incineration. Phase I coincides with Proto-Villanovan culture in Etruria; the beginning of Phase II is roughly tied to the beginning of Villanovan culture. The length of these periods is arbitrarily fixed to a large degree; Colonna prefaced all his dates with $\pm$ 25 years, which would allow for Meyer's objection that Phase II is too long and Phase III too short. Moreover, the work of Meyer and Toms[26] among others has shown the possibilities for effective relative chronologies, but the margin of error in both relative and absolute chronologies must remain high for the reasons indicated above.

Recent attempts have been made to challenge this system more fundamentally. At the lower end, Francis and Vickers have suggested that our dates for Greek pottery and buildings are too high.[27] The implications for Latin chronology are limited precisely because we have no way of telling how much time elapsed between a Greek pot leaving its place of origin and being deposited in a Latin grave or temple.

[25] Gierow 1964–6; Gjerstad 1953–73.   [26] Toms 1986.
[27] Francis (1990) gives arguments and bibliography; R. M. Cook (1989) is a response in favour of the orthodoxy.

Archaeological Prolegomena

These remarks have been intended to present the problems posed by the evidence as a whole and to act as a sort of caveat. The following account endeavours to observe the chronological framework as far as possible, and to offer more detailed treatments of specific necropoleis.

2
The Late Bronze Age and Latial Period I, c.1200–900 BC

To understand how Italian society developed in the various regions, it is essential to gain some perspective on the complex and far-flung pattern on trade and exchange throughout the Mediterranean: the necessity of beginning with the Mycenaean influence in order to understand later periods is stressed by Macnamara (1984; 421). It can be seen that the vigorous activity in the late Mycenaean period, though not necessarily all conducted by Mycenaean Greeks, had a most significant effect on southern Italy and Sicily. The central region of Italy, on the other hand, experienced the trade currents and external influences of the Late Bronze and Early Iron Age in varying degrees. Throughout the first half of the first millennium, for instance, Etruscan settlements were much more open to and affected by external influences than Latin settlements, but sites like Tarquinia and Caere lagged behind sites in southern Italy and the Po valley in the Late Bronze Age. The involvement of central Italy and of Latium in the Late Bronze Age was, as far as we can see, minimal. It was the changes in the south that had an impact on Etruscan society in the tenth century, and this development north of the Tiber was to affect the Latins in later periods. Only by going back to this early period can we assess the place of Latin culture in central Italy and the Mediterranean as a whole.

ITALY DURING THE MYCENAEAN PERIOD

At the period of the maximum expansion of Mycenaean influence in the fourteenth to thirteenth centuries BC, there are indications that parts of Italy and Sardinia were being explored and exploited, largely for raw materials. Some Mycenaean objects have been found in Italy, as in many places in Europe, but it is

The Late Bronze Age and Latial Period I 25

important not to over-stress the Mycenaean Greek element of this exchange; other peoples, the Cypriots for instance, may also have contributed much.[1] The archaeological evidence for the Mycenaean expansion into Europe has caused much controversy. It is difficult to distinguish between a Mycenaean import, a form that copies a Mycenaean prototype and a form that belongs to a European koine in which Mycenaean civilization participated but which it did not dominate. All three types of explanation might coexist, which leaves the methods by which the knowledge of types of artefact circulated at this period practically unattainable.

If the material found in Italy is sorted chronologically, and if the significance of the finds is not over-estimated, the evidence can appear undramatic, and some connections become very tenuous. Müller-Karpe[2] indicated the parallels between Aegean and European hut-urn forms, but the Aegean prototypes predate the European ones by some two hundred years.[3] Contacts with Sardinia and the Po valley are perhaps strongest in the twelfth century BC, at the very end of the Mycenaean civilization.

Yet there is every reason to believe that intrepid sailors ventured far from their homes in the late Bronze Age. Shipwrecks containing Bronze Age material have been found in a number of Mediterranean areas.[4] Mycenaean pottery has been found in considerable quantities in Cyprus, and also Anatolia, Egypt, and the Levant, often accompanied by Cypriot pottery, which would suggest that the islanders acted as intermediaries.[5] Sardinia also shows significant amounts of Mycenaean pottery, and it

---

[1] General accounts of the Mycenaean world are given by Stubbings, *CAH* ii (2), ch. 22a, 27; Hooker 1976, Treuil *et al.* 1989. See also contributions to Foxhall and Davies 1984. For Mycenaean contacts with the rest of Europe, see Harding 1984; Bouzek 1985; Musti in Acquaro *et al.* 1988: 21 ff., 113 ff.; Marazzi, Tusa, and Vagnetti (eds.) 1986; Smith 1987. On Cyprus, see below n. 21.

[2] Müller-Karpe 1959*a*, 1959*b*.

[3] See Bartoloni *et al.* 1987: 207 ff. for the typological similarities and the chronological gap.

[4] The Cape Gelidonyia shipwreck is discussed below; see Harding 1984: 62 nn. 21–3 for further discoveries. See also Buchholz in Heltzer and Lipiński (eds) 1988: 187–228 for references to the shipwreck at Ulu Burun (Kas). Another wreck has been reported at Haifa; see Purcell in Murray and Price (eds.) 1990, 54 n. 36, 37. This article is of general relevance to the subject. See Åström 1986 for a contemporary harbour.

[5] Harding 1984: 230; cf. Boardman 1980: 23 f.

has been suggested that the *nuraghi* characteristic of Sardinian culture in the late Bronze Age may have some connection with the Mycenaean palatial systems and their methods of monumental building; this must remain a hypothesis.[6]

For Sardinia the most significant evidence is that of copper ingots in a characteristic ox-hide shape which, according to recent scientific analysis, may have originated in Cyprus, despite Sardinia's own rich metal resources; the suggestion has been made that Sardinian tin attracted traders.[7] The connection with Sardinia ought not to be forgotten; the island enters history again in the sixth century with the take-over by Carthaginians, but its role in the Mediterranean metal trade may have remained steady.

Toward the end of the thirteenth century, there are parallel developments of bronze types in a number of European sites, in fibulae and in swords and axes, with particularly strong connections between Greece and northern Italy (Peschiera), dated to Late Helladic IIIB–C, that is, towards the end of the thirteenth century. Here it is especially difficult to prove Mycenaean priority; it is more significant to note that the Aegean, Italy, and the Urnfield culture of Central Europe are all connected through the Adriatic, across which bronze artefacts, amber, and pottery were exchanged between the three.[8]

The case of Frattesina in the Po valley is particularly interesting. Around 1200 there seems to have developed some kind of industrial centre, for although we have no Mycenaean pottery, and indeed the date is very late for Mycenaean Greek influence, we find elaborate bronze, ivory, bone, amber and glass ware, and even ostrich eggs. Some of these raw materials must have been brought in from outside, and perhaps some of the techniques. Although Frattesina is at the moment unique in Italy, similar sites may have existed along the Po valley. The astonishingly large size of Frattesina (around nine hectares) is an indicator of how advanced this area seems to have been.[9]

[6] Harding 1984: 49 ff. There are a number of publications on Sardinia; see Ferrarese Ceruti, 'La Sardegna e il mondo Miceneo' in Barreca *et al.* (eds.) 1985: 245–54; Lo Schiavo 1985; Balmuth (ed.) 1987; Gras 1985: 43–97.
[7] Gale and Stos-Gale 1987; cf. Ridgway 1991 urging caution.
[8] Harding 1984: 258 ff.
[9] On Frattesina, see the articles collected in *Padusa*, 20, 1984, esp. Bietti-Sestieri, 413–27, and Negroni Catacchio, 515–28 for the slight contacts between Frattesina and Etruria.

The Late Bronze Age and Latial Period I

Finally we should consider the fragments of Mycenaean artefacts found in Central Italy.[10] The extremely poor nature of the evidence may be due in part to the circumstances of archaeological research; the only fragments come from excavations rather than surveys, and there are no fragments at all from Latium. Nevertheless, this poverty may still be indicative. The evidence for Central Italy amounts to one pottery sherd each at San Giovenale and Monte Rovello, and five at Luni sul Mignone. The sherds are of poor quality and difficult to date, and since it has been suggested that Mycenaean pottery was being imitated in the south of Italy from as early as the fourteenth century, we cannot be sure of its provenance. There is a hoard of bronzes of Cypriot origin at Piediluco in south Umbria; the objects date from the twelfth century approximately, but they are not of uniform antiquity and were deposited in the tenth century, so they may have been used and broken elsewhere. There are also two fragments of *lastra fittile*, or worked stone, apparently bearing Phoenician letters and dated to the fourteenth century, which have been found at Campo di S. Susanna near Rieti in the Sabina.[11]

Not discouraged by the exiguous material remains, Peruzzi[12] has attempted to prove the extent of the Mycenaean presence in Rome and Central Italy by the examination of the alleged Arcadian settlement on the Palatine and by tracing Mycenaean roots in Latin words concerning weapons, buildings, textiles, agriculture, and religion. The etymological approach seems too fraught with uncertainty to justify a position so completely unsupported by archaeology.[13]

Harding concludes his book with the words 'I have tried to make it clear . . . that I regard the important question as being not: "Were there Mycenaeans in Europe?" but: "What was the significance of the export of Mycenaean material to Europe, in social, economic and technical terms?"'[14] For Central Italy the

[10] See Vagnetti's appendix to Peruzzi 1980; *Enea nel Lazio* 1981: 87 ff., esp. 107.
[11] e.g. *Atti Taranto* 1982: 30 for copies of Mycenaean pottery; Garbini 1985. See also Bietti-Sestieri 1985B. [12] Peruzzi 1980.
[13] Poucet 1985; 74–7, 128–32; Barber 1991: 263 f. has a similar list of words shared between Latin and (Mycenaean?) Greek, but has suggested that there may be a common ground of borrowing for both cultures.
[14] Harding 1984: 288.

issue of a Mycenaean presence hardly arises, but the more important questions are how any material reached Central Italy at all, and what was the effect of the decline of Mycenaean civilization on the area in the later twelfth century. Undoubtedly, the Cypriot–Sardinian connection is crucially important, and it is illuminated by the cargo ship which sank off Cape Gelidonyia, laden with copper ingots and scrap, on its way from the east Mediterranean to the Aegean in around 1200 BC.[15] The material weighed about a tonne,[16] and included 257 miscellaneous bronze objects from a number of areas. The movement of metal around the Mediterranean is clearly of importance at this early period, and Sardinia was probably a recognized source of copper and tin. Other significant items were amber, which would have been imported from the Baltic to Greece, and faience, which was widely distributed throughout Europe and Britain from the early Bronze Age, though it may have been the technique rather than the material which was the object of exchange.[17]

It is probable that the traders' natural routes passed through southern Italy and Sicily, where the density of Mycenaean influence is consistently greater than in Central Italy,[18] and it is possible that the spread of Mycenaean goods (or imitations) into the latter area may have been the result of local networks of exchange.[19] When the Mycenaean civilization went into decline, the systems in which it had participated did not. The Cypriots may have preserved the continuity,[20] assuming that they had not made the most significant contribution in the first place.[21] It has

[15] Bass 1967.
[16] This weight is strikingly similar to the total weight of bronze allocated to individual smiths in the Pylos administrative territory and recorded in the Jn series of Linear B tablets, as though this were a typical cargo. See Harding 1984: 48 with refs.
[17] Amber: see Harding 1984: 68 ff., 58–60 on its Baltic origins. Faience: id. 87 ff.
[18] Vagnetti (ed.) 1982; Whitehouse 1973, which suggests that the Mycenaeans may have stimulated urban development in southern Italy.
[19] See Marazzi, Tusa 1979 for models of exchange networks.
[20] Gras 1985: 98–111; cf. French in Marazzi, Tusa and Vagnetti (eds.) 1986: 277–82: 'this is the world of the much maligned Peoples of the Sea' (at 282).
[21] The bibliography for Cyprus is enormous. Relevant works include Lynn Holmes in Robertson (ed.) 1975; Karageorghis (ed.) 1986; Peltenburg (ed.) 1989; Tatton-Brown (ed.) 1989; V. Cook 1988; Karageorghis (ed.) 1989; Knapp 1990. See also Lo Schiavo, Macnamara, and Vagnetti 1985 (30–5, 71 for bronze handles on pots at Terni c.900 BC).

even been suggested that the fall of the palaces may have encouraged bronze-workers to adopt greater mobility, autonomy, and initiative in their search for raw materials and new outlets for their products. Some of these bronze-workers may have come westwards from Greece, others perhaps from Cyprus.[22]

It is striking that where external trade affected Italy most, there seem to have been economic and organizational changes, which are to be associated with a more developed luxury economy, itself an aspect of greater incorporation into long-distance trading networks. The development of Frattesina is a particularly noticeable example of this, but in southern Italy and Sicily, many of the sites which show Mycenaean pottery at roughly the same time undergo some sort of change in their settlement pattern, towards a sort of proto-urban system.[23]

It is essential to note that neither the inhabitants of Latium (where Mycenaean goods have yet to be found in any quantity) nor of Etruria (where the finds are exiguous) made this social development in the late second millennium. The significant change in Etruscan settlement patterns came around 900, and cannot therefore be associated with the Mycenaean period of expansion.

BETWEEN BRONZE AGE AND IRON AGE

Despite the endeavours of many brilliant scholars, the end of the second and the beginning of the first millennium BC in Central Italy remains a confusing time.[24] This is partly a result of the coexistence of a number of conflicting modern definitions, but only in part, because behind the rival nomenclatures lie a number of very difficult problems concerning the nature of cultural identity, the motive forces of cultural change, and the circumstances of cultural differentiation.

The term 'Villanovan' was used by Gozzadini for his discoveries at a cemetery near Bologna, and originates in the name of his personal estate in the neighbouring *comune*. Thus, it described the archaeological culture of one area, and this, as Ridgway puts

---

[22] Vagnetti 1983 at 181.
[23] Marazzi, Tusa, and Vagnetti (eds.) 1986: 13–17 (Puglia), 27–35 (Basilicata), 55–67 (Broglio di Trebisacce) for southern Italy; 93–100 with Holloway 1991: 34 ff. for Sicily.   [24] For a general synthesis see Bietti-Sestieri 1973.

it, 'is not a racial group, nor a historical tribe, nor a linguistic unit, it is simply an archaeological culture'.[25] In other words, we should avoid the concept of a 'Villanovan people' or of 'the Villanovans'; within a relatively uniform material culture there may in fact have been a number of different racial groups or a number of different dialects and we are not entitled without better evidence to proceed from the identification of a series of choices concerning the shape and decoration of pottery and metalwork to a claim about the uniformity of the people who produced them.

The term 'Proto-Villanovan' was coined by Patroni in 1937, again in order 'to describe certain cultural features, characteristic of a late stage in the Italian Bronze Age, in such a way as to stress not only their dissimilarity from what had gone before but also their status as a source of what was yet to come in the Villanovan culture of the Iron Age'.[26] Chronologically, the Proto-Villanovan culture relates to the Final Bronze period and Latial Period I; the Villanovan culture begins at the same time as Latial Period IIA, and is thought of as the start of the Iron Age.[27]

The examination of old and new material has blurred lines and distinctions; there is a much clearer continuity evident now between Proto-Villanovan and Villanovan in Etruria, and perhaps an increasing sense of the difference in Latium between the Alban Hills and other sites.[28] The pattern is complex, and the distinction between Bronze and Iron Age particularly misleading, since the actual predominance of iron is much later than its introduction and the metal characterizes periods neither by its presence nor by its use. Bronze remains more common than iron; before the latter became commonly used, a technology had to be developed to add carbon to the ore to give hardness. The iron must be heated in a charcoal furnace and then tempered to prevent brittleness. To ensure that the carbon has an effect at relatively low temperatures, it is necessary to work by laminating strips of metal (as can in fact be seen with some early weapons), and since these are not techniques used by bronze-workers, iron-

[25] Ridgway 1988: 640 f.; the quotation, which I have borrowed from this account, is from Clarke 1968: 12.   [26] Ridgway 1988: 628.
[27] Peroni 1988: 37.
[28] Bietti-Sestieri and Bergonzi in Peroni (ed.) 1980: 399–423 at 403.

working cannot have been easily introduced.[29] The rise of specialized workers of either metal, however, is bound to have an effect upon society. It is clear that bronze was used quite widely in the Late Bronze Age and well into the Iron Age, but before 1000 the evidence is not from graves but from hoards. It is only with the later extensive grave deposits that a broad distribution of ornaments and weapons is found in Etruria and Latium. It might be objected that this represents a change in the evidence rather than a change in the use of metal, but one could also argue that the societies had to possess sufficient bronze ware in order to make individual depositions a rational strategy, as well as being concerned in using personal wealth in the context of burial. The expansion of the bronze industry, which presumably centred on the Tolfa-Allumiere group and on Elba, where bronze and later iron goods have been found concurrently with the mainland trends,[30] is still based on local demands and conditions, but by the end of the Proto-Villanovan period this expansion was affecting the nature of society.

MODELS OF TRANSITION

In crude terms, the Final Bronze Age in Etruria and Latium succeeds the period discussed above, the period of the Mycenaean empire and the remarkable metallurgical koine which appears to have existed across large parts of Europe. Even in this period of cultural community, it is sometimes possible to recognize local variations on a general theme,[31] but it is largely true that regional characteristics are a feature of post-Mycenaean times. As has been suggested, to suppose the existence of a dominant Mycenaean cultural identity would be to misunderstand the nature of Middle Bronze Age society at a fundamental level, so the developments of the Final Bronze Age must be related to the demise of the Mycenaean empire in a different

[29] See Wertime and Muhly (eds.)1980, especially articles by Muhly, Waldbaum, and Snodgrass. Morgan 1990: 197 f. claims for Greece that metal was not commonly used in everyday life, but largely directly towards graves and sanctuaries.

[30] Bietti-Sestieri 1981, 1985B; Warden 1973.

[31] Bietti-Sestieri 1976/7: 204 n. 5 refers to an Italian axe in Germany in the 13th or 12th century.

way. A number of syntheses of the material have been offered, frequently with the intention of presenting a model for the dynamics of change in the Final Bronze and early Iron Age. Such endeavours have set a clear agenda for analysis of the archaeological material, particularly with regard to settlement size and patterns.

Peroni's standard article[32] is both more and less than a synthesis of the material; less, because it has been overtaken by more recent discoveries and gives no space to the Latin experience of the Final Bronze Age, and more because it is a model of the development of regional activity. Peroni describes seven interdependent features. There is a substantial increase in the number of archaeologically relevant sites in the thirteenth century in Italy, which is sustained and must represent a demographic expansion. From this factor, and from the evidence of new tools, such as stronger ploughs, horse-carts, bronze sickles and axes, possibly connected with deforestation, we can deduce a strengthening of the agricultural economy, both through arable agriculture prevailing over pastoralism, and, with new techniques, through the adoption of more intensive and stable forms of agriculture. Technological progress and the quantitative increase in bronze metallurgy is both cause and effect in agricultural development and is only explicable in terms of population rise. This latter factor implies that, in the later Bronze Age, sites should be larger (with three-figure instead of two-figure populations, Peroni suggests) and last longer. On this last point, although there does appear to be a genuine increase in the size of sites, which can be judged from settlement patterns and survey work, any population figures are bound to be hypothetical.

Peroni goes on to discuss the effects on the social structures of communities. For the Middle Bronze Age he posits patriarchal clans, for the Recent Bronze Age 'communities functioning in terms of family units that are economically, socially and juridically autonomous', and contrasts 'groups of a few dozen burials dominated by a few more important and richer depositions, almost always of males (in which we can reasonably recognize the chiefs of each clan, generation by generation)' with the large, generally undifferentiated and almost egalitarian communities of

[32] Peroni 1979c.

the 'Urnfields'. Yet at the same time, population growth and a wider diffusion of metallurgical forms from a specializing and stable artisan class bring strengthened markets, an increased acquisitive power, and the accumulation of reserves of wealth, either in agricultural forms which we cannot recover, or in the metallic hoards which occasionally we do find.

Peroni[33] has reformulated his position with specific reference to the Proto-Villanovan culture and the growth of major centres of settlement in Etruria, a process not paralleled in Latium.[34] For Peroni, in this article, the crucial issue is the nature of the ownership of the land, and specifically the move from collective ownership with produce redistributed according to a gentilitial hierarchy, to private possession of land and the means of production, rapidly and inevitably leading to a class structure and a new gentilitial system.

In the meantime, A. M. Bietti-Sestieri had produced an important response to Peroni's first article,[35] in which she argued that the late Bronze Age economy in Italy should be understood very much at the level of interaction of local centres, of individual and communal reciprocity and the economy of gift-giving.

In my opinion, the value of these articles lies in the models they offer outside their chronological contexts. Peroni's first article describes a kind of society which in Latium would be represented by settlements in Periods I and II, while his second article seems to me to offer valuable insights into the changes taking place in Period III, the Orientalizing period, and possibly later as well. It is very important to take the models together, since there is a problem in Peroni's description of an apparently undifferentiated, 'egalitarian' society (or a society in equilibrium, in the formulation of Bietti-Sestieri and Bergonzi)[36] and the accumulation of reserves of wealth. The first kind of gentilitial

[33] Negroni Catacchio and Peroni in Peroni (ed.) 1980: 27–46. Rittatore Vonwiller's own article 'La Cultura Protovillanoviana' in *PCIA*, iv, 1975: 11–41 was not so far-reaching; it was accompanied by detailed archaeological details of metal hoards by M.A. Fugazzola Delpino (43–9) and an extensive bibliography (51–60).
[34] Ridgway 1988: 640 f. gives a brief account of this phenomenon, stressing aspects of continuity.
[35] Bietti-Sestieri 1976/7. For Rome and the Alban Hills see 234 f. The account of Latial Period I in *Atti* 1980 is clearly based on this.
[36] *Atti* 1980: 64. This is perhaps a better formulation since we have no evidence for the equality of the sexes.

society outlined by Peroni would permit wealth distinctions not necessarily threatening the equilibrium of the community, but it would also suffer from the inherent danger of the region as a whole becoming open to a significantly larger influx of material wealth and opportunity for prestige, or settlements growing in size to make the previous communal system unworkable, or both.[37]

SETTLEMENT PATTERNS AND INDICATIONS OF HABITATION

Some time in the Late Bronze Age there seems to have been a change in the settlement pattern in Latium; sites had previously been chosen for their advantages with regard to natural features of the landscape, such as proximity to rivers and natural resources, but then settlers moved to sites which could be defended. This may indicate the beginnings of raiding and looting as significant activities for the Latins and possibly the people of the Sabina, but we cannot be sure.[38] This marauding might indicate the increased conspicuous availability of goods such as jewellery and weaponry, as we find in the graves of this period; conversely, the deposition of weapons in graves may reflect this activity.

A number of the sites which were established at this time continued in existence into much later periods. Rome, Lavinium (Pratica di Mare), Colle della Mola near Doganella di Rocca Priora, and the Polesini caves at Tivoli have all produced Middle Bronze Age material. Sub-Apennine pottery has been found at Ostia, Ardea, Colle S. Magno (Frosinone) and Osteria del Curato (Rome); later Bronze Age pottery at Colle Ripoli and Monte S. Angelo in Arcese; and later Bronze Age bronze objects at Rome, Palestrina, Tivoli, and Ardea.[39]

Many other sites in Latium continue through the Latial peri-

[37] The model of an influx of wealth disrupting a society and forcing it to adapt is used in Betteridge 1989 to explain aspects of the process of urbanization in the 6th century.
[38] The evidence for this move is given by Pacciarelli 1979; it was confirmed by M. Angle and R. Dottarelli in a paper delivered to the 4th Conference on Italian Archaeology in January 1990. A similar preference can be seen in Etruria at the same time; cf. Domenico and Miari's paper at the same conference (Domenico and Miari 1991). Bietti-Sestieri and Bergonzi (*Atti* 1980: 50) preferred to stress the continuing importance of natural resources. [39] *Atti* 1980: 48 with refs.

The Late Bronze Age and Latial Period I   35

ods, and this makes the settlement pattern of Latium different from that of Etruria after the beginning of Latial Phase IIA. The inhabitants of Latium occupied a large number of sites scattered across the region with a loose internal structure, whereas the settlers in Etruria were concentrated in a much smaller number of more densely populated sites.[40]

The general pattern of settlement in the Alban Hills seems to be a number of communities with associated necropoleis a few hundred metres from each other.[41] The necropoleis and settlement traces in the Forum (Temple of Antoninus and Faustina, Arch of Augustus, Regia, Forum of Augustus) and Palatine (House of Livia) seem to show an analogous pattern.[42]

The size of the communities can only be estimated; at Villa Cavaletti between forty and fifty tombs were found for Latial Periods I and IIA; at Osteria dell'Osa, seventeen incinerations were found, to which could be added perhaps a dozen other tombs from Period I. About twenty tombs from Period I were found near the temple of Antoninus and Faustina in the Forum at Rome, and about ten from the same date at Pratica di Mare. These are the best documented examples we have, and although we do not have full totals, they might be taken as supporting a two-figure population. However, if the necropoleis only contained part of the population this must be revised, or at least regarded as an unsafe guess.

Evidence for the nature of the settlements is limited. It is possible that caves were used as they had been in previous times[43] and continued to be in the Iron Age.[44] The hut-urns characteristic of burial goods at this time probably reflect the nature of some of the dwellings (though it is only at Ardea, on the acropolis, that we have post-holes of a hut associated with Bronze Age finds).[45] From the urns, a general picture of the huts

---

[40] The comparison is often made, e.g. *Enea nel Lazio* 1981: 92 f; di Gennaro 1979, 1986.   [41] See Colonna 1974: 293 for a map of the Alban Hills sites.
[42] *Atti* 1980: 48 with refs. Gjerstad 1953–73 on Rome and Gierow 1964–6 on the Alban Hills remain the standard collections of the evidence.
[43] Barker 1981: 99 ff. for Luni, Narce, and Grotta a Male in the Abruzzi.
[44] Gierow i. 10 f. for Iron Age remains in the Polesini caves and a Period III burial at Nemi.
[45] Gierow i. 17 f; the finds are a carinated bowl and a decorated sherd. The original publication was in Andrén 1961 at 39 f.

themselves may be reconstructed.[46] The framework was of wood, with an oval or circular floor-plan, between 10 and 14 feet across, with a door and sometimes a window, walls of wattle and daub, and a thatched roof.

The detailed survey of the area to the north of Rome around Antemnae, Fidenae, and Crustumerium, conducted by L. Quilici and S. Quilici Gigli, has contributed to our knowledge. Fidenae has evidence of Middle to Recent Bronze Age on two hills, separated by a small valley, but as yet nothing from the Final Bronze Age. Crustumerium has ceramic impasto from the Final Bronze Age on the site of the later settlement and also in the surrounding territory. The authors locate the Tutienses, a people that Pliny attests in his account of the vanished *populi Albenses* of Latium, in between the two sites, and the Latinienses near the site of Antemnae, and place their absorption into the more successful settlements at the beginning of the Iron Age. Dionysius (2. 53. 4) describes Fidenae as an Alban colony. There is an undeniable cultural community between the two areas in Period I but Dionysius' explanation is untenable.[47] It is possible that some people were attracted from the Fossa di Settebagni to the better defended sites, just as the Latinienses may have moved from the Parioli region of Rome to Antemnae or Rome,[48] but if we date the disappearance of these two *populi* to the beginning of Period IIA, further problems arise; there is no archaeological evidence at Antemnae before about 800, and it is hard to explain the survival of empty names for at least two or three hundred years into a period of literacy. The growth of sites in Period IIA does seem to show selection and concentration of settlement, but similar processes occur in subsequent periods.

It is also possible, especially in this area which was a natural

[46] Exhaustive catalogue and discussion in Bartoloni et al. 1987. See *CLP* fig. XVIA for a reconstruction. In appearance they were probably little different from the huts used by shepherds at the turn of this century, and photographed in Ashby 1986: 35 (Le Molette), 82 (Marcellina), 104 (Gabii), 177 (Ardea), 215 (Veii). Cf. Davico 1951. We should not forget that the huts may have had an élite status in this period, however lowly their uses in a much later time.

[47] See Quilici and Quilici Gigli 1986: 361–5; 1980 273–6. (Apart from the evidence in the Fossa di Settebagni, there have also been finds at Tor San Giovanni [see below n. 49]). The magnificence of the fieldwork and of the detailed publication of the finds at these sites is not vitiated by a faith in the written sources which seems to me misplaced.

[48] Quilici and Quilici Gigli 1978: 151–2.

route-way into the Sabina,[49] that some of these settlements were associated with exploitation of the waterways and the short-distance movements of animals; they may, in fact, have been seasonally inhabited areas, like the caves that were still used in the Iron Age and maybe some of the archaic sites in the Alban Hills and the Colle Ripoli.[50] In this way they may have preserved an archaeologically invisible existence of a sort for many years, into a time when they might be recorded for posterity. It is perhaps wise not to connect the rather fluid settlement pattern of this period with the literary accounts.

POTTERY, METALWORK, AND OTHER GRAVE GOODS

The vast majority of the ceramic pieces found in Latium from Period I come from the context of the burial ritual.[51] The consequences of this fact for the interpretation of the archaeological record have been touched on above. Much of the material comes from the Alban Hills, but it should be stressed that it was often discovered in disturbed deposits and without systematic excavation. Isolated finds and excavations subsequent to the synthesis of Gierow have not changed the general picture, however.

Until the recent excavations at Osteria dell'Osa, which have given us a much larger and more unified database that has been subjected to rigorous modern methods of analysis, it had been believed that incineration and pozzo-type burials were the characteristic of Period I, leaving the change to inhumation and fossa-type tombs to be explained. It now appears that the transition began earlier and was gradual, so that the choice of the form of burial may be an indication of social position or some other

---

[49] For work on this area, see Cardarelli 1979; Bietti-Sestieri *et al.* 1984: 18, 20; and recently *Il Tevere* 1986: 56 f. for Tor San Giovanni in the Middle Bronze Age (apparently not later) and Bartolini et al. 1987: 98–110.

[50] I have expanded here a suggestion made by Angle and Dottarelli see n. 38 above.

[51] This brief summary is based on *CLP* and *Atti* 1980; the former gives complete accounts of individual burials including reinterpretation of some of the material in Gierow ii (1), while the second gives a synthesis with a list of types and illustrations. Meyer 1983 and Bietti-Sestieri 1992: 21 ff. give similar accounts.

factor.[52] The hypothesis of invasion has long been discounted on the grounds that there is no secure evidence for it. It was a tenet of processual archaeology that one should search for motives for change other than migration wherever possible, and it is certainly difficult to make this the prime mover of the changes in burial ritual which occur in Central Italy at various times.

Moreover, the account in *CLP* which gives priority to the Alban Hills as the beginning of stable settlement in Latium, as well as the centre of the distinctive Proto-Latial culture, has also been superseded by important discoveries at Ficana, Aprilia, and Ardea, which appear to antedate the Alban Hills material. Most significant is the bronze hoard at Rimessone near Ardea, found by a young boy taking animals to pasture, and published by F. Delpino and M. A. Fugazzola Delpino.[53] It contained 1.5 kg of bronze: twenty-two fragmentary objects and three solid pieces. Among the objects were knives, axes, lance-heads, and fibulae; some of them were unused, some incomplete, some deliberately damaged. By detailed comparison of individual objects, a date of between the late eleventh and early tenth century could be fixed, and a strong cultural comparison with Cerveteri and the Tolfa Mountains, as opposed to the connection with Terni–Acciaierie established for the Alban Hills in the tenth century. As a whole this evidence is Proto-Villanovan rather than Proto-Latial, and thus raises the possibility of a significant difference between the Alban sites and those nearer the coast or on waterways.[54]

The ceramic material is closely associated with remains of food and drink from the burial ritual, and it is possible to associate certain pottery forms with certain types of food.[55] It must always be borne in mind that the buried pottery may have been of a better quality than that used daily, but we cannot tell for sure until a later date, when there are clearly fine and coarse wares coexisting.

The major elements of an incineration burial in Period I are the

---

[52] Bietti-Sestieri (ed.) 1979; id. 1985a. Pozzo tombs are well-shaped holes in the ground into which the container for the ashes of the deceased were placed; fossa tombs are ditches into which the body of the deceased was placed.
[53] *Il Bronzo Finale*, 425–52.   [54] *Atti* 1980: 66.
[55] *Il Bronzo Finale*, 415.

The Late Bronze Age and Latial Period I

hut-urn for the ashes, the large dolium or jar to contain this and the other offerings, and usually four or five pottery vessels of various sizes and shapes, sometimes but not always with incised decoration or a raised pattern like a net. The hut-urn may be replaced by a vase with a covering, sometimes like a hut-roof, or more rarely like a helmet.[56] These were placed in a hole or pozzo, which was sometimes lined with stone or tufa. It was filled in, and might be marked in some way on the surface.

The similarities between the Alban Hills and Rome in this period are very close, and these tombs are in general very similar to the kinds of burial and burial deposit found in the Tolfa Mountains, around Allumiere and Sasso di Furbara.[57] The presence of miniature statuettes, some with a hand extended or holding a bowl, must be part of the symbolism of the burial rite. Spindle-whorls are taken as an indication of female gender from this period right through the Latial periods. To a large degree this seems confirmed by the analysis of skeletal data at Osteria dell'Osa, though there is a danger of a circular argument in disputed cases—because there are spindle-whorls, the deceased must be female.[58]

As for the metalwork, the serpent fibula is the most common form, though others occur. Characteristic are miniature knives, swords, and lances. The gold ring in a fibula (*ad arco ingrossato*) and the separate gold ring discovered at Grottaferrata (Villa Cavaletti) T8 and now lost appear to be solitary examples of this metal in Period I.[59] The miniature armour is a sign of male gender; the serpent fibula is mostly male too, but occurs in the

---

[56] Bartoloni et al. 1987; G. Bartoloni 1985. For 'coperchio a tetto', see *CLP* 75 (Grottaferrata [Villa Cavaletti] T6); for 'coperchio conico apicato d'impasto' see *CLP* 80 (Grottaferrata [Boschetto]).

[57] These crucial details were worked out by Müller-Karpe 1959*a*. I follow the chronology of *Atti* 1980 for the development of Period I. There are also typological similarities with Pre-Hellenic I at Cumae. Reate and Poggio Sommavilla, and Falerii and Narce show some similarities with the Latin material, though the absence of hut-urns in the Faliscan region has been regarded as a significant difference. On Falerii see Colonna 1974: 295 f.

[58] For statuettes, see e.g. *CLP* 83 (S. Lorenzo Vecchio [Rocca di Papa]), a crudely modelled figure holding out its right hand with a carinated cup. For spindle-whorls see e.g. *CLP* 111 (Rome [Temple of Antoninus and Faustina] T. Q); Bietti-Sestieri 1992: 108.   [59] *CLP* 73 f.

Villa Cavaletti deposit with spindle-whorls; it is just possible that this is a joint male and female burial.[60]

BURIAL RITUAL AND SOCIETY

There are many aspects of the burial ritual and the material associated with it which will always be unable to be recovered; essentially, we lack a reliable control by which to justify the use of comparative material. But the nature of the necropoleis, and the presence of material evidence which indicates some level of contact with other parts of Central Italy, invite us to pose questions about the structure of society, and about artisan activity and exchange, questions which recur throughout the Latial periods. These questions can be regarded as directly interrelated. The unifying link is the burial ritual itself, which seems in some way to have mirrored the conditions of daily existence, and which also seems to have set up a structure of demand within the economy of the living.

One of the first issues to address must be the production of the pottery and metalwork found deposited in the burials. The evidence from the period of Mycenaean influence in the Mediterranean seems to imply specialized artisan activity, such as pottery made on a wheel in certain areas, possibly even to the north and the south of Italy, but there is no such evidence for Central Italy; in fact the evidence more plausibly implies an absence of direct Mycenaean contact with the area. Any specialized labour in Etruria and Latium at the beginning of the first millennium developed in response to local demand.[61]

The bronze hoard at Rimessone, with its strong similarities to bronze hoards in the Tolfa–Allumiere area, becomes central when one reviews the evidence. Leaving aside for the moment the

[60] *Atti* 1980: 58, from Müller-Karpe 1959*a*. Bronze razors have been found in miniature and normal size; the comparison of the two has proved valuable in establishing relative chronologies. The serpent fibula with the solid plate catch is the most significant link between the Alban Hills and the Terni–Acciaierie and Fucine Lake area in the Sabina, but there are also close similarities in knives and razors, both miniature and normal size.

[61] Bietti-Sestieri 1992: 36 stresses the role of the craftsmen; 'production and circulation apparently developed from a patrimony of ideas commonly shared by the metal craftsmen, rather than as a response to the specific demands of the local communities.' As will be seen below, this is a very plausible case, but one must also stress the role of the communities in encouraging further production, and possibly a degree of conservatism once the objects become part of a ritual.

purpose of the hoard, the material would seem to represent the activity of one or more specialists, at least in the case of the carefully decorated and quite complex fibulae.

The pottery is more difficult. Could it be that pottery was produced by a large number of people in the community? It is apparent from evidence from Period IIA at Osteria dell'Osa that two individual 'styles' can be identified for two separate groups, but it may not be necessary to make another move to identifying two 'hands'.[62] Anyway, the evidence should not be read back into Period I.

The issue can be approached from another angle, that is, from the nature and size of communities, and the meaning of specialization in that context. A very basic point may be made at the outset; in Period I, spindle-whorls may have been confined to female graves, indicating that spinning was the specialized labour of women. In later periods, where we have skeletal evidence, the gender connection does not always seem so close; the involvement of men might indicate a more extensive textile industry.

Estimating populations of settlements from necropoleis is very difficult. The exact relationship of individual necropoleis to individual settlements is not at all clear, and the amount of material which has been lost cannot be deduced. Even with the complete excavation of Osteria dell'Osa, we must be aware of the possibility that not all the dead individuals in a given community had equal access to burial in the necropoleis; this again is an unknown quantity.[63]

Similar problems arise with an attempt to derive a population figure from the size of the communities in question, but they are perhaps less severe. Although we are unable to define the precise limits of any site, none of the evidence we have from ceramic scatters, or anything else anywhere in Latium, would warrant a belief in a population much larger than a hundred or so. In such small communities, to be a specialized craftsman or woman may have been a highly honoured position, and knowledge may well have been a closely guarded secret.

There is no technical necessity for pottery to have been a specialized activity. G. Pulitani's recreation of the pottery methods of this period shows that they did not require specialized

[62] Bietti-Sestieri 1985.   [63] See above p. 19 f., and Morris 1987.

expertise or equipment.[64] However, we can look at metalwork and decorated pottery in another light. Colonna[65] makes an important point when he suggests that a potter was a 'depositario di una tradizione'. Of course this is only a suggestion, and might easily be denied on the same subjective grounds, but the manner in which the pottery form and decoration retain both a local pattern and a wider set of contacts and influence does seem to be significant. We might not expect Central Italy to develop widely divergent pottery traditions, but we must still explain why it did not and why it is that we can talk about the general similarities of pottery from Rome, Osteria dell'Osa, and even Veii.

If an artisan had a place in the system of burial ritual, the specialization of a craft occupation need not have been due to a technique beyond the ability of others (as it came to be with more sophisticated firing and decoration) as much as to an almost sacred knowledge concerning the maintenance of a certain tradition. These objects are of a magical significance,[66] representing in miniature the world of the departed; objects like the hut-urn were surely confined to ritual uses and the circumstances of this production may have been similarly unusual.

The argument for metalwork as a specialized activity is probably stronger, as has been suggested above, on the grounds of difficulty and complexity. The typological connections of the pottery are broadly with the metalliferous area of the Tolfa–Allumiere, but the typological connections of the metalwork are with Terni–Acciaierie, which may indicate that technique was of great importance and could be separated from the raw materials.

The coherence of the Latin burial rite appears to mark the area out from others in Central Italy; that is to say that, although there are cultural affinities with Etruria, between Latial Period I and Proto-Villanovan, burials in the Alban Hills in particular seem to have had a clear symbolism. The hut-urn and the practice of miniaturization seem to represent two important aspects of the magic of the ritual, and moreover, it may be suggested that the general absence of differentiation between tombs in one site and in the area as a whole leaves open the

[64] Bietti-Sestieri (ed.) 1992b: 439 ff. The process requires clay, dry weather, and wood for the fire.
[65] Colonna in Momigliano and Schiavone 1988: 294. This account conflates Periods I and IIA.
[66] Colonna 1974: 291.

possibility that unusual burials, like the Warrior burial at Lavinium,[67] indicate aspects of the social persona of the deceased. This burial, with armour and miniature weapons, may also indicate the increase in raiding and looting which can be seen in the settlement pattern at the beginning of the period. Differentiation by role rather than by wealth seems a clear possibility.[68]

It is likely that the limited wealth differentials between burials reflects limited resources and also a certain stability. If we could assume that only a part of the population was being buried in the necropoleis, it would suggest a society with a generally stable aristocracy, not fighting among themselves for predominance, or at least not using the burial ritual in that way.

Whatever the exact nature of the burial ritual, there can be no doubt that the practice of honouring the dead with a *corredo* implies a system of supply and demand, and the presence of amber and bronze indicate that this system was open to commodities from outside Latium, either as raw materials or as finished goods, possibly as part of a mechanism of trade or gift exchange between Latin sites and with sites outside, especially in Etruria, where this may have contributed towards the dynamic of change. Unfortunately, without much more and much better evidence we cannot construct adequate genealogies for the material that came to rest in Latin graves. The plausibility of this sketch must in part be judged by its compatibility with conditions in the subsequent, slightly better documented period.

[67] T21, see *CLP* 294 f.   [68] *Atti* 1980: 63.

3
Latial Period II, c.900–770 BC

The second phase of Latin culture begins around the end of the tenth and carries on into the eighth century. This is also the beginning of the Iron Age, though very little iron is found in Latium before the end of this phase. The period is contemporary with the beginning of Villanovan culture in Etruria, with which Latin culture has clear parallels.

In general terms, the period can be seen as one of consolidation. There is increasing wealth and increasing social differentiation. The customary division of the period into IIA and IIB somewhat arbitrarily indicates a point at which Latin civilization ceases to look back to its earliest traditions and begins to look forward to the orientalizing period. It seems undeniable that the development of a full aristocratic society in the eighth century is based on the advances of the ninth century towards stability. These advances grow out of the society described above for Period I.

THE TRANSFORMATION OF ETRURIA

As our knowledge of settlement patterns in Etruria increases through survey and excavation, generalizations become more difficult. Nevertheless, it remains true to say that there was a radical transformation of this settlement pattern at the beginning of the Iron Age, which was indicated by a concentration of population in a few major sites, which were not yet urban, but which provided the necessary basis for urban development. This change cannot be unconnected to social changes, nor can it be dissociated from wider economic developments in Central Italy. It is a change that has no contemporary parallel there. On the whole it is a remarkably uniform transformation, despite the destruction and abandonment that inevitably ensued.

It is important to stress that the general statement conceals a

Latial Period II

great diversity of experience, but that an unsupported archaeological record cannot be made to yield a narrative account of any complexity; in other words, we shall not always be successful in attempts to explain this diversity. Some smaller settlements do survive; it would be surprising if the settlement pattern changed neatly and without exception, but the exceptions do not alter the general impression.

The greatest confusion has been caused by the Swedish excavations at San Giovenale and Luni sul Mignone, two sites some 6 km from each other in the Tolfa–Allumiere district, and the necropolis of Sorbo at Cerveteri. According to the excavators, the Proto-Villanovan facies continues at these sites into the eighth century BC and cannot be regarded as a predecessor to Villanovan culture, but must be contemporary. This contention has been much disputed; the chronology is comparable to that of Gjerstad and Gierow and has been attacked often and fiercely.[1]

Potter[2] makes an important suggestion when he relates the material in these sites to a Faliscan site like Narce and to Latin sites like Rome, Pratica di Mare (Lavinium) and Ardea by virtue of their continuity from the Final Bronze Age into the Iron Age. This would imply that cultural choices are related to choices about settlement patterns and habits.

The Proto-Villanovan culture undoubtedly precedes the Villanovan, and no Villanovan objects have ever been found in Proto-Villanovan graves;[3] this is a significant argument for Villanovan culture succeeding Proto-Villanovan. The presence of Proto-Villanovan culture in Villanovan contexts, however, is increas-

---

[1] Østenberg 1967; Wieselgren 1969; Hellström 1975. (Meyer 1983: 82 f. has questioned the conclusions drawn from Luni sul Mignone. In his analysis, the main site has a clear continuity on the traditional scheme, and Phases 4A and 4B, which represent the Proto-Villanovan extension, belong to Monte Fornicchio, 1 km to the west, and Tre Erici, ½ km to the east, and are represented by a handful of sherds which might as easily be dated to the Sub-Appennine and Proto-Villanovan phases. He also disputes the dating of stratum 3B by a Proto-Corinthian sherd which he considers to be in an insecure context.) Thomassen (ed.) 1967–72; E. and K. Berggren 1980; Pohl 1977; Forsberg and Thomassen (eds.) 1984. Pohl 1972 is a brilliant presentation of a major necropolis, prejudiced at the end by a belief that the developments of the 8th century early orientalizing phase are to be attributed to the arrival of the 'Etruscans'. Bietti-Sestieri 1992a: 29 ff. gives an up-to-date account of the Etruscan sites; see also Stoddart in Champion (ed.) 1989, Rendeli 1991 for more general reviews.
[2] Potter 1979: 55–6.   [3] Ridgway 1988: 631.

ingly common, without a clear sense of stratigraphical continuity, but with an undeniable overlap in chronology. This conservatism has also been alleged for the Alban Hills as against the Latin sites of the plain, but again, only on the basis of a pottery analysis which has not been widely accepted.[4]

There may be explanations for cultural facies overlapping without resort to beliefs about different ethnic groups or invasions. Luni sul Mignone and San Giovenale both belong to the Tolfa–Allumiere group, and their Proto-Villanovan aspect is to be expected, but they also seem not to have participated in the move towards the larger sites; they continue to exist in the shadow of Tarquinia and Cerveteri until about the eighth century, when destruction layers and a clear hiatus may indicate a forcible absorption into the orbit of one or the other of these sites. (This in turn may reflect a conflict over the rich mineral resources of the area, which Cerveteri appears to have won.) They may have preserved a local and older tradition against the newer culture of the larger sites which were already moving towards urbanization.

We must therefore acknowledge that the form and decoration of pottery, and perhaps also the choice of incineration or inhumation, reflect social, economic, and settlement patterns and changes. This would be an unreliable index to change, but, if true, it would emphasize the crucial link between material remains and the nature of a society. Thus Proto-Villanovan culture would appear to preserve older traditions, even in more recent contexts.

This is not to defend the Swedish dates wholesale, for there can be little doubt that many are unacceptably low. Further work on the pottery and stratigraphy of these two sites may yield a more orthodox dating. On the other hand, even if the Swedish dating is too low, the suggestions made here about the connection between Proto-Villanovan material culture and settlement patterns and life habits still holds.

This does not bring us closer to an explanation of the appearance of Villanovan culture and the concentration of settlement that accompanied it. We should also note that, although this process is of immense importance, the creation of the territories

[4] Gierow 1983.

Latial Period II

of sites like Veii, Cerveteri, and Tarquinia is perhaps even more significant, and much harder to fix chronologically.[5]

Bietti-Sestieri addressed this problem in a very important article, connecting the change from diffuse to concentrated settlement with the exploitation of mineral resources.[6] In the twelfth and eleventh centuries, metalwork is fairly uniform and the resources are not controlled; by the tenth century we begin to find artisans producing local styles, and increasing contacts with northern Italy, Sicily, and Greece. As demand increases, so does organization and control of the resources, and the small village communities become less able to cope with the complexity of the situation, which leads to the development of larger settlements. Population growth and an increase in social differentiation also have a part to play in this network of factors.

The expansion of supply and demand must have involved a more organized system of distribution and exchange. Indeed it is the principle of organization that is at the heart of the transformation of Etruscan society, for a growth in organization both requires and inspires a change in society, leading eventually to the urban state, though Bietti-Sestieri rightly stresses that the Etruscan sites of the early Iron Age represent not urban settlements but the establishment of the preconditions for the development of an urban phase.[7] Moreover, just as we should not believe that the countryside of Italy was deserted except for urban foundations in later times, so we should not be surprised to find at sites like Luni sul Mignone and San Giovenale (whose excavators candidly acknowledge their lowly status) a continuity of settlement and a maintenance of earlier tradition, notwithstanding the development of other more advantageously positioned sites.

As regards the development of Etruria as a whole, our knowledge has increased remarkably since the initiation of the British School at Rome field surveys. In 1961 Ward-Perkins could write as follows: 'There is nothing from the Ager Veientanus to suggest that it was the scene of any substantial settlement before the occupation of Veii itself by groups of early Iron Age farmers, a part of whose material equipment relates them unequivocally to the Villanovan peoples of coastal and central Etruria.'[8] The

---

[5] Potter 1971: 56.   [6] Bietti-Sestieri 1981.   [7] Bietti-Sestieri 1981: 263.
[8] Ward-Perkins 1961: 22.

concept of 'Villanovan peoples' is now awkward; but the important issue here is that seven years later, after further finds, Ward-Perkins was able to show that the picture was different. Further survey was to show that the Ager Veientanus did in fact show signs of late Bronze Age settlement along its river routes, even though, at that time, it may have been heavily forested.[9]

In 1982 di Gennaro and Stoddart published a catalogue of all known proto- and prehistoric sites in southern Etruria; there were 61 in all.[10] By this time, di Gennaro had been able to state that the major Villanovan centres had already been populated before the period of concentration.[11] In 1988 Barker and Rasmussen were able to show 16 possible and 5 probable pre-Etruscan sites around Tuscania,[12] and to conclude that 'the critical phase of settlement shift from a relatively undifferentiated system to the hierarchical system dominated by the major centres such as Tarquinia and Vulci lasted less than a hundred years within the ninth century'.[13]

This still raises subjective issues; in 1985 A. Guidi regarded Etruria and Latium as having quite different settlement patterns; in 1986 di Gennaro was stressing hitherto unknown degrees of similarity. Guidi based his opinion on a technique of spatial analysis, the rank-size rule,[14] and saw Latium undergoing the changes that affected Etruria in the tenth century some two hundred years later in the eighth century. Following Bietti-Sestieri, I prefer to regard its mineral resources as the significant element in the Etruscan transformation. The development of Latium is quite different; it has different causes and followed a different trajectory. The similarity which di Gennaro could trace affects most regions at some stage, when the issue of defensibility

[9] Kahane, Threipland, and Ward-Perkins 1968: 14–17.
[10] Di Gennaro and Stoddart 1982: 1–21.
[11] Di Gennaro in *Il Bronzo Finale* 267–74: Vulci (Lago artificiale, La Città); Tarquinia (Hencken 1968: 410, fig. 410. Unpublished material from R. E. Linington (Poggio sopra Selciatello. Cività); Cerveteri (T163 from the Fondo Chiani burial at Sorbo); Veii (Casal del Fosso, cf. Kahane, Threipland, and Ward-Perkins 1968: 15). [12] Barker and Rasmussen 1988: 38.
[13] Ibid. 40.
[14] By this method, settlements are ranked in descending array and settlement size plotted against this. The process is completely arbitrary when there are no indications of rank clearly expressed in contemporary sources; Guidi shows the difference between the numerous small sites of Latium and the fewer larger sites of Etruria, but the method proves little. See Guidi 1985.

Latial Period II

of sites becomes important, and this links Latium to Etruria only in the same sense as it links Latium to most regions.

In conclusion, the transformation of Etruria was a process of concentration of settlement on certain major sites, which still allowed the existence of other areas with their own culture. Expansion rapidly followed concentration, with the institution of the hierarchical system which existed in the region for many centuries. These changes were motivated by the more systematic exploitation of Etruria's mineral resources, and this has its roots in the impact made on Central Italy by the larger systems of the Aegean and their vicissitudes, and the demands of Central Italy itself; meeting these demands was itself a factor in the transformation of the whole region, providing opportunities for development which Latium was to exploit in later periods.

Crucially, this transformation is not centred around iron; although iron was beginning to appear in Etruria in the ninth century, bronze was still the commonest material by far. The transformation of Etruria through the early Villanovan period must meet an already existing need, such as the Proto-Villanovan graves show, and make the region sufficiently advanced that, during the orientalizing period, it is able to develop the iron resources of Elba in particular, but also the Tolfa–Allumiere, and thus participate in new trading opportunities. The development of iron may itself reflect a growing availability of bronze, and a consequent lowering of its status value. In all these developments, the Latins, who had no mineral resources of their own, could only follow their neighbours.

ROME AND THE ALBAN HILLS

Latial Period II is usually divided into two halves, as suggested by Müller-Karpe,[15] in order to resolve the cultural anomalies of the period through chronology; the characteristic features of IIB were later than those of IIA. Colonna[16] supported the fairly rigid division but preferred an explanation in ethnic terms; the changes were brought about by new settlers. Discussion of the issue with regard to the Etruscan sites we know indicates that these solutions may both underestimate the complexity of the situation.

[15] Müller-Karpe 1962: 25–7, T44.   [16] Colonna 1974: 301.

The reason for the division is the substitution of fossa-tombs for pozzo-tombs across the broad range of Latin sites in the ninth century BC. By Latial Period IIB (830–770 BC in the standard chronology) the fossa-tombs predominate, along with a range of pottery which shows a clear evolution from the forms of IIA. The division of the period is in some ways unfortunate, for the changes can be regarded as a process rather than a break, but the coincidence of the beginning of Period II and of the Villanovan period in Etruria provides a suggestive comparison.[17]

The change between Periods IIA and IIB is most noticeable at Rome and the sites in the Alban Hills; at Rome there is a change of cemetery, and in the Alban Hills a decline in quantity of tombs and material. Meanwhile, in other parts of Latium, there appears to have been a general rise of new sites. Although the material culture of Latium does not improve dramatically, there does seem to have been a consolidation, which might have been due to the development of agriculture and stable settlements, as well as the improvement of the metallurgical industry of Etruria.

The tombs from Period IIA at Rome were all from the Forum, and included both incinerations and inhumations.[18] The material from the Alban Hills is sporadic and scattered.[19] The cultural affinities of the two areas in Period IIA are slightly different from those in I; the number of forms is, in fact, slightly smaller. Pottery in IIB changes little from IIA, but remains comparable with Central Italian forms; it is hard to say whether this is simply an issue of inherited traditions or of continuing contacts.

Metalwork, on the other hand, has become more common and its forms more standardized, which is possibly an indication of centralized or mass production. The fibulae *ad arco ingrossato* with their incised decorations are found in almost all female

[17] See Close-Brooks and Ridgway 1979 at 109 for Rome IIA contemporary with Veii I.
[18] Cremations T, GG, R, V, X, S, T; inhumations B, HH, PP, KK, P, II from *Atti* 1980 and Meyer 1983. Gjerstad, *Early Rome*, ii. 19 f. has a quite different order, which shows that both his absolute and his relative chronology are now thought problematic.
[19] See Gierow ii(1): 31 ff. for Grottaferrata, 285 ff. for Castelgandolfo; 63 f. for Villa Cavaletti T4 (cf. *CLP* 77 f.) and T7 (cf. *CLP* 78 f.). Both these tombs were cremations, as Gierow discovered on examining the material; this fact was not mentioned in the reports and further details have been lost because they were excavated before the arrival of G.A. Colini and A. Mengarelli to supervise the work. For their report see *NSc* 1902: 135 ff.; cf. Pinza 1905 coll. 350 ff.

Latial Period II

tombs in Latium, and are also very common in Veii (Phase IIA) and Cerveteri. Contacts with Cumae are also possible.[20] Amber is found in Latium too, and this must indicate direct or indirect contact with long-distance trade, since amber is not found naturally in Italy.

Inhumation as opposed to incineration is a part of the Villanovan cultural facies, and links it with the 'Fossakultur' of Central Europe, with which it is broadly contemporary.[21] Consequently, it was thought to indicate an invasion from the north; even as recently as 1974, Colonna maintained that the introduction of inhumation at Rome was connected with the presence of Sabines. This is not well supported by other evidence, which shows that the change occurred across the region and also elsewhere (including Campania), and a change in burial pattern might have been prompted by a number of reasons, such as a desire to place more emphasis on social groupings in a necropolis, as we seem to find at Osteria dell'Osa. That the change had social implications, if not social reasons, may be indicated by the continuation of cremations at Quattro Fontanili, Veii, for high-status individuals into Villanovan IIB (Toms).[22]

Incineration did not cease immediately at the end of Period I. The transition from I to IIA is in fact rather confused, with a number of incinerations surviving into the ninth century. However, as inhumation begins to dominate, the significance of incineration must change; at Osteria dell'Osa incineration seems to be a mark of prestige, perhaps honouring the 'founders' of social groups.

With regard to the Alban Hills, recent work by P. Chiarucci and others has shown that the decline of the area during Period II was not as sharp as has been supposed, and that the area was not completely abandoned.[23] Nevertheless, there are only two tombs in the Alban Hills which can be dated to Period IIA and one for

---

[20] Bietti-Sestieri 1992*a* stresses the Campanian connection; see 62 ff.
[21] See e.g. Hencken 1968: 439 ff., 541 ff.
[22] Toms 1986: 65.
[23] The evidence is brought together in Gierow 1983; for Period IIB we now have Albano Laziale, Via Virgilio T1 (Chiarucci *DocAlb* 2, 1974: 28–39, id. *Colli Albani*, 72–4). To this account should be added the necropolis at Colle dei Capuccini e di Tofetti and associated settlement material for Periods I to IIB in Chiarucci 1987.

IIB,[24] and the great majority of vases from the mixed find groups from Marino and Grottaferrata (which indicate disturbed tombs) belong to I and IIA. Even though the evidence is partial and the circumstances of its recovery not good, this seems to show a general stagnation at least, if not an actual decline, and crucially, it is dated to a period when settlement in other parts of Latium was developing strongly.

The changes in the burial ritual may not be unconnected to this decline, for the general disappearance of the rite of inhumation indicates that the tightly coherent burial practices which had characterized the Alban Hills culture were no longer the exemplar for the rest of Latium. If the growth of sites in the plain and elsewhere cannot be unconnected to the transformation of Etruria, the decline in the importance of the Alban Hills will also be related to the development of links with areas along river and land routes bypassing the relatively inaccessible sites in the Hills.[25] Defensibility was not the only issue in the choice of sites in Period II; accessibility and the command of natural resources are clearly also important.

The situation at Rome is distinctive, though one must stress that the evidence is disputed. The evidence is partial because excavations have always been hampered by the presence of later Roman material. Most of the tombs were uncovered at the turn of the century. Pinza, Gjerstad, and Gierow all believed that the Esquiline necropolis was contemporary with the Forum–Palatine complex, but this is now rejected. Instead, it is generally believed that there was a transition, gradual or sharp, from the Forum–Palatine to the Esquiline, which took place at the latest during IIB, when the earliest Esquiline tombs begin.[26]

By the eighth century we have traces of huts (probably not for human habitation) and child burials in the Forum; again the evidence is lacking to show whether there was settlement in the area immediately after the necropolis was abandoned, or after a space of time.[27] If there was continuity, then one might assume

---

[24] IIA: Castel Gandolfo T1 (Gierow ii(1) 326 f.), and Grottaferrata (Villa Cavaletti) T4 (op. cit. 48 ff.). Also a tomb at Lanuvium, Tramway Station 1 (op. cit. 370 ff.). IIB: Albano Laziale, see n. 16 above.

[25] Bietti-Sestieri 1992a: 70 ff. gives an account of the interregional contacts of this period. [26] Holloway 1994: ch. 2.

[27] Meyer 1983: 134 for huts and child burials under Regia. Doubts have been cast upon Gjerstad's presentation of the Equus Domitiani area by Ammerman 1990, and Brown's 'huts' at the Regia (Brown 1976) were probably animal pens.

Latial Period II

that the Romans as a community started to bury their dead in the Esquiline and Quirinal necropoleis instead of the Palatine/Forum area, apart from some of their children.

If the burial place used by the settlers at Rome shifted during the latter half of the ninth century, it may follow that the settlement was to some extent unified around its necropolis (however loose the unity may have been), rather than a number of autonomous settlements. In this case, the concentration of settlement that permitted this uniform action must have its roots in the late ninth century. A parallel may be drawn with the suggestion made below that the Osteria dell'Osa necropolis was used by a number of the communities around the Lago di Castiglione.

In Etruria, sites like Veii and Tarquinia have been thought of as having a patchy settlement, with concentrations of ceramic scatter within the sites indicating separate settlements. A similar and contemporary development in the shape of settlements can be seen at Fidenae and Crustumerium, where the settlements gradually encroach upon each other. The pattern would have been the same at Rome, with settlements on a number of hills, probably including the Velia. It is important to note that the Etruscan sites maintained separate burial grounds to some extent simultaneously (Quattro Fontanili and Grotta Gramiccia at Veii, for instance), but they come together in a very different way and are much larger. Consequently, they are large artificial conglomerations in which communities might well be expected to stay separate. The Latin sites, on the other hand, are much smaller, and were contiguous from a very early period; their co-operation is at once more gradual and more natural.

It is possible that one reason for these changes in the internal ordering of Rome, and also a contributing factor to the growth of settlements elsewhere in Latium, was the move of people away from the Alban Hills. There is no clear evidence for this, however, and even if the hypothesis were in some part correct, it should not be used to prove the historical basis of the Roman legends concerning the foundation of Rome from Alba Longa.

Since the material remains from Rome are still of poor quality, though increasingly standardized, there seems to be no reason to assume an economic expansion, but there does appear to be a general stability, perhaps derived from a firmly based exploitation of the land. Wheat, barley, millet, and various forms of beans, as well as remains of pigs, sheep, fish, pigeons, and turtles, have been found in Roman tombs from Period IIA;[28] there is some similar evidence from Osteria dell'Osa and Satricum.

The most significant fact, however, is that it is only at Rome that we see the relationship between settlement and burial undergoing a radical spatial shift, which may indicate at this early stage the capacity of this site for growth and realignment within its own territory.

THE DEVELOPMENT OF SITES OUTSIDE THE ALBAN HILLS

The complexity of settlement patterns in Central Italy at this vital period should not be underestimated and there is a danger in attempting a synthesis too soon;[29] fortuitous or planned discoveries may easily upset what must be only a tentative account. At the same time, this makes it important to give as much evidence as possible, in order not to simplify.

The apparent decline of the Alban Hills through Periods IIA and IIB, both in the rigour of their funerary practices and the number of inhabited sites, is to be contrasted with the flourishing of a number of sites elsewhere in Latium, on the coast, on the plain, and on the banks of the Tiber and its tributaries. Some of these sites appear to be quite new, like Tibur, but most, and perhaps all if we had a deeper knowledge of their archaeology, have some traces of settlement in earlier times, but exhibit expansion in this period.[30]

The necropolis at Osteria dell'Osa begins in IIA, though there are some traces of Bronze Age settlements a short distance away at Castiglione. Guaitoli[31] seems to attribute the change to a general move towards elevated sites.

[28] Meyer 1983: 107; Bietti-Sestieri 1992a: 233 ff.
[29] Detailed discussion of Osteria dell'Osa is in the next section.
[30] Fidenae, for example, has Middle Bronze Age antecedents and then a hiatus until the end of the Bronze Age, but the archaeological record here is not an adequate basis on which to ground beliefs about the vicissitudes of the site through time (see Quilici and Quilici Gigli 1986). There does not apear to be any support for clear and widespread breaks in the settlement pattern of Latium; it must be stressed that even the Alban Hills were never completely abandoned.
[31] Guaitoli 1984: 374.

Latial Period II

The sites which command the coastal plain are well represented in the ninth and early eighth centuries. Lavinium has earlier settlement traces, but its necropolis appears to expand during this period, and there is also some still unedited evidence which may indicate early hut-dwellings.[32] Ardea also has evidence of very early huts,[33] and there was a small settlement nearby at Torre S. Anastasio, which may have been an offshoot from Lavinium.[34]

Satricum (Borgo Le Ferriere) is one of the most interesting Latin sites, which has been thoroughly excavated over a number of seasons by the Dutch School at Rome. It has one hut from towards the end of IIB, and also burial evidence. There are also rubbish pits and cooking areas (previously confused with the separate settlement areas) which appear to belong to this general late IIB phase of growth. This area gives us precious information about the non-burial, domestic culture of Satricum; it is suggested that an area was set aside for cooking, and the domestic utensils found there can be seen to be of a similar type and make to contemporary grave goods, but of less variety. Unfortunately, the sample is probably too small to permit confident assertions about the differences between the two. The greater variety of the grave goods may indicate that some objects were made specifically for burial, but on the whole the objects seem to represent reasonably faithfully the conditions of life.[35]

Guaitoli compares the development of these sites with that of Cerveteri, Tarquinia, and Vulci.[36] It is interesting that at Satricum there is a fibula *ad arco bifido* which has a parallel at the Tomba Osta at Cumae. This may indicate a coastal route between Latium and Campania, which probably linked up with the Etruscan sites, and was exploited in the orientalizing period.[37]

[32] Fenelli 1984: 35–44. [33] Morselli and Tortorici 1982: 79 f. n. 56.
[34] Guaitoli 1977; Guaitoli, Piciarreta, and Sommella 1974: 97. The site is near the present Lido di Lavinio.
[35] For the hut see Maaskant-Kleibrink *et al.* 1987: 54 ff., 90 ff. Cf. also Maaskant-Kleibrink and Olde Dubbelink 1985; Mengarelli in Pinza 1905: coll. 377–87. For a contemporary burial see *CLP* 335 f., T.XVII. This, one of the earliest tombs from the site, is a late cremation with miniaturized pottery; but see *Atti* 1980: 48 for a tentative attribution of this and T.XVI (n. 38 below) to Period IIA.
[36] Guaitoli 1977.
[37] See *CLP* 335 for the connection; the fibula is in T.XVI (an inhumation with full-size bronze armour). Cf. Hencken 1956: 157, figs. 12–13.

A number of other sites develop through Period II which have control over land or water routes between Etruria and Campania, or Latium and the Sabina. There is burial evidence from Ficana and Praeneste, and Guaitoli suggested that the rise of Velitrae, Tusculum, and Tibur should be dated to this period, and that their importance as military or commercial sites should be recognized.[38]

The necropolis of Castel di Decima was revealed in rescue archaeology in the 1970s. It also begins in Period II, with burial evidence increasing with time and, most important, an artificial *agger* or rampart which by associated material has been dated to the first half of the eighth century BC.[39] This might be connected with the appearance in IIB and III of real armour in tombs, instead of miniaturized armour.

It would be natural to associate these developments with the expansion of the major centres in Etruria, and the emergence of Veii as a factor which stimulated the development of routes through the Fossa di Malafede and the Fossa di Galeria to Campania. The existence of settlements along these natural routes suggests an inland route connected perhaps to Veii, with a coastal route used by the Etruscan port settlements. Transport by sea may have remained the more significant method, but clearly the transformation of Etruria entails changes in the network of economic relationships throughout Central Italy, which again entails further changes.

Aspects of this process must also be sought within Latium itself. Those sites which began early in the Iron Age show a marked increase in population, which is gauged by the increase in recovered burials (Rome, Osteria dell'Osa) and the increase in the size of sites (Fidenae, Crustumerium, Ardea). The defensibility of sites is already a factor by the late Bronze Age, but the *agger* at Castel di Decima, if correctly dated, is the first monumental reflection of this. Continuing this process, the orientaliz-

---

[38] Guaitoli 1977.
[39] Guaitoli 1979; 1984: 369 ff.; date supported in Morselli and Tortorici 1982: 121 ff. This would be the earliest known *agger*; the suggestion that the *murus terreus* at Rome belongs to the 8th century cannot be substantiated. The examples at Ficana and Acqua Acetosa Laurentina are dated to slightly later in the 8th century, again by associated material, whilst those at Anzio, Borgo Le Ferriere, and Ardea are put in the late 7th to early 6th centuries.

ing period sees a much greater emphasis on defence and military weapons as grave goods. The development of sites along the Tiber (Fidenae and Crustumerium) and the Anio (La Rustica and Tibur) reflects increasing contacts with the peoples in the hills. The movement of livestock may be another factor and it is significant that sites like Cures Sabini, Palombara Sabina, and Rieti show a development similar to that of Latin sites. The stone circles around tombs at Tivoli, a typical Sabine custom, may reflect the merged culture of this area. One can also see contacts with the Faliscan and Capenate areas.

This said, we should also acknowledge that Period IIB does not show dramatic improvements in material culture, but rather a standardization of forms and a reduction in the number of types of pottery. It may best be described as a period of stable consolidation.

OSTERIA DELL'OSA

Excavations began at this site under the direction of M. O. Acanfora; twenty-two tombs of the late ninth and first half of the eighth centuries were explored and published.[40] The excavations continued under the direction of A. M. Bietti-Sestieri from 1973, and by the time of the publication of the 1979 catalogue, over 200 tombs had been excavated, dating from the early ninth to the late seventh centuries. The catalogue presents about thirty of these tombs.

Some further results are incorporated in *Atti* 1980; a further article appeared in 1984 and an English account in 1985, which contained significant new material and crucial new interpretation. By this stage the number of tombs excavated had reached about 350. In 1992 Bietti-Sestieri published the complete excavation of some 600 tombs, giving full details of the anthropological study of the skeletons by Becker, the grave goods, with comparisons with other Latin and Italian material, and plans of all the tombs. A companion volume in English gives a summary of the findings. These publications are invaluable tools for students of Latin archaeology, and make it unnecessary to present more than a brief account here.[41]

[40] Acanfora *et al.* 1976.
[41] Bietti-Sestieri (ed.) 1979, (ed.) 1984, 1985, 1992*a*, *b*; Holloway 1994: ch. 8.

Bietti-Sestieri's standpoint is clear; in her article of 1985 she stated that her concern was 'essentially with the specific problem of the change in funerary ritual and ideology as an indicator of social change', and reference is made to the work of Binford and Tainter. I have already tried to show why the approach of Binford among others has made the study of necropolis evidence so central, but it will be valuable to test the specific aspects of these methodologies against a specific instance.

Binford made the claim that there was a direct relationship between a society's funerary practices and the 'form and complexity of the organizational characteristics of the society itself' because tombs are symbolic representations of the 'social persona' of the individual, but focused only on those attributes thought to be worth representing after death. Tainter suggested that a community employed an 'energy expenditure' on the funeral directly proportional to the individual's rank, an expenditure which should be judged by the whole treatment of the body.

However, Ucko criticized this approach, pointing out that a single cemetery site may well not contain a representative sample of the population using it from the point of view of sex, age, social status, cause of death, or physical condition at the time of dying; that there is a variation in the treatment of the dead within all cultures as well as between cultures, making comparisons hazardous; and that burial practices are not necessarily stable or closely correlated with other aspects of social structure or belief.[42] Ucko stresses the complexity of the issues and the need for a variety of approaches. Further useful comments on methodology are made by Morris in his latest work, which stresses that burial evidence reveals ritual to us rather than the society itself, and we have to build into our interpretation the presentation of social reality in such special contexts.[43]

Topography and Physical Characteristics

The necropolis at Osteria dell'Osa is part of a very complex settlement pattern around the Lago di Castiglione, which has formed inside the crater of an extinct volcano.[44] The area is a

[42] Ucko, 1969–70. See Curti 1987 for an application of the theory to Osteria dell'Osa.   [43] Morris 1992.   [44] Bietti-Sestieri 1985: 138.

smaller example of the sort of settlement found in the Alban Hills. Exploration of the area as a whole has been limited; it comes into the survey work conducted by L. Quilici which centred on Collatia. The Temple of Juno at Gabii (the urban site which was formed out of the disparate settlements in the area) has been excavated by the Spanish School at Rome, but few other sites in Latium offer such opportunities for intensive survey and excavation.

The area has seen dramatic physical changes. Volcanic activity took place in the Pleistocene period, and subsequent erosion and collapse formed an area of capellacio and tufa into which the necropolis was dug, since it formed a less resistant soil.

The original meaning of 'Osa' is water, and the Fosso dell'Osa may represent the water course which helped to form a lake. By the tenth century AD the ravages of malaria had left deserted the ancient village and the Benedictine church and convent of S. Primitivo (later S. Primo). The Castiglione *castellum* was built on the site of Gabii in around AD 1200; four of its towers and the lake are clearly visible on the map of Eufrosino della Volpaia around AD 1500. The area was in the hands of the Colonna family for a while and passed in 1614 to the Borghese family, who began a large-scale drainage operation, still incomplete in 1880. The modern canal network was built in 1907.

The most significant aspect of the geography of the region would be the absence of the lake in antiquity; no ancient source mentioned it and, if it is a late formation, Osteria dell'Osa and Castiglione would have been in more direct contact in our period.

The area is also an important meeting-place for a number of roads. The Via Prenestina ran east–west through this area, and it is very likely that there was an early road connecting the area to the river Anio only 4 or 5 km away. L. Quilici, however, appears to think that the site was not on a major transhumance route.[45] This does not mean that the site had no connections with the interior of Italy before transhumance became important, but we are reminded that the fortunate discovery of the necropolis here is not an indication of the importance of the site in prehistoric times.

[45] *Ricerca* 1979: 14 ff. Quilici 1974: 444.

The Necropolis and Settlement Evidence

In 1889 A. Cozza published details of the chance discovery of an inhumation of a man within an oak trunk.[46] The associated finds were of hand-made bucchero, two vases with geometric decoration, a bronze coppa, and a large amphora of 'argilla biancastra' which was not locally made. This should date to Period IV and Pinza suggested that it might be part of a larger necropolis.

This necropolis has now been partially revealed. It is in the area between the Via Prenestina and the Via di Poli, which separate at the village of Osteria dell'Osa. The densest cluster of graves is to the north, nearest the intersection; the graves are more diffusely spread to the south-east. The necropolis must have been between two and three hundred metres long at least. Significantly, as at Castel di Decima, it is not easy to see a chronological basis for the expansion; all parts of the necropolis have yielded a continuity of tombs through the various phases, though there is an important Period III group which is isolated from the rest.

The evidence begins with the late incinerations which belong to Latial Period IIA, that is around 900 BC. The evidence begins to decrease from Period III onwards, though the burials which we do have show fully the changes and developments which affect the rest of Latium. None of the IVA burials are particularly wealthy in the context of some Latin burials—there are no gold objects, for instance—but they do show a significant advance in the number of goods found. After IVB the necropolis evidence from all over Latium comes to an end.

The analyses of the gender and age of the corpses permit us to say something about the conditions of life. The preservation of the skeletons is not good, partly due to the practice of secondary deposition of goods, which led to the disturbance of the skeletons. This in itself sheds an interesting light on the Latins' view of the dead; honouring the spirit would seem of more importance than preserving the integrity of the corpse. It is not unusual in some societies for the mourning process to be marked by a later exhumation of the corpse.

I have given the results of the work done on the age and gender of the corpses in the last part of this chapter. Taken as a whole, we

[46] Full details in Bietti-Sestieri 1992b.

find a concentration of burials in Period II and then a gradual tailing off. There are slightly more female than male burials, and rather more burials in Period IIB than in Period IIA, which suggests the slight increase in the population of the settlements using the necropolis that one would expect. The number of children found in the necropolis in Period II is less than one would anticipate in a time of high child mortality; on the other hand, there is a concentration of female deaths at the young adult age, which probably represents the cruel toll of childbirth. Analysis of a much smaller sample of thirty graves at Caracupa on the eastern side of the Lago di Castiglione give roughly comparable results.[47]

The evidence for the settlements to which the necropoleis were attached is far less clear. The necropolis at Castiglione appears to have erased traces of settlement in its own confines; the fragments of pottery from the end of the Middle Bronze Age come from just outside. As at Fidenae, there is a gap until the end of the Bronze Age, and neither of the necropoleis have Period I material, though survey work by Guaitoli has indicated the presence of material indicating settlement around the south-west and south-east of the crater from this time.

The foundation of the necropolis at Osteria dell'Osa seems to indicate that settlement had become more stable; perhaps the position of the area had encouraged temporary residence as a stopping-place, until the developing economic conditions of the late Bronze Age, and possibly demographic increase and shifts in the distribution of population made permanent settlement viable.

Tortorici stated that he thought it unlikely that Osteria dell'Osa had a connection with Gabii, and he has been proved right, for the concentration of settlement is a phenomenon of the seventh century, subsequent to the flourishing of Osteria dell'Osa. Until that time communities seem to have been small and scattered, maintaining a short distance between each other, in a manner very similar to the settlements in the Alban Hills.

It is the society of these small, autonomous, but in some sense interdependent sites which we must endeavour to reconstruct from the burial evidence, and it is important to try to establish the relationship between the settlements and the necropoleis.

[47] For Castiglione, see Bietti-Sestieri in Bietti-Sestieri (ed.) 1984: 160–70.

There are two basic possibilities; that Osteria dell'Osa and Castiglione represent one community each, or that certainly Osteria dell'Osa and possibly Castiglione served a number of communities in the area.

We must take into account A. M. Bietti-Sestieri's brilliant analysis of a cluster of tombs in the north-west of the cemetery, which seems to have been the earliest part. Bietti-Sestieri was able to identify two groups, centred on a few cremated male depositions, which set up a cultural pattern for the tombs around them, and this traditional distinction was maintained over perhaps as long as a century. The two groups comprised twenty-five and thirty-six tombs respectively, and ten further groups have been identified as belonging to either the north or the south lineage.

In the northern group, four cremations *a pozzo* have a central place and are comparable in a number of ways. The pit filling includes a large slab of yellowish travertine crust, usually just above the mouth of the dolium. There was also an offering of food, some three or four ovicaprine ribs. They contain fibulae (serpent fibulae with disc-foot), quadrangular razors, and spearheads. Only one of the four has a hut-urn. The pottery associated with the burials is accurately made and has some plastic decoration; it is suggested that it represents a banqueting service.

In the southern group, which has five cremations, the pit-filling usually contains two or three small white pebbles, and a ring of pebbles around the upper layer. The mouth of the dolium was covered with an impasto lid; only one has any meat (a fragment of deer femur); there are fibulae (serpent fibulae with symmetrical feet), one lunate razor, and spears which are cast in one piece, rather than having sockets for wooden handles as in the northern group. All have hut-urns, but the pottery is less accurately made, mostly undecorated, and entirely without plastic decoration.

In the fossa tombs around the cremations, the fibulae remain mutually exclusive, and the pottery follows the same pattern; the northern group has accurate decorated pottery, while the southern group has more inaccurate and plain vases. The surrounding burials form a complex mix of men, women, and children, with some early cremations with miniaturized goods which do not appear to belong to the groups, and some later cremations with normal-sized goods which do; the ritual remains exclusively male.

Sex and age are distinguished by personal ornaments; this is the same for both groups, and the associated groups. Bietti-Sestieri identifies what becomes an increasingly standardized *corredo* which she calls a 'weaver-set', comprising two jugs, a cup, a fibula, and several spindle-whorls and spools, which is entirely confined to female burials.

The burials of men appear not to have complete sets of vases and to be in peripheral positions, which may suggest that they were younger; interestingly, infant girls are buried with personal ornaments, but not all infant boys, which, together with the presence of rich female graves, would appear to suggest that females were important from the time of their birth, whereas males grew into importance, or perhaps had to earn it. It is also worth noting that, whereas the pottery in the incineration burials appeared to have been made especially for the ritual deposition, the pottery in the inhumations was of a more domestic nature and some showed signs of use prior to deposition. The hut-urns and the spindle-whorls indicate the two important daily activities of carpentry and spinning, which have left no material traces, though they need not indicate that the deceased practised either craft. Some older adults have a large amphora with a cup inside, which might indicate their control over the distribution of food and drink resources in the community.

In the later groups, the senior males are increasingly found on the periphery of the group rather than at the centre. This may be a way of making clear the territoriality of the grave groups. The development in Period III of one major group isolated from the others would be the outcome of such a process.

Bietti-Sestieri concluded in 1985 that 'these data seem to indicate that the community of Osteria dell'Osa at the beginning of the Iron Age is based on a relatively simple "egalitarian" kinship structure, whose basic unit can probably be identified as an extended family.' Instead of regarding the two groups as reflecting two kinship groups within one community, however, it might be possible to see each kinship group as constituting a settlement, with two distinct but linked settlement areas represented in one necropolis. In some sense the Esquiline necropolis at Rome may also have been a shared necropolis for a group of loosely linked settlements, and a similar development might be suggested for Fidenae and Crustumerium.

This would obviate the awkwardness of believing in nine roughly contemporary heads of two families in one settlement, if that is what the male cremations represent, but it might also imply that the rite of burial in the necropolis was itself a privilege, since a settlement size of twenty or thirty people over the space of a century is rather hard to believe. This would indicate social divisions which are archaeologically invisible, unless we can find the burials of others excluded from the necropolis.

It may be significant that the *corredi* from Castiglione have less metalwork in them than those from Osteria dell'Osa, which might reflect a different tradition or an economic reality based on the greater size of Osteria dell'Osa, or the fruits of cooperation between two settlements.

One may imagine that a number of settlements grew up around the Castiglione crater in the Final Bronze Age to take advantage of agricultural possibilities, and perhaps also some increasingly frequented route-ways. Although autonomous, the settlements could hardly have been unaware of each other, and may have begun to cooperate in various ways from an early date. The egalitarianism of the earliest settlements may be an illusion, and it is quite possible that differentiation by role occurred early on, and further development of a hierarchy was in process by around 900.

The necropolis at Osteria dell'Osa may have served one or two communities. Around 900, nine males were accorded cremations in two groups with similar *corredi*. These were the first of a number of burials; they acted as the centres for two distinct groups, which were defined geographically in the cemetery and by mutually exclusive uniformity of *corredi*.

One presumes that the cremations represent heads of families or the like. What is significant is their belonging to a larger group; this group might be a sort of tribe, a precursor of the later gens, or it might be a settlement. Later cremations may represent the successors to these heads. Women were always regarded as important; men seem to have had to earn their position, perhaps through initiation rites at certain ages, which might at a later date be reflected in the *sodalitas* group. Weaponry for battle, but also perhaps for the hunt, marks fully incorporated men;

and the anomalous male burials with female goods or the peripheral male burials may represent those who failed to reach a certain age or to accomplish certain tasks, or perhaps simply younger brothers.

We can see from the evidence a society divided in a number of ways: by age, gender, and role certainly, and perhaps also by membership of certain larger groups. Burial ritual, of which we can recover only a part, seems to lay emphasis on these defining characteristics. The form of burial is used to make a statement about the importance of an individual, with cremation, which requires the most energy, always representing high status, and it is also used to make distinctions between individuals. The retention of fine distinctions in *corredi* for a century, or three to four generations, may indicate a stable and conservative society. It may also indicate a society operating at a certain level of tension, and needing to preserve distinctions which fade out at a later stage.

One might even argue that the introduction of inhumation, a burial ritual requiring less energy, represents an opening of the necropolis, which was previously restricted to those to whom a cremation was accorded; but the presence of certain individuals as founding figures as it were may indicate that exclusivity remained. It may have remained necessary to belong to the right family. It is interesting that D'Agostino in his publication of several hundred early Iron Age tombs from Pontecagnano in Campania, considers the possibilities both of an unequal society and of restricted burial grounds, but this is still in the realm of hypothesis.[48]

We may also make some hypotheses about the nature of artisan activity. We do not know whether the pottery and/or metalwork was produced by specialist artisans, though this seems possible and even likely. More important, the evidence shows that a material culture and its tradition were regarded as a vital means of maintaining distinctions between groups and of establishing the internal homogeneity and integrity of the individual group. This must raise large issues concerning our understanding of minor variations in pottery and metalwork form and decoration, for it can be seen that these variations may in some

[48] D'Agostino and Gastaldi (eds.) 1988: 238 f.

instances have been conscious choices for the purpose of self-definition, and the intentionality of burial depositions is underscored once again.

Consequently, the artisan's position is not simply that of meeting a demand for a certain object, but of supplying and maintaining an identity for a group of people, and the issue of external influences on culture might be rooted in the need for variation, the deliberate adoption of the foreign in order to reinforce the localized unity of the group.

In this regard, it is interesting to note that in IIB there is a general standardization of pottery and metalwork throughout Latium, even granted that Osteria dell'Osa shows how important the slightest variation could have been. It is important not to see the settlement pattern of Latium changing dramatically at long intervals, with one stage of concentration at the beginning of Period I, a general realignment at the IIA/IIB transition, and then widespread synoecism in the seventh century. The abandonment and unification of small sites may have been a constant process, and the standardization of material culture may reflect the community of numbers of sites.

It is possible to regard Period IIB as a period of solid but gradual establishment and stability after the growth in IIA. The succeeding period transforms the situation, introducing clear signs of inequality, and perhaps the exacerbation of tension between the family and the community, which is at its sharpest when groups move towards unity and urbanization, leaving family units struggling to find new ways of maintaining and expressing their differentiated roles and status.

Osteria dell'Osa: Evidence

In the following tables and graphs I have set out the evidence from Osteria dell'Osa, using the anthropological data presented by Becker in Bietti-Sestieri (ed.) 1992b. I have only used individuals who were assigned a definite gender, though many of these were themselves open to uncertainty. I have rounded down ages where there was uncertainty; this included 11 individuals. I have excluded individuals whose date was quite uncertain. In the tables, Rows II, III, and IV represent individuals whose date could not be assigned more precisely, but in the graphs I have assigned all of those in II to the IIA group.

The tables and graphs are therefore not to be taken as accurate reflections of the community of Osteria dell'Osa, merely illustrative depictions of the kinds of trends and proportions which can be seen at the broadest level, given the degree of inherent uncertainty with regard to the anthropological data. The graphs show in particular the tailing-off in numbers of burials and also in non-adult burials after Period II.

Age-groups:

1: 0–18   5: 41–50

2: 19–22   6: 51–60

3: 23–30   7: 61–70

4: 31–40   8: 71+

TABLE 1. *Burials of males by age and period at Osteria dell'Osa*

	1	2	3	4	5	6	7	8	?
II	2	–	–	1	1	2	2	–	2
IIA	3	–	2	–	2	–	–	2	2
IIA1	5	4	2	4	9	–	5	5	–
IIA2	2	1	4	3	7	7	2	3	–
IIB	10	5	2	6	9	5	5	1	–
IIB1	1	–	1	9	6	4	13	5	–
IIB2	4	1	1	–	3	4	5	4	–
III	–	1	3	–	1	1	1	3	1
IIIA	1	1	–	–	4	1	2	3	2
IIIB	1	–	–	–	3	3	1	1	1
IV	–	–	–	–	–	–	–	–	–
IVA1	–	1	1	–	–	2	1	1	1
IVA2	–	1	–	–	1	3	3	1	–
IVB	–	–	1	–	4	–	4	6	–

TABLE 2. *Burials of females by age and period at Osteria dell'Osa*

	1	2	3	4	5	6	7	8	?
II	1	–	1	4	7	1	4	3	4
IIA	3	1	–	5	1	–	2	1	–
IIA1	2	4	5	6	6	3	6	5	–
IIA2	2	2	6	4	5	4	1	8	–
IIB	5	2	8	5	5	7	2	3	6
IIB1	5	3	9	20	8	5	4	2	–
IIB2	4	1	5	11	6	5	9	7	1
III	2	1	–	–	1	1	–	2	–
IIIA	–	–	2	–	2	3	5	3	–
IIIB	–	–	2	2	4	2	3	3	1
IV	–	–	–	–	–	–	–	1	1
IVA1	–	–	–	1	3	3	3	4	4
IVA2	–	–	–	2	1	–	1	–	–
IVB	–	2	2	1	2	2	2	1	1

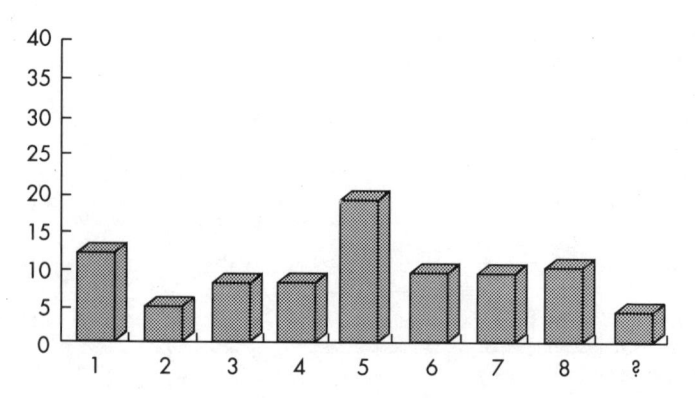

FIG. 1. Male burials in Period IIA at Osteria dell'Osa

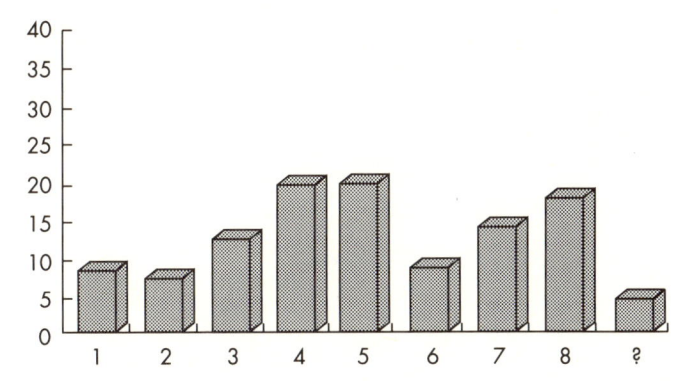

FIG. 2. Female burials in Period IIA at Osteria dell'Osa

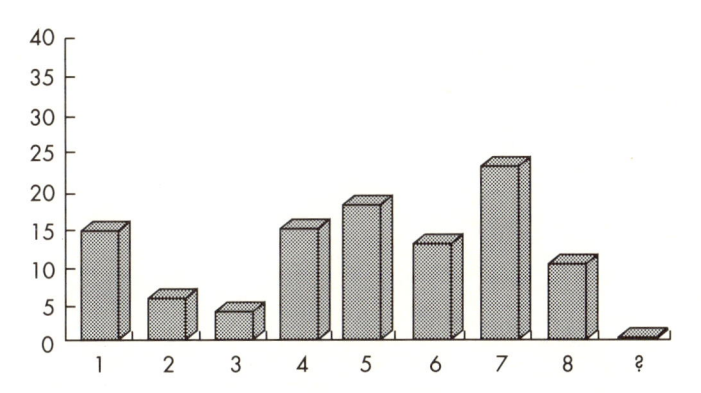

FIG. 3. Male burials in Period IIB at Osteria dell'Osa

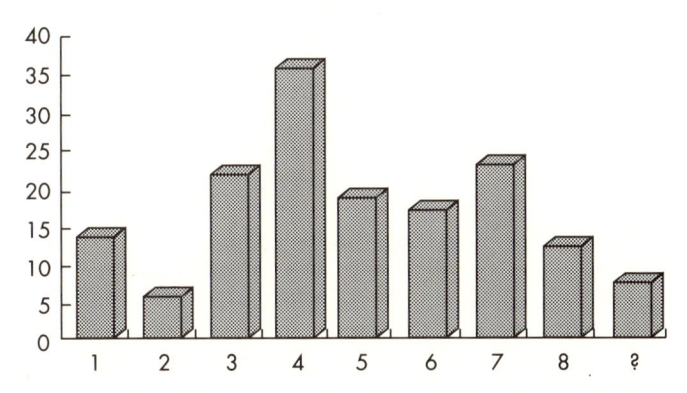

FIG. 4. Female burials in Period IIB at Osteria dell'Osa

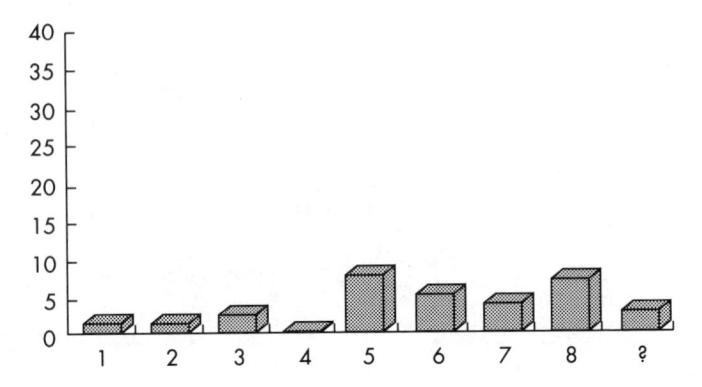

FIG. 5. Male burials in Period III at Osteria dell'Osa

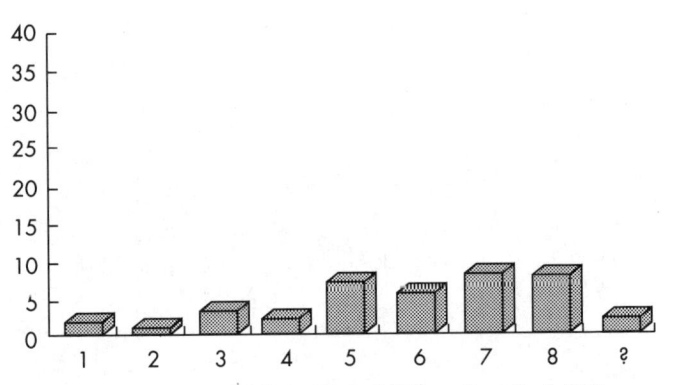

FIG. 6. Female burials in Period III at Osteria dell'Osa

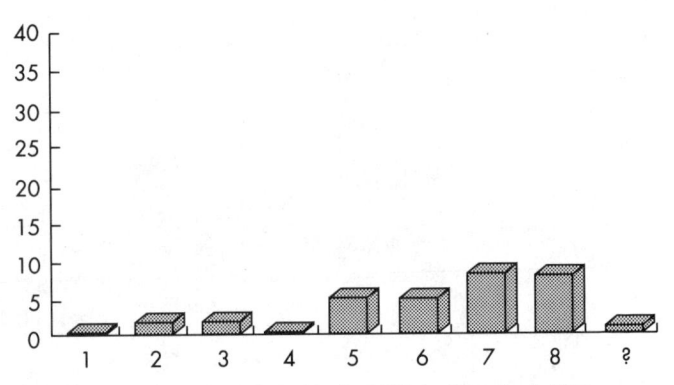

FIG. 7. Male burials in Period IV at Osteria dell'Osa

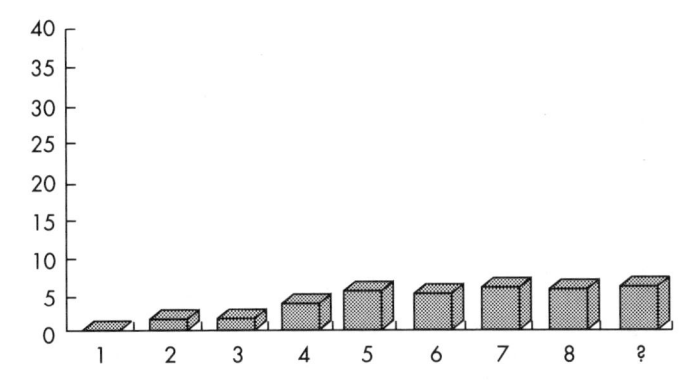

FIG. 8. Female burials in Period IV at Osteria dell'Osa

4
Latial Period III, c.770–730 BC

In the eighth century the entire Mediterranean was caught up in an accelerated trading network. At its heart was the expansion of the Phoenicians into the western Mediterranean, and the colonial adventure of the Greeks was also a significant stimulus to development. In Chapter 2 it was suggested that the presence of the Mycenaeans on the coast of Italy was a stimulus to the development of 'urban' sites, especially in the south and the Po valley. The same process is even more clearly visible in the eighth century, as southern Italy, Etruria, and Campania reacted in varying ways to the presence of Greeks in Italy, and of eastern goods and customs which permitted greater display and greater differentiation between those who could imitate the sophisticated foreign customs, and those who were excluded, at least for a while.

It is not possible here to give a complete account of the Mediterranean experience in the eighth century, but it is important to consider the nature of this trade and exchange in so far as it may have affected Latium. There is a debate about the extent of contact between Latium and the rest of the Mediterranean in the early first millennium; some scholars place the degree of contact very high, others are more cautious.

The actual presence of the Phoenicians and Greeks in Rome and Latium in the eighth century BC may in fact have been very limited. On the other hand, the impact of these peoples on Italy as a whole is undeniable, and Latium does seem to have been affected by the development of its neighbours. This is a microcosm of the Mediterranean experience as a whole; short-range contacts and overlapping spheres of influence were more important than long-range dynamics, and we should not envisage a central exclusive initiative of either the Greeks or the Phoenicians.[1]

[1] See Whittaker 1974 for a rejection of the concept of monopolies at this time.

Indeed, in this context, it is worth reconsidering the generally held belief in migrant artisans from across the Mediterranean. Evidence for individuals or groups leaving their homes to take up residence in another country and pursue their craft is limited to one or two places where the burial evidence allows us to pick out the existence of settlers through their distinctive burial customs; this is how we know that Phoenicians settled in Pithecusa along with the Greeks. There is no such evidence in any of the Latin burials, though that may say more about the exclusive nature of the burial rite.

There is no reason to doubt that some migration did take place occasionally; but if the extent and complexity of trade in the Mediterranean can be shown, it also makes sense to stress imitation, which can be demonstrated quite clearly in Central Italy. A pot which looks Greek was not necessarily made by a Greek potter. The general implication of a belief in complex and continuing trade currents from Phoenicia to northern Africa must be that individual regions participated in different ways to differing degrees.

It is important to distinguish between the level of contact at which this sort of interaction may plausibly have taken place and the level of contact at which it may not. Trading without personal interaction of any sort is attested in ancient sources as well as inherited systems of gift giving. This has been called 'silent trade' and is discussed in detail by T. R. Smith, where it is suggested that such a form of trade is largely used by long-distance traders to 'avoid the difficult, time consuming and potentially dangerous face to face exchange with alien peoples'. When possible, this would be replaced by trade through 'cross-cultural brokers' and eventually through 'trade enclaves', the peaceful settlement of foreign traders in an indigenous community.[2]

Hence, a model of interaction which sees the sites as simply stopping-off places may undervalue the contacts made and their consequences, but it is not always the case that imports carry with them the cultural baggage of their place of origin. Goods may not always be carried by their makers; they may frequently change hands before their final deposition. As indicated before, one of the consequences of believing in considerable trading activity in

[2] Smith 1987: 145 ff.; quote at 147.

antiquity is that one envisages many links in every exchange; an object need not be carried by compatriots of its maker.

It has recently been claimed that the considerable number of Egyptian scarabs found at Pithecusa, especially in children's graves, may indicate a Phoenician habit of using apotropaic amulets.[3] The evidence for this is very strong and indicates that a single type of object has borne its original cultural meaning for two other civilizations, Phoenician and Greek.

Complex cultural messages can be passed through intermediaries, the 'cross-cultural brokers', and wine-drinking or the use of perfume may be examples; the alphabet and literacy may be others. This is in no way meant to diminish the importance of the colonies in southern Greece or Pithecusa, or the orientalizing movement as a whole. The diffusion of objects and customs is undoubted, but because the trading movements of the eighth century were so considerable and far-flung, we can now move away from the rather monolithic view of Greek objects and customs being passed on by Greeks and only by Greeks. The miscellaneous contents of various shipwrecks are a metaphor for the variety of influences exerted on various Mediterranean shores.

The Phoenician move westward seems to have been a response to an increasing need for raw materials in the land-locked Neo-Assyrian empire.[4] After the decline of Mycenaean expansion, the Cypriots appear to have played a major part in the Mediterranean, trading as far west as Sardinia.[5] As pressure from the Neo-Assyrian empire grew, Phoenicians took over some of this activity. It is often suggested that the Phoenician involvement in the west had a 'precolonial' phase; contacts were made with Cyprus, Greece and Italy.[6] These contacts were a stimulus to certain

[3] De Salvia 1978. The suggestion was taken up and used by S. Frankenstein in a paper entitled 'Phoenicians and Greeks: A Western Venture' given in the Ancient History Seminar Series 'The Origins of Graeco-Roman Culture: Around Black Athena' at the Institute of Classical Studies, London, in spring 1990.

[4] A modern comprehensive account of the Near East in this period is much needed; the contributions in *CAH* iii (1) give an important overview. The contributions of Postgate and Frankenstein in Larsen (ed.) 1979 are crucial. See now Purcell in Murray and Price (eds.) 1990; Gras, Rouillard, and Teixidor 1989.

[5] For a general account of Cyprus in this period see Karageorghis, *CAH* iii (1) ch. 12. See also Gras 1985: 98 ff., and Bisi 1986. For Phoenician goods in Sardinia at an early date see Matthäus 1989; the picture is more complex than a simple series of thalassocracies.

[6] See in Acquaro *et al.* (eds.) 1988, the articles by Mazza, Bisi, and Bondi.

parts of Greece, which appear to have been developing aristocratic societies again after the relative impoverishment of the Dark Ages, with a need to emphasize and secure their position by competitive display and expenditure, and by the possession and conspicuous consumption of luxury items, which could only be fulfilled by participation in the new trading opportunities.

An early and crucial stage in this general expansion was Pithecusa, the first Greek colony on the Italian coast.[7] The archaeological record of Pithecusa shows an immense pluralism, and it is quite possible that the colonists were not only Greek but contained an admixture of other ethnic groups. There are early Greek imports, which increase in number after around 725; there is a great deal of imitation Greek pottery as well, some of which may have been exchanged with Italians on the mainland. It is also suggested that Pithecusa took iron ore from the island of Elba off the Etruscan coast.[8]

By the seventh century the site seems to have served its purpose and been overtaken by the coastal site of Cumae, which had greater agricultural resources; by this stage, Pithecusa had perhaps established the trade networks and assisted the integration of the mainland area.

PHOENICIAN AND GREEK CONTACTS WITH CAMPANIA AND ETRURIA

The impact of the first colonies on the Italian mainland can be judged by the presence of eastern Mediterranean imports. For south Italy, contacts seem to have lapsed a little after the Mycenaean age, but this may be illusory. At Satyrion and Porto Cesareo there is Greek pottery from the ninth century and Laconian Geometric sherds; there are chevron skyphoi at Scoglio del Tonno; Egyptian trinkets at Torre Galli, Crichi, and Torre del Michelicchio, and a fine Phoenician bowl at Francavilla Marittima. It is the continuity here that is important, enhancing the possibility of settlement succeeding trade.[9]

In Campania itself we have a reasonable amount of evidence, but in a poor state. We have little from the first layers at Cumae;

[7] See Ridgway 1992 for a complete account.
[8] Ridgway 1992: 105, 108.
[9] De la Genière 1979 at 77.

its foundation date of c.740 has to be surmised.[10] At Capua there are Geometric cups from the mid-eighth century on, and a little later, Egyptian faience; the same is found at Calatia. This evidence, poor as it is, at least indicates the movement of goods inland, we must presume from the two colonies.[11] For the region further south, D'Agostino has given a list of Greek-style pottery in the Valle del Sarno. Of nearly twenty types, the vast majority are from Italy itself, either Etruria (a krater perhaps from Bisenzio) or far more commonly from Pithecusa itself. Some pottery seems to be local to the area.[12]

For Etruria, the Quattro Fontanili cemetery at Veii has produced seriated tombs,[13] stylistic analysis of the Greek pottery,[14] and scientific analysis.[15] The results indicate a period in which the chevron skyphos was popular; most of the Greek imports fall in this period, but scientific analysis has reduced their number in comparison with those of Veientine or Campanian origin. Moreover, there are less than twenty Greek-style fragments under analysis (representing the majority of those sherds which could be identified) out of 651 tombs and several thousand objects.

This does raise doubts about the extent of the Greek impact on mainland Italy in the eighth century BC. Ridgway makes the highly significant observation that the general absence of Thapsos or Aetos 666-type cups in Etruria may be an indication that the exchanges were not wholly profitable. The Greeks and Phoenicians may not have found what they were looking for.[16]

On the other hand, the evidence from Osteria dell'Osa seems to suggest that some pottery forms were moving northwards into Latium. One may consider here the inscription on an impasto vase found at that site in the tomb of an elderly female, which may spell out the name of a person or a deity. The excavators set the vase in the context of contacts with Campania and the south and suggest that it gives evidence for the diffusion of the Greek alphabet in Italy; the vase, dated to the end of Period IIB, is the

[10] Frederiksen 1984: 62.   [11] Johannowsky 1969.   [12] D'Agostino 1979.
[13] Toms 1986.   [14] Descoeudres and Kearsley 1983.
[15] Ridgway 1988 with full refs.
[16] On the complex issues of Greek pottery in Italy, apart from the works cited above, see also Vallet (ed.) 1982, (esp. Coldstream and his summary at the end; also D'Agostino, who suggests the possibility of an unequal exchange between native Italians and the over-optimistic Greeks); Torelli 1987: 145–60.

earliest of its kind yet found. This again shows movement and mobility and the importance of the contacts with the Greek world, but it is difficult to know how much further one may go with such an isolated piece of evidence.[17]

DEVELOPMENTS IN LATIUM IN PERIOD III

Burial evidence outside Rome and Osteria dell'Osa is rather limited in this period; important finds have been made at Campo del Fico,[18] and at Torrino, which seems to be a small family burial ground.[19] The major archaeological finds are of huts and the earliest fortifications. Both indicate stable settlement, an awareness of the community as in some way unified, and also an acknowledgement of the need for defence.

Communities which show their first traces in this period include Antemnae; the necropolis at Castel di Decima grows in this period (T23 is Period III), but most of the burials there are IVA. Other communities, like Tibur, Fidenae, and Crustumerium, consolidate, while the Alban Hills area continues to decline.[20]

We can begin to see more of the settlements themselves from this period. Huts have been found at Lavinium (Pratica di Mare) and Satricum. During the eighth century at Lavinium, the valley settlements appear to have been abandoned for more elevated sites near the acropolis, and there is the possibility that some defensive works were created. Huts (A, C, E) and infant tombs (8, 5, 1, 2) can be attributed to Period III or early IVA. To the north-west of the settlement one eighth-century furnace has been discovered, from which it is clear that the ceramic ware was fired by direct contact with the flame, at a low temperature, and thus gained its characteristic brownish-black colouring.[21]

At Satricum, a number of huts excavated in the nineteenth century may have belonged to the early eighth century BC; we have more secure modern reports for Huts I and II, which contained domestic and perhaps imported pottery, and a number of animal bones.[22]

[17] See Bietti-Sestieri, De Santis, and La Regina 1989–90; Appendix 2 below.
[18] *Enea nel Lazio* 1981: 13 F.   [19] Bedini 1985.   [20] Gierow 1983.
[21] Fenelli 1984 at 331, 341.
[22] Maaskant-Kleibrink *et al.* 1987: 54 f., 61 f., 90 f.

One important aspect of the development of huts is the clear move to bury children within settlement areas and not in necropoleis, as shown by the figures from Osteria dell'Osa in the previous chapter. This has been seen by Bietti-Sestieri and de Santis as a form of spatial control; it may have been a way of establishing long-term control of a site, and the authors connect it with the rise of aristocratic families.[23] We may also note the earliest fortifications; a ditch and an *agger* at both Castel di Decima and Acqua Acetosa Laurentina are dated by associated pottery to the eighth century BC.[24]

Ceramic production is still largely by hand, but there is a clear increase in the number of forms and styles of decoration, some confined to small areas, like the amphorae with crested handles which show four different forms, one of which is not found outside Castel di Decima. This may suggest the existence of specialists within settlements.

Another completely new aspect of pottery production in this period is the use of purified argilla clay, turned on a wheel and then painted. Most of this is found at Rome, but it is also found at Tibur, Decima, and La Rustica. It is not possible to say whether Rome was the only place of production, as Bedini and Cordano suggest, for we do not know that artisans were static and attached to just one site; it is equally plausible that men who worked outside Rome sometimes came there and discovered new forms and techniques which had been learnt.[25] However, Rome was probably the channel for this new knowledge and skill, though the amount of material found hitherto would not justify seeing Rome as more than an important point of transit across the Tiber; it does not merit the status of an *emporion*.

There is also an increase in the use of bronze in the period, which suggests access to better supplies of the raw material than in the previous one. Iron is also used, and the various sites seem to have a fairly uniform quality of objects. There are also items which combine a number of different materials, like wood,

[23] Bietti-Sestieri and De Santis 1985. See Sourvinou-Inwood 1983 for a reverse development in the burial of children (from houses to necropoleis) indicating similar social processes in 8th-century Greece.
[24] Survey and full references in Guaitoli 1984. For Castel di Decima see Guaitoli *et al.* 1974, Bedini and Cordano 1975; for Acqua Acetosa see Bedini 1980, 1984.   [25] Bedini and Cordano in *Atti* 1980.

amber, and bone, and also some use of silver for personal ornaments, though gold remains extremely scarce and was perhaps not worked locally. This general increase in manufactured items represents on the one hand the new skills and techniques of the artisans, and on the other a continuing and developing demand for new and different objects. The greater variety of fibula forms is particularly noticeable, and at the same time the maintenance of gender distinctions. There is an increasing number of arms and shields in *corredi*, and even some chariots made of wood, bronze, and iron. The chariot emerges in the following periods as a particularly visible indication of prestige for both sexes.[26]

The bronze hoard at Ardea is an important piece of evidence for the use and distribution of the metal at this period. The significance of this collection of worked and unworked bronze on the outskirts of the settlement, and apparently lacking any religious connotation, has been much discussed. The two most likely suggestions are that it represents a sort of premonetal currency, or, more plausibly, that it is a collection of bronze intended for reworking. This would explain the disparate nature of the items—there is no standard weight, for instance—and the fact that some of the items appear to have been deliberately broken, in order to facilitate melting down.[27]

ROME

Though exiguous, the remains from Rome allow us to see the earliest traces of the settlement's future importance. We can see the growing wealth of some burials, which may well belong to a social élite, and also growing external contacts in the harbour area. The organization of the settlement also becomes clearer. The evidence can be divided into two parts: the archaeological evidence of tombs and the pottery in the Forum Boarium, some of which may be Greek, and the references in the literary sources to fortifications which have been assigned to the eighth century by some scholars by analogy with fortifications elsewhere in Latium. The general evidence from tombs indicates increased

---

[26] This general account is based on that of Bedini and Cordano in *Atti* 1980.
[27] *CLP* 312–16. The use of bronze for domestic tools and the absence of iron need not be significant indicators of the non-establishment of ironworking, since they may have been hoarded separately. On chariots see Galeotti 1988.

wealth and social differentiation, and this holds for men, women, and children. Particularly noticeable is the jewellery and an early chariot-burial.

Meyer lists forty tombs from Rome as belonging to Latial Period III; one is from the Quirinal, two from the Via Sacra, and two from the Via Gioberti at the westernmost edge of the Esquiline, from which hill come the remaining thirty-five.[28] All the tombs had some objects; we find bronze personal ornaments and iron weapons. The absence of material imported from abroad, except for amber and an ivory necklace, is striking. Some of the material may have come from Etruria; on the whole it is carefully, sometimes expertly made, showing the advance of artisan activity in this period.

The Greek-style pottery from S. Omobono consists of seven fragments of skyphoi (one a Thapsos-type), six fragments of closed-shape vases, one fragment of a kotyle, and one of a globular aryballos. When E. La Rocca presented them in *CLP* (367 f.), he inclined to believe that some at least came from Euboea or the Cyclades; the Thapsos skyphos and the aryballos he assigned to Pithecusa and Cumae respectively.[29] More recently, G. Bartoloni has suggested that the supposed Greek fragments may in fact be Veientine, and she rejects the idea that there was a Greek *emporion* at Rome, or a community of resident artisans.[30]

[28] See Meyer 191, who gives references to Gjerstad, *Early Rome*, ii. The tombs, in the order given by Meyer, are: 51, 49, 58, 22, (Osteria dell'Osa 19), 23, 39, 89, 45, 19, (Osteria dell'Osa 23), 91, 21, 25, 30, 31, 13, (Osteria dell'Osa 32), 44, 3, 6, 94, 14, 86, 87, Quirinal II, Via Sacra MM, 84, (La Rustica XI), 100, 102, 103, 98, 123, (Osteria dell'Osa 33), 74, (Castel di Decima 23), 110, 115, 8, 119, 99, 127, Via Sacra M, Via Gioberti 1, Via Gioberti 2. They are all published in full in Gjerstad, but once again it is necessary to stress that Gjerstad's analysis resulted in a false absolute and relative chronology. Meyer's list shows no discrepancies with the presentation of material in *CLP* 1976, though he does incline to making Period III longer than Italian scholars do. Of the tombs, twelve appeared to have been female, ten male, and five either contained a man and a woman or else had anomalous grave goods. The identifications were made by the typology of the *corredi*; no anthropological data are available. The two Via Sacra tombs and the two tombs on the Via Gioberti were all of children. T58 and T127 may have been very late cremations; the presence of an iron dagger in the latter would suggest a male. There is also a late cremation at Castel di Decima (T322). See *Atti* 1980: 109.
[29] Cf. also La Rocca in Vallet (ed.) 1982: 45–54.
[30] Bartoloni in Cristofani (ed.) 1987: 46; cf. Isler 1983: 23 ff. for the Veian tradition. *Atti* 1980: 107 supports a Pithecusan provenance.

Latial Period III

This conclusion is supported by the results of Ridgway's analysis of the Quattro Fontanili material, which indicated how quickly the Etruscans began to imitate Greek pottery very successfully.[31] On the whole, as Bartoloni rightly insists, we should think of Rome and Latium as a less wealthy region than Etruria, a situation which continued into the seventh century.[32]

Turning to the settlement itself, we find evidence for habitation in the form of three huts on the Palatine near the Scalae Caci, measuring approximately 5 m by 4 m, and one under the atrium of the Domus Augustana;[33] these are comparable with the two huts found at Lavinium.

The evidence concerning Rome's early fortifications is less straightforward. We rely upon literary references to the *murus terreus* and the Tigillum Sororium to build up a picture of a defended Rome. Such defences are clearly possible for this time; there is a ditch and an *agger* at Decima and Acqua Acetosa which have associated eighth-century pottery, and Anzio may have similarly early fortifications. There is an *agger* at Ardea and one at Satricum from the seventh century, and one was attributed to Servius Tullius at Rome. Walls do not seem to precede the seventh century.[34]

Varro places Rome's *murus terreus* on the Carinae, which was the beginning of the Sacred Way (LL 5. 48). The topography of this area is confused, but the general suggestion is that the wall and the gate known as the Tigillum Sororium defended the Forum area against incursions from the east.[35] Unfortunately, neither the wall nor the gate is securely dated, and it is important to note that, although the construction of such a defence implies a sense of communal obligation, the wall was not an enceinte. Later evidence for a wall between the Velian and the Palatine hills shows that the settlement was still not unified,[36] but there was a greater sense of communal responsibility as a growing population brought the small nuclei of people into closer contact with each other.

---

[31] Ridgway 1988.   [32] Bartoloni in *Etruria*, 47.
[33] Gjerstad, *Early Rome*, ii. 48 f., 63 f.   [34] Guaitoli 1984.
[35] Coarelli 1986: 111 f.
[36] For this wall, see *GRT* 79 ff.; below Part II Ch. 10

OSTERIA DELL'OSA

The significant developments in the social structure of the Latin communities are represented in the necropoleis of Osteria dell'Osa and Castel di Decima by the increase in prestige goods buried with the corpses and also by the internal articulation of the tombs, which appears to show a deliberate attempt to preserve family units even in death. By now, it need scarcely be said that the evidence is scanty and the interpretation can only be tentative.

At Osteria dell'Osa, Latial Period III is represented chiefly by a group of tombs in its centre which appear to start in Period IIB. The *corredi* do not distinguish gender, age, and family roles, and are relatively poor (15 per cent are without *corredi*), though they do preserve a general uniformity that would seem to suggest the unity of the group. There seems to have been a deliberate attempt to indicate relationships and relative importance by the spatial distribution of the tombs instead. Tombs do seem to have been well marked from early times, and superimposition of graves is rare and generally confined to periods of difficulty or poverty. At this site there is evidence for the deliberate juxtaposition and superimposition of tombs, a situation which foreshadows the development, both in Latium and more consistently in the great Etruscan necropoleis, of family burials in chamber tombs. The whole group seems to have been orientated around pairs of tombs, one male, one female, rather than the previous system where the male cremation was central. The superimposition of tombs, up to a sequence of three, which are also in a chronological series, would appear to indicate linear descent. A number of the female graves are relatively wealthy, with a higher number of personal ornaments, compared with a number of tombs which have no funeral outfit at all.

Bietti-Sestieri and others have seen at this time the development of the gentilitial system in society, a development out of the family units of the late Bronze Age settlements into larger and more socially differentiated units within which the extended family with its clients was the most important element. The degree of contiguity between kinship group and settlement is an important question; clearly enough, by the late eighth and seventh centuries it is seldom appropriate, since settlements have grown so much in size. The term gentilitial should not be taken as indicating *gentes* similar to those of the classical period, since we are probably not justified in seeing a straightforward continuity from the archaic age to the institutions of later centuries; it is arguable, however, that this is an early stage in the evolution of such institutions. The value of Bietti-Sestieri's discoveries here is to show the self-definition of what appears to be a kinship group by the inhabitants of Osteria dell'Osa. Such self-definition would have become increasingly important as communities grew larger. The presence of armour in a number of Period III tombs may indicate an increase in belligerence, another factor promoting internal cohesion. The development of Rome and sites on the Tiber like Antemnae and Fidenae, and those on the western coast like Castel di Decima and Satricum, may have challenged Osteria dell'Osa's prosperity.[37]

[37] See Bietti-Sestieri (ed.) 1979: 163 ff.; 1984; 1985*a*; 1992*a*: 199 f.; 1992*b*: 785 ff. See also p. 66 ff. above.

5
Latial Period IVA, c.730–630 BC.

This period is often called an orientalizing phase in Latium, as well as in Campania and Etruria, because of the influence of eastern models on the style of pottery and metalwork. Although there is little firm evidence for the permanent presence of Greeks or others from the eastern Mediterranean in Etruria or Latium, luxury objects from the east and imitations of them are frequently found in tombs, and there can be little doubt that contacts between the east and the west were close.

Interpretation of the evidence remains difficult though. On the standard chronology, Period IVA is very long (c.730 to 630 BC), certainly when compared with Period III (which the standard Italian chronology may have left too short), but it is hard to trace development through the period. It seems that all the most important aspects of the period as regards rich burials and the first stone buildings occur at the end, from 650 BC on, which makes it difficult to define the transition to IVB. Moreover IVB, with its limited material evidence, is itself very much a transition to the sixth century, clearly a quite different sort of world. The division between IVA and IVB is rather arbitrary, and the end of IVB is defined only by the cessation of burial evidence, which had already become scarce, and not by a dramatic change in material culture. I follow for convenience the standard divisions made in a continuous process of social and material development.[1]

Despite the population growth of most Latin sites of this period, suggested by settlement patterns and the complexity of social structures, the grave evidence is scanty. It has been suggested that this is partly because tombs of this period were closest to the surface and most damaged by ploughing and other later

[1] Meyer 1983 suggests that IVB should begin c.650 BC, but this is somewhat arbitrary.

activities, but it is worth noting that necropoleis tended to expand horizontally and not through imposing tombs on top of each other, except in unusual instances. Other explanations are needed.

More significantly, the major collection of material from Castel di Decima remains largely unpublished and evidence from Rome is limited. On the other hand the immensely wealthy tombs of Praeneste, almost the only tombs we know from this site, are unparalleled in Latium in the degree of wealth and the amount of gold and silver they contain. Whether this gives an untypical picture of Latin aristocracy is less easy to say, for they fit easily into the tradition of princely tombs in Central Italy, and it may simply be a matter of chance that others have not been located. Nevertheless, such displays can hardly have been common.

One useful approach to this period is to trace the visible dominance of local aristocracies, engaging in the conspicuous consumption of wealth and in forms of peer-polity interaction like gift-giving.[2] From this period of wealth one moves into the alleged Tarquinian dominance at Rome and to the sixth-century change from expenditure on burials to the building of temples and large domestic structures, like the houses beside the Via Sacra at Rome.

As I suggested above, this fits into a general tradition of wealthy tombs in Central Italy during the seventh century. Such tombs are often called princely (*tombe principesche*), though the term is misleading to a degree, since we cannot be sure that all the sites also had regal dynasties. These tombs are found in Etruria and Campania, and we shall see that some are clearly connected; the Praeneste tombs contain objects whose exact partners are found in tombs elsewhere. Such tombs are not unknown in the Greek world or, for that matter, in other parts of Iron Age Europe; there is at least the potential for regarding such displays as part of the transition towards proto-urban culture.[3]

[2] Mauss 1954 was the major statement of the anthropology of gift-giving. Morris 1986 applied these insights to one part of the Aegean. Two different approaches to the theoretical and historical issues are offered by Renfrew and Cherry (eds.) 1986 and Rowlands, Larsen, and Kristiansen (eds.) 1987. The latter treatment focuses on commodities and broad trade and exchange movements, and also on production and the supply of demand.

[3] D'Agostino 1977 for Italian tombs; for other Iron Age examples see, for instance, Millett 1990: 38 ff. (Britain); Hedeager 1992: ch. 3 (northern Europe).

We have seen that Period III evidence tends to indicate a degree of social differentiation, and certainly towards the end of IVA and IVB the ability of some members of society to obtain very significant amounts of luxury goods is evident. The following account begins with the settlements and focuses on the sanctuary site at Satricum, and the hut and remains found at Ficana. The burial evidence is then discussed, with particular emphasis on Praeneste.

THE ARCHAEOLOGICAL EVIDENCE.

The settlement patterns of IVA sites do not appear to change dramatically until towards the end of the period, when stone buildings and fortifications become more common. There is a general consolidation of the already existing sites, and it may be observed that, at Fidenae and Crustumerium, separate areas of habitation begin to encroach upon each other, one assumes because of an expansion of population.[4] This trend may also be assumed at Rome and elsewhere, and must have deepened the unresolved tension for autonomous sites within a loosely identifiable settlement area.

Fortifications were built in this period at Ficana, Lavinium, and Satricum.[5] The development of sanctuaries and huts runs parallel; this indicates an advanced technique, but more important, a display of permanence and a move towards more centralized settlements. Early houses may have developed into cult places. There are a number of identified votive deposits, and at Satricum, Lavinium, and possibly Ardea we have the first stone buildings on sanctuary sites, replaced in the sixth century by larger edifices.[6] There were huts at Tivoli, Satricum, and Ardea, and also on the Palatine at Rome, where there were also major earthworks and, late in the period, walls at the foot of the Palatine. The stone house at Ficana was built about 650 BC.[7]

[4] This may best be seen from the appropriate maps in Quilici and Quilici Gigli 1980, 1986.
[5] Guaitoli 1984. The evidence for the first pavement of the Comitium is given in Coarelli 1986: 120 f., and there dated to the late 7th or early 6th century; this too is evidence of communal awareness and activity, though it postdates the remarkable earthworks earlier in the 7th century.   [6] See Colonna 1984.
[7] See *Roma e il Lazio*, 196 ff. with references.

Satricum and Ficana are the most instructive examples. The complex evidence from the temple area at Satricum indicates the existence of a central hut (or perhaps a cult place) with a hearth from the ninth century. It measured about 7 m by 4 m, and was replaced around 650 BC by a rectangular building (the *sacellum*) about 10 m by 6 m in stone, possibly with terracotta roof decorations. Associated with the building is a votive model of it; one side is open, which makes it recognizably a temple rather than a domestic building. The progress from hut to temple on one site is found later at Velletri, Lanuvium, and Gabii, and parallels Drerup's analysis of the development of houses with hearths into cult places in Geometric Greece. There are a number of votive objects, including local and Etruscan pottery, miniaturized pottery, beads, iron and bronze fibulae and rings, and including some gold and *aes rude*, faience including Egyptian scarabs, and ivory. Some of this material clearly belongs to a deliberate votive deposit.[8]

The building uncovered at Ficana is roughly contemporary with the *sacellum* at Satricum. It is about 12 m by 6 m, divided into two rooms. The roof was tiled, an unusual luxury for the time, and the house may have had a portico. There was no trace of a hearth, but tableware, coarse kitchenware, storage pots, cooking pots, weights, spools, and spindle-whorls were found. In a nearby rubbish tip were found a number of pieces of pottery which appear to have been discarded afer a fire. They include four holmoi, thirty drinking vessels, including a kotyle with very fine and unusual decoration which seems to be imitating a metallic form, a number of plates, cups, and other containers. Some of the items appear to have been hung up, and some of the drinking vessels and holmoi may also have had associated metal implements, like those preserved at Praeneste.[9] A. Rathje concludes that this is a banqueting service, an indication of the life of the aristocracy. Many of the objects are typologically similar to those found in burials, indicating that whatever we find under-

[8] Chiarucci and Gizzi 1985: 117 f. for the *sacellum*, 127 ff. for the votive deposits and the earlier hut. Cf. Drerup 1969, esp. 123–8. Wikander 1988 dates the introduction of roof-tiles in the Hellenistic and Italic world to c.675–600 BC. Their weight was an important factor in stimulating architectural development; their chief advantage was the reduction of the risk of fire. Beijer 1991 identifies local pottery production at Satricum.   [9] Rathje 1983; ead. in Murray (ed.) 1990: 279–88.

ground we should assume to have existed in greater quantity above ground.

The use of wine, an import from the east which probably began in the eighth century, became most important in the seventh. There were vines which were native to Italy, but they do not appear to have been cultivated, a situation vividly described by Homer in his account of the island of the Cyclopes (*Od.* 9. 116 ff.), located to the west of Greece, where vines grow but are not cultivated, and Polyphemus is an undiscriminating drinker; if this is a vague reference to Italy, it is unflattering to the inhabitants. Wine was used in life and in a funerary context, as the evidence from Rome, for instance, shows.

The nature of the house itself remains problematic. It is possible that further work will uncover cooking areas outside the house; at Satricum there were such places away from the huts.[10] This would explain the absence of the hearth but the presence of the domestic items. We cannot tell whether the presence of the banquet service so close by indicates that the house was used for such occasions. It may be appropriate to mention here Aristotle's account of the Italian *sussitia*, though the value of this statement is hardly proved by the Ficana find.[11]

The Ficana finds in particular, to which may be added some still unpublished but evidently wealthy tombs,[12] are part of the general phenomenon of the appearance of visibly wealthy groups within Central Italian society. To some extent this could already be identified in the eighth century, especially in Etruria and Campania, but by the seventh century the phenomenon is more widespread and more pronounced. This seems to be the result of increasingly large and complex social groups coming into contact with new opportunities for expressing their internal hierarchies. It took about a century for the impact of the Greeks on the Italian coast to become fully evident in Latium, but it stimulated a reaction, so that in the seventh century there was a demand for those sorts of goods which the eastern contacts could bring. If the demand existed, it is likely that it also stimulated the move towards greater productivity and a greater profit from agricul-

---

[10] Maaskant-Kleibrink and Olde Dubbelink 1985.
[11] Ar. *Pol.* 7. 10. 1329b, on the practice of *sussitia*, given by Italus king of the Oenotrians who converted them from *nomades* to *georgoi*. Aristotle refers to the Tyrrhenians as sharing in this custom. [12] Rathje 1983: 26.

ture and other economic pursuits for at least some members of society to be able to obtain these objects. Such a process must undoubtedly have led to significant changes in the social structures of Latin sites, changes which become clear in Period IVB.[13]

The divisions in society were expressed in both the world of the living and the world of the dead. The so-called princely tombs of Central Italy, apart from the wealth which they contain in the *corredi*, must also represent great funerary occasions, with members of other areas perhaps present, and certainly they could scarcely avoid the attention and sometimes the awe of their own people.[14] Yet the Ficana finds indicate the need to recognize the exotic and beautiful personal ornaments as being worn as a form of display during one's life as well. The funeral is merely the culmination of a lifetime's conspicuous self-presentation. It would appear from the evidence of an earlier period at Osteria dell'Osa that the graves were revisited after burial, so even the funeral was not the final act.

Most sites show some tomb evidence; only a few will be discussed here. A characteristic of Roman burials at this time are the depositions of young children in oak trunks with considerable numbers of grave goods and also evidence of a ritual meal in the form of carbonized grains of emmer and spelt, barley, horsebeans, and grape pips. There are four such burials by the Via Sacra; there are also two adult depositions on the Esquiline.[15] The presence of grape pips is of obvious importance, for although it seems clear that vines of some sort had existed in Italy for thousands of years previous to this moment, there is no earlier evidence for their cultivation, and this is important confirmation of the Ficana evidence. That wine is a commodity which can mark out one's social status quite as clearly as the bronze fibulae and the 400 beads buried in Via Sacra 220-1 has often been pointed out.[16]

---

[13] By this I mean to indicate the emergence of historical leaders from outside Latium, the organized structures of religion and a sort of politics, the development of unified settlements, and so forth.

[14] See D'Agostino 1977 for comparative material.

[15] The tombs are Esquiline 105, 95; Via Sacra K, I, G, AA; all are described and illustrated in Gjerstad, *Early Rome*, ii. Meyer also includes T214 under the Equus Domitiani (Gjerstad, 82 f.) but the material is too scrappy here to be reliable.

[16] See Gras 1985: 367 n. 2. Phoenician amphorae in Central Italy from 720 BC on are listed at 318 f. Grape pips have been found at Rome, Gabii, and Ficana.

Somewhat surprisingly, these finds at Rome, wealthy as they are, do not match the large collection of material discovered at the end of the last century at Riserva del Truglio, near Marino in the Alban Hills. There are twenty-seven tombs here from IVA and three from IVB, most of which show a strikingly high number of metal objects; though there is no gold or silver, one brooch appears to have originated in Phrygia. Some tombs have over two dozen fibulae. The ceramic evidence is also rich; there are no imports but a range of local and imitated styles, both hand-made and wheel-made, often coinciding in the same deposition. There are a number of Egyptian faience scarabs here, as in Satricum.[17] There is also a mixed find group with large numbers of objects similar to those found in the tombs. It is clear that iron is now at least as frequent as bronze.[18]

What is remarkable about this find, of course, is that in the previous two periods it had seemed that the whole area of the Alban Hills was in considerable decline, though not completely abandoned. Suddenly at this one site we find a resurgence of wealth which continues for well over a hundred years, and, with the exception of the Praeneste tombs, is among the richest. It is noteworthy that the site does not seem to have evidence of any chariots such as have been found at Castel di Decima, Acqua Acetosa Laurentina, and Ficana,[19] but it does have amphorae, cups, and skyphoi, such as one might associate with wine-drinking. The extraordinary amounts of metalwork found here are a mystery, but since we can make a very strong and clear link between Praeneste and Caere in Etruria, it may be that we should see here a revival of the link with the Tolfa–Allumiere area, a link which existed back in Period I, and which may never have lapsed entirely.[20]

One further outstanding tomb may be mentioned, the tomb at Lavinium on which was built the later so-called 'heroon of Aeneas'. The body was placed in a tufa coffin, over which was

---

[17] A partial survey of these items in Latium is given in Hölbl 1979 ii. 150 ff.
[18] Gierow ii (1), 145–232. For Phrygian fibula in T29, see *CLP* 97 no. 17.21.
[19] Galeotti 1988; the instances cited are Castel di Decima T15, 101, 50, 100; Acqua Acetosa Laurentina T70; Ficana T32.
[20] Whatever the interpretation of the evidence at San Giovenale and Luni sul Mignone, the material would indicate some continuity of settlement in the heart of the Tolfa–Allumiere region, and the 7th century may see a dispute over the area between Caere and Tarquinia.

constructed a tumulus. This rich deposition again contains no gold, but large amounts of pottery. There is an oinochoe of Proto-Corinthian type and some pieces of bucchero; the rest is more clearly local. There is one silver fibula and considerable amounts of bronze and iron, including some armour, which would suggest a male deposition. There are also fragments of a chariot of some sort.[21] We may reasonably conclude that wealth was distributed throughout Latium, among a certain social group, the members of which may have had contacts among themselves and in other areas of Central Italy, and may also have been in competition with each other for prestige.

All these patterns are borne out in the evidence from Castel di Decima, as far as it is known. In the synthesis of the evidence given by Bartoloni, Cataldi Dini, and Zevi in 1982, which is the most recent account, the authors claim that some 300 tombs have been found in this necropolis, which makes it comparable in terms of numbers with Osteria dell'Osa, but its dates are from the end of IIB (T132) into the seventh century, roughly speaking, a century later. The foundation of the site seems to show the importance of the routes running through the Fossa di Malafede and the Fossa di Galeria to Veii in one direction and Campania in the other. The tombs are wealthy and show a considerable amount of bucchero, indicating strong trading links.

The general orientation of the tombs is north-east to south-west, and they are not regularly spaced but grouped in clusters. The early inhumations are topped with tufa, and there are also some empty tombs with irregular orientation, which may represent cenotaphs. Women predominate in numbers; the earliest tombs include some unusual multiple burials of up to three persons, and individual tombs, either male or female, can be regarded as being in a central position and of the earliest date in their groups. In the eighth century an attempt seems to have been made to keep personal ornaments and ritual objects separate at the time of deposition, but this practice was later abandoned (though maintained at Laurentina and Riserva del Truglio). Gender differentiation is clear, with spindle-whorls a very typical mark of a female tomb, and some weapons in male tombs. It is noticeable that the authors have not been able to identify indivi-

[21] *CLP* 305 f. no. 102.

dual groups in the way that Bietti-Sestieri has done for Osteria dell'Osa.

Even in the earliest tombs there is evidence for contacts with the east, with Egyptian scarabs (one, in T266, dates from the tenth or ninth century BC, which is an interesting indication of how much time might elapse between production and deposition of an object) and faience, as well as a clear Euboean influence on the local pottery. Period IVA tombs at Castel di Decima contain a mixture of goods, with jewellery, weaponry, and ceramics; there are about twenty objects at least in each of the published tombs. Gold and silver are rare, but not absent. Male burials seem particularly splendid, with weapons and chariots being abundant. With regard to the pottery, T15 is remarkable, and so far unique in Latium, for having at least four vessels which are of Greek origin; a fifth may be Pithecusan. The burial is of a male, also contains a chariot, and is from the late eighth century. There is also a Proto-Corinthian kotyle in an early seventh century male deposition (T152). Bucchero is very common.

Analysing the material from Castel di Decima is difficult, but it does seem to be evident that the necropolis, and presumably the community, followed a somewhat different development from that of Osteria dell'Osa, even in the same periods. The latter shows more wealth in Period IIB than in III, while the rich burials of the former are concentrated in Period IVA. At Castel di Decima, differentiation of gender, possibly of age through different combinations of weapons, and status are important, whereas in at least one part of Osteria dell'Osa they have ceased to be so. Osteria dell'Osa seems to develop through the advantages of its natural position from an early period; Castel di Decima seems more reliant on a trading route developing, and from the beginning there is a considerable emphasis on weaponry in grave goods, which may indicate that trade was sometimes a hazardous business, or that trade and banditry slipped easily into one another.[22]

---

[22] See *NSc* 1975 for the detailed publication of some of the tombs, and cf. Bartoloni 1974; Zevi 1977; Bedini 1977; Bartoloni, Cataldi Dini, and Zevi 1982; Holloway 1994: 114–20.

PRAENESTE

The amazing wealth of the Praeneste tombs is quite unparalleled in Latium, but their familiarity has perhaps reduced the sense of surprise that they should still occasion; nothing comparable precedes or succeeds these finds.[23]

The Cista Ficoroni was unearthed as early as 1738, but it was in the nineteenth century that the great discoveries were made. The Tomba Barberini was found at Columbella in 1855, followed by the Tomba Castellani in 1861. In 1876 an excavation financed by the Barberini brothers brought to light the tomb named after them. We also possess some items from tombs that were not documented.

Unsurprisingly, it was the precious objects which most concerned the nineteenth-century excavators, and sadly, the rest of the necropolis is still largely unknown. Pottery remains are scarce, though there are fragments of impasto, bucchero, and Proto-Corinthian-style ware in the Tomba Bernardini. It seems most likely that this gap was a result of the concerns of the excavators, who operated in a rather hurried fashion, but it may yet prove a peculiarity of these tombs or of the whole necropolis.

One of the most famous pieces of the collection is the beautiful gold fibula which bears the inscription *Manios : med : vhe : vhaked : numasioi*, i.e. *Manios me fecit Numerio* or *Numisio* (Manios made me for Numerius). Unfortunately, so much doubt has been cast recently on the authenticity of this piece that it must be discounted, at least for the time being.[24]

It is not only the wealth of the *corredi* here that impresses one, and the fact that gold is not found in anything like the same quantities anywhere else in Latium; it is also the variety of styles and provenances for the objects. If it is a sign of prestige to be able to command goods from exotic and distant places, then the Praenestine nobles succeeded dramatically.

Outside influences can be detected in two aspects: first the direct import of goods from outside Latium and secondly the

---

[23] Canciani and von Hase 1979; Denismore Curtis 1925; Bordenache and Bartolini 1975 on the Tomba Castellani. Cf. also *CLP* 213 ff.; Holloway 1994: 156–60. See Markoe 1985 for the Phoenician bowls.
[24] Guarducci 1980. Cf. Trümpy 1983, Cornell 1991: 16 (accepting it as genuine) Holloway 1994: 161 ff. Trümpy does not claim to have proved authenticity. For other aspects of the collection see Emiliozzi 1988.

use of motifs of decoration which are native to other areas. The burials are inhumations in large ditches, and the Tomba Bernardini in particular showed the retention of a distinction between ritual objects and personal ornaments, the latter being closer to the body in a shallow ditch within the main grave, which was itself lined with tufa. All the large tombs are dated to the second quarter of the seventh century, that is, to the end of Period IVA, and have much in common with each other. We have one indication of the identity of the occupant of a tomb; a silver bowl in the Tomba Bernardini bears the inscription *Vetusia*. Torelli has identified this as an Etruscan version of a name, and a connection has been made with the *tribus* Veturia, placed by Taylor to the south of Rome along the right-hand bank of the Tiber down to the coast, an area straddling important communication and exchange routes across Latium between Etruria and Campania.[25]

The jewellery of the Tomba Bernardini is a perfect match with that of the Tomba Regolini Galassi at Caere in style and date, and also with tombs at Cumae.[26] Characteristic of the style is gold work with plastic decoration of animals, whose details are outlined in granulated gold. There is a strong connection with craftwork from Lydia, but the dispersal of these luxuries seems closely tied to the phenomenon of Phoenician colonization, and the presence of eastern craftsmen around the Mediterranean. It has even been suggested that the style was created in the Lydian area as a response to demands from clients. The hair-clips which have been found remind one of Thucydides' reference to the hair-clips of the Ionians and Athenians (Thuc. 1. 6), and there is a double-sheathed fastening which has brought comparison with an object described by Homer (*Od.* 19. 225 ff.). Lions, griffins, and sirens are the standard decorations in the tombs, in various combinations; the presence of griffins and sirens on a bronze cauldron from the Tomba Bernardini has no Italian parallel, but there is an identical object at Olympia in Greece. We know from Herodotus and from archaeological evidence of other Etruscan objects from this period at Delphi.[27] The fibulae prompt

[25] Torelli 1967: 38 ff.; 1987: 130 ff.; Cornell 1991: 16 ff.; Prosdocimi 1979: 379–85; *CAH* vii (2), 285. For the tribe see Taylor 1960: 42.

[26] Canciani and von Hase 5 ff.; cf. Pareti 1947; Marshall 1911 for Caere.

[27] Contemporary Italian fibulae and Greek imitations in Olympia listed in Gras 1985: 662; id. 664 f. for early 8th-century helmets at Delphi and Olympia.

comparison with sites in Etruria, Latium, and Campania; there are also phalerae of gold and silver from the trappings of a horse.

All the tombs have large containers and cauldrons, some of solid metal, and others which originally had a wooden framework covered by exquisitely decorated plate. There are a number of silver kotylai and oinochoae which were probably used for wine; and also silver plates, some of them gilded, with Cypriot origins. One plate in the Tomba Bernardini has on it the figures of Osiris and Horus and an inscription in Phoenician. Some of the silver cups and bowls, including the one with the Vetusia inscription, were probably made in Caere.

The bronze artefacts come from a variety of sources; some, like the cauldron with griffins and sirens, have north Syrian decoration, others can be traced to Campania or Euboea, others again to Vetulonia and north Etruria. One can clearly detect the interchange of forms between ceramic and metallic vessels which seems to have begun in Period III. There were also at least four great bronze shields in the Tomba Bernardini alone; this sort of object is also found at roughly the same time in Etruria and Umbria, Rome, Cumae, and Campania.

Some of the ironwork was part of assemblages of armour and of chariots, and is associated with very distinctive ivories of a high standard. We have ivory lions, engraved scenes, figures, and rings, and also skilful combinations of ivory and other material. The ivory seems to have come from north Syria or Phoenicia, though it is also possible that some of the decoration was executed in the Greek colonies or in Etruria.

Finally we should note the quantities of glass and amber in personal jewellery, rather disappointing fragments of pottery, faience, and some traces of leather and bone; it appears that a whole lamb may have been sacrificed in the Tomba Bernardini. There do not seem to have been any of the firedogs and spits which are so common in Etruria and at Pontecagnano, and which have sometimes been seen as having a monetary value.

Denismore Curtis published a detailed and exemplary account of the Tomba Barberini in 1925, and suggested that the closeness of the parallels with the Tomba Regolini Galassi at Caere in particular would lead one to regard the occupant of that tomb as an Etruscan prince who had moved to Praeneste. This would fit with Ampolo's description of Central Italian society as 'open', permitting mobility at least to the members of the élite, though it remains possible that the similarity is a product of a particular instance of trade and exchange.[28]

The reasons for such an extraordinary display of conspicuous consumption of wealth are debatable. Assuming that the goods were in some sense owned by the deceased and were not presents after death, it may be that these burials represent a way of disrupting the accumulation of wealth by an individual family, or even mark that disruption when there are no legitimate heirs. Nevertheless, the most obvious explanation is that the funeral was being used to underline the status both of the deceased before death, and also that of those whom he or she left behind as relatives, and it seems at least possible that this display was not intended merely for the other people in Praeneste. Of course one's understanding of these burials is determined partly by whether one believes that they were as unusual in Latium at that time as they are in our archaeological record, and whether it is more than sheer chance that we do not have more such graves from other Latin necropoleis.

Even with the considerable amounts of material which we do have, any detailed deductions about Latin society will be difficult. It is perhaps unreasonable not to believe that there were similarly rich groups of people elsewhere in Latium, and that the Praenestine nobility and their counterparts in Latium possessed rich goods which they did not deposit in graves and which have therefore disappeared. It is also unreasonable to suppose that the accumulation of wealth from abroad was fortuitous or not linked to an ability to offer something in return, for, although there is a tendency to underestimate reciprocity or symmetry in early exchange networks, partly because we are so often ignorant of their nature, this is a tendency which can be pushed too far. The concentrations of wealth which we see in this period are significant indicators of the development of an organized exploitation of labour and resources, and of the social processes which can lead to personal wealth like reciprocal gift-giving. We can add the development of fortifications as another indication of the greater organization of communal effort, and it is not inappropriate that the period also shows the first buildings on sacred sites;

[28] Ampolo 1970/1; 1976/7.

Latial Period IVA

the establishment of religious buildings and probably a calendar of festivals is a very important element in the transformation of Latin society and becomes even more noticeable in the succeeding period, when it may be argued that the expenditure of wealth was diverted from funerals to the community, with the construction of large temples in the sixth century BC and the clear existence of an organized religion in which sacrifice was an important element, and which seems to have been controlled by and to have supported the standing of the aristocracy.[29]

[29] Two festivals are described in Ampolo 1981*b* which seem concerned with the definition of the city-state as newly founded. Many priesthoods were the prerogative of some sort of defined aristocracy from the 6th century, and the origins of this may reach back further.

6
Latial Period IVB, *c*.630–580 BC

Period IVB is a vital phase of transition between the pre-urban society of IVA and the urban society of the later sixth century; this aspect of transition is not particularly well illustrated by the material remains, which are far less impressive than those of IVA, and do not yet have the monumentality which marks, as well as anything, the urban period. The nature of this transition will be discussed from the other side in Part II, and what follows is an attempt to follow the process through chronologically.

The most confusing aspect of this period is that there is a significant decline in the wealth of burials and in their number. Our evidence is much more restricted than before. Soil erosion and damage from ploughing and other activities cannot be the whole explanation. We know, after all, that there are very few burials in Latium which belong to the later sixth and fifth centuries, and this cannot be the result of the loss of material but only of deliberate strategies of disposing of the dead, which no longer included the conspicuous underground depositions of previous times.[1]

The record is not completely blank for IVB, however, and the most important change is the first use of chamber-tombs, which were to become such a distinctive part of Etruscan burial practices in later centuries. The most significant such tomb is at Osteria dell'Osa, and it may represent an extended family, thus connecting with the ninth- and eighth-century-burials which used a different method to indicate lines of affinity even in death.[2] There are also very interesting collections of chamber-tombs just

---

[1] See Colonna 1977, 1981*b*. The first article refers to sumptuary legislation of the 5th century, the second suggests deliberate attempts to define a Latin community by contrast in funerary ritual to Etruria. See also Bartoloni 1987.

[2] Osteria dell'Osa T62; Bietti-Sestieri (ed.) 1979 187f. There were at least eleven depositions, with homogeneous material of argilla depurata, bucchero, silver, iron, and bronze with close parallels to Veii.

Latial Period IVB

to the south of Rome, around Acqua Acetosa Laurentina and Castel di Decima.[3]

The chamber-tomb is an important concept because it relates to the monumental buildings which were to be constructed all over Latium in the sixth and fifth centuries, and also because the focus on social groups was to be redefined over the same period. The extent to which the natural family unit, especially at the aristocratic level, was preserved or changed in the course of urbanization is discussed below.[4]

With respect to settlement patterns, there is little change that can be detected; on the whole, choices of sites had already been made and were adhered to, the major change being the waning of sites like Castel di Decima, which seem to have fallen within the tribal area set by Rome in the late sixth and early fifth century.[5]

It may be possible to see an important change taking place in the internal structure of settlements, as suggested by C. Ampolo in an important work of synthesis.[6] Ampolo suggests that during this period, sites develop their centre and divide the rest of their area into units to which he gives the name *pagi*; this term is found in antiquarian sources with respect to early Rome, and in particular in the fragment Oxyrhynchus Papyrus 2088, which refers to the 'Servian' reorganization of the city.[7] Bedini has suggested that the discoveries of chamber-tombs at Tor de Cenci near Castel di Decima represent a *pagus*, and one can argue that these monumental tombs represent the aristocrats who became patricians at Rome and gave their name to the tribes (these should fall in the Voltinia or Aemilia).[8] The same might be said for those at Acqua Acetosa Laurentina and Casale Massima. These sites, especially Castel di Decima, appear to decline after the end of the sixth century, though burials without *corredo* continue at some.

One very significant reason for the articulation of major settlements must have been the rise in population; there seems to have

---

[3] Bedini and Ruffo 1981 for Torrino; Bedini 1980 for Casale Massima; Bedini 1981 for Acqua Acetosa Laurentina; Bedini 1988–89, 1990 for Tor de Cenci.

[4] See further below, p. 189 ff.

[5] *Atti* 1980: 165. The identification of Castel di Decima and Politorium originated with Nibby. It is discussed in Poucet 1985: 122–3.

[6] *Atti* 1980: 165 ff.; Torelli in *CAH* vii (2) 30 f., and articles by Ampolo and Capogrossi Colognesi in Momigliano and Schiavone 1988.

[7] For this document see Thomsen 1980: 14 ff. with references.

[8] Bedini 1990; see below p. 194 f.

been a steady increase from the tenth century onwards, and despite the absence of proof, one would assume that it continued into the fifth century and beyond, not least because the size of settlements, and the building projects undertaken, rises continuously and simultaneously across these years, and this cannot be entirely due to a better organization of labour.

These developments can be seen at Satricum, for example, where the old huts are replaced by a proper house, as happened also at Ficana and Ardea. The cult centre of Mater Matuta continued, and although the temple was not built until the middle of the sixth century, there is evidence for a continual development of the site before this period, indicating an important theme in Latin settlement history, which is the perpetual ordering and re-ordering of the cult centre and its practices; the archaeological counterpoint to the understanding reached by religious historians of the Protean transformations of Roman belief. Conservatism is a concept out of place in both religious belief and religious building.[9]

It is at Rome that the developments can be seen most clearly, through material remains and some reliable hints from literary tradition. The chronology of the last three kings of Rome is dubious; the durations of their reigns are suspiciously long (thirty-eight, forty-four and twenty-five years respectively). Moreover, the Romans were surely capable of inventing a plausible myth around their buildings and a hazy recollection of the past.[10] The whole story of the Tarquin dynasty must be treated with some care but we may assume that, from the sixth century onwards, there was a united entity which knew itself as Rome, though its definition may have been rather vague. Rome was large, and its appearance by the beginning of the Republic probably marked it out from all its Latin and some of its Etruscan neighbours, but within its loose boundaries there must have been a very large amount of agricultural or even uncleared land; settlement was probably quite dense on some hills, perhaps far less so in valleys liable to be marshy.

The development of Rome from period IVB into the sixth century is shown in Part II, so that for the moment it is suffi-

[9] Chiarucci and Gizzi 1985: 117 f. for the *sacellum*, 87 f. for the first phase of the temple; also Colonna 1984 at 402 ff. [10] Purcell 1989: 165.

cient to indicate the extent and nature of the evidence. For the most part, this shows a rearrangement of what previously existed, possibly occasioned in part by natural destruction. The huts on the Palatine near the Scalae Caci appear to have been destroyed, but there are architectural terracottas found here which suggest either a continuation of habitation or else the institution of a cult. There is a child burial dated to this period from underneath the Aula Regia of the Flavian palace, and on the other side of the hill Carandini has found contemporary building work. Near the Temple of Antoninus and Faustina, the area of the old necropolis continues to have huts upon it, though now of a more elaborate plan, and some child burials.[11]

The most significant development of this period, which made possible the building works described below, has only just been revealed by the core samples and environmental research conducted by Ammerman. He has shown that Gjerstad's account of the so-called Equus Domitiani area erroneously identified huts and semi-permanent dwellings from evidence which should be interpreted differently. He also showed that the central area of the Forum valley between the Palatine and Capitoline slopes would have been under constant threat of flooding, if not a permanent marsh, until the later seventh century, when a massive landfill was attempted, raising the level of the ground by as much as 2 m, onto which was laid the first surface pavement of the area, probably in the sixth century. The Cloaca Maxima of the same period must then be seen as part of a programme of cooperative effort over many years; the landfill shows a number of layers which confused Gjerstad. Ammerman estimates that the landfill may have involved between ten and twenty thousand cubic metres of soil. Only after this landfill could the Via Sacra and the Forum assume the importance which they did.[12] It is worth noting that the literary tradition records the unrest and distress caused among the Romans by Tarquinius Superbus' building programme; later

[11] For the Palatine huts and the architectural terracottas, *Atti* 166, Gjerstad *Early Rome*, iii. 56 f.; for children's burials, Bietti-Sestieri and De Santis in Bietti-Sestieri, Pontrandolfo, and Parise (eds.) 1987; *Atti* 1980: 166, Gjerstad, *Early Rome*, iii. 70–1, *CLP* 122 f. (child buried under Aula Regia with two bucchero kylikes, five coppe, two or three impasto olle, three aryballoi piriforme di argilla figulina); for the wall discovered by Carandini see *GRT* 79 f., 97 f.; Holloway 1994: 100 f.
[12] Ammerman 1990.

Romans clearly appreciated how much work must have been involved in creating the sewers, for instance.[13]

During Period IVB the huts beneath the Regia disappear, possibly due to flooding, and are replaced at first by a ditch for sacrifices and votive deposits, and later by the first stone-built Regia.[14] Nearby, in the atrium of the Vesta, was found a votive deposit dating largely from this period, which fits with other votive deposits found on the Velia, Campidoglio, and Quirinal, largely of miniature pottery but also including metal objects.[15] The relative poverty of the deposits themselves presumably conceals the importance of the cults, for most of these received a monumental enshrinement in the later sixth century. Another indication of the importance of religion at this time is the introduction of sacred elements to the topography of the Forum Boarium, with at least four strata of votive deposit underneath the archaic temple at S. Omobono.[16] This probably reflects to some extent the growing recognition of the importance of this part of the settlement to the community as a whole.

Hardly to be distinguished from these developments are those in the Forum itself; the first pavement may be dated to around 650 BC, and the second to c.625 BC. This latter reached as far as the Comitium area; around 600 there was built a stone structure which is probably to be identified as the Curia Hostilia. Around 580 the votive deposit at the Lapis Niger began; the religious text possibly dates to the second half of the sixth century, and the whole complex, later adorned with an altar and a column, has been identified by Coarelli with the Volcanal. This is very close to the original Ara Saturni, which almost certainly existed in some form in IVB.[17]

The consequences of these developments are the new existence of a clear and defined centre for Rome along the Forum valley; it is quite likely that some aspects of the Roman triumph, which seems to have been imported from Etruria around this time, were also intended to focus attention on this area.[18] Moreover, there

[13] Dion. Hal. 3. 67; Livy 1. 56. 1–3; Pliny *HN* 36. 107.
[14] On the Regia see Brown 1967, 1974–5; Coarelli 1986: 56 f.
[15] Gjerstad, *Early Rome*, iii. 359 ff.
[16] Coarelli 1988: 208 ff., *GRT* 114, 129 f.
[17] Coarelli 1986: 119 f., *GRT* 54 f. Ara Saturni, see Coarelli 1986: 199 f., with date at 224 f. Curia Hostilia, ibid. 140 f.
[18] For the triumph see Coarelli 1988: 414 f.; Bonfante Warren 1970.

Latial Period IVB 103

seems to be a coming together of the various functions of a settlement, quite naturally based on religion. The massive landfill is a dramatic example of the labour resources which could be called upon, and must mark a significant stage in the development of the city as an urban settlement.

For the first time, there is the possibility of finding evidence relating to the production of material goods, in the form of inscriptions on pottery in particular. The interpretation of this evidence is not at all straightforward. The Duenos vase, the only piece surviving from a votive deposit on the Quirinal, is particularly contested:

*iouesat deiuos qoi med mitat nei ted endo cosmis virco sied
asted noisi ope toitesiai pacari uois
duenos med feced en manom einom duenoi ne med malos tatod.*

It has been suggested that Duenos is the name of the maker of piece, three miniature ollette joined together, and made out of buccheroid impasto. The alleged organization of artisans into *collegia*, attributed to Numa but almost certainly later, is often adduced here. It is also possible that the name is equivalent to 'bonus', and is a reference to the high social status of the dedicator.[19]

There are a number of other inscriptions on various objects, which indicate first that the art of writing had become widespread to some extent, and that it may have been a requisite for some craftsmen to know how to write; and secondly that some objects were literally texts from this period on; that is, they were intended to be read and not just looked at. The various messages indicate the increasing presence of Etruscan in Rome, either in terms of important people, artisans, or simply Etruscan objects.[20]

Specialized and perhaps local craftsmen leave their mark in unusual places, most astonishingly in a gold dental fitting found in the mouth of a corpse at Satricum, probably buried at the beginning of the sixth century.[21] This is a particularly significant

[19] For the Duenos vase, see the recent *GRT* 20 f. with refs.; Cornell 1991: 9.

[20] For epigraphical evidence, see Appendix 1. The contributions to *Gli Etruschi e Roma* 1981 are central; see also Cornell 1991. The 'textuality' of objects is a theme of Thomas 1992 ch. 5.

[21] Pot 1987: 35–40; XII Tables 10.8 (Cic. *Leg.* 2. 60) for burial regulations regarding gold tooth fillings.

find because it indicates that, although the incidence of metal objects in tombs declined dramatically from the previous period, there was no corresponding drop in technical ability or in the availability of precious metals. A further indication of this may be found in the beautiful jewellery in a female tomb of the late sixth century at Fidenae.[22]

There is a considerable amount of continuity between IVA and IVB in terms of pottery forms, though the incidence of bucchero and imitation bucchero does increase.[23] The large number of aryballoi gives a material indication of the rise of olive cultivation in Central Italy, which may well have changed the nature of farming, not only because of the increased demand for land, but also because of the organization of labour needed; it is 'notoriously biennial', and so would have affected agricultural strategies. The olive would have grown fairly easily on hill-slopes (provided that they were cleared), but the marshier valleys would have required effective drainage.[24] Its presence in Latium, along with that of the vine, undoubtedly affected strategies of conspicuous consumption and luxurious living. Olive pips have been found in quantity in a sixth-century context underneath S. Omobono.

Period IVB does mark an advance on the preceding period, but its character as a transition between the full orientalizing phase of IVA and the urban development of the later sixth century makes it hard to separate from either. The absence of great material wealth in any context perhaps signals a period of uncertainty, as earlier strategies give way to newer ones; the late and rich female tomb discovered at Fidenae may indicate that here the older ways were still being observed. The chamber-tomb at Osteria dell'Osa and the burials of children within houses at Rome and elsewhere may also be symptoms of the dissolution of life based on the community, in favour of a more stratified and unequal society, in which there were a number of overlapping divisions according to various criteria, one of which may have been the family defined

[22] For the Fidenae jewellery see *GRT* 260 f. with references.
[23] *Atti* 1980: 178 f.; Colonna in Momigliano and Schiavone 1988: 303 f. See Ginge 1990 for two vessels from Satricum, possibly made in Etruria, showing Near Eastern influences and decorative motifs from metal prototypes.
[24] *Atti* 1980: 31 f., 43 f.; Osborne 1987: 45 f.

for purposes of inheritance. It remains probable that since the evident wealth of IVA is picked up in the second half of the sixth century, in the intervening period there would have been a good deal of public display and extravagance.

7
Lines of Interpretation

This conclusion to Part I draws together the general trends so far identified. The first section is a discussion of luxury goods in the area; the second is a brief attempt to indicate the way in which the economy of Latium worked; the third is an account of the development of society in Latium from the archaeological evidence.

THE IDENTIFICATION OF LUXURY GOODS AND THEIR ROLE

The term 'luxury goods' is intended to describe commodities which are not necessary to life, and which have a greater material value, and greater prestige status, than any equivalents they may have. Thus jewellery is an inessential item, and a gold cup has greater value than a cup made of pottery. The absence of a non-burial context to use as a control is an acute difficulty for the identification of luxury goods, because the value and prestige of a commodity changes over time. Increased contact with Greece and the eastern Mediterranean by the sixth and fifth centuries made Greek and imitation Greek pottery less rare, and therefore less of a luxury, than it had been hitherto; and the introduction of the cultivation of olives and vines into Central Italy would have made the use of their products more common; it is difficult to trace accurately the spread of luxuries through society.

With some caution, we may begin to analyse the evidence presented above. In Latial Period I there are very few objects which we would immediately identify as luxury goods, and indeed there is little differentiation between *corredi* either in quantity or quality. On the other hand, apart from the large dolia,[1] we have no fragments of coarse ware. Therefore, either

[1] On dolia see Gjerstad, *Early Rome*, iv. 98 f.

the only pottery used was that found in burial contexts, or there was in daily use a less refined pottery. It is also possible that plates, cups, and so on were fashioned out of wood and have not survived.

The nature of the Period I pottery seems to indicate its particular appropriateness for the burial context (there is uniformity and miniaturization, which suggests that it was created together, and with the intention of acting as proxy), and so we might suggest that this pottery was itself special. The presence of metal miniatures would seem to imply the same, since these proxies appear to have no daily use, except perhaps as a sign of gender and status.

This is not necessarily to be equated with the suggestion that the pottery and metalwork was a luxury, which could only be maintained if it could be shown that some proportion of the population was not buried with this form of *corredo*, indicating that it was not a necessary part of the preparation and rituals of death for all members of the community. This is hard to do. Certainly, in Period I there do not appear to be any burials without burial goods in the necropoleis, and at other times these are sufficiently rare that they may indicate something other than poverty.

The sample we have is perhaps too small to permit any significant conclusions about status differentiation, but the absence of weapons and of 'female' fibulae in the same tomb seems to indicate a stricter gender differentiation than was maintained in later periods.

In Period IIA there is the added complication of the change from incineration to inhumation. A model of explanation for this, involving invasion or immigration, has been rejected as unlikely; it is unsupported by current theories of social and cultural change, and, more important, by the evidence, for there is no material indication of a change in population patterns. Both Period IIA and IIB seem to indicate a growth in the number of forms of commodities found in graves, but also a standardization; that is, there are more types, but the types are more widely found. The evidence from Osteria dell'Osa in particular indicates that, even in Period II, there was a sense of status differentiation, initially expressed by the choice between cremation and inhumation while the two practices coexisted, and a sense of identity operating to distinguish neighbouring groups.

It is very important that Period III does not show a considerable amount of foreign imports, though one might otherwise have expected it. Given the busy activity in the Mediterranean in the eighth century, one must ask why Latium shows such a small degree of direct influence from abroad. The answer may lie in the organization of Latin society with regard to obtaining precious luxury goods.

Although it may be suggested that Latin society was in some way divided from as early as the late tenth century on, it does not follow that this social division was always accompanied by a sophisticated exploitation of the lower section of society for the benefit of the upper. One would suspect instead that this development was the result of the first wave of outside influence on Latium in the eighth century, when foreigners came prospecting for mineral wealth, bringing new luxuries with them to the coast of Campania and Etruria. The desire to become a part of this economy, and the success, seems to have led throughout Central Italy to a more aristocratic society; one deduces this from the greatly increased wealth apparent in the seventh century, which may have been the result of a greater surplus production in Italy.[2]

There are two possible alternatives to this model. One is that Greeks and Phoenicians gave away precious objects without return, which seems nonsense. A second is that, by the seventh century, the Mediterranean had a surfeit of luxury goods, and that they had become debased. However, there seems no evidence for this in contemporary written sources from the seventh century and shortly after in Greece. Homer, Hesiod, and the accounts of the early tyrants at Corinth, for instance, indicate that wealth was highly prized, but largely in the hands of a few. At the beginning of the sixth century, the problems of debt-bondage at Athens do not seem related to a debased luxury economy. Anyway, in eighth- and seventh-century Central Italy, precious objects do not seem sufficiently common for one to

[2] Bietti-Sestieri 1981 makes similar arguments for the 10th century and before in Etruria, when the motive force was the Mycenaean/Cypriot trading network; I hope I have indicated a continuity between the late Bronze Age and the orientalizing period.

believe that all members of society owned gold and silver, though by this stage bronze fibulae may have been common.

Perhaps a more significant indication of the rarity of precious metals is the imitation of them in pottery, which appears to begin in Period III. Bucchero in particular copied metal forms, its burnished black being reminiscent in a way of silver; and pottery was occasionally gilded or silver-plated. This process seems especially common for symposiastic vessels (found outside the burial context at Ficana), and both Greek and Phoenician metal objects are found in imitation; sometimes the originals are also found in Central Italy.[3] This imitation may indicate that more members of society were engaging in the use of status symbols, even though they could not all afford the authentic metal versions, or it may indicate the desire to use substitutes for metals in burial depositions.

Chronology is important here. There is no doubt that there were banqueting services in existence in Latium by the last decades of the seventh century, but one issue is whether the cups and amphorae of the late eighth and early seventh century indicate a similar degree of Eastern impact. In fact, although brocchette, anforette, painted decoration (e.g. chevron cups), moulded decoration (e.g. spirals on amphorae, possibly an imitation of metalwork), and the use of the wheel all indicate the lasting influence of the first presence of Greeks and Phoenicians, the real and deep impact seen at the material level in exotic imports, and at the level of social behaviour in the adoption of symposiastic rituals, seems later, and more plausibly associated with the massive presence of Greeks in Sicily and southern Italy from the end of the eighth century on. This might indicate that the practice of imitating metal through pottery had a different significance at different times and in different parts of society.

Positive evidence for symposiastic customs in Latium is clear for the sixth century, when there are Greek imports and imitations showing symposiastic scenes or with inscriptions indicating

[3] Rathje 1990: 281 f.; see Rasmussen 1979, esp. ch. 4 for some decorative motifs shared by ceramic and metal objects (ribbing, stamped motifs, dotted lines, fans, incision especially of palmettes and animals). Ström 1983, reviewing this book, makes an even stronger case for the connection, saying that bucchero is often closer to a metal original than impasto, so the imitation was directly from metal and not through the impasto ware.

drinking, such as the olla from T115 at Osteria dell'Osa from Period IVB with the inscription *salvetod Tita*. In earlier periods this is less certain, but it is hard to explain the Ficana banqueting service and other imitations of Graeco-Phoenician pottery or metalwork forms without reference to some sort of drinking ritual, probably connected in part with the funeral, since there are seventh century tombs with grape pips attested. One might wish to connect this with the prohibition of *circumpotatio* at funerals in the later Tenth Table; the word is presumably a calque of the Greek *perideipnon*. Gras suggested that wine-drinking practices from the early seventh century are to be connected with earlier practices like the sacrifices and milk-drinking at the Feriae Latinae, and points out that the move from these primitive practices to something similar to a symposium also marks a move from the association of individuals to the gathering of a certain social group, the aristocracy. On the other hand, we cannot date the inception of the Feriae Latinae, and social stratification had clearly begun before the seventh century. It is also worth noting that the Latin 'symposium' was not all that similar to a Greek one; people appear to have sat up, and wives were allowed and may have been accorded much respect. Comparisons with the Etruscans, about whose practices we know equally little, may be more just, and if the primary influence is Greek, it was not absorbed without alteration.[4]

From a different angle, in the eighth and seventh centuries there is an increased amount of warrior equipment in the outstanding tombs, culminating in the great chariot burials at the end of the seventh century, as well as the development of fortifications at a number of Latin settlements.

A full history of Latin armour has yet to be written, but just as D'Agostino found difficulty in identifying the hoplite in southern Etruria, so also in Latium the evidence seems to point towards a fairly individual approach to warfare. In early cremations weaponry is usually miniaturized, and it is possible that, with rather limited access to worked or unworked bronze, the actual weapons were of too much value to the community to be buried. In the early cremation of T21 at Lavinium, there is an

---

[4] Rathje 1979, 1990; Gras in *Modes du Contact* 1067–75. For Osteria dell'Osa T115 see *GRT* 100 f.

almost full panoply of armour, some of it full size, which is striking. Throughout weapons appear to be honorific, at first strictly male as far as we can tell, but later found also in female burials, and it is interesting that the great shields in the Praeneste burials were probably far too weak to be used in conflict. Similarly the chariots are not confined to male burials; though some are chariots of war and some chariots for luxurious transport, there is no clear gender differentiation.[5] Iron tends not to be used much before the seventh century; it could be very brittle unless properly treated. Weapons are not found in every male burial at any period, though they seem particularly common in Period III.

Our evidence is clearly flawed by the absence of burials with *corredi* in the later sixth century, when there are suggestions, largely based on our understanding of the Servian army, that a form of hoplite warfare was introduced in Latium, as well as in Etruria. It has been pointed out that forms of communal fighting are not unknown outside Greece, but the inspiration may well have come from southern Italian colonies. There seems relatively little indication that the army did not begin as, and remain, a vehicle for aristocratic display. The Republican centuriate assembly, which was based on the military organization, was heavily weighted towards the upper classes, and a striking panoply from Lanuvium early in the fifth century could only be the possession of a leading person in the community.[6]

Around the seventh century there is the beginning of a massive change in domestic architecture, with stone houses replacing huts at Ficana and Satricum, for instance, as well as in Etruria. By the sixth century the practice of building in stone has become more widespread and is used for temple constructions. If the first houses really are private domestic buildings, and not primarily public buildings (for it remains possible for an essentially private building to have a public function as well), then these may be regarded as ultimate luxuries, requiring a great degree of organized labour. The association of a banqueting service with a building at Ficana might indicate some sort of *andrion* or male mess.

Thus the eighth and early seventh centuries are characterized

[5] See Bartoloni and Grottanelli in Rallo (ed.) 1989: 55 ff.
[6] D'Agostino 1989, 1990; Torelli in *CAH* vii (2), 35 ff.

not so much by their 'orientalizing' (which is more properly descriptive of the late seventh and sixth centuries) as by their social evolution. This earlier period must prepare the way for the markedly unequal society of IVA and onwards. Whereas the social differentiation at the beginning of Latin civilization may have been in some way communally accepted, and the luxuries of that time the gift of the community, it seems more likely that the luxurious life of the aristocracy from the later seventh century on was based partly on the systematic exploitation of the human resources of the community.

This can be seen in terms of a changed role for the luxury commodity. At first it seems to be a mark of the community's hierarchy; later it becomes part of an individual's self-presentation; and finally it becomes part of a 'political' act, emphasizing the power of an individual or her or his family with respect to the rest of the community.

At the second stage, military prowess and the spoils of looting were probably central; at the third stage, it is the surplus production and human resources of the community which are exploited to provide the prestige goods that mark out the position of the few. The crucial indication that this may be true is the existence of a defined hierarchy in Etruria and Latium in the historical period.

It is important to bring out the unproven assumptions underlying this account. At the outset, there is an assumption of an agreed social hierarchy, close in a way to a social contract.[7] The relatively stable settlement strategy adopted from c.1000 BC on in Latium must have been at least a semi-voluntary response to the conditions and potential of the area. The Latins could have continued as constantly fragmenting semi-nomadic warrior bands; the move towards communities which tended towards expansion rather than fission is a crucial one.[8] Some members of the community, by heredity or by their own deeds, may have acted as protectors of the rest, and it would appear that, in time, aristocrats came to demand their privileges and to separate themselves from the community; some similar process is often

[7] This is assumed by Peroni 1979c, 1988.
[8] This is brought out by Claessen and Skalník in Claessen and Skalník (eds.) 1978 at 21 f.

assumed for the origins of hektemorage in Attica.⁹ This is the beginning of the exploitation which must underlie the conspicuous consumption of the seventh century on.

The nature of the burial ritual, with its specific goods and spatial distribution, may indicate that the act of burial within a necropolis context was itself confined to a proportion of the population of Latium, and that the differentiation within a necropolis indicates further shades of status differentiation within this small group.¹⁰ The proportion of the Latin population which obtained this privilege would have decreased over time with a growing general population; the question of where the rest of the dead disappeared to has not received an immediately plausible solution, though Cornell has suggested that, in the past, burials without *corredi* may have been found but not recorded, and they would be difficult to assign to a period. The limited number of tombs without *corredi* in the necropoleis recently excavated is still striking.

It must be stressed that there is no evidence that necessarily indicates reserved burial rites in Latium, and the small size of communities in the tenth century, followed by the corresponding increase of population and necropolis size, means that there is no reason to assume this until the disparity in the figures in the seventh century. However, there are indications of status differentiation in the later tenth century, and these may have been connected in part with the transition from cremation to inhumation; it is not unreasonable to assume a hierarchy from the beginning of stable settlements. The act of burial, which clearly had implications for one's social prestige by the seventh century, may have had similar implications at an earlier date. It is impossible, given the poor data, to trace any changes in the extent to which burial was reserved at different periods; the process seems to accelerate in the course of Period IVA.

As for the military aspect, it is important to keep this in perspective; organized military activity is unlikely before the late eighth century, when there is the earliest, though sparse, evidence for fortification by ditch and rampart. Military pro-

⁹ See, for instance, Forrest 1978: 45 ff., 147 ff.
¹⁰ See Morris 1987 for the original argument, and D'Agostino in D'Agostino and Gastaldi (eds.) 1988 for Pontecagnano.

wess, which is not necessarily hereditary, is not a good long-term basis for individual authority. However, the ability to command a military force from one's dependants could be a very significant asset. The Praenestine nobles may never have used their panoplies, but they presumably indicate the ability to raise a force of men. If this is a reasonable supposition, we have further indications of an aristocracy forming groups of dependants to bolster their position.[11]

It is worth noting that more optimistic commentators have given exchange of gifts and redistribution a more prominent part than exploitation of others. The importance of gift exchange was stressed at the outset; I do not believe that aristocracy can have survived without a firmer economic base than this. Yet it is fair to stress that the luxury commodity has a plural significance, as was stated above; as a mark of honour, a means of indicating gender or status, as a means of storing wealth or regulating the amount of luxury objects in circulation, as a form of currency, as a gift, and as an expression of power. Many of these roles can exist simultaneously, and no doubt they did. If agriculture operates within history as a shaping factor, so does the production of and demand for luxury objects; subsistence and wanton expenditure coexisted in antiquity as they do today. These two aspects of Latin economy are discussed in the next section.

SURPLUS PRODUCTION AND SUBSISTENCE ECONOMIES

The general view of agriculture in the archaic period, and for much of the classical period in some parts of the Mediterranean world, is that only a basic subsistence could be gained from the earth, and that many larger settlements had to supplement their local production with imports, or expand by colonization.

Agricultural activities in Latium change crucially when vines begin to be cultivated in the eighth century BC; they are different again in the villa economy of the late Republic and the early Empire. Use of the land and of natural resources is a dynamic

[11] On military developments in Etruria, see D'Agostino 1989, 1990; Cels-Saint-Hilaire and Feuvrier-Prévotat 1979.

factor, not a stable given; the environment, as the Pompeians discovered and as we are now discovering, cannot be taken for granted.[12]

The area is defined by natural boundaries, the Tiber, the valleys of the Sacco and the Liris, the Garigliano, and the Tyrrhenian Sea. These boundaries are clear geographical markers, but not obstacles to invasion or barriers to contact. The present shape of Latium is due largely to the volcanic activity of the Alban Mountains between 130,000 and 30,000 BC. These created the tufa of the hills themselves and part of the alluvial plain of Latium; the limestone hills around Praeneste and Tibur are of an earlier foundation.

The region is particularly well supplied with water; the two major river systems are those of the Tiber and the Sacco–Liris, with their numerous tributaries. They are irregular, and far from ideal as regards navigation, but they seldom dry up. This had the consequence of making some areas marshy, and malaria was a terrible scourge until the drainage programmes of the past century,[13] though the system of *cunicoli* probably began in the sixth century BC, and medieval neglect of the land may have made this more of a factor in recent times than in antiquity.

Some deforestation may have been necessary before agriculture could be feasible in a number of sites; it is quite possible that this process continued long after the archaic period, which raises a question about the nature of settlements. Even when settlements were protected by fortifications from the seventh century on, part of the land enclosed may have been uncleared, and certainly part of their territory. The soils of the region, derived as they are from limestone or volcanic deposits, are not outstanding for their fertility, but are adequate, given the unavoidable exigencies of subsistence agriculture. Large-scale arable farming is practised today towards the coast, with vines and more intensive market gardening in the hills to the north and east. Strabo (5. 3. 5)

[12] My account is based on those of Quilici 1979 and Bietti-Sestieri and Ampolo in *Atti* 1980. Toubert (1973) i. ch. 2–3 gives an interesting account for the early Middle Ages, with reference to a wealth of documentation from the period, but it is not possible to make a direct comparison with earlier times. The most accurate maps are those of the Istituto Geografico Militare.

[13] Ashby 1927: 49 f. the introduction of malaria is often dated to the 5th century BC, e.g. in Ogilvie 1965: 395.

described the region as fertile except for the marshy regions near the sea. In antiquity, timber and stone resources may have been of greater economic importance than agriculture; quarrying still continues near Tivoli, and tufa from Fidenae and stone from Gabii were used at Rome.

However, agriculture was the primary activity of prehistoric times, and it is unlikely to have ceased being so for the majority of Latins. Our knowledge of the crops and animals of the prehistoric period comes from the detailed analysis of exiguous remains in tombs; it would appear that some sort of ritual meal accompanied the funeral.[14]

Until the eighth century, cultivation was largely confined to cereals and vegetables. Between the eighth and sixth centuries, viticulture, olives, new and better cereals, rotation of crops, and new technology[15] were all introduced. Latium seems a little behind its Italian neighbours early on; the new world of the orientalizing and archaic eras may have had the confidence to experiment and develop which the earlier, grimmer world of subsistence farming had lacked. Beans and chick-peas were present from the earliest times, and there must have been ingenious use of natural herbs and edible fungi.

The contribution of animals to the economy was large. The widespread religious practice of sacrifice may have furnished an important supplement to diet, but it is also clear that traditions like that of Hercules and Cacus, and cults like the Lupercalia, Parilia, and Suovetarilia, which seem to be of a relatively early date, are connected to the protection of animal husbandry.

Very important claims were made for the status of transhumance in early Italy by Barker,[16] but recent studies have tended to be more cautious,[17] and this region was never noted for its

[14] On the significance of food and drink in the context of death see De Martino 1958: ch. 6.
[15] Ampolo in *Atti* 1980: 34 dates the introduction of new metal technology into agriculture to the 8th century BC, in disagreement with Peroni 1979c.
[16] Barker 1981, 1989.
[17] See the contributions of Ampolo and Garnsey in Whittaker (ed.) 1988. Whittaker sums up the conclusions of the book on pp. 3–4 with three important statements: (i) pastoralism must always start from agriculture; (ii) specialized pastoralism must be accompanied by specific political conditions; (iii) an economy founded on pastoralism is not infrequently an economy of relatively high involvement in the market.

pastoralism. Large-scale movement of large numbers of animals is almost certainly out of the question before the mid-Republic, but small-scale movements are highly probable. This allows the possibility of early contact, and possible conflict, between the people of the plain and the peoples of the hills around.

The most important animal was the pig, for despite its general lack of utility (it produces only meat and perhaps pigskin leather), it will eat anything. Ovicaprine animals are next in frequency. Bovine animals were not much used for meat, and to slaughter one was originally a great crime, which indicates their importance in other contexts, and perhaps their exchangeable value, for they are expensive to rear.[18] Use of milk and cheese, and also of fish in this well watered area, adds some balance and variety to the diet, and hunting of animals and birds must have been an important part of daily existence. The likelihood is that most early Latins practised a form of mixed economy to protect themselves against bad years. Food shortage must have been as endemic and chronic in prehistory as in classical times, but the conditions in Latium were not unduly harsh.

Two issues may be raised in this context, and both are well stated in N. Purcell's essay on 'Mobility and the Polis'.[19] The first is the importance of general movements of people: 'There is no real reason to assume that in human history the settled cultivator is the norm. Stability is not the base, the usual state from which mobility departs.' The consequence of this ought to be that stability is a calculated response to conditions, and would not be made unless it were practicable.

The second is that, even within stable settlements, people are not static:

Mobility has often been part of the flexible ecological response: nomads are now seen as pastoralists engaged with a wide range of environments and so much involved with others exploiting adjacent riches in different ways, whether they are hunter gatherers or arable cultivators, as to be regarded as in some sense a part of the same society, which is not to obscure the fact that the symbiosis need not, unfortunately, be peaceable.

[18] *Atti* 1980 44 f. for evidence of animal bones; 46 for the proscriptions against killing oxen.
[19] Purcell in Murray and Price (eds.) 1990: 29–58; quotations from 41, 42; cf. Campanile (ed.) 1991.

To this may be added the contribution of artisans, for although we are not yet able properly to assess the mobility of the artisan in Central Italy, standardization of forms of products indicates a continuing general tradition across the area, and it seems fairly evident that some artisans from Phoenicia or even Greece did set up contacts with Etruria at least, and a few may even have come to be resident at some stage.

In short, settled conditions of life are chosen in preference to nomadism for a reason, and the conditions of such a life, in a relatively sparsely populated and fertile area like Latium, cannot have been particularly harsh. Again, one must retain a sense of perspective; death and starvation would never have been far away, and life was short for the majority.

A. Sherratt has brought out succinctly two ways in which the issue of surplus in the economic conditions of world trade before AD 1500 has been treated:[20]

> In one of these, the movement of goods from place to place is a consequence of increased prosperity: the achievement of a surplus in primary production releases local products for exchange on a wider market, permitting the acquisition of foreign goods which are desirable, though inessential. In the other view, it is the drive to acquire exotic items which stimulates the increased production of local items necessary to acquire them. In this conception, trade is more than just a consequence of increased efficiency: it is the motor which drives the whole system.

Crucially, the latter approach focuses attention on the broadest possible view. Unlike an 'evolutionary' approach, which moves from the local markets through to the broader processes, as if one followed from the other, the second view stresses cupidity, and the desire to participate in large economic processes.

Now there are a number of reasons for a community, or for a group within a community, to create some sort of surplus simply for local reasons. Yet the production of an agricultural surplus of any sort (even in a region like Latium, where it was relatively easy to do) in fact requires a considerable stimulus; as Boserup showed,[21] intensification of a basic agricultural economy

---

[20] Sherratt (forthcoming); I am grateful to Dr Sherratt for allowing me to benefit from his work before publication. See Sherratt and Sherratt 1993; Bernard Knapp 1993. [21] Boserup 1965 esp. 53 ff.

requires a very significant shift in attitudes to work and to the land. The development of ironworking, which made itself felt from the late eighth century on in Central Italy, would have done much to improve tools, and the introduction of the cultivation of vines and olives would have been at least as significant.

Yet, if we examine what reasons Latin communities had to produce a local surplus, we face some difficulties. It may make sense from the beginning for the community to endeavour to create a surplus with which to reward their chief people; but this is different from individuals or a particular group in a community endeavouring to command a surplus with which to acquire luxury commodities for themselves. This is quite a different matter, and involves quite a different view of the community. It is clearly connected with the practice of 'euergetism', which seeks to command wealth from the system in order to return it to the system, and in order thereby to have one's own position recognized if not improved, and one's person honoured.

On a very large scale, this is part of the economic dynamic of Neo-Assyrian and Neo-Babylonian 'requisitioning systems', which often worked to provide a king with sufficient resources with which to reward his subordinates, and thereby justify and retain his own position. On a very small scale, Latin communities may have produced a surplus in the tenth and ninth centuries in order that their chief people might redistribute it among the community. But the result of the large-scale process was the establishment of a large number of core–periphery relationships though the Mediterranean. 'Basically the effects of the need to meet the constantly increasing demands of the requisitioning system . . . was to intensify in each society the means of producing a local surplus, whatever these had been'.[22] The process worked from the heart of the Middle East to Phoenicia on the coast, and thence to Greece and the West. The importance of Sherratt's second explanation is to stress that there was a return process, in the desire to belong to this system, as Athens and Euboea demonstrated in their cultural flowering in the eighth century to meet the Phoenician traders; as Etruria demonstrated in the rapid exploitation of its mineral resources from the mid-eighth century on, which possibly entailed a conflict between

[22] Purcell in Murray and Price (eds.) 1990: 38 f.

Caere and Tarquinia over the Tolfa–Allumiere resources. (This sort of process no doubt contributed to the military development of Central Italy and of Greece, in which context one naturally thinks of the Lelantine War in ninth- or eighth-century Euboea.) One presumes that there must have been some benefits for the community which belonged to this system of core and periphery, but these are most evident in sixth century Latium with the development of massive public buildings. Of course we have no proof that any of these were funded by private individuals or families, but this interpretation would clearly connect with the decline of ostentatious burials. For a brief while, the wealth which came from the Mediterranean exchange system was lavished on a few individuals, but then it was lavished on the community. This coincided with the urbanization of settlements, with their politicization.

The nature of the surplus that was created in Central Italy is not easily identified. It must be stressed that Latium was always a poor relation of Etruria, for the very clear reason that Etruria had far greater mineral resources. We should probably think in terms of cattle and sheep, textiles, and possibly human beings. Anyway, the mere extension of the system afforded possibilities for more individuals, Phoenicians and Greeks. It is also important to see in accumulations of wealth like the Tomba Bernardini, or displays like the Ficana banqueting service, the personal determination of individuals to profit themselves and their communities; Sherratt's arguments have the merit of moving away from pure abstraction.

There is some evidence for surplus production in Latium. There is the eighth century bronze hoard at Ardea, which may represent some form of collected wealth, though this is a rather dangerous example.[23] More reliable indicators are the fact of settlement stability, of growth and synoecism, which indicate the pooling of resources. The obverse of this is warfare and plundering, gaining wealth at the expense of other communities. Finally, there is the practice of gift-giving, so well attested for archaic Greece. Some system of reciprocal obligation seems likely for Central Italy as well, and it would explain the spread of exotic luxury goods into the centre of Italy. Ultimately, the best

[23] See above, p. 79.

evidence for surplus production is to be found in the votive deposits and ritual sacrifices involved in Latin religion, frequently identified above; I shall discuss the temples of Latium at a later stage.

We may also consider these issues in the light of the theoretical accounts of long-distance trade, discussed by Smith.[24] Such approaches are particularly useful for understanding the relationships between Latium and its neighbours. This account takes up a number of the ideas used by Karl Polanyi and his followers. First, there is the distinction between 'primitive economies' (with pervasive social control of production and distribution) and 'archaic economies' (with transactions concerning wealth and disposal of land). These distinctions can only be a sort of shorthand, and the theoretical entities are often insufficiently flexible to fit the variety of situations appropriate to a real community or chain of communities, but Polanyi's fundamental insight that early economy is 'embedded' in society, so that understanding of one brings understanding of the other, is important. For instance, the three modes of exchange in primitive economies are reciprocity, redistribution, and market exchange, and the reciprocal processes of gift exchange have been shown to have links with kinship ties.

Central to these concepts of long-distance trade is the port of trade, which acts as a neutral place for the interaction of two different cultures. From this one may go on to theoretical models of distribution systems. Of those applicable to this period, three sorts are relevant; network systems in which exchange is direct and uncommercialized, central place systems around a single centre with partially commercialized and administered markets, and dendritic systems characteristic of externally oriented trade.[25]

The mature dendritic system, with a functional stratification of centres, import and export of goods with other regions, and redistribution of goods within the region seems far too complex a system for Latium before 600 BC, but a less sophisticated

[24] See Smith 1987: 53–67. On ports of trade see also Humphreys 1978: 31–75.
[25] Smith defines dendritic systems as systems in which all lower level centres are tied to a single higher level centre in a chain that is entirely vertical. Therefore the system forms a tree-like (i.e. dendritic) pattern. Crucially, the system is entirely externally oriented.

version in which the centre merely performs more of the same functions than the rest, and collected goods are only exported, and only imported goods are redistributed seems more appropriate. Even so, one must be cautious; there is little evidence of the direct presence of Greeks or Phoenicians in Rome before the seventh century, and Rome's position prior to this need not have been so predominant as to make a simple network system inapplicable.

In fact, it is the situation in Central Italy as a whole which seems to give the proper scale, and although this was on the edges of the major Mediterranean networks, these can be seen to have affected the area quite considerably and to differing degrees. Southern Italy was directly affected by the early movements of Mycenaeans and others, and that Etruria was affected is shown by the transformation of its settlement pattern around 900 BC. Then Etruria shows little real development before the major exploitation of its mineral resources began in the eighth century, when it began to import and imitate Greek pottery sooner than Latium, while at Rome there appears to have developed a production of argilla figulina for the rest of the area.

The theoretical models must go hand in hand with the archaeological evidence; Latium does not show as quick and as deep an impact from outside as Etruria. As we accumulate more evidence through archaeology, the picture becomes more complex, and the interdependence of different regions more evident.

By about 600 Latium had a developed economy and society quite different from that which existed at the beginning of the millennium. All the evidence indicates that an aristocracy had evolved, capable of exploiting the resources of the individual communities, and anxious to participate in the trading exchanges of Central Italy. The second part of this thesis is concerned with the further development of individual communities, both at an economic level (which is again best indicated by archaeology) and in their social institutions, for which one has to rely more heavily on literary accounts.

THE DEVELOPMENT OF LATIN SOCIETY

The Late Bronze Age remains at Ficana, Aprilia, and Ardea are significantly earlier than the Rome–Alban Hills group, and it is quite likely that the first sites in Latium were near the coast or on waterways. Advanced bronze-working techniques were already practised, possibly on these sites, and Etruria at least had been affected to some extent by the Recent Bronze Age contacts between Sardinia and the eastern Mediterranean.

The establishment of a Latin culture, centred on Rome and the Alban Hills and distinct from the general Proto-Villanovan culture, was an important development. The growth of regional identity (the Faliscan region was separate from both Proto-Villanovan and Proto-Latial, and continued so) probably indicates an increase in population to an extent sufficient to support such a cultural choice, and also a conscious change of settlement pattern, towards stability. This cultural koine is the justification for treating Latium as a reasonably unified region with some sense of identity from an early period; the unity was gradually more clearly expressed.

At this period communities were small, but possibly not quite egalitarian; with limited material possessions, small distinctions are important. The communities tended to gather in small groups, as at Rome and Fidenae, for instance. Despite their proximity, only hundreds of yards apart in both these instances, a degree of autonomy may have been maintained. The evidence for Osteria dell'Osa in the ninth century indicates slight differences in material culture distinguishing groups.

The organization of these communities is largely a mystery. Many authors stress the gentilitial nature of early society, but this requires further definition. By the ninth century, some communities would have been quite large, large enough to contain more than one extended family or clan, though the small clusters of chamber tombs at Tor de Cenci, like that at Malagrotta in Etruria, may simply represent one extended family. Larger communities were obviously more complex.

The evidence from Osteria dell'Osa and Castel di Decima from the ninth and eighth centuries would support a view of socially differentiated communities, with a class of wealthy families, to whom was entrusted, or who attained, the office of warfare. The length of their tenure of such privilege may not have been great. Within this class the family was a further vertical division, though there was no doubt continuous endeavour by families to outdo each other in life and in death.

In fact, one could propose a model that places the greatest legal and social development of the family, as a group distinguished from the community, in the seventh and sixth centuries, connected with monumental domestic architecture, intramural burial of children, and chamber tombs. One may note that, at a parallel stage in the development of the Greek polis, the treatment of the dead also changes, with more defined groups of burials, and also with the beginning of child burials in formal necropoleis; previously, in direct contrast with the Latin practice, they had been buried inside houses.[26]

In other words, some small communities, perhaps comprising a few clans with their dependants, developed into large urban settlements, with a number of such clans, and a much larger group of dependants. The need for a clan, and emerging families within it, to preserve and reinforce its identity after such a commingling of peoples would have driven them towards the more striking displays of individuality such as the Praenestine tombs and the houses at Ficana and Satricum (and, more notably, those on the Palatine at Rome, described below).

At the same time, this must have created an even stronger aristocratic class, and this is connected, for instance, with the considerable evidence for the growth of symposiastic rituals. Religion may have played a part in this, but it seems very likely that it was turned to the benefit of these social conditions; the administration of ritual and cult was to become largely the province of the nobility.

Of course, the synoecism of smaller communities would have been preceded by links facilitating this union, perhaps creating tensions that could only be resolved by such a union. In particular, intensification, and the drive to acquire an ever greater surplus in order to participate more fully in external trading contacts, as well as to preserve one's position amid increasing local competition between and within communities, may have made larger settlements appear an attractive means of producing a greater surplus. The Praenestine exotica and the Ficana banqueting service are both chronologically in the transition period to more fully urban conditions, and indicate both sides of the process.

[26] For these developments see Sourvinou-Inwood 1983.

In Part II an important issue will be the development of social institutions within communities when the social organization as a whole changes radically, from a pre-urban to an urban state, to use a convenient terminology, and one which has been significant for Greek history in the roughly contemporary period.

The evidence cited in the preceding chapters has shown the first stages of Latin culture, followed in Period II by a significant increase in settlement. In Periods III and IVA there were major building works for the first time, an increase in the wealth of burials, and some indications of greater military activity. Aristocratic display is at its height in the late seventh and early sixth centuries (late IVA and early IVB), and by this time communities had become more closely knit. The self-definition of community and aristocracy are the themes of these four centuries, and Part II seeks to examine the further development of both.

PART II
Rome and Latium in the Sixth Century BC

8
Latium: The Archaeological Evidence

A number of recurring themes dominate the archaeology of Latin sites in the sixth and early fifth centuries; domestic architecture, temple buildings, and votive deposits. There is a notable absence of any secure evidence concerning land use, and it is quite obvious that the houses of which we know represent no more than a small part of the habitations on the various sites. One presumes that they represent the houses of the aristocrats because of their size and permanence, in which case we are ignorant, as so often, of how and where the rest of the populace lived.

We may begin with the three sites on the Via Salaria to the north of Rome. Antemnae[1] has a large number of roof-tiles, ceramic ware, copper, and bronze, which seems to represent an increase in the number of buildings and an intense occupation, perhaps the most flourishing period of the city. In addition to the large numbers of buildings seen by Lanciani before the construction of the nineteenth-century fort, some of which may have had upper storeys in clay or rough bricks, there were found cisterns, wells, and a drainage system, which inspire comparison with the drainage of the centre of Rome at a similar period. There may also have been an internal road, part of the network joining the site to Rome. A wall and ditch protected the settlement; the wall may have encircled the site though possibly not of a regular height. An antefix of the Juno Lanuvina type has been attributed to the site and seems to date from the early fifth century, indicating a sanctuary preceding the Hellenistic phase, which is the earliest we know from other evidence.[2] This particular type of

---

[1] *GRT* 152 ff.; Quilici and Quilici Gigli 1978: 157–62; Mangani 1988; *Enea nel Lazio* 48 f.
[2] For the sanctuary, see Quilici and Quilici Gigli 1978: 43 f.; for the antefix ibid. 48 f.

antefix has also been found at Falerii Veteres, Fidenae, Rome, and Satricum. There are considerable quantities of bucchero on the site too, and Holland conjectured the existence of a ferry crossing from the course of the river here. Consequently, the site may have had a remarkable range of commercial and cultural contacts with sites in Latium, Etruria, and even Faliscan and Sabine territory. Its relation with Rome has been variously estimated and will be discussed below.

Fidenae[3] prospered even more in the sixth century. Development is concentrated on the Collina di Villa Spada and the hill directly to the north of it, and an immediate parallel might be drawn with the development of the Palatine, Velia, and Capitoline hills in Rome within a united settlement. Miniature vases and an antefix representing Juno Lanuvina, again from the fifth century, seem to indicate the presence of a sanctuary on the main hill, though there is no firm indication of a forerunner of the Republican forum. There are indications of fortifications and a road network centred on the Villa Spada, in relation to the domestic buildings inferred from foundations; the way road 36 runs parallel to the tufa foundations of the building at site 35 reminds one of the route of the Via Sacra in front of the houses at the foot of the Palatine.[4]

The wealth of Fidenae may also be gauged from the beautiful jewellery found in a late sixth century female grave, comparable to some jewellery from Praeneste, which of course had a past tradition of wealth and outstanding crafted goods.[5] We are reminded that Fidenae may have been much richer in previous centuries, but that its wealth may not have come to light in archaeological reports; on the other hand, of course, it may be that Fidenae's prosperity was a result of increased trade and opportunities in the sixth century.

Even more striking than the development of the main settlement is the great increase in the territory of Fidenae. Every attempt seems to have been made to fulfil completely the agricultural potential of the area, and the presence of roof-tiles in the surrounding country may well indicate reasonably permanent

[3] *GRT* 155 ff.; Quilici and Quilici Gigli 1984: 378–98.
[4] Cf. also Castagnoli 1972; Rykwert 1988.
[5] *GRT* 10.4 260 ff. Cf. also Ammanato, Di Gennaro, and Pulimanti 1985; Di Gennaro and Messineo 1985.

dwellings. The greater part of the settlements outside the town are groupings of a larger or smaller number of dwelling-places, and the inhabitants seem to have been buried in the area which they worked. It is significant that the rich burial referred to above came from the centre of the site on the Villa Spada, while the outlying burials away from the formal necropolis are not as wealthy. Many forms of ownership and organization can be suggested, from the cooperation of a group of families to one family per area, or one family dominating a number of free, semi-free, or slave workers. It seems clear that the settlement pattern is closely tied to the road network.

In 504 BC, according to the sources, Claudius arrived from the Sabina with a number of his clients, and were settled in their own tribe, the Claudia, adjoining the Clustumina which was founded slightly later.[6] It is unfortunate that this major event has left no trace in the archaeological record despite the hypothesis that Fidenae may have lost part of her territory, thus affording an explanation for her constant support of Veii against Rome. However, the two well fortified sites just to the south of the Tutia (114) and on the Mons Sacer (214) may indicate more unsettled conditions.

There is a similar pattern at Crustumerium,[7] with dense settlement both inside and outside the walls right through to the end of the fifth century. Scatters of roof-tiles attest settlements in the surrounding territory, which tend to follow the route-ways, again well developed. This area was to become renowned for its fertility, and already *cunicoli* had been built for drainage. Bronze votive figurines have been found in a grove which was later sacred to Mars, which probably indicates the necessity of defence of the roads, the settlement, and its agricultural produce; similar offerings have been found at the Lapis Niger at Rome, at the extra-urban sanctuary at Gabii, and at Lavinium. It may be that the creation of the Tribus Clustumina gave Rome a corridor of influence bypassing the disloyal Fidenates, but there is surely no doubt that the tribal system indicates that Rome was quite properly aware of these three powerful sites. It is also significant that we are quite unable to trace a distinct

---

[6] For Claudius and his *clientes* see Livy 2. 16. 4, Dion. Hal. 5. 40, Plut. *Popl.* 21.

[7] Quilici and Quilici Gigli 1986: 281–9; *Enea nel Lazio* 49 f.

Sabine culture in any of these sites, although Crustumerium is excluded by the editors of *GRT*.

The site of Gabii represents the archaic synoecism of a number of separate communities, of which Osteria dell'Osa and Castiglione were two. Whether the site of this first town was the same as that of the town in the late Republic and the Empire remains unclear; Guaitoli maintained a continuity, but L. Quilici remains sceptical, preferring the old suggestion that the archaic city was in the area to the east of the crater, destroyed by later quarrying.[8]

Excavation has revealed little from the major temple to Juno Gabina, which was important in the succeeding centuries. The size and outline of the sixth-century temple are unknown, but a certain amount of material has been discovered, including an archaic antefix of a female head, impasto and bucchero pottery, some Geometric and Corinthian style Etruscan pottery, part of a Corinthian olpa, seventeen fragments of Attic vases, mostly of the fifth century and of undistinguished quality, and a later fifth-century Egyptian scarab made of agate. The evidence shows a steady diminution in the amount of material from the end of the sixth century and through the fifth, and little of it is clearly votive in character, compared with the material which begins in the fourth century. It has been suggested that the antefix was deposited as a votive at a later date. This pattern of decline may be related to the effects of aggressive wars.[9]

Some fortification walls have been discovered, and also a temple outside the walls. This single-roomed temple is dated to the early sixth century, and is just under 5 m by 9 m in size. It may correspond to a temple to Apollo mentioned by Livy (41. 16), but this cannot be proven. A collection of bronze kouroi and korai has been found. They are mostly about 8 or 9 cm in height, and correspond closely to similar figures found in Rome (Lapis Niger) and Satricum, Privernum, and Lavinium. A terracotta of a harpy was also found which corresponds to temple decorations on the temple at Vignale in Falerii.[10]

In the preceding period, Acqua Acetosa Laurentina was notable for its considerable necropolis; in the sixth and fifth centuries

[8] *GRT* 159 ff. (L. Quilici); Guaitoli 1981a,b.
[9] Almagro-Gorbea 1982: 603 ff.; id. 1981; *Enea nel Lazio* 43 ff.
[10] Colonna 1984: 400 f. with bibliography.

the site, now well defended, does not show much burial evidence, but it does have three stone-built houses, apparently destroyed early in the fifth century after a brief existence. The houses are datable by associated pottery, which is for the most part unexciting, though it has yielded two inscriptions and some imported material.

One building is relatively well preserved; it is separated from its neighbour by a very narrow corridor. It has four rooms at the front and two at the sides, with an open space in the middle occupied by two wells and a cistern, related to a drainage canal. The rooms vary in size from about 2 m by 2.3 m to 3 m by 4 m, and it has been suggested that one was for stabling animals and another for a kitchen. The second house was about 13.5 m by 8.5 m in all, and the lines of the third are almost impossible to ascertain. All three had tiled roofs and show the same methods of construction, either of squared blocks of stone or of piles of small stones, and sometimes both together. All three seem to open on to the same street. The third house was destroyed by a chamber tomb built in the early fifth century, and there are other such tombs on the site.[11]

Ficana, a site believed to have been destroyed by Ancus Marcius (D. Hal. 3. 38), has been located on the heights of Monte Cugno. Its natural defences were strengthened by an *agger* in the eighth century. Settlement within the site was considerable; huts, buildings, and tombs have been found. In the open spaces in between one might expect artisan activity or agriculture. The huts have associated child burials largely from the seventh century.

During the sixth century these huts were replaced by buildings, also with child burials or *suggrundaria*; about a dozen have been found, three clearly associated with one house; they are slightly smaller than those at Satricum, for example. Pottery is largely standard Latin forms, though there is also the seventh-century banqueting service described above. The site seems to show a decline in the late sixth and fifth centuries.

A hut has also been found outside the *agger* near the bottom of a river, which was presumably connected with a valley route, the river traffic, and a road from the Monte Cugno site. The first

[11] *GRT* 171 ff. with bibliography; see esp. Bedini 1981 for the houses; id. 1983.

phases of settlement on this site belong to the later seventh century, but the house itself was first constructed in the early sixth century, and it was abandoned in the early fifth century. It is unusual in shape, with three rooms in a row.[12]

Lavinium was a flourishing site in the sixth century, and a number of very important archaeological discoveries have been made there. The site was fortified in the seventh century, with a wall enclosing approximately thirty hectares and a gate which seems to have been connected with the road that led to Ardea. Exploration within the walls has been somewhat limited, but houses have been found on the site of previous huts, and there are indications of planning around the central roads and the terrain of the settlement, which was much closer to the sea in antiquity than it is now, and possibly more marshy. There is evidence of drainage work on the site. The edifices so far discovered seem to be functional, either as houses or as places of artisan activity; a number of kilns have been found on the site.[13]

Outside the walls, a number of important religious sites have been found. About three kilometres away is the sanctuary identified as that of Sol Indigetes, which shows material from the ninth century but has a concentration of terracottas and ceramic ware from the fifth century on; later authors associated this site with the burial place of Aeneas. Closer to the town is the 'Heroon of Aeneas', a seventh-century burial mound, unusual in its own right, which was the focus of continuous interventions at later periods. The first of these is marked by a sixth-century bucchero oinochoe, which postdates the rest of the material in the tomb, but is much earlier than the more extensive fourth-century interventions.[14]

The sixth century also saw the beginning of the massive sanctuary marked by thirteen altars. Altar XIII, and those under IX and VIII are the earliest, and belong to the sixth century; they were constructed of tufa, almost certainly painted, and represent a fusion of Greek models and Latin techniques. These early altars, like the rest, are aligned along a north–south line. Associated with the altars are various painted cups from Greece,

[12] *GRT* 178 ff.; Cataldi 1981, 1984; Pavolini 1981; Jarva 1981; on *suggrundaria* see Gjerstad 1954*b*.
[13] *GRT* 182 ff.; Castagnoli (ed.) 1972, 1975; Guaitoli 1981*c*; Torelli 1984.
[14] See Cornell 1977 for a careful summary.

Latium: Archaeological Evidence 135

including two from Sparta, local pottery, a number of bronze kourai and kouroi, and the bronze plaque with the inscription (in reverse):

> Castorei: Podlouqueique
> qurois

which is to be taken as a reference to Castor and Pollux, the Dioscuri. By altar VI was found a late sixth-century kore of exceptional beauty and complexity, in the manner of Ionic examples, shown holding a mirror like those found at Praeneste. The sanctuary as a whole has been variously interpreted, sometimes as a sanctuary of the Penates, sometimes as a sanctuary of Aphrodite. Close to the thirteenth altar was a house, first built in the sixth century. It had two doors and a portico and was rebuilt after a fire, at a date certainly before 450 BC The original plan was retained but further rooms were added; some of them may have been unroofed. Around 450 BC the house was destroyed in the reorganization of the area, which also involved the construction of altars V and I–IV. Domestic bucchero and impasto ware was found in the house, as well as a kiln, and also a piece of lastra fittile showing a lion. The house cannot easily be dissociated from the altars, but it appears that it was not a temple itself.[15] To the north-east of the settlement was found the sanctuary of Minerva, which shows ceramic and bronze votives from the sixth century, but also a concentration of material from the fifth century onwards. A vast collection of fourth-century terracotta figures was found at this sanctuary.[16]

It would appear that Lavinium's port contributed both to its prosperity and to the openness to foreign innovation which is shown by altar forms, the kore found by altar VI, and of course the import of the Dioscuri. Lavinium would certainly have participated in the trade along the coast to and from Campania. The clay of the site is still used because of its high quality, and recently the use of the territory for agriculture has been indicated by the discovery of a number of settlements.[17]

Ardea maintained a strongly fortified and strategically placed

---
[15] For the altars see Castagnoli 1975, for the Dioscuri, ibid. 441 ff.; for house see *Enea nel Lazio* 169 f., 183 f.   16 *Enea nel Lazio* 187 f.
[17] For the Greek influence on Lavinium, see Torelli 1984: 203 ff., Dury-Moyaeres 1981.

settlement in this period, split into three sectors; the acropolis, Civitavecchia, and Casalazzara. The fortifications are variously dated from the eighth to the fifth centuries, and no doubt underwent constant renovation.[18] The temple of the acropolis had its first phase in the sixth century; in the fifth century it was refashioned at about the same time as the building of the temple on the Civitavecchia plain; a third temple followed on the Colle della Noce. The temple on the acropolis was probably that of Juno, and measured 24 m by 33.4 m. It had three cellae, which occupied a third of the length, and then an empty central area and a double pronaos, both equal thirds of the length. A similar plan was followed in the later temple on the Colle della Noce (21 m by 35 m) which was probably dedicated to the Dioscuri. This leaves the temple of Hercules in Civitavecchia (approximately 32 m by 35 m), the inner plan of which has not survived. These three monumental temples, according to Colonna, 'made Ardea the most notable city in Latium in the fifth century as regards sacred architecture'. All three had very similar architectural decoration, leading Colonna to speak of a 'local school'. Contemporary with these developments are those in urban architecture on the site.[19] Nearby on the Colle della Banditella, a tufa altar has been found from around the end of the sixth century, similar to those found at Lavinium, and perhaps identifiable with the federal sanctuary of Venus, the 'Aphrodisium', mentioned by a number of authors as being close to Ardea.[20]

Lanuvium overlooked the plain dominated by Ardea and Satricum, and was directly connected with Antium. Lanuvium may well have been in the forefront of the fighting with the Volscians; an extraordinary warrior's tomb from the early fifth century has been found, with a helmet with eyes marked out in gold and silver, and anatomically shaped body armour. The first phases of the temple to Juno Lanuvina came in the sixth century. Around 500 BC it took monumental form, with three cellae and dimensions of around 16 m by 24 m. Antefixes of a female head and a Silenus have been found. Juno protected the city in war and

[18] *GRT* 192 ff.; *Enea nel Lazio* 10 ff.; Morselli and Tortorici 1982. See Melis and Rathje 1984: 390 f. for the houses.   [19] Colonna 1984: 409 ff.
[20] *GRT* 195.

through promoting fertility, and there was also a connection with flocks of sheep and goats which were sacred to her.[21]

Velitrae is situated on the south-western slopes of the Alban Hills, and sites from the early Colli Albani culture were situated here; for the late archaic period, the most significant aspect of the settlement that we know of is the temple under S. Maria delle Neve, which yielded remarkably beautiful architectural terracottas, directly comparable to those found at Rome and Cerveteri, as well as a votive deposit with Greek imports (kylikes from Attica and Sparta, and a bronze kore from Chiusi). The first phase of the temple appears to be sixth century, with a fifth-century refurbishment (it had three cellae and measured about 11.5 m by 13 m). Other, more tenuous indications of cult activity in the surrounding territory have also been found, but little of the material is incontrovertibly archaic.[22]

Valvisciolo on the Monte Carbolino, near the site of Caracupa where a large necropolis was found, is an extraordinary settlement, massively defended by a series of terraces rising up a slope of 200 m in height and 500 m in length. The terraces are brilliantly constructed for preventing easy attack, with defended gates, and the whole structure is reckoned to be of late seventh-century construction at the earliest. Within the settlement of Valvisciolo itself was a votive deposit from the late sixth and early fifth centuries.

This massively defended site has been connected with Norba at the forefront of Latin–Volscian hostilities. It may be that the terraces should be dated to the sixth century, since the earlier date is based largely on the date of material used for infill, and therefore not only not contemporary with the wall, but perhaps quite significantly later.[23]

Norba itself, high up in the Monti Lepini, had two acropoleis with their own walls and a regular internal plan. The site appears to have taken this form at the end of the sixth century. Considerable amounts of pottery have been found scattered, including

[21] *GRT* 196 ff.; Chiarucci 1983; Colonna 1984: 406 f.
[22] *GRT* 199 ff.; Mancini 1915: 68–88; Crescenzi 1981; Museo Civico di Velletri (Cataloghi dei musei locali e delle collezioni del Lazio, vi, 1989). Colonna 1984: 402 f. for temple; Åkerstrom 1954, Cristofani in Cristofani (ed.) 1987: 97 f. for architectural terracottas.
[23] *GRT* 209 ff.; Quilici and Quilici Gigli 1987; Mengarelli and Paribeni 1909.

some of a votive nature near the temple of Juno, which also produced architectural terracottas, among them a head of Juno Sospita from the early fifth century.[24] Signia, another site of strategic importance in the Monti Lepini, has powerful walls from the fifth century and a temple which has produced some architectural terracottas. Its identification as a temple of Juno Moneta is insecure.[25]

Circeii represents the southernmost limit of Latium Vetus, a vital promontory for the sea voyage along the coast, and also well-placed to oversee the coastal land-route. Tarquinius Superbus was supposed to have used it as a garrison for both land and sea (Livy 1. 56. 3, Dion. Hal. 4. 63), and the association of the place with the enchantress Circe may be an indication that it was a hazardous point in a sea journey. Its ancient settlement is unknown, though there is an archaic sanctuary at Colle Monticchio, refashioned in the early fifth century, about the time of the recorded capture of Circeii by Coriolanus and his Volscians (Livy 2. 39, Dion. Hal. 8. 14, Plut. *Cor.* 28).[26]

Anagnia, situated in the valley of the river Sacco, had a naturally defended acropolis, and has also provided a major votive deposit near S. Cecilia. It is interesting that the town was thought to be the chief one of the Hernici, yet the votive deposit is very similar to Latin examples. It contains a number of fragments of impasto, (Etruscan and later Campanian) bucchero, Attic Black Figure and Etrusco-Corinthian pottery, and a large range of personal ornaments in bronze, iron, bone, and glass paste.[27] The existence of relatively wealthy sites south of Rome may indicate a general increase in material wealth throughout the region in the later sixth century. The contacts with the south and with the interior of Italy are strengthened, only in part peacefully.

Finally Satricum, the famous site on the river Astura, defended naturally and by some fortifications of the sixth century, had an acropolis with a temple to Magna Mater and important domestic buildings. A temple and other houses have been found to the west

[24] *GRT* 214 ff.; Quilici and Quilici Gigli 1988; Savignoni and Mengarelli 1901, 1903, 1904; *Enea nel Lazio* 67 f.   [25] *GRT* 219 ff.
[26] *GRT* 217 ff.; *Enea nel Lazio* 70 ff.
[27] *GRT* 223 ff.; Mazzolani 1969; Bidditu and Bruni 1985; Gatti 1986, 1987, 1988, 1990, 1993; *Enea nel Lazio* 60 f.

at Macchia S. Lucia; the fortifications enclose an area of some forty hectares.[28]

The best preserved house (Building A) had roof-tiles, a pebbled floor, a well or cistern, a storeroom which included kilns for pottery, and a portico. The first phase is early sixth century, and the second phase comes after a destruction in the middle of the century. It is now dated as contemporary with Building C and the first phase of the monumental temple, and although the plan is not completely regular, there seems to have been a clear attempt to build three houses and the temple on the same orientation around 540 to 530 BC. The first phase of Building A produced an almost square edifice, about 25 m by 24 m, with a number of rooms about 4 m by 5 m, a blind wall, and a courtyard. The walls seem to have been of wattle and daub on stone foundations. The second square building (Building B) between Building A and the temple, probably looked over a piazza and an altar, since there was a long-standing votive deposit there. Building C was built on the other side of the temple. The houses, which are properly compared to houses of a similar plan at Acquarossa, seem to have gone into decline c.500 BC, and a connection with the activities of the Volscians in the area has been drawn. Concerning Building A, Maaskant-Kleibrink wrote, 'Judging from its size and position, it would seem possible that it was a "Regia" resembling that in Rome. However, the finds recovered from the building make this less likely. The pottery is that of a regular instrumentum domesticum.'[29]

The first phase of the Satricum temple to Mater Matuta, which was built on the site of the previous sacellum and votive deposit, dates from the third quarter of the sixth century, had a single cella, and measured perhaps 8 m by 21 m; there was then a reconstruction around 530 BC to form a larger single cella temple about 16.5 m by 27 m; the third phase, dated to the early fifth century, was much larger, measuring about 21.4 m by 34 m, with three cellae. There were different phases of architectural terracottas, and it is by these that we are able to make these datings. Those of the third temple include the merely decorative, as well as various heads, a harpy, a 'typhoeus' (a man with wings, and

---

[28] *GRT* 230 ff.; Maaskant-Kleibrink 1987; Chiarucci and Gizzi 1985.
[29] Maaskant-Kleibrink 1987: 95 f.; quote at 95.

legs ending in snakes) and two groups in which a satyr is seen raping a maenad. The sixth-century votive deposits are largely of impasto, bucchero, and Etrusco-Corinthian pottery vessels of various shapes.[30] The main temple site has yielded large and important quantities of pottery in a deposit dating from the seventh century. In a recent publication of unstratified finds, Greek imported pottery made up about fifty vessels out of over 5,000, i.e. roughly 1 per cent. The proportion is probably an important indication of the rarity of these imports.[31] This is the general pattern in Latium, as this account should have indicated. Only Lavinium, a port itself, can be shown with any confidence to have had direct contact with the Greek world. Some sites in the south may have had contacts with Campanians; others quite possibly obtained their Greek goods through Rome, with which they had other demonstrable contacts, notably in architectural terracottas, or Etruria, whence a large amount of bucchero was imported. Bucchero and Etrusco-Corinthian pottery formed the greatest proportion by far, over 3,500 vessels, i.e. 70 per cent. This must represent a very significant exchange between the two regions; there was no reason for Etruscans to make such massive donations at Satricum.

The site has also produced a fifth-century necropolis with over forty tombs, the largest in Latium from this time. The tombs are characterized by the unusually large numbers of locally made pottery vessels found in each *corredo*. It is interesting to note that the site is reported to have come under Volscian control in the fifth century; if this is reliable, then it would indicate a difference in burial practices between Latins and Volscians at that time.[32]

Some general conclusions can be drawn about the lifestyle of the Latins in the sixth century. In almost all the sites there was some religious establishment, and most of these found a permanent stone building in the late sixth century. This is roughly contemporary with the first appearance of stone-built houses, and both seem to contribute to the rise of town-planning. Fortifications were important in this period; the choice of sites had

---

[30] De Waele 1981; Colonna 1984; Maaskant-Kleibrink 1987: 34 f.; Rendeli 1989. Full account of terracottas in Knoop 1987; cf. Lulof 1991.   [31] Stibbe 1984–5.
[32] Heldring and Gnade 1987; Gnade 1992.

been determined long before by considerations of defensibility, but natural protection no longer seemed sufficient. On the other hand, there was also a development in most areas of the capacities of the countryside for agriculture. No doubt there is some connection; intensified agriculture needed more defence and excited more attention from others. Greater surpluses would have permitted increased exchange, and raiding would have had a significant impact. Finally, although we know of more burials from the late sixth and even the fifth century, these are still rare, and nothing inclines one to doubt the general statement that patterns of burial across Latium changed in the course of the sixth century.

Specific details about the nature of domestic and sacred buildings in the archaic period can also be given. In general, there are two types of houses; those nearest the centres of settlements tend to be the largest, often made of two rows of rooms on either side of an open courtyard, with either a blind wall or another set of rooms at the back. Houses outside the city, like those at Ficana, seem to be constructed of a single row. All the settlement sites show a degree of conscious planning, given the nature of the site, and perhaps conforming largely to already existing route networks. It is possible that some of the houses which we know, or some similar to them, had the same functions as the Regia at Rome, but it is much clearer that the larger buildings were the homes of the wealthy and noble families of Latium.[33]

Through the period we can see a development in temple architecture and decoration, from the early single cella temples to the Tuscan-style temples with three cellae, and columns, which were on a much larger scale. The number of refurbishments of temples is striking; some sites clearly maintained their sanctity, but this made them the focus of repeated demonstrations of the ability of the Latin settlements to match advances in other parts of Central Italy, and re-express their religious concerns in the most up-to-date of ways.[34]

It is worth noting at this point that the Tuscan style of temple, with a tripartite structure and three cellae at the rear, does not

[33] On houses in general see Melis and Rathje 1984.
[34] On temples in general see Colonna 1984; Cristofani 'I santuari: tradizione decorative' in Cristofani (ed.) 1987: 95 ff.; Rendeli 1989.

have parallels with the Greek temples already being built in the south of Italy. Far closer parallels are to be found in Phoenician and Punic temples, which also seem to have been tripartite. One example is to be found at Kition on the island of Cyprus; others may be cited from Punic Sardinia. There is a temple to Bes at Bithia, and two temples at Monte Sirai, one on the tophet. Punic temples, it is suggested, had a vestibule, a central area and a *penetrale*, sometimes divided into two cellae for Melqart and Tanit.[35] On the other hand, the traditions of architectural terracottas as decoration appear to have originated in the Greek south of Italy and in Campania. Temples seem to show the same syncretizing trends as religious belief.[36]

[35] Karageorghis 1976: 76; Pesce 1961 fig. 7; Barreca (ed.), 1985: 317; *Ichnussa* 376.
[36] Douglas van Buren 1921, 1923, 1926; also Wikander 1986.

9
Etruria: The Archaeological Evidence

Some aspects of the archaeological evidence for Etruria are given here as a counterpoint to the more detailed presentation of evidence from Rome and Latium.[1] In general, the Etruscan evidence shows more variety of local exotic ware, and more imported material in terms of types and quantity. The funerary evidence from Etruria is considerably greater and more elaborate than that from Latium, and only Rome is on a scale comparable with the great Etruscan centres.

By the end of the seventh century the major Etruscan settlements were fairly advanced; they were developing orthogonal planning and there are other suggestions of a unified approach to the layout and organization of the community, through religion, fortifications, and clearly demarcated trading areas.[2] Orthogonal planning was probably connected with augural practices, though there was a *spectio* along the Via Sacra in Rome, a city notorious for its lack of orthogonality.[3]

Beyond this there was also a development of the countryside around the cities, as was dramatically illustrated by the cellar or storeroom from the sixth century found in the territory of Veii.[4] One may assume that smaller settlements were being founded to exploit the agricultural potential of the area, and support for this has been given by the Tuscania survey.[5]

The small settlement of Acquarossa seems to have developed rapidly from the later seventh century on, and by the sixth century we find outstanding monumental buildings in Zone F,

---

[1] General accounts in *Rasenna* 1986; Torelli 1985; bibliography in Serra Ridgway 1991.   [2] Torelli in *Rasenna* 46 f.
[3] Colonna in *Rasenna* 433; Coarelli 1986: 100 ff.
[4] Murray Threipland and Torelli 1970; a cellar or storeroom with 6th-century pottery, a little of it imported.   [5] Barker and Rasmussen 1988.

at least two of which (A and C) can be reconstructed with some confidence. These alone have terracotta friezes of a type reminiscent of those found in the Forum Boarium at Rome; it has been suggested that they were made on the site, but that the moulds for them had been brought in, perhaps from Cerveteri, since the quality of the moulds seems to have been greater than the quality of the friezes produced. While a number of the houses found at both sites are roughly rectangular, with a row of rooms next to each other, and comparable to the house found at Ficana, the two buildings in Zone F at Acquarossa are much larger and have a more complex ground-plan. It seems reasonable to contrast these buildings with the Regia at Rome and the houses found at Satricum; unfortunately, the finds inside them are largely of architectural remains, and there is nothing to give a clue as to their function. They may have had a religious aspect or they may have been palaces; they may indeed, as Torelli suggested, have begun as palaces and then been made public religious buildings in the crisis at the beginning of the fifth century, which saw the power of the aristocracy threatened.[6]

In terms of social development, there is much significance in the development of the Etruscan armies on the basis of a sort of hoplite organization, a development which is comparable to the expansion of luxurious burials to a greater number of individuals. Previously, it has been suggested, Etruscan warfare was based on the principle of individual combat, and thus very much the province of a few aristocrats. Opening this up to a wider group is a significant breach of the tight grip which a small section of society had had over the whole; yet it is still far from suggesting an egalitarian society, and Torelli in particular has shown eloquently and interestingly how Etruscan cities maintained an oligarchic society for a long period after what appears to have been a crisis in the early fifth century.[7]

One extremely important development is the introduction of a form of coinage around 570 BC in the form of bronze bars, which have been discovered in the fascinatingly heterogeneous cargo of

[6] For Acquarossa see Wikander and Roos 1986; Østenberg 1975; Stopponi (ed.) 1985; Wikander and Wikander 1990.
[7] D'Agostino 1989, 1990; Torelli 1985; see also Torelli 1983.

a ship wrecked off the island of Giglio during the sixth century. Recognizable coinage followed in the early fifth century.[8]

Another significant development is the increase in the number of tombs found in the cities, from a few very wealthy ones to a number of tombs, sometimes as many as a hundred, which may not be as spectacular as their predecessors but are clearly in the same tradition. A number deliberately echo domestic architecture, and parallels to this can be found in Faliscan and Sabine territory. This expansion of the practice would seem to indicate some loosening of the control of a tight aristocracy, and the spread of affluence. It is significant that it is not so marked in central northern Etruria, where the contacts with the Greek world were perhaps not as strong. No doubt the slight decrease in conspicuous consumption of wealth in tombs was more than offset by the development of notable public and private architecture.[9]

One significant indicator of the increase in the possibilities for affluence is offered by the ports at Gravisca (Tarquinia) and Pyrgi (Cerveteri). Both ports have large sacred complexes which also show the presence of a wide range of traders from the Mediterranean in the sixth and fifth centuries. At Pyrgi the gold sheets indicate clear Punic influence; at Gravisca the names found on pots offered as dedications in the temples correspond closely with names found at Naucratis in Egypt, and contacts have been assumed with Corinth, Aegina, and Athens.[10]

At Pyrgi,[11] there appears to have been a small temple built around the mid-sixth century, but replaced at the end of the century by a much larger complex. The whole was oriented in the direction of the road to Caere. One temple was dedicated to Leucothea or Ilithyia. Leucothea was the Greek goddess of the dawn, and her temple is mentioned in connection with the sack of Pyrgi by Dionysius in 384 BC.[12] The temple was rebuilt again around the middle of the fifth century, at which time it gained the

---

[8] Bound and Vallintine 1983; Bound, 'Una nave mercantile di età arcaica all'Isola del Giglio', in *Il Commercio Etrusco Arcaico* 64–70. The wreck contained Corinthian and bucchero ware, Phoenician amphorae, and at least two metal ingots. See also Cristofani in *Rasenna* 139 f.; Parise, 'La prima monetazione etrusca', in *Il Commercio Etrusco Arcaico*, 257–61. [9] Torelli 1983; 48 ff.
[10] Moretti 1984; Torelli 1971, 1977, 1982. [11] Coarelli 1988: 331 ff.
[12] Ps.-Arist., *Oecon*. 2. 2. 20 = 1349b; Polyaen. *Strateg*. 5. 2. 2; Aelian *Var. Hist*. 1. 20.

famous architectural relief apparently depicting two scenes from the myth of the Seven at Thebes.

Beside the second temple, which was built at the end of the sixth century in the reorganization of the whole area, was a small open space with a circular altar and a well,[13] and it is from here that the three well-known sheets of gold were recovered, two of which are inscribed in Etruscan and one in Phoenician. Although not all the details of the inscriptions can be deciphered, it seems beyond doubt that they represent a deed of dedication by one Thefarie Velianas, the king of Caere, to the goddess Uni-Astarte.[14] A contemporary inscription on an argilla vessel bears the word *Unial*, the genitive of Uni. So there can be little doubt about the name of the deity worshipped in this temple, and the identification with Astarte suggests that she was for the Etruscans a goddess of sexuality and fertility, and may in important respects have been comparable to the deity Fortuna worshipped in Rome and particularly associated with Servius Tullius. The architectural decoration seems to have reminiscences of decoration on temples to Aphrodite in Cyprus, and in this context it may be relevant that the inscriptions on the gold leaves were in eastern Phoenician as opposed to Carthaginian Punic.[15]

At Gravisca[16] there are signs of cult activity from the early sixth century; a sacellum to Turan was built about 580 BC, and then a larger building, which seems to have been attached to a house, was constructed around 530 BC In about 470 BC, the area was cleared for a larger sanctuary. Torelli suggested that the house belonged to an aristocrat or even a king, and that the removal of this personal control of the cult was another significant indication of the revolutionary changes in Etruscan society at the beginning of the fifth century. From the numerous Greek objects found with inscriptions, it is clear that the Greeks equated Turan with Aphrodite. Some 120 Attic vases have been found, and around 110 from the Greeks in Italy, together with a unique cache of about 3,000 lamps. Gras made an important revisionist statement concerning this site, in which he suggested that the link with Tarquinia should not be overstated (though it should

[13] Coarelli 1988: 357 ff.
[14] For the texts see *TLE* 873, 874. See also Pallottino *et al.* 1981; Coarelli 1988: 328 ff.   [15] Verzár 1980.
[16] Colonna (ed.) 1985: 141 ff.

not be excluded either); the major connection in the third quarter of the sixth century, he suggests, is with Caere and the trade route north to Gaul; only at the end of the century did the site assimilate more to the culture of Tarquinia, which in the previous hundred or so years should be seen as closely connected with Tuscania.[17] Gravisca's status as a Greek *emporion* would explain some cultural divergences from inland sites.

The religious buildings at these two ports are of such evident importance that Torelli for one has been led to suggest that trade was controlled through the medium of religion.[18] One interesting inscription on an amphora deposited in the temple of Aphrodite at Gravisca has the words *udrie metrie*, that is, a fair measure of liquid.[19] The role of temples in the trade of the ancient world is not easily understood, though the individual sanctuaries attested at Naucratis may indeed suggest that such places contributed to a sense of local identity in trading. In other words, the independent trading of adventurous individuals with little reference to a local centre gave way to a more organized exchange system in which centres like Corinth and Athens preserved their own interests. In this context it is interesting to note the change in the nature of pottery imported to Etruria, which has often been noted, with the early predominance of Corinth giving way in the course of the sixth century to the predominance of Athens.[20]

There was not only a crossover of material goods; ways of life and styles of architecture were also shared with the larger world of Italy and the Mediterranean. The striking architectural terracottas which have been mentioned in connection with Latin temples are also found in Etruscan sites on sacred and domestic buildings. The ultimate source of this development seems to have been Magna Graecia and Sicily, where a number of beautiful and elaborate friezes have been found, directly comparable to those of Central Italy; but the contribution of Campania was considerable and includes the provision of some of the moulds.[21]

[17] Gras in Bonghi Jovino and Chiaramonte Treré (eds.) 1987: 141–52.
[18] Torelli in *Rasenna*, 47.   [19] Torelli 1977: 400 f.
[20] Cristofani in *Rasenna*, 124 ff.; Spivey and Stoddart 1990: 84 ff.
[21] Andrén 1940 remains the fundamental collection; cf. also Cristofani in Cristofani (ed.) 1987: 95 ff.; for connection with Magna Graecia, see Roncalli in *Rasenna*, 595 ff. Comments in Heurgon, 1969: 9–31 are relevant; cf. Bonghi Jovino in *Atti* 1989: 667–82. For Campania see Frederiksen 1984: 174 ff.; and for 6th-century friezes from Metaponto strikingly similar to the Roman examples, see Frederiksen 1976–7: 53 ff. figs. 10, 16.

As Cristofani showed through his approach to art in sixth-century Etruria, culture had a vital role in defining social status and allegiances.[22] The orientalizing, especially of the coastal cities, is partly a function of their involvement with the trading links through the Mediterranean, but it is also a reflection of the desire which Etruscan families had for a certain manner of artistic endeavour; one can see the development from the seventh century of local styles of vase painting and tomb painting which show some similarities in content. It must be of some significance that little of this artistic independence was shown in Latium. To speak of the austerity of Latium in this respect may not be the whole answer.

Crucially, the number of sites explored in some detail in Etruria allows us to make quite precise comparisons which reveal a diversity of culture in the region; from the coastal sites with their considerable Greek imports and their debt to Greek artistic patterns to the more isolated inland sites, importing imitation Greek pottery like that of the Micali painter and developing their own styles, and then north to important sites like Volaterra and Murlo, which appear to make contact with the Greek world rather later, and turn their attention more to the north of Italy and southern Central Europe. We can also compare the astonishing concentration of tomb paintings in Tarquinia, and apparently in only one of its necropoleis, with exciting developments in pottery at Cerveteri and the emergence of that site into the Greek historical record.[23]

The nature of Etruscan exports, the basis of the economy which allowed the Etruscan cities to participate fully in these trading links, is as ever obscure, but there can be little doubt that the mineral resources at Elba in particular were important.[24] Bucchero as well is found far afield, and no doubt it was used as a container as well as an object in its own right.[25] We may underestimate how much could be gained from control of shipping routes, and piracy was probably a lucrative endeavour.

Gras has collected the evidence for Etruscan activity in south-

[22] Cristofani 1978.
[23] There are countless books on Etruscan art; important treatments include Brendel 1978, Spivey and Stoddart 1990, Bonfante (ed.) 1986. On tomb paintings see Steingräber (ed.) 1986; also Blanck and Weber-Lehmann (eds.) 1987 for some paintings which no longer survive; Spivey 1987 for the Micali Painter.
[24] Spivey and Stoddart 1990: 77.   [25] Rasmussen 1979 143 ff.

Etruria: Archaeological Evidence   149

ern Italy and Greece.[26] The material evidence is admittedly fairly poor; very few objects have been found, even in Sicily. More significant is the early fifth-century stele from Lemnos, which appears to be written in a language at least related to Etruscan, and the finds at Olympia and Delphi, which do seem to be Etruscan votives from the early fifth century, at the time when the Etruscans, with the assistance of the Carthaginians, were engaged in battles against Greeks. After the defeat of the Etruscans in a sea battle off Alalia, the directions of Etruscan development seem to have changed towards the mainland routes, south into Campania and Lucania, and north into central Europe, and Greek imports tail off later in the fifth century. The evidence in Greece must represent something more than the activities of a few individuals; it is a late and brief phenomenon, but important none the less.

Three general conclusions can be made. First, both Latium and Etruria exhibit an increasingly sophisticated pattern of settlement, both within their urban sites and in the territory; this may imply an increase in population and in exploitation. Both areas seem to have had an aristocratic hierarchy, though the one in Latium used public buildings instead of funeral display, whereas the one in Etruria used both to indicate its supremacy. Public buildings of a religious and a secular nature are increasingly common; apart from the temples mentioned above, Staccioli has suggested that there was a sort of Regia at Aquarossa,[27] and Torelli has identified an equivalent of the Comitia Calabra in a temple to Uni in Tarquinia;[28] neither is certain.

Secondly Latium, including Rome, seems to have been dependent on Etruria, and not an independent participant in the trading activities of Central Italy. Thirdly, contacts with Greek and Punic civilization were close and frequent, and undoubtedly transformed Italian society, but they do not seem to have been imposed, and Etruscans and Latins seem to have been able to choose what they wished to emulate. For a brief while, towards the end of the sixth century, contacts between the various cultures were very close, but then differences seem to have emerged, and there was a drifting apart.

[26] Gras 1985: 391 ff.; Lemnos 615 ff.; Delphi 681 ff.
[27] For instance, in Staccioli 1976.
[28] Torelli in Bonghi Jovino and Chiaramonte Treré (eds.) 1987.

10
Rome: The Archaeological Evidence

This chapter is a brief account of the archaeological evidence from Rome from the early sixth to the early fifth centuries. The evidence is arranged in four sections. The first attempts to show the evidence for Rome's settlement pattern. The second is concerned with the religious buildings and sites in Rome; the social and political implications of religion are the subject of a later chapter. The third section focuses on the Forum area, and then on the Via Sacra leading out of the Forum, and the other roads in Rome. The final section is an account of the Forum Boarium. A concluding section summarizes the evidence for the unity of Rome, the main focus and purpose of the building activity, and the extent of non-Latin influence on the settlement.

As I have explained in my introduction, I have endeavoured to base my account so far on the archaeological evidence, and to leave aside the literary evidence for the early history of Rome, believing that its reliability is weak. When we come to the sixth century, however, it is less easy to be so dogmatic. There are coincidences between the literary and archaeological evidence which are hard to explain away, and many of the dates for the foundation of temples and for other events come from the written accounts, occasionally with the welcome agreement of the material record.

According to the ancient sources, chief among whom are Livy and Dionysius, Rome came to have at least two Etruscan kings, Tarquinius Priscus and Tarquinius Superbus. Between them came the obscure figure of Servius Tullius. In this period, Rome developed its institutions and its topography; the second Tarquin in particular is associated with major building works. It is striking that these works in Rome before the Republic do indeed fall in the sixth century, and for various reasons we may assume that Rome attained considerable political sophistication at the same time.

Unfortunately, we cannot be absolutely sure that the later authors were doing more than guessing at the achievements of these obscure kings. It is interesting that the earlier kings tend to be pigeon-holed as 'military leader' or 'religious reformer'. If information was organized through the construction of ideal types of leader for these kings, something similar may have occurred with the later ones. So Tarquinius Superbus takes much of the credit for a late sixth-century expansion of Roman influence in Latium and southern Etruria, while his predecessor Servius Tullius is regarded as the great political founder, who reorganized the city into four tribes or regional areas.

Servius is mentioned a number of times in the following pages, but he remains a very obscure figure. He is not clearly Etruscan; nor is he a Roman patrician. He has been plausibly associated with a military supporter of the elder Tarquin, much as Gelon rose to the Syracusan tyranny through being the cavalry commander of another tyrant. At the same time, he became the object of much speculation in antiquity, as is shown by the fanciful accounts of the prodigies which attended his birth. He was said to be descended from a slave, which is likely to be an invention based on the similarity of his name to the Latin word for slave (*servus*). His rise to the kingship is therefore regarded as a product of great good fortune. He is closely associated with the goddess Fortuna.

Where the boundary lies between fact and fiction is unclear. If Servius did in fact build temples to Fortuna, did someone work out that he must therefore have been very lucky, or did his luck lead to his being associated with temples to this deity? We cannot tell. What I think is irrefutable is that Rome expanded dramatically in the sixth century; that she did so under the influence of some powerful figures who most likely included the three recorded kings; and that the archaeological evidence presented below indicates some aspects of what Rome looked like, as well as the creation of buildings and areas which reflect the growing political maturity of the community.

DEFINING THE CITY

By the end of the sixth century, Rome exhibits sufficient characteristics to be regarded as an urban settlement, on any sensible definition. Its festivals and fortifications indicate a unity between the various parts of the settlement. Its social and political development is advanced, and based on the organization of a large territory. It has an effective military system. It cannot make much sense to simplify a complex process, which can be traced back at least as far as the building of the first defences in the eighth century, and pick a point at which Rome becomes an urban settlement, but we are able to trace some stages in the development.[1]

Fortifications are an important indication of the self-awareness of a community. To build fortifications requires communal effort. It also requires a recognition of what needs to be defended, a definition of territory; and it implies a concept of other settlements as potential threats to be guarded against.

Rome may have had an earthen rampart towards the east from quite an early period, which would not distinguish it from its neighbours.[2] According to the sources, Servius built a wall around the city for defence, and this wall has been assiduously sought by some archaeologists. Numerous remnants of a wall in Grotta Oscura tufa were indeed found, but already by the end of the nineteenth century there were suggestions that this edifice was not in fact the Servian wall, but a defensive system built after the catastrophe of the Gallic War, and certainly not until after the capture of Veii in 396 BC, since Veii controlled the Grotta Oscura quarries.[3] Indeed some sections around the Aventine seem even later than this, belonging to the Second Punic War and the civil disorders of 87 BC.[4]

[1] See Ampolo 1980-2 for some aspects of this; also Drews 1991. The bibliography on the early state is considerable. An early formulation was made by Childe in 1950, based on a comparison between Near Eastern and Meso-American centres and smaller communities. Smith in Ucko, Tringham, and Dimbleby (eds.) 1972: 567-74 analyses the Roman situation in terms of association and internal exigencies eroding the basis of the patrician dominated settlements. Further definitions are to be found in Claessen and Skalník (eds.) 1978 and Cohen and Service (eds.) 1978.   [2] See Holloway 1994: ch. 7 on the issue of Rome's walls.
[3] See Thomsen 1980: 222 f.; the identification was upheld by, among others, Lanciani and Jordan, and refuted by Richter and Pinza. Richter had showed that the letters on the wall could not date to the 6th century; another argument was adduced by Tenney Frank (1924: 113 ff.) that Veii controlled the quarries of Grotta Oscura, and that Rome could not have afforded to purchase so much stone at an early period; nor would Veii have given it as a present for the fortification of a rival city.
[4] See Säflund 1932; Lugli 1933 at 44 f.; id. 1934: 132 ff.; id. 1957: 264 ff.

Rome: Archaeological Evidence 153

In addition to the Grotta Oscura sections, there were parts of the wall constructed in capellacio. Säflund[5] argued that these belonged to the post-Gallic War period as well, possibly even to the repairs of 87 BC, but Gjerstad[6] thought that some of the cappellacio may have belonged to an earlier defensive system, preceding that of the aftermath of the Gallic War. This system, he believed, defended the individual hills, and did not form a circuit of the city.

The picture is further complicated by the account given in the sources of a great *agger* of earth, like that at Ardea, which was also attributed to Servius. Säflund[7] attributed a section known as Agger K to this period, but it might just as easily be a part of the fortification work after the Gallic War. Gjerstad then focused attention on the section Quirinal G, which was excavated by Boni at the beginning of this century. In the second stratum Boni found a fragment of an Attic red-figured kylix, dated by scholars like Beazley and Paribeni, with some caution, to the early fifth century.[8] However, the fragment does not date the *agger*, since it is a solitary indication and might just as easily have been brought from somewhere else at a later date, when the soil for the *agger* was being collected.[9]

The conclusion must be that there is no archaeological evidence at all for a wall or rampart around Rome until the fourth century.[10] Ampolo suggests, more cautiously, that although an 11 km perimeter wall is quite implausible for this date, there may in fact be some early fortifications which were taken over in the later construction.[11] Gjerstad's suggestion of individual hill fortifications is supported by Carandini's discovery of the Palatine wall, which seems to separate it from the Velia, although in none of its phases was this wall alone adequate for defence.[12] Circuit walls

---

[5] Säflund 1932: 243 ff.   [6] Gjerstad 1954: 56 f.; *Early Rome*, iii. 27 ff.
[7] Säflund 1932: 122 ff., 163 ff., 231, and 248 f.
[8] Beazley quoted in Gjerstad 1951 at 414 n. 10; *Early Rome*, iii. 40 n. 3; Paribeni quoted in Alföldi 1964: 321 n. 6.   [9] Quilici in *GRT* 40.
[10] Coarelli 1986: 112.
[11] Ampolo 1986: 446 f. Cf. Todd 1978: 14, who assigns the first rampart to the early 5th century. Cf. Valditara 1986 who accepts the ancient tradition uncritically.
[12] Some details concerning this wall are now to be found in *GRT* 79 ff.

were the answer to more developed warfare than that of the sixth century.[13]

If Gjerstad was right to see a system of fortifications of individual hills, then we might presume that these protected areas of habitation and burial. The *murus terreus* indicates the possibility of a more general defence, possibly from an early period. The settlement pattern of Veii and Fidenae, among other sites, suggests a patchy settlement of land with areas either unused or with an agricultural function that has left no archaeological trace.[14] Beloch calculated an area of 426 hectares within the fourth-century walls; in the sixth century this may have been settled in a similar way.[15] In other words, one might see an early general defence of the settlement and also continuing defence of individual regions, the hills representing fortified refuges for a diffuse population.[16]

In this context we must also consider the Pomerium or sacred boundary of Rome. Momigliano summed up this issue succinctly when he said, 'Strictly speaking we do not even know what the Pomerium was and when it became an accepted notion.' Ancient scholars had similar difficulties; they tended to use an etymological argument to place it *post murum*. Of course, if there was no circumvallatory wall in the sixth century, either the wall and the Pomerium were unconnected, or else the Pomerium was fixed independently of the walls. It has been argued that the Pomerium was clearly fixed at the Forum Boarium, so that the port there was

[13] For an account of Etruscan and Latin military organization in the archaic age, see D'Agostino 1989, 1990; see above, p. 110 ff. It seems highly unlikely that a full-scale siege could be conducted by any Central Italian state much before the 5th century, especially of a settlement as large as Rome undoubtedly was. The accounts of sieges in Livy and Dionysius seem hopelessly anachronistic. This does not mean that there were no assaults on settlements, or that some defences were not necessary.

[14] For Veii see Ward-Perkins 1961; for Fidenae see Quilici and Quilici Gigli 1986.

[15] Ampolo in Momigliano and Schiavone (eds.) 1988 for the figures and comparisons. Beloch's original calculations were in Beloch 1886; for other Latin sites see Guaitoli 1977.

[16] For references to walls around Rome in the regal period, see Cic. *De Rep* 2 11 (all the kings); Flor. 1. 4; Aur. Vict. *Vir Ill* 5. 2 (Ancus Marcius); Livy 1. 36. 1; Dion. Hal 3. 67. 4 (Tarquinius Priscus); Livy 1. 44 3; Dion. Hal. 4. 14. 1 (Servius Tullius); Strabo 5. 3. 7; Dion. Hal. 4. 54. 2; Plin *NH* 3. 67. POxy 2088 on the reign of Servius Tullius at line 15 contains the letters: *]dita est eaque Roma muro[*, suggesting the building of a wall.

Rome: Archaeological Evidence 155

in a sense extra-urban. Walls attributed to the sixth century have been found in this position, and even later walls observe this line.[17] Carandini's discoveries may be relevant here. Tacitus (*Ann.* 12. 24) indicated that the Pomerium originally circled the Palatine, and he may preserve here a memory of the old wall.

We come finally to festivals, which have been thought to indicate various stages of the growth of Rome. We must assume that a religious festival can in some way preserve as it were a photograph of a particular period in time, and not become so changed over time as to make the original details unrecognizable.[18]

One such festival is the Lupercalia. At one stage it was thought that the Luperci ran around the Palatine hill, and this was taken as giving Tacitus the evidence for the Pomerium, which he assigned to Romulus. Even if the interpretation of the ritual was correct, this would only have told us something about Tacitus' method, and would not have constituted a very convincing proof that the Pomerium originally took this course. In fact it has been shown that the Luperci did not run around the Palatine, but ran up and down the Via Sacra, which is roughly the same area in which the ritual of the Equus October took place. The festival thus has no bearing on the extent of Rome at any time.[19]

The festival of the Septimontium might appear to have more potential, but it is similarly problematic. The canonical seven hills of Rome were variously given by scholars in antiquity, and there is some reason for suggesting that the canon was invented by Varro. It is at least possible that the festival referred to two *saepti montes*, the Palatine and the Velia, to which a sacrifice was made on the day of the festival. The hypotheses which could arise

[17] Momigliano 1963: 100; Magdelain 1990: 155–91; Ruggiero 1990 for the Forum Boarium walls.
[18] This image is used by Fraschetti 1984.
[19] The topography of the Lupercalia was explained by Michels (1953). The bibliography is extensive; see Ulf 1982. Originally Preller (1858), convinced that the ceremony was a *lustratio*, assumed that the Luperci made a circuit of the city, and Jordan and Hülsen (1878–1907, ii. 269) identified this with the Pomerium around the Palatine described in Tacitus (*Ann.* 12. 24). The central texts are Varro *LL* 6. 34 and Augustine *De Civ Dei* 18. 12, which may well be based on Varro. As Nilsson said (*Latomus*, 15, 1956, 133–6 at 133), Michels 'a montré que l'opinion répandue, selon laquelle les Luperques couraient autour du Palatin, n'est pas justifiée et que, par conséquent, les conclusions tirées de là ne sont pas fondées'. For the Equus October see Ampolo 1981*b*.

out of such a belief are numerous; it might refer to a very early state of affairs, or to a divided settlement, or to the predominance of these hills in the sixth century. What it would not do would be to indicate anything about the extent of the city.[20]

The best indication of unity is probably the Equus October festival, which is discussed below in the context of the Regia, for this ceremony appears to connect the Via Sacra with the Campus Martius, and the competition between the Sacravienses and the Suburanenses seems to indicate regions of the settlement.

Finally, we know of a number of processions around Rome and its territory. The problem with using these as evidence is that our belief in the date of their formation depends largely on our belief in the extent of Rome's territory at any given moment, so that one is immediately involved in a circularity. The mysterious ritual on 16 and 17 March, which involved a procession to the twenty-seven Argeorum Sacraria and then the casting of twenty-seven puppets into the Tiber on 14 May, has been variously interpreted. The Capitoline and the Aventine hills are not included in either list. It would make sense to see this as repre-

[20] The basic ancient accounts of the Septimontium are Varro *LL* 5.41 and Festus 474, 476L. On Varro see Gelsomino (1975, 1976), who suggests that Varro invents much of the tradition of the seven-hilled settlement. Festus is quoting Antistius Labeo, but this has become garbled. The main quotation gives eight hills, not seven. There is a definite statement about seven hills in Paulus' epitome of Festus 458L, but the original Festus is unfortunately corrupt, and Paulus was an unreliable conveyer of his source. Various attempts have been made to solve the contradiction; Wissowa (1904) pointed out that the Subura and the Succusa, a summit on the Caelius, were frequently confused, hence the introduction of the Caelius may have been a gloss on the Subura which was a valley rather than a hill. This was followed by Gjerstad (1962: 23–4; cf. *Early Rome*, v. 38–41), and by Park Poe (1978), whose historical reconstruction seems fanciful. The other approach is to reject the tradition of seven hills altogether, as do Holland (1953) and Poucet (1960, 1967b), who offer the alternative etymology. Apart from Antistius Labeo's statement that a sacrifice was made to Palatuar and Velia on the day of the festival, the 11 December, there are only two other references to the ritual, one in Plutarch (*Quaest. Rom.* 69), and the other in John Lydus (*De Mens.* IV 155). Ampolo (1981b) explains the veto on using yoked animals on this day which elicits Plutarch's question by reference to Festus 92L, which gives the sound of a yoked animal as a bad omen, and claims that this is one of the *auspicia propertvia* and thus appropriate to the Septimontium procession. However, even if Ampolo is right, the phrase which he invokes is only present by supplement in one manuscript of Festus 286L, and given by Festus as *pedestria auspicia* (Festus 287L). Leading off from Festus 284L on *publica sacra*, Fraschetti 1984 suggests that the Septimontium was not a festival for the whole populus but only for the *montani*; the *pagani* would have similarly specific festivals.

senting the four regions whose creation is attributed to Servius in the sixth century, as Varro's evidence suggests.[21]

There is also the nexus of sacrifice and ritual shared between the Amburbium (of which we know practically nothing), the Ambarvalia, and the ceremonies of the Fratres Arvales, which may or may not be identical. The Ambarvalia involved a sacrifice at certain places around the perimeter of the Ager Romanus, and Quilici and Quilici Gigli attractively suggested that a sacrifice may have taken place at Antemnae, but this can only be conjecture. The Fratres Arvales focused their cult at the grove of Dea Dia at the fifth milestone on the Via Campana.[22]

With the battle of Lake Regillus, and the creation of the twenty-one tribes (seventeen rural tribes in addition to the four urban tribes attributed to Servius Tullius) it becomes clear that the definition of territory had reached an elaborate and vital solution. The roots of this must presumably lie in the past, and possibly back in the earliest firm settlements in Latium in Latial Period I. As time goes on, however, these boundary rites take on a new degree of importance, and by the sixth century they are part of the self-definition of the urban state; they became poliadic festivals.[23]

The archaeological evidence does not clearly support a circumvallatory wall around Rome, and other evidence which has been adduced to indicate definitions of the Roman territory are problematic. Yet there can be little reasonable doubt that Rome developed both an internal organization and, together with that and the extension of its territory, a concept of the city limits.

[21] Details of these mysterious rites are given in Scullard 1981. For the procession, see 90 f.; for the sacrifice 120 f. Plutarch (*Quaest. Rom.* 86) calls the rite the greatest of the purifications.
[22] There are magisterial comments on the ritual of the Arval Brethren in Syme 1980: 103 ff. Most importantly, he states (107) 'there is no sign that any of the antiquarian writers knew the text of the Arval Hymn. Their paraded and derivative scholarship would have been dismayed.' Further treatments of the complicated relationship between this rite and other figures of Roman mythology can be found in Radke 1972 and Olshausen 1978, which places the foundation of the ritual in the 6th or 5th century BC and contains an extensive bibliography. In Strabo 5. 230 there is a reference to an Ambarouian at 'Festoi' and other places. Scullard 1981: 124 f. discusses public and private Ambarvalia, but Kilgour 1938 denies that there was a connection between this ritual and that of the Arval Brethren.
[23] The concept of poliadic festivals is exploited in de Polignac 1984.

These need not have been accurately defined at every single point, but it is likely that certain areas, the Forum Boarium in particular, were defined through boundaries.

TEMPLES AND SANCTUARIES

No other Central Italian settlement has yielded as much evidence for religious sites as Rome, though this abundance has not made Roman religion any more intelligible.[24] It is not possible to mention every site in this account; the intention is to indicate the importance of religious building in Rome.

Undoubtedly, many geographical features of the original settlement may have been cult places from early times. Some such place is the Lupercal, a natural but still unidentified cave on the Palatine slope.[25] King Numa was supposed to have met the nymph Egeria at the Lake of Camenae;[26] the Lake of Juturna and the spring at the Tullianum, as well as the Lacus Curtius and the drainage works of the Cloaca Maxima all had recognition of some sort in ritual or myth;[27] there is also the Fons Cati on the Quirinal. These water routes must have been extremely important indicators of boundaries if the early settlement was a divided one; they would also have provided necessary water for agriculture, pasture, fishing, and of course for the humans. It is evident that the vagaries of the water system caused great difficulties in the lower-lying parts of the Forum valley, which were probably under water at least some of the time until the first pavement of the Comitium area, and indeed perhaps longer, since there is no reason to assume that the drainage was immediately successful. Sadly, there is little in the archaeological record to tell us how these natural features were honoured until later times.

There are two sanctuaries reported by Gjerstad on the Quirinal, which he claims were in existence from the Iron Age. One, under Sta Maria della Vittoria, has a particularly large votive deposit of ceramic, bronze, and iron objects, including some

[24] For accounts of Latin temples, see Zevi, 'I santuari di Roma agli inizi della repubblica', in Cristofani (ed.) 1987: 121–32; Quilici, 'Forma e urbanistica di Roma arcaica', in *GRT* 29–44; Rendeli 1989.   [25] See Ulf 1982: 29 ff.
[26] Livy 1. 21. 3.
[27] See esp. Coarelli 1986 and the account below, p. 166; see Steinby 1989 for the Lacus Juturnae.

from the Republican period; there was a generally similar deposit at S. Vitale (the old Villino Hüffer), of which only the enigmatic Duenos vase was preserved. These are important indications of the gaps in our knowledge; both were chance nineteenth-century discoveries, and neither can be assigned a deity. The absence of architectural remains may indicate that they remained as open-air sanctuaries.[28]

Finds of architectural terracottas on the Cispian hill and on the Esquiline (these latter appearing to come from the same mould as some terracottas found at Velletri), were taken by Gjerstad as evidence of temples on these hills. Again they are unidentifiable; it is, however, worth considering whether these may not in fact belong to domestic buildings, since discoveries at Acquarossa, Murlo, and Ficana have indicated the growing wealth of private accommodation.

At roughly the same time as the second stone Regia was destroyed by fire, between 575 and 550, a similar disaster befell what was to become the House of the Vestal Virgins; this much we infer from a deposit of largely domestic items found in a pozzo on this site. Once again, the distinction between domestic and religious building is hard to maintain. The tradition claims that the house of Vesta goes back to the time of Numa; even if the origin of the Vestal Virgins does precede the sixth century, which would not be unreasonable though it must remain hypothetical, we have found nothing on this site which is an unambiguous indication of religious activity.[29]

The chance discoveries in the S. Omobono area have focused attention on the Forum Boarium as an area of cult activity, and the finds have excited many scholars because they go some way towards indicating the validity of the sources about Servius Tullius.[30] At the site were found various friezes, terracottas, and statues,[31] and there are also some fragments of Greek pottery, making up a deposit of around a hundred such fragments from the late seventh century on. The sixth-century fragments amount to only a handful. They should probably best be considered along with Gjerstad's summary of around 500 pieces of

[28] Gjerstad, *Early Rome*, iii. 145 ff.; Bartoloni 1989–90.   [29] *GRT* 62.
[30] Speculations discussed by Thomsen 1980: 260 ff.; cf. Grottanelli 1987.
[31] For details see Appendix 2.

Greek pottery found in Rome during the sixth and early fifth centuries. The pottery comes from Attica, Corinth, Sparta and east Greece, with Attic predominating in the second half of the sixth century but tailing off in the fifth, a pattern which is matched in the coastal sites of Etruria, though the speed of the Roman decline is a little quicker.[32]

The interpretation of the area is complex. Coarelli suggested that there were two temples in the sixth century, as there were in the fourth century, but the second has yet to be found. Thomsen believes that the original temple was dedicated to Mater Matuta, and that Fortuna was only given an equal place when the two temples were constructed in the fourth century; he supports this with the evidence of animal bones from a sacrificial pit, which preceded the first temple; some of the animals appear to have been pregnant, which is a feature of the cult of Terra Mater. Thomsen actually goes so far as to dismiss all connection between Servius and Fortuna as the product of later speculation, and thinks that the Mater Matuta temple was the original Servian foundation. The problem with this is that the second temple of Fortuna, being an unknown quantity, may in fact have been equal to that of Mater Matuta, but we simply do not know.[33]

Champeaux accepts the Servian connection, as does Coarelli. Champeaux stresses the Latin nature of Fortuna, seeing the goddess as related to the stages of a woman's life, and therefore to fertility and fecundity (of fields as well as women) and as a poliadic deity, guarding and protecting the city.[34]

Coarelli rejects the supposed autochthonous Italian culture of the cult, propounded by Champeaux, and concentrates on the connections of the cult with the east, in particular by comparison with the sanctuary at Pyrgi, which is the port of Cerveteri. This sanctuary, as we know from two gold tablets in Phoenician and Etruscan, as well as the material remains, consisted of two temples, one to Uni (who, it has been suggested, was equivalent to Mater Matuta and Leucothea) and one to Astarte (equivalent to Fortuna).[35]

[32] For S. Omobono see *Enea nel Lazio* 1981: 124–30; for other Greek imports see Gjerstad, *Early Rome*, iv. 514 ff.; Meyer 1980, 1983: 160 ff.
[33] Thomsen 1980: 260 ff.; Holloway 1994: 10 f.
[34] Champeaux 1982: 281 ff., 437 ff.
[35] Coarelli 1988: 328 ff. For Pyrgi see Pallottino *et al.* 1964; Colonna (ed.) 1985: 127 ff.

There are difficulties with Coarelli's identifications and connections. He strengthens his case by pointing out that the Punic deity Melqart was worshipped at Pyrgi, and the Graeco-Roman deity Hercules, who has similar functions and attributes, was worshipped in the Forum Boarium. Bonnet[36] doubts the connection at Rome, and Coarelli's argument is largely based on ingenious articles by van Berchem, which use very late evidence about the Melqart cult and the practices at the Ara Maxima.[37] The presence of a Hercules statue in the S. Omobono sanctuary cannot prove this connection.

It is very difficult to say how deep the foreign influence was at Pyrgi and at Rome, and of what date. The bilingual tablets at Pyrgi discussed above, coupled with evidence for a treaty between Etruria and Carthage, and then Rome and Carthage, may indicate quite a close contact.[38] Pyrgi, being on the coast, was clearly open to considerable influence from foreign traders. Rome, on the other hand, was not on the coast, and shows a fairly limited exposure to external influences. Champeaux could show specific Latin connotations to the Fortuna–Mater Matuta complex, and the Phoenician aspects of the cult at Pyrgi must have fitted some aspects of already existing Etruscan deities. Heracles seems to have come from the Greeks in southern Italy, probably only in the sixth century, and possibly first to Etruria. Goddesses of fertility abound in the Mediterranean. Later experience and writers embellished and defined vaguely overlapping spheres of myth and religious activity. The equivalents which Coarelli uses (for example, Uni = Mater Matuta = Juno Lucina) are likely to have been vague, and elaborated at a later date. The Greek aspects of the cults of Ino–Leucothea and Palaemon–Melicertes found in Cicero and Ovid are perhaps of this nature.

Coarelli's strong interpretation would suggest a great interchange of religious influence and information between Phoenicians, Greeks, Etruscans, and Romans in the mid-sixth century.

[36] Bonnet 1988 278–304.
[37] Van Berchem 1959–60, 1967. Dalley 1987 tentatively identifies the spread of the cult with Phoenician mining activities, which might suggest connections with Pithecusa or through Elba.
[38] Hdt. 1. 166–7 for Carthage and Etruria fighting together against the Phocaeans; Ar. *Pol.* 3. 1280a36 ff. for treaties between Carthage and Etruria; Pol. 3. 22 ff. for the Carthage–Rome treaties.

Bonnet, in contrast, suggests that the Carthaginians 'ont implanté, plus ou moins autoritairement, les cultes de Melqart et d'Astarté chez leurs alliés étrusques',[39] but that their influence did not reach as far as Rome. If the fundamental aspects of the cults are to do with fertility and the city, it might be suggested that, both at Pyrgi and in the Forum Boarium, which were open to foreign trade, there already existed cults which could be understood in terms of Phoenician or Greek deities, and that by the late sixth century, contact between Phoenicians, Greeks, and Etruscans was sufficient to leave its mark on religious buildings, and that this filtered through, directly or indirectly, to Rome. The artistic influence from Etruria on Rome is undeniable.

The religious activity itself seems to indicate partly the continued importance of agriculture, as well as the institution of rites of passage, and a concern with the continuation of the city through reproduction, which focused on women. This can easily be paralleled in the Greek world. It is worth mentioning the tradition that Servius founded a number of other temples to Fortuna, a tradition found especially in two passages in Plutarch.[40] Coarelli and Champeaux tend to believe that there is some small degree of truth in this tradition; Thomsen dismisses it completely. All three scholars accept that the shrine to Fors Fortuna on the other side of the Tiber, in what is now the district of the Porta Portese, was roughly contemporary with those in the Forum Boarium. This cult has interesting connections with artisans, slaves, and enfranchisement, though it is difficult to say whether this is part of the actual conditions of the time, or simply another part of the myth of Servius' servile origins. It is significant that, even in the early Empire, Servius and Fortuna had much significance; the statue in the Forum Boarium temple was acquired by Sejanus and placed in the temple of Fortune which formed part of Nero's Domus Aurea. This indicates as well as anything that the regal period was under discussion and revision in the early Empire, which may well have affected our sources in ways we are unable to identify.

[39] Bonnet 291.
[40] Champeaux 1982: 268 ff.; Coarelli 253 ff.; Plutarch, *Quaest. Rom.* 36, *Fort. Rom.* 10, 322 f.–23a.

Most of the remaining temples that we know of in Rome offer less detailed information. There was a temple of Fides on the Capitol; a temple to Juno on the Arx, to Juno Sospita on the Palatine, and to Juno Lucina on the Cispian; there were temples to Quirinus and Semo Sancus on the Quirinal, which were regarded as part of the Sabine inheritance of Rome; on the Velia were the temples of the Penati and of Vica Pota; and outside the Pomerium, outside the city unit, there was built a temple to Diana on the Aventine, which became very important in the struggles between the Romans and the other Latins, and was attributed again to Servius Tullius. This temple was compared to the great temple of Artemis at Ephesos, partly because of its federal aspect and partly because of the cult image, which was also adopted by the Phocaeans and thus transported to Massilia.[41]

It is important to stress that the evidence for the antiquity of these temples is very weak, and that many may very well have been founded in the fifth or fourth centuries.

It is also interesting to note that a number of these buildings were said to have been originally the houses of kings or important political figures. On one hand this often explains why we hear of them; on the other it raises once more the issue of the relationship between domestic and sacred buildings in Central Italy.[42]

There were also a number of sanctuaries and shrines of various kinds, both public and private. It would appear that the great

---

[41] Thomsen 1980: 292 ff. and below.

[42] See the over-optimistic account by Quilici in *GRT* 29 ff.; and cf. the discriminating accuracy of Platner and Ashby 1929. See also Lugli 1952–69. The evidence is as follows: Fides, attributed to Numa (Livy 1. 21. 4, Dion. Hal 2. 75, Plut. *Numa* 16); Juno Moneta (Livy 7. 28. 4–6 for the dedication of a temple in 344 BC on the site of the destroyed house of M. Manlius Capitolinus; only from Plutarch *Camil.* 27 do we have the information that the geese that betrayed the secret attack of the Gauls in 390 belonged to Juno Moneta, implying, perhaps wrongly, the previous existence of a cult here); Juno Sospita (Ovid *Fasti* 2. 55. 9 without date, and perhaps betraying confusion with the Magna Mater on the Palatine, since there was another later Juno Sospita cult below the Palatine); Juno Lucina (Varro *LL* 5. 49–50, 74; Dion. Hal. 4. 15, ascribed to Titus Tatius); Quirinus (temple dedicated 325 BC, Livy 10. 46. 7, Pliny *HN* 7. 213; Paulus 303L for mention of a sacellum on the same spot which may be earlier, or may indeed be the temple wrongly described); Semo Sancus (built by the last Tarquin but not dedicated until 466 BC, Dion. Hal. 9. 60. 8; Plut. *Quaest. Rom* 30, Pliny *HN* 8. 194 for the statue, distaff, and spindle of Tanaquil); Penates (in the house of Titus Hostilius, Varro *ap. Non.* 531, Solin, 1. 22, Dion. Hal. 1. 68. 1); Vica Pota (in the house of P. Valerius, Livy 2. 7. 12); Diana (Varro *LL* 5.43, Livy 1. 45. 2–6, Dion. Hal. 4. 26).

family or village groups who had coalesced to create the city maintained some of their own rituals, which were not transferred immediately to the larger unit. There was, for example, a private cult of Hercules at the Ara Maxima, and there were many others, as will be shown later.

The Argeorum Sacraria, twenty-seven in all according to Varro, were divided among the four regions of Rome; sadly, we do not have locations for all of them.[43] A full list of other known sanctuaries is instructive, since the number (around twenty) is so high, but we cannot tell, of course, if some were of more recent date.[44]

From this account, which is not exhaustive, it may be deduced that by the sixth century, there was sufficient religious vitality in Rome to sustain a large number of temple buildings and ritual activities. A dense concentration of such buildings may have helped to define the city area, and sharing cults may have helped to give the unit a social cohesion. Moreover, the amount of public building, combined with the size of Rome, indicates an ability to control human labour resources which we do not find anywhere else in Latium. This is best demonstrated by the remarkable amount of building work undertaken at the end of the sixth and the beginning of the fifth century, much of which was attributed to Tarquinius Superbus, though it is not surprising to find major public works associated with a ruler who was portrayed as a typical Greek tyrant.

Most remarkable of all is the great temple of Jupiter Optimus Maximus, together with Juno and Minerva, which was built on the Capitoline hill. It seems that an earlier shrine to this triad was dedicated on the Quirinal; the later temple was of vast dimensions (approximately 61 m by 55 m), and the only parallels one can draw that are roughly contemporary are with Magna Graecia (Paestum) and Sicily (Agrigentum and Selinus). It was probably built out of native tufa and had three cellae, with altars and statues of the deities. There can be little doubt that this vast and imposing edifice must have overshadowed the federal sanctuary of Jupiter on the Alban Hills, which did not have a temple, and one suspects that this may have been part of the intention.[45]

---

[43] See Varro *LL* 5. 45 f.   [44] See Stara-Tedde 1905; Edlund 1987.
[45] See *GRT* 75; Colonna in Cristofani (ed.) 1987: 64 f.; Castagnoli 1978: 37–45; Gjerstad, *Early Rome*, iii. 168–89.

Other temples include the Ara of Saturn, identified by Coarelli with the Volcanal, near which a votive deposit has been found, though it is rather poor.[46] The temple was supposed to have been built out of the *bona Porsennae* and the *bona Tarquiniorum* (booty won by war or confiscation), and it is interesting that the temple was also the place of the public treasury of the Romans, the Aerarium Publicum. Parallels can be found for placing the financial wealth of a city in the hands of the gods. Not long after, in 495 BC, a centurion called M. Plaetorius was given the honour of dedicating a temple to Mercury on the Aventine; the day of dedication, the Ides of May, became a festival for merchants (*mercatores*), but Zevi sensibly suggested that, to begin with, there was probably a connection with grain rather than high finance and commerce.[47] The Temple to Ceres, Liber Liberaque, dedicated by Sp. Cassius in 493 after a particularly bad famine in 496, became another plebeian centre; it was also placed on the Aventine, but its artistic inspiration was strongly Greek, suggesting that, whereas in earlier days association with foreign ideas had been the privilege of the upper classes, as time progressed, not only did those of a lower social class absorb these ideas, they also appropriated them, perhaps along with a desire for the new freedoms of the Greek world.

Contemporary with these events, and perhaps of similar inspiration, was the vowing of a temple to the Dioscuri in *c*.496 by the dictator Postumius after the twins appeared following the battle at Lake Regillus, which was dedicated by his son in 484 BC. The temple was placed in the Forum near the Lacus Juturnae, where the twins were supposed to have watered their horses, and measured about 27 m by 34 m. This temple has been firmly dated to the early fifth century by archaeological investigation.[48] Importing two Greek divinities to celebrate a Roman victory over her Latin neighbours must have had great significance at the time.

---

[46] Sciortino and Segala 1990; terracottas from the temple are presented in *GRT* 68 ff.   [47] Zevi in Cristofani (ed.) 1987: 125 ff.
[48] Nielsen and Zahle 1985.

THE ARCHAIC FORUM

The Comitium and the Volcanal

The focus of activity in the Forum was the area of the Comitium to the north and at the foot of the Arx.[49] Almost certainly, this area would have been marshy ground until the drainage of the Forum, monumentally achieved by the Cloaca Maxima, attributed to Tarquinius Superbus, but attempted earlier, as Ammerman has shown. The Forum is the area of the Lapis Niger, but also of the Republican Curia, Rostra, and Tribunal—in other words, the centre of political activity until the radical reorganization of central Rome by Julius Caesar. There were eight successive pavements of this area, and the last one was by Augustus.[50]

Only the first two pavements definitely come into our period. The first was directly on top of the soil, and beneath it was found a fragment of the handle of a large bucchero vessel, possibly a kantharos; and also other fragments of pottery, some early impasto, and one of Corinthian argilla, according to Boni (this may not now be a secure attribution, since pottery identifications have changed, and the piece itself has been lost).[51] On top of the pavement were found some tiles, which presumably belonged to a building associated with this area, which had suffered fire damage before the second pavement was built. Coarelli associates this with the first Curia. The second pavement had associated bucchero and red-slip ware (notably a bucchero kylix). The archaic inscription was probably set up at this time, on a raised pavement of irregular tufa blocks from the Capitoline. Gjerstad dated the first pavement to around the beginning of the fifth century, but Coarelli places it a century earlier; the second pavement is associated by Gjerstad with the rebuilding after the Gallic fire of 390 BC, but placed by Coarelli around the middle of the sixth century.[52]

---

[49] The Forum has naturally attracted an enormous bibliography which is thoroughly presented by Coarelli. The excavations of Boni were sadly not fully published at the time, though both Gjerstad and Coarelli consulted his notebooks. Work is still progressing; see, for instance, Giuliani and Verduchi 1987 for the area of the so-called Equus Domitiani; and *GRT* for the excavations on the Palatine.

[50] Coarelli 1986: 119 ff.; Gjerstad 1941; *Early Rome*, iii. 217–59. For Boni's original excavations, see the accounts in *NSc* 1900: 295–340.

[51] Boni op.cit. 333–4; Gjerstad 1941: 147; *Early Rome*, iii. 220 n3; Coarelli 1986: 120 f., 127 f.

[52] Coarelli 1986: 129 f.; Gjerstad 1941: 148–9; *Early Rome*, iii. 220.

Rome: Archaeological Evidence 167

Gjerstad associates the third pavement with the building works of C. Maenius around 338 BC.[53] Two raised areas north of the Lapis Niger inscription were created, with three steps leading up to them; the inscription and probably an altar stood in the middle, and at a different orientation, which shows that this area was already being preserved. The pottery included some Etruscan black glaze, and also a mid-Republican oil lamp, which is probably intrusive, and belongs to the large altar constructed at a later date. The other pottery supports a date around the end of the sixth century and the beginning of the fifth. If the archaic inscription does not belong to the second pavement, it is unlikely to be later than this third one, because of the construction of the two raised platforms around it, which Coarelli identifies with the Rostra and the Graecostasis. The next pavement was probably built around the middle of the fourth century. Additional support for Coarelli's dating comes from the material found in a votive deposit under the Lapis Niger, the oldest objects of which were dated correctly by Gjerstad to the second quarter of the sixth century.[54]

Finally, there is the archaic inscription itself, on a block of Grotta Oscura tufa, about 61 cm high and with a base of 47 cm by 52 cm. The block has four main faces and a small fifth face, and the writing runs vertically and in boustrophedon fashion. In *GRT* the text is presented as follows (though their own drawing shows that the last line must begin *LOIV*):

1) *quoi hon[—/—]sakros es/ed sord [—]*
2) *[—]..ahas/recei:i[—/—]euam/quos:r[—]*
3) *[—]m:kalato/rem:ha[—/—]od:iouxment/a:kapia:dotau [—]*
4) *[—]m:i<:>te<:>r.[—/—]m:quoi:ha/uelod:nequ[—/ —] od:iouestod*
5) *[—]lou<i?>quiod[—].*[55]

The text has been variously interpreted. In 1949 Goidanich restored the text as if the cippus represented a law about burial places (*lex sepulcri*), and was associated with the sepulchre near the temple of Antoninus and Faustina, which, he suggested,

---
[53] Coarelli 1986: 130 f.; Gjerstad 1941: 150.
[54] For details of votive deposit, see *GRT* 54 ff.   [55] *GRT* 3.1.39, 58 f.

continued at least as far as the Lapis Niger.⁵⁶ In 1969 R. E. A. Palmer produced a different text and interpretation; he translated it as:

Whosoever [will violate] this [grove], let him be cursed. [Let no-one dump] refuse [nor throw a body —]. Let it be lawful for the king [to sacrifice a cow in atonement]. [Let him fine] one [fine] for each [offence]. Whom the king [will fine, let them give cows]. [Let the king have a —] herald. [Let him yoke] a team, two heads, sterile —. Along the route —. [Him] who [will] not [sacrifice] with a young animal—in a—lawful assembly in a grove —.⁵⁷

The text is interpreted as a boundary marker in the grove that once grew in the Comitium. The first offence over which the king had the right to exert his authority was a violation of the grove; then some sort of purificatory chariot-race is mentioned, analogous to those sponsored by the Arval Brethren at the Grove of Dea Dia. Since the king was forbidden to see anyone working, there is a penalty stipulated for the violation of this festival.

Palmer goes on to date the inscription to after 509 BC, the legal sanction for a *kalator* representing the curtailment of the powers of the king. He compares the text with two laws on holy groves, one from the late fourth century found at Luceria, and one from the second half of the third century found near Spoletium.⁵⁸ Both forbid violation of the grove (by dumping refuse or a dead body or offering sacrifice for dead parents in the first instance, by cutting the grove on any but the proper day in the second). The expiation and the powers to exact this are then laid down.

Palmer's interpretation was radically different from that of Dumézil, who rejected it, partly on the grounds that Palmer's restorations were too wild.⁵⁹ Crucial to Dumézil's account are two texts from the classical period; Cicero *De Div.* 2. 36. 77, where, after recalling a precaution adopted by M. Marcellus for

---

⁵⁶ Goidanich quoted in Degrassi 1949: 59–61, from P. C. Goidanich, 'L'iscrizione arcaica del Foro Romano', *Memorie Accademia d'Italia*, 3 (1943) 317–501. ⁵⁷ Palmer 1969.
⁵⁸ Luceria: CIL i. 401, *ILS* 4912; Spoletium: CIL i. 366, *ILS* 4911. Cf. Cato *De Agr.* 139 on the proper procedure for pruning a grove, and also Festus 33lL. The procedure is also illustrated by *ILS* 5037 at the grove of Dea Dia: 'He sacrificed two sacrifical sows on an altar before the grove in order to cut the grove and begin the work' (*ante lucum in aram porcas piaculas duas luco coinquendi et operis faciendi immolavit*). ⁵⁹ Dumézil 1979; cf. id. 1964, 1970b.

Rome: Archaeological Evidence 169

protecting himself against unpleasant auspices, Cicero adds: 'It is similar to that which we augurs advise, that the cattle be ordered to be unyoked so as to prevent a *iuge(s) auspicium*.'[60] Paulus (226L) tells us that: '*iuge(s) auspicium* is when yoked cattle dung together.'[61] The second text is Varro *LL* 5. 47, which describes the Via Sacra as the route 'along which the augurs are accustomed to set out from the citadel in order to observe the auguries.'[62] This interpretation makes the stone refer to an augural procession down the Via Sacra, which requires that no cattle should be seen under the yoke, since this is a bad omen.

Coarelli does not offer a new text but considers the inscription in a slightly different way.[63] He describes the *kalator* or herald as a servant of the king; the office is usually associated with pontifices and flamines. However, the so-called School of Heralds (*Schola Kalatorum*), identified by an imperial inscription, was found near the Regia.[64] He states that the function of the herald was *comitia calare*, which he derives from a passage in Aulus Gellius on the Comitia Calata which itself was derived from the jurist Antistius Labeo.[65] We know of curiate lictors from inscriptions, and Botsford and Coarelli assume that these are the same as the *kalator*, though the ancient sources do not make this equation.

The Comitia Calata met in the Curia Calabra on the Capitoline Hill, as a non-voting assembly, gathered under the presidency of the king (or the *rex sacrorum* under the Republic) to hear the proclamation of the Fasti; this ceased when the Fasti were published in 304 BC. Similarly passive as the Comitia Calata which met under the Pontifex Maximus to witness the inauguration of the *flamen Dialis*, the *flamen Martialis*, and the *flamen Quirinalis*, and perhaps of the king and later the *rex sacrorum*.[66] Mommsen

---

[60] *Huic simile est, quod nos augures praecipimus, ne iuge(s) auspicium obveniat, ut iumenta iubeant diiungere.*
[61] *Iuge(s) auspicium est, cum iunctum iumentum stercus fecit.*
[62] *Per quam augures ex arce profecti solent inaugurare.*
[63] Coarelli 1986: 178 ff.
[64] A list of *kalatores* from AD 101/2 (CIL vi. 32445) and an inscription reading *[in] honorem domus Augustae kalatores pontificum et flaminum* (CIL vi. 37167, *ILS* 4970), pieced together from two fragments of uncertain but clearly imperial date.
[65] Aulus Gellius 15. 27: see Botsford 1909: 152–67; Taylor 1966: 8 f.
[66] Varro *LL* 6.27; cf. Festus 42L; Macrobius *Sat.* 1. 15. 9 f.; Botsford 1909: 155 n. 5.

believed that the witnessing and ratification of wills twice a year (perhaps by vote), which was another task of the assembly, took place on 24 March and 24 May, days designated in the calendar as Q(*uando*) R(*ex*) C(*omitiavit*) F(*as*).[67] Other ceremonies before this body were *adrogatio* (where a person who was his own master consented to pass under the paternal power of another, which involved *detestatio sacrorum*, forsaking the religion of the family of his birth); *transitio ad plebem* and *co-optatio in patres*, under the Republic at least; i.e., those changes of allegiance which required the abjuration of one's previous social or religious ties.

Botsford and Taylor assumed without argument that there was a close connection between the Comitia Calata and the Comitia Curiata, but there does not appear to be any ancient evidence to support this point of view. It may well be that the structure of the Comitia Calata was identical with that of the Comitia Curiata and that the significant difference was that the former always met under a priest (not necessarily the Pontifex Maximus, as has sometimes been assumed); this might explain why they met in the Curia Calabra on certain occasions. This, it must be stressed, is only a hypothesis.

All these connections will be of little importance anyway if the assumption that the Comitia Calata was summoned by a *kalator* is rejected, but it does seem appropriate to have a mention of this official in a place where an important assembly of the Roman people met, for purposes which may very well have preceded the foundation of the Republic. The argument that, because this inscription almost certainly predates the Republic, the functions of the Comitia Calata (which is alluded to by a single word, and that not securely) were similarly ancient is clearly tenuous, though the conclusion might be correct. It would indicate the existence of a political institution for the representation of the community, that community being Rome, divided into *curiae*, and would further support the belief that Rome was an urban institution.

Common to all the accounts is the belief that there is a clear reference to the Rex in the word *RECEI* (the C is equivalent to a G, and this should be a dative case). This is generally taken to be

[67] Mommsen 1859 241 ff.; Watson 1971: 8.

the proper king of Rome before the reorganization that left a *rex sacrificulus* or *sacrorum* without any political power. To this should be added the late sixth-century bucchero coppa found near the Regia with the inscription *REX* on the inside. Now Coarelli showed quite convincingly that the complex around the Lapis Niger was the same as the Volcanal. The fragment of Attic pottery showing Hephaestus (the Greek equivalent of Vulcan) contributes to a rather circular proof of the identification of the Volcanal. The literary evidence comes from a number of sources which indicate that the Volcanal and the Comitium were closely connected at the least; for instance, Livy 2. 10 reports a statue of Horatius in the Comitium, while Dionysius of Halicarnassus 5. 25. 2 places it 'in the best place in the agora', and the author of *De Vir. Ill.* 11. 2 places the same statue in the Volcanal.

It is also Dionysius who tells us that assemblies were held at the Volcanal.[68] If the *kalator* of the inscription can be related to the summoning of the Comitia Calata and other forms of assemblies, and the identification of this part of the city with the Volcanal is correct, then we may suggest, with due caution, that the paving of the area and the setting up of the cippus represent an early definition of public space for public purposes, possibly the gathering together of the people for acts that affected the whole community, such as the publication of the calendar, sacrificial or purification rituals, the inauguration of priesthoods and perhaps the office of the king, and the witnessing and ratification of wills and adoptions.

The Via Sacra and Via Nova

The Volcanal area, although of great importance in the archaic period, was only part of a complex topography. The axis of the Forum valley was marked by the Via Sacra,[69] which ran from the foot of the Arx up to the Carinae; its exact definition, much discussed by Coarelli and others, may well have become unclear

[68] Dion. Hal. 6. 67; cf 7. 17.
[69] Coarelli 1986: 11 ff. Coarelli's topography has not been universally accepted; see Purcell 1989: 159 n. 15 for disagreements. Coarelli's route takes an impossibly steep turn up the Velia, and the alternative route to the arch of Titus suits the augural line of sight perfectly well. A strong criticism of Coarelli's position was made by Castagnoli 1988.

by later antiquity, but a shorter version clearly began at the Regia.

The importance of this axis cannot be underestimated; along it was enacted the gruesome festival of the Equus October, perhaps a sort of purification ritual comparable to the Lupercalia. It also represents the *spectio* for augural sighting, from the Arx to the Alban Hills, which would have been easily visible on a clear day. It was the path taken by triumphal processions, which, it has been suggested, had their origin in another purification ritual imported from Etruria, perhaps as early as the archaic period.[70] The route seems to have followed the natural contours of the Forum (which tells against Coarelli's reconstruction of the eastern end by the Basilica of Maxentius and Constantine) and is probably of great antiquity, accumulating more significance as time passed. On the other hand, it may only have been clearly demarcated after the landfill of the late seventh century which Ammerman has discovered. There is the typical mixture of the practical, the religious, and the political about this feature of Rome.

The settlement of Rome seems to have been effectively divided by route-ways by the sixth century; running off the Via Sacra are the Clivus Capitolinus, and the Vicus Iugarius leading to the Forum Boarium. The Vicus Tuscus leads from the Signum Vortumni towards the port (and there may be a route from it up onto the north-east of the Palatine), and seems to indicate the Etruscan influence on the settlement. Both probably represent the area of securely habitable land that preceded the landfill. The Nova Via (which cannot easily be dated) runs from the Vicus Tuscus to meet the Via Sacra at the Porta Mugonia; in between these two roads are found the Regia and the Vestal Virgins' complex.

A recent reconstruction suggests that the Via Sacra becomes the Vicus Cuprius around the Lucus Streniae and the Tigillum Sororium; this leads up to the Fagutal. Thence one road, the Vicus Orbius, later the Vicus Sceleratus after Tullia's horrid crime of driving her chariot over her father Servius, ran up to the Oppius hill, where Servius' house and the cult of Fortuna Virgo were to be found.[71]

[70] Bonfante Warren 1970; Versnel 1970.   [71] *GRT* 79–85.

That this major route complex is so vividly present in the myths of Servius Tullius, particularly of his death, may be significant, a suggestion that the settlement was now (for the first time?) an organized unity. The replacement of internal divisions in the settlement by an articulated settlement pattern may be a triumph of the sixth century.

Another aspect of the relation between Rome and its kings was the association of various houses with them. The Casa Romuli was on the Palatine and the House of Augustus was built nearby in a deliberate act of identification. Numa had one house on the Quirinal (an indication of his 'Sabine' origin) and one near the temple of Vesta, which one is inclined to associate with the Regia, or the Domus Publica. Tullus Hostilius was placed on the Velia, his house becoming the Temple of the Penates, generally associated with the fall of Alba Longa. Ancus Marcius lived at the top of the Via Sacra by the Aedes Larum; Tarquinius Priscus opposite the Temple of Jupiter Stator, and at the foot of the Palatine; Servius Tullius by the Temple of Fortune on the Oppian, and not far from the Temple of Diana on the Esquiline; Tarquinius Superbus on the Fagutal.

This represents the account of Solinus, which probably owes something to Varro and is the most complete we have. Earlier accounts are not as polished. There are some alternatives; the house opposite Jupiter Stator was also associated with Tarquinius Superbus. Servius Tullius was reckoned by some to have had two houses, one on the Esquiline to make it sufficiently dignified to be allowed into the city, and the one on the Oppian.[72] Coarelli picks out a general move eastwards, and the Servian house is explicitly connected with the expansion of the city boundaries. It is also interesting to note the identification of many of the houses with a particular deity.

The extent to which this is a late and arbitrary fiction to demonstrate the gradual extension of the city under successive kings is hard to assess. Certainly this is part of the truth—it is no accident that Solinus' late account is also the most complete—but the existence of sixth-century houses by the Via Sacra (which have not been assumed to be regal) indicates that there may very well have been early houses in some of these places. The possibility of

[72] Coarelli 1986: 56 ff.; Solinus 1. 21. 6.

confusion (and transition) between houses and temples may explain some of the religious identifications. Apart from the Palatine houses, there was also an archaic house under the temple of Antoninus and Faustina, on top of the necropolis; this has been identified with the second house of Valerius Publicola, which he built after destroying his first house on top of the Velia (thought to be a sign of wanting sole rule), near the sanctuary of Vica Pota (the old Victoria). The house is significantly close to the richest child burials in Latium, and it is intriguing to note that the *gens* Valeria were singled out by the right to bury their dead within the city of Rome. The cautious combination of archaeological finds and literary testimony may at least suggest that we should not underestimate the spread of archaic domestic architecture in Rome.

The Regia,[73] fancifully described as the house of Numa by Solinus, was the site of the cult of Mars and Ops Consiva , as well as being part of a complex of rituals which also involved the cult of Vesta and the Vestal Virgins. The association with kingship is strengthened by the discovery in the area of the pottery fragment with the word *REX* on it. The Regia, together with the Domus Regis behind the Atrium of the Vestal Virgins and the Domus Publica, which was somewhere on the Via Sacra, were in Republican times the homes of the Pontifex Maximus and the Rex Sacrorum who appear to have shared the religious duties which had been performed by the king; it is thus appropriate that the site was associated with Numa, the king most closely connected with religion.

Some of the architectural terracottas found here are directly comparable with others found in the Comitium area and attributed to the first Curia; they are dated to the early sixth century and may represent scenes from the story of Theseus and the Minotaur, but this has been challenged, in my opinion correctly. There is indeed what appears to be a composite figure, but this is quite a common motif in the friezes of Central Italy, a motif which might have travelled from southern Italy without the attached myth, or which may represent an indigenous belief or custom (like a ritual dance) of which we have no other trace.[74]

[73] Brown 1967, 1974–5, 1976; Coarelli 1986: 56 ff.; Torelli in *CAH* vii (2), 30–51.
[74] For the architectural terracottas see Cristofani in Cristofani (ed.) 1987: 95–120; Frederiksen 1976–7: 53 f. for similar examples from Metapontum.

The discovery of great palaces in Etruria is an important parallel to the Regia and the aristocratic house near the Palatine, as Torelli has recently made clear.[75] Murlo (late seventh to early sixth century), and Acquarossa (mid-seventh century, then rebuilt in the third quarter of the sixth century), have colonnades, rooms, and architectural terracottas directly comparable with those in Rome, with some shared symbols which may or may not be borrowed from the east. Acquarossa in particular has the same asymmetrical plan as the Regia. The same procession with a 'Minotaur' motif has been found at temple B at Pyrgi from the late sixth century; the Regia examples are notably early in this sequence.[76]

To assess the significance of the archaic Regia, it is necessary to return to the festival of the Equus October. There are a surprising number of sources for this festival, considering the scarcity of evidence for most early religious festivals. Esentially the ritual requires the annual sacrifice of a horse and involves two areas of the city, the Campus Martius and the Regia. The significance of the sacrifice has been much debated from antiquity on.

Polybius[77] tells of a ritual in the Campus Martius, in which a war-horse is killed by a throw of a spear; he attributes the suggestion that this is a commemoration of the Trojan War to Timaeus and dismisses it, suggesting that the ritual is a common practice on the outbreak of a war, and that the manner of the horse's death is taken as an indication of the future course of the war.

Plutarch[78] makes the festival the subject of one of his 'Roman Questions'; he picks out the sacrifice of a victorious chariot-horse, the sprinkling of blood from its tail on the altar of the Regia, and the fight over the horse's head. Plutarch envisages three possible reasons for the festival: the commemoration of the Trojan War, the connection between the war-horse and Mars the war-god, and a symbolic punishment of those who run away in war.

Paulus also has the first two explanations. Festus gives the longest account, mentioning the sacrifice of a victorious chariot-

[75] Torelli in *CAH* vii (2), 30–57.
[76] For Etruscan parallels see above; Stopponi (ed.) 1985.
[77] Polybius 12. 4b.   [78] Plutarch *Quaest. Rom.* 97.

horse, the race with the tail to the Regia, the fight over the head between the Sacravienses, who will fix the head to the Regia if victorious, and the Suburanenses, who will fix it to the Turris Mamilia. The sacrifice is to Mars, but without reference to the sack of Troy. Paulus also has a confusing notice about the sacrifice of a horse in the Campus Martius on the Ides of October 'for the success of the crops' (*ob frugum eventum*).[79]

Almost every aspect of this evidence has become the starting-point for lengthy and unresolved arguments. The most fundamental concerns the nature of the god Mars; Dumézil has insisted on the purely military aspect of the god, against the many scholars from Mannhardt on who have believed that Mars was originally an agrarian deity.

The Equus October festival has been quite an important part of the 'agrarian' interpretation, but Dumézil[80] has suggested that the Turris Mamilia indicates that the Suburanenses represent the enemy, an enemy which was once the *gens* Mamilia from Tusculum, who supported the exiled Tarquins and fought against Rome at the battle of Lake Regillus. This might be true, but it seems rather hard to believe; one feels that the prominence of the Mamilii in early Roman history may be one of many later glorifications of a family through its own 'historical' account of itself, and anyway, the erection of a Turris Mamilia, apparently near the Campus Martius, might just as easily be connected with the acceptance of the family, and then of the town of Tusculum, into the full Roman system in the fourth century.[81]

Apart from Devereux's highly speculative arguments on behalf of the agrarian interpretation,[82] there is the phrase *ob frugum eventum* in Paulus; but Paulus also says that the horse is 'suitable for war'; if fertility were the issue, surely a bull ('suitable for bringing forth crops') would have been sacrificed. As Dumézil shows, the phrase must indicate thanks for the protection of Roman land and crops over the year.

Another possible argument could be made with reference to the anointing with blood of the altar in the Regia. The Regia contained

[79] Paulus 197L; cf. Festus 295–6L, Paulus 326L. [80] Dumézil 1975.
[81] For various points in the history of the gens Mamilia, see Humbert 1978: 158, 330; L. Mamilius was given citizenship in 458 for his heroism, could this be the origin of the Turris Mamilia (Livy 3. 29. 6, Humbert 175)? The Tusculans probably received full citizenship in *c.*380 BC. [82] Devereux 1970.

a Sacrarium Martis with the spears and shields of the god, and also the Sacrarium Ops Consivae. Ops was the god of abundance and fertility, particularly with regard to cereals. There is no proof that the Equus October had anything to do with Ops Consivae, nor that Mars and Ops had a functional connection, but the protection of settled agricultural land by military force must have had a long history, and the juxtaposition seems appropriate.[83]

In this way, then, one can see a potent connection of military and agricultural activity, and the Regia is properly the centre of a number of seasonal festivals which mark the beginning and ending of the agricultural and military year. The ritual may have existed in some form before the construction of the Turris Mamilia; it may belong to the early Republic, and have nothing to do with the kings at all. It is tempting, however, to regard it as early, and it fits with other evidence cited for the self-awareness of Rome as a community. Moreover, the agricultural focus is a reminder of the patchy nature of settlement in Rome, and of the constant concern with the larger territory.

There was another sacrifice to Ops 'in the Forum' on 23 August and 15 December (perhaps the explanation of Plutarch's curious slip in assigning the Equus October to the Ides of December); this may very well have taken place near the Volcanal and the Ara Saturni, since Saturnus was also associated with fertility. He was regarded as the inventor of agriculture, and his altar was close to the Volcanal on one side and the Mundus (the most direct access to the Underworld) on the other, to which was made an offering of grain. Not far away was the Ficus Ruminalis, where farmers brought their young livestock and which had strong connotations of fertility. None of this can be dated; we cannot assume that it is all early.

At the beginning of this account of the Regia, reference was made to Solinus' list of the 'houses of the kings', of which the

[83] For Ops see Pouthier 1981). The festivals are: Consualia 21 August; Ops Opifera 23 August; Opiconsivia 25 August; Opalia 19 December (Opi ad Forum, according to the Fasti Amiterni, Degrassi 1963: 199). If there is one explanation which covers all these festivals, the apparent doubling of temples, and the shifting allegiances between Ops and Consiva, and Ops and Saturnus, it may lie in Pouthier's syncretistic approach; I suspect that the issue was always complex, and that Fowler may be right to see the phrase *Opi ad Forum* and Macrobius' connection of Ops and Saturn as later confusions; see Fowler 1899: 273; 1911: 412; cf. York 1986: 194 f.

Regia was one; and comparison has been made with palaces in south Etruria of this period. Rome itself had other major houses, recently uncovered by Carandini on the Palatine, and now published in *GRT*.[84]

What is given in *GRT* is an imaginative reconstruction of one house, using comparisons with other houses and chamber tombs in Etruria. This shows a series of rooms, including a banqueting room, around a central courtyard with an impluvium and cistern. The drainage system runs into the drain along the Via Sacra. The house is roughly 17 m by 35 m in size and with rooms on a first-floor level.

In front of the house were some small rooms, perhaps like the shops attributed by Livy 1. 35. 10 to Tarquinius Priscus; 'It was the same king too who divided up sites around the forum for private individuals to build on, and erected covered walks and shops.'[85] The old shops (*tabernae veteres*) were on the south side of the Forum; they were burnt in 210 BC (Livy 26. 27. 2). These may not have been the only *tabernae* of their period (a period not necessarily correctly pinpointed by Livy); the 'shops' in front of the archaic houses faced onto the Via Sacra, and it is possible that there were similar buildings on the other side of the road, on the southern slopes of the Velia, which are now lost. Their function is quite unclear. A long garden seems to have run along the eastern side of the house.

These details are mostly speculative, and a full publication of the actual finds is awaited, but the Etruscan instances show that such domestic architecture is not necessarily unthinkable in Rome at this time; a sixth-century impluvium has been found at Rosella. The implications of these finds for our understanding of the structure of Roman society at the end of the sixth century will be discussed below. This complex system of roads, sanctuaries and places of political significance ought to indicate the extent to which the topography of Rome was being used for the purposes of the community. The prominence of palaces, and it will be argued of temples too, is an indication of aristocratic dominance over the settlement.

[84] *GRT* 4.2., 97 f.
[85] *Ab eodem rege et circa forum privatis aedificanda divisa sunt loca; porticus tabernaeque factae.*

THE FORUM BOARIUM

Recent excavations and a thorough and most original treatment by Coarelli afford the opportunity of a fairly detailed understanding of one of the most important settlements in the city of Rome throughout its period of prosperity.[86] It marked the entrance into Rome from the Tiber, and must have been the focus of many activities which were to transform the city, while it retained its appellation of 'Cattle Market', which may indeed have been its original function.

The Forum Boarium and the numerous associated edifices were situated between the Circus Maximus and the Theatre of Marcellus, just opposite the Tiber Island, where the river runs closest to the centre of Rome. The port marked both a place of crossing and of transshipment of goods intended to proceed up the Tiber, and it retained its importance even after the development of the port facilities at Ostia, as is shown by the great Trajanic reorganization of the area.[87]

It seems reasonably clear that the Forum Boarium had an early connection with the trade in salt, which gave the Via Salaria its name. This road ran north-east from Rome along the Tiber, passing through the settlements of Antemnae, Fidenae, and Crustumerium, and on into the territory of the Sabines. The name of the road, neither a personal name (like Appia) nor the name of a destination (like Praenestina), has been taken as an indication of its extreme antiquity.[88]

Salt is a vitally important commodity; 'essential, irreplaceable, and sacred'. It was essential for the nutrition of animals and the preservation of animal products, and was consequently a strong link between Rome and the pastoralists of the Sabina.[89]

There are two salt-beds on the coast near the mouth of the Tiber, one on the Latin side, the other on the Veian side. The latter seems to have been connected to Rome by the Via Campana,

---

[86] Coarelli 1988 with full bibliography; Palmer 1990.
[87] For the importance and nature of the Tiber, see Holland 1961; Le Gall 1953, *Il Tevere* 1986.
[88] For the Via Salaria see Martinori 1931; Quilici and Quilici Gigli 1978, 1980, 1986; Radke 1973 with bibliography.
[89] On salt see Braudel 1984 i. 209; cf. iii. 123 for a discussion of how much Venice benefited from her enormous salt trade: 'Every year more than 40,000 horses came from Hungary, Croatia and even Germany to load Istrian salt alone.'

which led to the Pons Sublicius, along which were situated the shrines of Fors Fortuna and Dea Dia, which may date back to the sixth century BC. Ancus Marcius was credited with the foundation of Ostia and the salt-beds around it, as well as recovering the Janiculum for Rome and building the Pons Sublicius. Only the Veian salt-beds show signs of having been worked in the sixth century, but the argument from silence for the other salt-beds, little explored as they are, is invalid. It would be interesting to know the extent of Rome's control of the Tiber, including the Etruscan side, in antiquity, but it is unlikely that we shall gain such information. In the context of such general ignorance, Coarelli's belief that the connection between the Forum Boarium and the salt trade goes back to the Bronze Age can only be a bold hypothesis.[90]

Coarelli also endeavours to prove that there was a port at the Forum Boarium in the archaic period, which other scholars have denied. Once again, the implications are far-reaching, since, if there had been no such port before the fourth century, when the evidence is irrefutable, Rome's contacts with the outside world will necessarily appear less strong than has been thought. Equally, however, it is not true that the existence of a port would itself prove the simultaneous establishment of trading contacts with every trader who could make his way up the river.[91]

In order to prove his point, Coarelli has to resort to some dubious arguments. The cult of Portunus is present in the 'Numan' calendars;[92] there are indications in the sources of the import of grain to Rome from the early fifth century. Coarelli also uses a reference in Procopius to the 'ship of Aeneas' which was

[90] See Ogilvie ad Livy 1. 33. 9; Meiggs 1973: 16 ff., 479 ff.; Alföldi 1962; Holland 1961: 145 ff.

[91] Heurgon in Jehasse 1973: 551–2. Heurgon also suggests that Rome was without maritime ambitions until the late 4th century and the foundation of Ostia, and before this relied on the port at Caere. The belief that Rome did not have a port in the city goes back at least as far as Säflund 1932: 175.

[92] On Portunus see Coarelli 1988: 113 ff.; Holland 1961: 141–78. Holland suggests that Portunus was related by function to a ferry crossing over the flooded Velabrum (and thus in some way connected with Vortumnus, whose name was taken by Varro and others as derived from *a verso amne* (from the turned-back river). This may well have been wrong, but it indicates the area's propensity to flooding). See also Holland 1962 (Portunus did not have a key [*clavis*] but a rudder); Shipp 1951: 244–6 (Portunus, like Neptunus, originally a god of inland waters).

kept in the Roman Navalia, the description of which indicates that it was compatible with an archaic Greek penteconter. That the Tiber could be navigated by such a vessel is not in itself proof that it was.[93]

It seems unlikely that any evidence could be used as categorical proof that there was a port on the Tiber connected with the Forum Boarium in the archaic period; but considerable archaeological material has been found here which could not have originated in Rome. The development of harbours at Pyrgi and Gravisca, and the exploitation of natural resources in choosing and fortifying settlements, shows that Central Italians were not unaware of the world in which they lived. Whatever the nature of the Forum Boarium's resources in the sixth century, it is impossible to believe that its natural excellence as a place of contact was not acknowledged and used. Whether Greeks and Phoenicians came up the river to Rome in numbers is an entirely different question, which can only be approached through the amounts of imported material in Rome and Latium, or new finds of inscriptions.

The picture would be significantly altered if we had any significant evidence from Ostia before the fourth century. There are some terracotta fragments from the fifth century which probably indicate settlement, and some scraps of pottery, including a fragment of Attic red-figure ware, but these were first attributed, probably correctly, to fishermen or shepherds.[94]

The relationship between the Forum Boarium, the Portus, and the Pomerium is bound to remain unclear, because the Pomerium itself is an unsolved problem. Coarelli believes that the Pomerium does follow the 'Servian' walls, and draws the important conclusions that the Portus had to be outside the Pomerium, but the Forum Boarium was inside, so that the walls and the Pomerium take a course parallel to but not the same as that of the bank of the Tiber.[95]

The implications are significant; the Pomerium is drawn to include in the city area, the area under the protection of the gods, part of the city which was given over to activities of

[93] Procopius *BG* 4. 22. 7–16, Coarelli 1988: 125 f.
[94] Gras 1985: 237 n. 206 with references.
[95] Coarelli 1988 16 ff.; 385 ff., on the importance of the Porta Triumphalis and the triumphal entrance into the city.

exchange, but it excluded an area which was necessarily open to the comings and goings of merchants and other foreigners. Eastern parallels are significant; temples and trade were not separated, and the word *panegyris*, originally connoting a religious festival, took the secondary meaning of a marketplace.[96] Excluding the port would be an acknowledgement that the nature of the area made it unsuitable for inclusion inside the stable city boundary; it has a liminal status, which may be reflected in the deity Portunus, if he represents the entrance into the city.

Combining the evidence that we have, it would appear that in the sixth century the Forum Boarium was an important part of the structure of Rome in its economic and religious aspects. On one hand, there is a reasonable supposition that the area handled salt from the mouth of the Tiber which was intended for inland Italy, and this was perhaps only one of a number of commodities exchanged in the archaic period (oil, wine, cattle, sheep, and their products in terms of meat, leather, and wool come to mind). Moreover, the votive deposits here and throughout Latium indicate an increasing amount of imported pottery, especially from Etruria, and also, though not necessarily directly, from Greece, some of which at least may have been containers rather than or as well as ornamental objects. It is impossible that Rome and Veii at least were not in close contact at some level by the mid-sixth century, as the evidence of shared architectural decoration shows.

On the other hand, considerable building activity took place in the area in the sixth century, contemporary with and along the same lines as that in the main Forum area. The parallels are so striking that it is tempting to see a conscious building programme, though this may imply shared concerns and a continuity of intention among a series of dominant groups or individuals, rather than the predominance of a single one.

Moreover, the nature of the religious building here seems to indicate the conscious understanding of the area as one in contact with other areas. The cosmopolitan figure of Hercules, worshipped at the Ara Maxima in the Forum Boarium, may be an indication of this. Coarelli's Greek and Near Eastern parallels may very well be overly ingenious, but it is quite possible that Rome was trying to match or keep up with developments across

---

[96] Silver 1985: 7 ff.; Nilsson 1955–61: 826 ff.

Rome: Archaeological Evidence 183

the river. Certainly the decorations of buildings (both religious and domestic) and of pottery show knowledge and imitation of Etruscan models which are not confined to Rome.

CONCLUSIONS

Three major conclusions arise from the collection of evidence. First, it makes no sense not to regard Rome as an urban settlement by the late sixth century. By this time Rome had become a unified entity, though it preserved a sense of regions within it. This may have been reinforced by the division of the city into four, allegedly made by Servius, but it is also evident in the curial system. There are some indications of the inception of politics in the city with the establishment of the comitium area and perhaps the indication that the Comitia Calata was operating at this time.

Secondly, the building work which was carried out in the sixth and early fifth centuries clearly shows the ability to organize labour and resources. The focus on religious buildings and wealthy houses, which is also to be found in the rest of Latium as well as Etruria, indicates the aristocratic bias of society at Rome.

Thirdly, we may attempt to define Rome's cultural connections, and its place in the economy of Central Italy and the Mediterranean. There is clear evidence of influence from Etruria at all levels, which ties in with but does not substantiate the tradition that Rome was under Etruscan kingship for much of the sixth century. Greek and Punic influence is less easy to trace. This pattern will also be found in the later study of epigraphical evidence. The implication might be that such traces of external influence as we can see were passed on through Etruria. The issue of influence on religion is most important, and the best conclusion seems to be that the indigenous religious beliefs could interact with others and foreign practices and iconography could be adopted. So both Etruria and Latium were open to the cult of Heracles, probably passed from southern Italy, and the parallels with the cult of Melqart were employed in Etruria at least. The extent of cultural borrowing is difficult to gauge, but it was probably greater in Etruria than at Rome, and there is no clear indication of direct contact between Rome and the Punic civilization, though it is likely at some level late in the sixth century, as

Polybius' account of Rome's first treaty with Carthage would indicate (Pol. 3. 22). It is unlikely that cults were imposed; rather there was a considerable degree of syncretism.

The presence of Greek pottery can be used in this argument. It seems that most Greek pottery in Rome is found in votive contexts, and in sanctuaries. The amount of Greek pottery so far found in Rome is much greater than that found in any other Latin site. Different factors affecting recovery make comparison of numbers with Etruscan sites too dangerous, but the proportions of pottery in Rome and in Etruria at any given time seem comparable.[97]

Johnston has suggested that the predominance of Greek marks on imported pottery over Etruscan marks 'does not encourage the notion that any large part of the total trade from Greece to Etruria was in Etruscan hulls', but fails to include southern Italian Greeks or natives in his list of possible 'middlemen'.[98] In the third and last quarter of the sixth century, when imports of Attic pottery were at their height, it seems unreasonable not to expect the presence of some mainland Greeks in Etruria (as is clearly attested by the Gravisca inscriptions discussed above) and also in Rome; but Latium as a whole is at the end of a long trading link, with a number of participants, and has only a small role itself.

The presence of Greek pottery in particularly wealthy tombs and in sanctuaries would seem to indicate that the pottery had some prestige value in Latium, though its value in Greece has recently been questioned. It appears that the levels of Rome's imported pottery are closely tied with those of coastal Etruria, and fall off in the fifth century; this would indicate again that the commodity came through Etruscan sources, and that, as that region looked increasingly northwards and away from the Mediterranean after its naval defeats, Latium's line to the eastern imports was to some extent cut.

[97] Meyer 1980; Humphries 1978: 118, 291 n. 42.
[98] Johnston 1985; cf. id. 1979 for Greek marks.

11
Rome and Latium in the Sixth Century

The purpose of this final section is to try to combine the archaeological evidence which has been compiled in previous chapters with the literary and documentary evidence which exists for the sixth century BC. I wish to focus on three aspects, beginning with the social structure of Rome and Latium. It is clear enough that archaic Latium contained groups of different social status, and some of the tensions this created came to a head in the Struggle of the Orders from the fifth century on. Some of the social groupings can be identified, and their possible relevance to the archaeological record will be explored here. In the second place, we have reasonably good evidence for laws and treaties in the Latin world. Examining the legal evidence allows us to make hypotheses concerning the status of the Latins. We may also try to gain a very basic understanding of patterns of land ownership as one of the most important structural aspects of Latin society. Finally, religion is prominent in the archaeological record because of the many temples that have been discovered; the combination of literary and antiquarian material can help to give an outline of the context of this religious activity. In other words, I wish to indicate the sorts of areas in which archaeological and literary evidence seem to come together fruitfully. In so doing, I shall not attempt to solve the many problems of the sixth century, but only to indicate broad areas of interest.

THE ORGANIZATION OF SOCIETY

Certain aspects of the social structure of archaic Rome can be deduced with a fair degree of confidence. There can be little doubt that there were kings in sixth-century Rome; apart from the literary tradition, the Lapis Niger inscription and the pottery sherd with the word *REX* found under the Regia imply the existence of kingship in Rome in the sixth century, though our understanding of the kingship is not thereby enhanced. It appears that the kings were part of the patrician aristocracy, but rather stood above and outside it. Parallels for the kingship might be sought in Greek tyranny, but the literary accounts are so infected with the Greek literary tradition themselves that it is hard to be sure.[1]

The three last kings of Rome are associated with a certain amount of military activity, and Tarquinius Priscus and Tarquinius Superbus, notoriously, are of Etruscan origin. This fits with the plentiful Etruscan material evidence in Rome. One is tempted therefore to think in terms of warrior chiefs, who, with the aid of a military force and a degree of charisma, forced themselves to the leadership of Roman society, and created, or continued to create, a senatorial aristocracy which conspired to remove the last of them and establish the Republic.[2]

In addition to the monarchy, social stratification and the conspicuous consumption of wealth existed among the aristocracy of archaic Rome and in Latium too. There is no evidence to suggest any kind of economic decline in the sixth century, although wealthy burials are uncommon. The construction of temple buildings and other private architecture across Latium in the sixth century, as well as stray pieces of evidence like the gold tooth filling at Satricum, or the wealthy burial at Fidenae, as well as the evidence of votive deposits, indicates quite clearly that there was no shortage of luxury items or of disposable wealth.

One may suggest therefore that the cessation of wealthy burials is connected with new forms of expenditure; that for social reasons, wealth was redirected into public building. It is striking that a similar development occurred in Greece in the eighth century; Snodgrass says, 'there is a big social change with the redirection of attention towards the communal sanctuary and away from the individual grave.' At Corinth, for instance, the reduction of wealth in burials coincides with the foundation of temples to Apollo and Poseidon.[3]

[1] Momigliano in *CAH* vii (2), 87–96.
[2] Cornell in *CAH* vii (2), 257–64.
[3] Snodgrass 1980: 53–4, 99; Coldstream 1977: 174, 252–3.

It is sometimes suggested that the cessation of wealthy burials was connected with early legislation of the sort to be found in the Tenth Table, which sets a limit to expensive burials, and is supposed to have been based on Solonian laws from Athens. However, wealthy burials cease almost a century before the Tenth Table, and sumptuary legislation was rarely successful in antiquity. The change in the burial habits of the Latins should be seen as a cultural choice, not a result of legislation to curb display.[4]

The redirection of resources from burials to temples is an indication of the élite making its mark on the urban culture of Latin settlements. Burial expenditure is impressive, but a family rarely maintains its identity for longer than four generations,[5] and the display only lasts for the period of the funeral, though the rise of chamber tombs in the seventh century may be an attempt to overcome this disadvantage. The temples and palaces of the sixth century, on the other hand, were more visible and more directly involved in the life of the settlement; temples certainly formed a focus in many Latin settlements. The temple is a continuing part of the inhabitants' life, and moreover it is a depository for rich offerings that are clearly visible at all times, not hidden in the ground. The cultural choice to move to expenditure on conspicuous buildings is deeply bound up with the evolution of an urban society. The desire for more permanent memorials may also represent the evolution of a more stable aristocracy. These are the processes (rather than burial legislation) that are indisputably contemporary with the temple phenomenon.

What is most striking about the temple building of the sixth century is the number of stone structures which succeeded each other in a very short period of time; as we have seen, in Rome, Satricum and elsewhere a number of edifices had two, three, or even four phases before 500. On occasion it seems that this is due

---

[4] On the Tenth Table Cornell 1979–80: 83, Colonna 1977: 131 ff., and Ampolo 1984a all believe in unwritten prototypes of the law; cf. Toher in Raaflaub (ed.) 1986, who does not. I have benefited from discussing these issues with Prof. Toher. It is important to repeat that there may have been some wealthy burials in the 6th century. The imported Parian marble sarcophagus found on the Esquiline and dating to the late 6th century is one example; see *GRT* 252, Holloway 1994: 22 ff.

[5] Morris 1987: 90; Salares 1991: 202–3 on descent groups.

to fire or destruction; whether it is also part of the competitiveness of society, constantly updating and improving sanctuary sites, is more conjectural. Significantly, temple building and refurbishment appear to slow in the fifth century, when there were attempts to curb excessive display, and the economic climate was less buoyant.

It is also significant that, in Etruria in the sixth century, it seems that temple building accelerated, as in Latium, but burial expenditure did not decrease significantly; there are more, slightly poorer burials.[6] This may well be an indication that temple building was a way of differentiating a narrow élite from a wider group. It is also perhaps a sign of the inequality between Etruria and Latium; there was enough wealth in Etruria to continue burial expenditure, and to build splendid temples and palaces, but in Latium only one or the other was possible. This may also indicate that in Latium the wealthy and the aristocratic élite were synonymous, but in Etruria more people were becoming reasonably wealthy, and seeking to participate in the cultural display of the élite.[7]

Other indicators of wealth are harder to pin down. In so far as any weight can be placed on the presence of Greek pottery, it would appear that Latium as a whole lags behind Etruria and Campania, and that the closest contacts with the outside world came through Rome.[8] Rome acts as a sort of gateway settlement between Etruria and Latium, redistributing Etruscan and Greek pottery through the region. We ought not to underestimate direct contacts between Fidenae and Crustumerium with Veii across the Tiber, nor contacts to the south, with the Greek and Etruscan settlements in Campania and Magna Graecia. We have little firm evidence of material exchange with the south, since much of the Greek material may have come from south Etruria. The closest contacts, for which the evidence is partly the Greek pottery at Anagnia, the remarkable warrior display at Lanuvium, and other scattered material remains, but also the literary tradition of emabassies to the south in the fifth century, and the foundation of the temple of Ceres Liber Liberaque, which is clearly based on

[6] Torelli in *Rasenna* 48 ff.
[7] Raaflaub in Raaflaub (ed.) 1986: 198–243.
[8] Meyer 1980.

a parallel Greek triad, seem to have begun when the Etruscan mediation ceased; this may have encouraged or left room for more Latin involvement.[9]

The evidence seems to suggest that wealth in Latium was concentrated in the hands of a few. Throughout the five hundred years before the foundation of the Republic, the trend is towards greater production and an extraction of surplus, and the conspicuous consumption of wealth by an élite; this reaches its visible peak in the late seventh and early sixth centuries with the princely tombs, but I suggest that it continued with the major building works of the sixth century. The aristocracy of this period shared much with that of preceding generations and it is important to define as closely as possible the manner in which wealth was extracted from the many for the few. In previous times, the intensification of agriculture was an important means by which this occurred; by the sixth century the process may have become more thoroughly institutionalized, so that the literary records of the fifth century give a picture of ties of *clientela*, the problems of debt-bondage (*nexum*), and a privileged political and religious group dominating society; similar processes have been suggested for Etruria as well.[10]

Fundamental to all modern discussions of social organization is the institution of the *gens*. We know from the Twelve Tables that the *gens* was not simply an agnatic inheritance group; it was something larger.[11] Unlike the *familia*, there is no early evidence for a chief of the *gens*.[12] The extent to which the *gentes* incorporated the whole of the Roman population is also unclear; the patricians' claim that they alone could be organized into *gentes* seems to be false.[13]

The *gens* is an extremely shadowy institution, which, by the first century BC, had begun to lose much of its importance. The ancient sources are not clear about the nature of the *gens*, but their

[9] The most significant contacts with the Greeks in S. Italy mentioned by our sources are connected with famine and the need for grain; they are discussed in Garnsey 1988: 158 f. and Frederiksen 1984: 164–6. The embassy to Sicily occurred in 492 BC. For Ceres Liber Liberaque see Momigliano in Raaflaub (ed.) 1986: 188 ff.
[10] Drummond in *CAH* vii (2), 161, 215 f.; Cornell ibid. 329 ff; for suggestions of similar practices in Etruria see Torelli 1974/5: 33 ff., 1987: 87 ff.
[11] XII Tables 5. 4–5, misunderstood by Cic. *De Inv.* 2. 148.
[12] Franciosi 1984: 83 ff., 128 f.
[13] Livy 10. 8. 9; Momigliano in *CAH* vii (2), 99.

ignorance should not necessarily be taken as evidence that, in a much earlier period, it was of central importance. It is fair to say that it is not merely whim which has led scholars to emphasize the gentilitial nature of early Roman society. We shall see clear evidence in this section for the link between the *gentes* and religion, and religion is indivisible from politics in Roman and Greek society. We may note that many of the Roman tribes which were in existence by the beginning of the sixth century have names of important *gentes*. We may even say that, although the patrician claim to have a monopoly of the *gentes* is difficult to believe, the very fact that such a claim was attributed to them may itself be an indication of the importance of the institution. We may therefore attempt to present a model of the *gens* which seems to fit the available evidence.

In Attica before the time of Solon, the conspicuous consumption of the few was funded through pyramidal structures, in which the chiefs were supported by large numbers of dependants. If we follow the model that Forrest provided for Attica, we might associate the *gens* as a structural unit of society and the *clientes* as dependants in some way, who also provided the surpluses which allowed conspicuous consumption by the élite. The assumption here is that *clientes* were in some way tied in to the larger group of clansmen, rather than having an allegiance simply to individual members. This élite would most likely have been formed by the heads of the respective families connected through the *gens*. Such alliances might be formed through marriage, since it appears that the *gens* is an exogamous group.[14] Members of a *gens* might be found in a number of settlements; hence Vetusia in Praeneste, Valesios in Satricum, and the Claudii in Etruria. This may be the central aspect of the 'openness' of Latin society.[15]

In Rome, these *clientes* must have been citizens, for the Twelve Tables give provision against the defrauding of a *cliens*. One should think in terms of mutual support, with the major burdens of military leadership and political and religious representation being undertaken by the leaders, while the produce of the *clientes*, and their numbers in battle, acted as support. Gradually

---

[14] Franciosi 1988: 27 ff.
[15] Ampolo 1970/1; 1976/7 coined the phrase of an 'open' Latin society, indicating the mobility of the upper class across Central Italy.

the claims may have become more one-sided, especially when the conspicuous consumption of a few turned to the construction of temples and private palaces.[16]

The way in which the *plebs*, a group which became of central importance in the fifth century with their struggle for representation, fits into their structure remains unclear. There seems no reason to assume that some plebeians were not also dependants, nor that some, perhaps late arrivals in Rome during its expansion, were not. The view of Momigliano and Richard tends to suggest that the *plebs* should not be defined by identification with any social group, but rather as a political movement. Their grievances included the grievances of *clientes*, but that does not mean that the two groups are identical.

The expenditure at the centre and by the élite led inevitably to problems of debt, which were part of plebeian concerns in the fifth century and leave a mark in the Twelve Tables, where the provisions for the recovery of a debt, even to the extent of debt-bondage and enslavement of the debtor outside Rome, were laid down. This is very reminiscent of the problems of hektemorage and debt which Solon had to deal with at the beginning of the sixth century in Attica.

This is not to suggest that all *clientes* were badly treated or in debt; on the other hand, it is unlikely that the problems attested in the mid-fifth century were new. Nor would they have been confined to Rome; we hear of the *clientes* of Appius Claudius from the Sabina, and the existence of the *clientela* system in Latium seems very probable, given the existence of élite clans or *gentes*. The extent of the building programme at Rome, and perhaps the added factor of kings who needed to outstrip their aristocratic competitors in the game of prestige, may have exacerbated the problems there.

One important aspect of the social and economic structures of Latium is the system of land tenure. Much of Latium throughout the period would have been marshy, wooded, or scrub land, offering opportunities for some uses, but little for arable farming. Land of such a nature may not have been clearly demarcated, but there seems to have been a gradual reclaiming of land for

[16] Forrest 1978 summarizes the parallels in Greece.

agriculture, as shown by the spread of land use around Fidenae and Crustumerium. The tradition states that Romulus distributed Roman land to the Romans, and there may also have been public land for general use, but the fifth-century problems over land would seem to indicate that there was an appropriation of territory by the wealthy. The origin of the private ownership of land is unclear, but it is enshrined in the seventh of the Twelve Tables. The issues are well presented by Diósdi, who suggests that land was originally the property of the *gentes*, not legally as Mommsen thought, but through a kind of power position, a material relationship lacking legal protection. He deduces from the custom of *ercto non cito* (the non-division of ownership in the partnership of family heirs after the death of the head of the family) discussed by Gaius (*Inst.* 3.154) that this gentilitial ownership gave way to family property.[17] This still left problems for the poorer members of society.

Another approach to the nature of Latin society is through the evidence of onomastic structures.[18] An anonymous ancient author, apparently heavily reliant on Varro, propounded the view that the earliest inhabitants of Latium and elsewhere only had one name, like Romulus. Until the mid-seventh century in Etruria, inscriptions also bear this out.

According to our source, it was under the influence of the Sabines that a second name was added, the *nomen* (the first name thus becoming the *praenomen*) which represented the clan or *gens* to which the individual belonged. The third name, the *cognomen*, was not added until much later. Again the inscriptions bear this out; the double name is standard in Etruria throughout the sixth century, and is also attested in the Satricum inscription.

[17] Capogrossi Colognesi in Momigliano and Schiavone 1988: 263 ff.; Drummond in *CAH* vii (2), 118–24; Cornell, ibid. 325–9. Varro *RR* 1. 10. 2; Pliny *HN* 18. 7 give the details of the supposed Romulean distribution. For detailed discussion see Diósdi 1970; cf. also Betteridge 1989, who suggests that the process of urbanization emancipated the individual; Diósdi thought that a basically autarchic peasant economy necessitates the concentration of property. Both positions are to some extent true, but the legal private ownership of land at the time of the Twelve Tables, and the preceding 'power position' of the *gentes* have in common the effective dominance of an élite.

[18] See Mommsen 1864: 1 ff. for a basic account; the Varronian fragment is in Funaioli 1907: 331 ff. See also Schulze 1904, Rix 1972, Heurgon 1977 (focusing particularly on inscriptions).

Rome and Latium

The *cognomen* is to be distinguished from a patronymic, which explains the three names found in Faliscan inscriptions and also in the Tivoli dedication.

This apparent development, significantly faster and more consistent in Etruria than Latium if the epigraphic evidence is to be believed, has been central to many arguments about the nature of early Italian society. The gentilitial *nomen* precedes the familial *cognomen*, and has therefore been taken as proof that the *gentes* or clans were of greater importance than the family unit, and may even have existed before the state. If the argument holds, it ought to hold for the entire region.

The *gens* also had a part in inheritance, where *gentiles* inherited if there were no *adgnati*. Although this is not proof of the autonomous existence of the *gens* (it only shows that the *gentiles* were recognizable in the same way that the *adgnati* were), it may be taken to show that families operated within the larger framework of the *gens*. The *gens* probably had a military aspect too, since the Fabian clan at least went to war as a group. *Gentes* are also said to have had burial grounds exclusive to the clan.[19]

Mitchell has attempted to compare the *gentes* with the Greek *genos*. As Bourriot and Roussel pointed out, the *genos* has a religious role, and even if the exact organization of the *genos* belongs to the period of the polis, Lambert is right to stress that there was always a need for religious and inheritance groups.[20] The same may be said for the *gens*, in that it is likely that it had significant precursors, though the clans of the eighth century were probably unlike those of the sixth in some respects. It would make sense, for instance, to see the groups at Osteria dell'Osa as in some ways prototype *gentes*. As indicated above, the *gentes* have an important territorial aspect, and one might suggest that individual communities in Rome and other Latin sites that eventually came together into urban settlements may have been formed of one or more clans. It is therefore not necessary to postulate *gentes* existing before the state. The onomastic evidence

[19] Cic. *De Off.* 1. 17. 55; *De Leg.* 2. 22. 55; Livy 40. 38. 4; Plin. *Pan* 32; Franciosi 1984: 37 ff., discussing those *gentes* which cremate and those which inhume.
[20] Mitchell 1990; Bourriot 1976; Roussel 1976. Doubts expressed by Lambert 1986, esp. at 279: 'the fact that in the historical period *phylai* and *phratriai* were integral parts of the polis does not imply that they must have had their origin at the same time as the polis'; cf. Lambert 1993: 267 ff.; Kearns 1985 on continuities.

suggests that the larger association was expressed at a later stage; it may in fact be a product of the more complex social organization of the seventh and sixth centuries, but had less formal antecedents, which crystallized into a gentilitial system.

In the course of the sixth century, and consistently from then onwards, the *gens* seems threatened from the inside by the smaller family unit. It would appear that, over time, some families within the clan grew to have greater power than others; disparities of talent and wealth would explain this, and would have prevented the clan from acting as a coherent unified body. By the late Republic and early Empire, although the *gentes* still existed, and perhaps preserved some of their traditions, little was known about them; the law on *gentes* had become obsolete by the time of Gaius' *Institutes*. The power of the Roman *paterfamilias* becomes dominant, and this has led many modern scholars to trace the basis of Roman civil law to the individual father, and to leave aside the *gentes*, which, as Franciosi has frequently argued, may well be misleading.[21]

Evidence from archaic times for the *gentes* in Latium is limited. The gentilitial *nomen* is certainly an important aspect, and it is one of Franciosi's arguments for the clan originally having more importance than the family. Most important, the recent discovery at Tor de Cenci perhaps gives us some indication of the functioning of a small community just outside Rome, probably roughly in the *tribus* Aemilia.[22] The tombs there, grouped around two central inhumations, the persistence of burial for some centuries, the care with which the tombs were left undisturbed by later quarrying, and the apparent function of the place as a *compitum* or crossroads, if not a full *pagus* centre, led the excavators to suggest that there may have been a gentilitial hero cult here, as at the heroon at Lavinium, and perhaps a number of other chamber tombs in Latium. The settlement was probably inside the Roman tribal region by the early fifth century; the individuals buried here may well have been major figures in a *gens*, perhaps with branches in Rome itself. If the ceremony of the Lares was performed here as at other *compita*, it may have been in

---

[21] On families within *gentes*, see Franciosi 1988 3 ff., 1989 7 ff. For Gaius see Gaius *Inst* 3. 17. For the origins of law, Kunkel, Kaser, and Wieacker accept the *paterfamilias* line; contra Franciosi 1984: 13 ff., 1989: 49 ff.

[22] Bedini 1988–9, 1990.

honour of deceased aristocrats, as death continued to be appropriated and used by the élite.

The issue of hero or ancestor cults in Latium is worth considering further. Apart from the tombs at Tor de Cenci, there is also the re-use of the tomb later known as the Heroon of Aeneas at Lavinium.[23] The tomb was originally constructed in the seventh century, and the first intervention, marked by a piece of bucchero and other objects, came in the sixth century. Chamber tombs in general preserve a sense of family identity; and we have seen at Osteria dell'Osa respect for ancestors in the early ninth-century cremations, in the superimposition of tombs in the eighth century, and again in the seventh to sixth century chamber tomb. It is quite possible that rituals or sacrifices were made at chamber tombs; according to Dionysius (Dion. Hal. 4. 14. 3), Servius Tullius ordered that statues of heroes should be erected at *compita* and honoured every year.

It may be possible to compare this limited evidence with what we know about Greek cults. In the eighth century, in the Argolid and in Attica, both regions similar in size to Latium, Mycenaean tholos tombs were reopened and worshipped, with the political intention of laying claim to territory or representing separatist tendencies, according to Whitley.[24] It is not impossible that the chamber-tombs to the south of Rome, at Tor de Cenci, Aqua Acetosa Laurentina, and elsewhere also represent the political interests of *gentes* centred at Rome. The potential for connecting ancestor cults, or at least the preservation of the memory of ancestors, with gentilitial cults is obvious, and the fact that such treatment is restricted to a few would reinforce the aristocratic control of such practices.

In the late eighth and early seventh centuries, some very wealthy tombs were established at the West Gate of Eretria; a heroon was built in the early seventh century, and sacrifices appear to have been made there for a further century.[25] The possibility that tombs like those at Praeneste, or at the Heroon at Lavinium, itself outside the community but near the site of the Thirteen Altars, in some way marked boundaries or represented a

---

[23] *CLP* 306, and above.
[24] Whitley 1988; cf. Snodgrass in Gnoli and Vernant (eds.) 1982: 107–19.
[25] Coldstream 1977: 196 ff.; cf. Bérard in Gnoli and Vernant (eds.) 1982: 89–105; de Polignac 1984: 127 ff.

focus for the community is strong. Bérard connected the cult of the hero with the formation of the city, and it is interesting that the Greek hero cults began in the eighth century, when the polis was beginning to emerge, while the wealthiest Latin tombs and the examples we have been discussing emerged in the late seventh century, when a very similar process was taking place in Latium. Bérard said of the Greek examples that 'les cercles aristocratiques . . . savent faire parler le mort pour justifier leurs initiatives politiques,' and the same point could be made for Latium.[26]

From this cursory survey, we can see that Latin society had clear vertical divisions, and that many of the political and social divisions reflected central structural issues like the ownership of land. This is consonant with the archaeological record, which has shown conspicuous consumption by an élite, and has indicated that many settlements were formed by the synoecism or absorption of distinct areas of inhabitation. It is therefore plausible that the organization of society should have reflected the territorial interest of its members.

We ought at this point to examine other forms of organization which can be suggested for archaic Rome. According to the tradition, Romulus divided the Roman people into three tribes and thirty *curiae*. The three tribes are largely a mystery, but the *curiae* are slightly more accessible, because they survived into the early Empire.[27]

It is usually assumed that the *curiae* were formed from the *gentes*, the evidence being the apparently gentilitial names of the Acculeia, Faucia, and Titia (though none are prominent *gentes* in later records), and a passage in Gellius taken from Laelius Felix, in which it is stated that an assembly organized by *genera hominum* ('kinds of men') is curiate. This shows that the *curiae* were based on kinship groups, but not necessarily on *gentes*, though the connection is at least plausible. Some of the rural tribes of Rome have names shared with prominent *gentes*, which reinforces the territorial aspect of the *gens*, and the likelihood that it is a central institution in the structure of the population.[28]

[26] Bérard op. cit. at 102.
[27] Momigliano 1963: 108 ff.; Palmer 1970.
[28] Taylor 1966: 8 f.

The Comitia Calata, which met at the Curia Calabra on the Capitol and ratified wills, changes of status from patrician to plebeian and vice versa, and seems to have been the body that 'elected' or formally acknowledged the king (a function which probably continues in the curiate authorization of *imperium*) is generally thought to have been organized by curiae. The *curiae* had their own religious functions, in particular the Fordicidia and Fornacalia, which appear to be archaic agricultural festivals. They had their own chiefs, the *curiones*, and the Curio Maximus, who was the main chief, was always a patrician. The members met together for dinners, and a Claudian phase of the Curiae Veteres, a building presumably used for this purpose, may have been uncovered at the corner of the Palatine.

There are indications that the *curiae* also had a territorial definition; two of the known names (Veliensis and Foriensis) are topographical; the Fornacalia may include a purification of boundaries, and Dionysius explicitly says that Romulus apportioned land to them (Dion. Hal. 2. 7. 4). The conservatism of the organization, and its eventual decline in favour of the centuriate assembly, may be connected with a persisting and increasingly anachronistic territorial definition.[29]

Momigliano made the exciting suggestion that the curiate organization at Rome could be compared with the Tabulae Iguvinae; the special relationship between the Petronii and Hondus Iovius, and the Vucii and Jupiter may indicate two *gentes* with their special religious centres emerging from the larger groups; it is equally possible that the *gentes* already had their religious connotations.[30] It should be sufficient to conclude that the *curiae* represent an early organization of Roman society which has the political role of defining the citizen body and ratifying authority within it, and which may also be based on an early territorial division of the Roman territory. It is worth mentioning that an inscription indicates that *curiae* also existed at Lanuvium, and probably elsewhere, at a later date. They may also have been present at Tibur and in Etruria.[31]

Another social group is attested in the late sixth-century

---

[29] Palmer 1970: 131–40 implies that the *curiae*, not just the tribes, were flexible enough to admit members from the wider Ager Romanus of the early 5th century.
[30] Momigliano 1963: 115 ff.   [31] CIL xiv. 2114, 2120 for Lanuvium.

Satricum inscription, with the mention of *suodales*.[32] The nature of the *suodales* is unclear, but it is most likely to represent some sort of age group, or a band similar to a Greek *hetaireia*. The connection of Valesios with the *gens* Valeria found at Rome is difficult to resist, and if the inscription is the base for a statue, then such a dedication might also suggest an élite context.[33] Two sorts of compatible groups might be suggested. The *suodales* might be a sort of warrior group, which would fit the weaponry often found in graves of an earlier date. There is also sufficient evidence of wine drinking and symposiastic institutions in the sixth century and earlier to support that connection. Both, from Greek parallels, are resolutely aristocratic in nature.

So far, there is archaeological, epigraphical, onomastic, and institutional evidence for organizations in Latium, which divide the whole population and reveal an aristocratic stratum of society. There may well have been more groups, like the early *collegia*, attributed to Numa. The military organization attributed to Servius Tullius may be late in its details, but a division of the army into cavalry and others, according to wealth and status, is very likely; this is borne out by the division of the army into the *classis* of fully armed troops, and the larger group below that qualification (*infra classem*). The presence of infantry armour and cavalry accoutrements in wealthy burials is amply attested in the archaeological record in Rome and elsewhere, and must have been a central aspect of the organization of society.[34]

I have stressed throughout the importance of the *gens*, and in particular I have attempted to show that it is at least consistent with the evidence to see it as having a degree of autonomy, rather than being a purely administrative or legal aggregation of individuals and families who otherwise operated independently. I wish to pursue this by indicating the centrality of the *gens* in the religious life of early Rome.

The suggestion has often been made that, at Rome, many cults

---

[32] Versnel in Stibbe *et al.* 1980; Versnel 1982. Tac. *Ann.* 1. 54 reports a group known as the *Sodales Titii*, supposedly descended from Titus Tatius, and discussed by Versnel 1980: 111.   [33] See Appendix 1 for further details.
[34] For Numa's *collegia* see Plut. *Num.* 17. 1–4; Pliny *HN* 34. 1; 35. 46; Momigliano in *CAH* vii (2), 101, regarding them as one of the elements that prepared for the emergence of a unified plebs. On the Servian army see Thomsen 1980: 144 ff.

originated with one or two *gentes*, and that each *gens* had a deity of its own.[35] The existence of religious worship based on the *gens* indicates that it had a more than superficial degree of unity, but there is little to indicate when this religious practice began. The case of the Potitii and Pinarii, who surrendered the cult of Hercules at the Ara Maxima in 312 BC, is an important indication of its antiquity.[36]

Festus gives a clear enough division of Roman cults (284L): *Publica sacra, quae publico sumptu pro populo fiunt, quaeque pro montibus, pagis, curis, sacellis; at privata, quae pro singulis hominibus, familiis, gentibus fiunt.* The case of the Potitii and Pinarii is an instance in which a private sacrifice became a public one, and it may not have been an isolated instance.[37]

Numerous instances of such cults can be adduced; a few will be mentioned here. Cicero gives a significant indication of private clan religion; in *De Har. resp.* 15. 32 he asks *L. Pisonem quis nescit his temporibus ipsis maximum et sanctissimum Dianae sacellum in Caeliculo sustulisse? Adsunt vicini eius loci; multi sunt etiam in hoc ordine qui sacrificia gentilicia illo ipso in sacello stato loco anniversaria factitarint,* and he is here referring to the *gens* Calpurnia, though others may have shared the temple with them.[38]

Macrobius mentions other examples (*Sat.* 1. 16. 7): *sunt praeterea feriae propriae familiarum; ut familiae Claudiae vel Aemiliae vel Juliae vel Corneliae.*[39] The *gens* Claudia does seem to have clearly private rites, according to Ateius Capito, the Roman jurist who wrote on sacrificial ritual and is quoted by Festus; *Propudialis porcus dictus est, ut ait Capito Ateius, qui in sacrificio gentis*

---

[35] Altheim 1938: 137 ff.; de Marchi 1896, 1903 ii. 1 ff.; Fustel de Coulanges 1980: 94 ff. See also Westrup 1954; Otto 1909; de Francisci 1959: 170–1.

[36] Livy 9. 29. 9; North in *CAH* vii (2), 622.

[37] 'Public sacrifices are those done through public expenditure for the people, such as those for the hills, *pagi*, *curiae*, and sanctuaries; whereas the private ones are those for individuals, families and *gentes*.'

[38] 'Who is unaware that recently L. Piso destroyed a great and most sacred shrine of Diana on the Caeliculum? The neighbours of that place are present here; there are many in this order who performed the annual rites of their *gens* in this designated place.' On Cicero's *De Har. resp.* see Lenaghan 1969; v. ad loc. for this passage. The Calpurnius Piso was the consul of 58 BC (PW 90).

[39] 'There are other festivals besides that belong to families, like those of the Claudii, or the Aemilii, or the Julii, or the Cornelii.' Macrobius uses the word *familia* where one would expect *gens*.

Claudiae velut piamentum et exsolutio omnis contractae religionis est (Festus 274L).[40]

To this evidence may be added a couple of passages from Cicero concerned with Clodius' *transitio ad plebem* and adoption by Fonteius. In his speech *de domo sua*, which is a deliberate attack on Clodius, and therefore likely to be full of exaggerations, Cicero indicates that the pontifical college had to consider the adoption in the light of any possible diminution of the *sacra* (13. 34; 14. 36), and he complains, *probate genus adoptionis; iam omnium sacra interierint, quorum vos esse debetis; iam patricius nemo relinquetur* (14. 37).[41] Cicero may well be exaggerating, but he can only be referring to the Claudians, so this is an indication of their special *sacra*.

We have already seen that the *transitio ad plebem* took place before the Comitia Calata, which dealt with wills and adoptions. It would appear that part of the rejection of one's clan was the *detestatio sacrorum*; as Servius said, *consuetudo apud antiquos fuit, ut qui in familiam vel gentem transiret, prius se abdicaret ab ea in qua fuerat et sic ab alia reciperetur* (*ad Aen.* 2. 156).[42]

Some cults are attested by historical accounts, which may have been inspired by a cult activity. For instance, according to Livy (5. 46), in 390 BC when Rome was besieged by the Gauls, C. Fabius Dorsuo set off from the Capitol to the Quirinal, wearing his toga in the Gabine fashion for a sacrifice, and carrying the *sacra* in his hands, performed the ritual on the Quirinal, and returned through the enemy lines. The sacrifice, Livy tells us, was *genti Fabiae* (for the *gens* Fabia). We have a quotation in Appian from Cassius Hemina (fr. 19P ap. Appian *de reb. Gall.* fr. 6), who said that the cult was of Vesta, but Ogilvie in his commentary suspects that this may be due to Cassius' interest in this deity. We also know that the *gens* Fabia provided some of the Lupercales together with the *gens* Quintilia (Festus 78L), and this may be sufficient to connect the clan to this particular hill;

---

[40] 'The *propudialis porcus* is so called, as Ateius Capito tells us, because in the sacrifices of the Claudian *gens*, it is the atonement and discharge of any religious contract.'

[41] 'Approve this kind of adoption; soon all the rites, for which you are responsible, will die; soon there will be no patrician left.'

[42] 'It was the custom among the ancients that whoever moved family or *gens* first abdicated those in which he had been and so was received by the other.'

the deity may have been Faunus, as suggested by Altheim. The Fabii also claimed descent from Hercules (Plut. *Fab. Max.* 1). When Quintus Fabius Maximus was called back to Rome from the conflict with Hannibal, we do not know whether it was for the *sacra* of his own *gens*, or because his presence as dictator was necessary for state cults (Livy 22. 18; Polybius 3. 94).

There is a very interesting reference to gentilitial worship in Dionysius (9. 19. 3), in connection with the *gens* Fabia when they were defending Rome from Veii. The account in Livy, and the one preferred by Dionysius, is that the Fabii were slaughtered after foraging too far from their camp, but Dionysius also has a version which says that the Fabii were returning to Rome to perform a 'traditional sacrifice, which the Fabian *gens* had to perform'. He rejects this because the rites could have been performed by others of the same clan who were advanced in years, and had remained in Rome; and even if all the members of the *gens* had left Rome, it was only necessary for three or four to return to Rome to perform the rites for the whole clan. It may be that Dionysius is here reflecting the practice of the late Republic and early Empire. Even if he is right in rejecting the story, it would show that gentilitial cults were being performed at Rome by small numbers even in his day, private rituals which might easily be left unmentioned in our sources, but which might nevertheless have had great antiquity.

As for the rest of the evidence, it is to be gathered from stray references and allusions. The private cults of the *gens* Julia are best known. It may be that they had some private worship of Romulus, through whom they traced their ancestry back to Aeneas and thence to Venus; we hear of a statue *inter arcem et Capitolium* ('between the Arx and the Capitol') (Pliny *HN* 16. 69. 216; Gell. 5. 12. 1). Servius (Ad *Aen.* 10. 316) indicates worship of Apollo. Symmachus (330. 10 Seeck) writes [the gods] *ipsas nobilium divisere gentes: Pinarios Hercules occupavit, Idaea mater legit hospites Scipiones, Veneriis sacris famulata est domus Iulia*,[43] but one is inclined to wonder whether both these are not the product of Augustan propaganda and the emphasis on Venus and Apollo in the poetry of Vergil and Horace.

More secure is the worship of Vediovis, whom Weinstock

---

[43] 'The gods even share the *gentes* of the nobility: Hercules takes the Pinarii; the Idaean mother chooses the Scipios as hosts; the Julian house ministers Venus' rites.'

identifies as Iulus, at Bovillae, which was also revived by Augustus (Tac. Ann. 2.41; 15.23). This cult is attested, uniquely, by an inscription at Bovillae from around 100 BC which runs:

VEDIOVEI PATREI GENTILES IULIEI
VEDI[OVEI] AARA
LEEGE ALBANA DICATA.

There is, however, no guarantee that the Julian involvement in the cult is much older than the inscription.[44]

Of the four *gentes* mentioned by Macrobius as having *feriae propriae*, we have discussed the Julii and the Claudii. With regard to the Cornelii we have no other information, although it may be significant that they never cremated their members, as we are told by Cicero (*De Leg.* 2. 22) and Pliny (*HN* 7. 187). The fourth of the clans is the Aurelia. It was alleged that the Aurelii were of Sabine origin, and they worshipped Sol.[45]

The conclusion that may be drawn from this evidence is that some Roman cults may have had their origin in worship by *gentes*, and that senior members of a *gens* probably had religious duties, possibly from a very early date. This may contribute to an understanding of why so many priestly offices appear to have been restricted to patrician families in the early Republic; this seems fairly clear for the *rex sacrorum*, the *maiores flamines*, the Luperci and Salii, the augurs, fetials, *pontifices*, and *duoviri sacris faciundis*.[46] Without entering the vexed issue of the nature and formation of the patriciate, it does seem clear that the aristocracy at Rome controlled much of the religious life of the city.

THE LEGAL ORGANIZATION OF ROME AND LATIUM

The first treaty between Rome and Carthage, reported by Polybius and dated to 509 BC, gives us some of the earliest information concerning the relations between Rome and the Latins. It may have been an example of certain agreements which Aristotle

---

[44] 'The Julian *gentiles* to Father Vediovis: An altar to Vedivis declared by the Alban law.' Weinstock 1971: 4–12; CIL I² 807 = XIV 2387 = ILS 2988.
[45] Richard 1976; Festus 22L.
[46] Beard in Beard and North (eds.) 1990: 19. Mommsen 1864–79, i. 69–127 gives an account of the priesthoods; individual priesthoods are discussed in detail in Wissowa 1912.

mentions, or a formal setting out of their terms; it may have been inspired by the change of government at Rome, and by the uncertainty of the Etruscan position at the end of the sixth century. The treaty is sworn between Carthage on one hand, and Rome and her unnamed allies on the other, and there is also mention of states who are subject to Rome. This formula of Roman dominance may reflect Roman claims at the end of the sixth century, and these may well have been a contributory factor in the unrest that led to the Latin revolt at Lake Regillus. The result of this battle has been variously interpreted; the Romans claimed it as a victory (Livy 2. 20), but Cornell suggests that the result was far more even, and that the battle, together with the external threats to Latium, put an end to Roman expansion.[47]

Two fundamental reorganizations of Roman society occurred in the sixth and fifth centuries; the first was the group of measures attributed to Servius Tullius, and the second was in the aftermath of the victory at Lake Regillus. Both are central to the history of Latium as well as Rome. The details of the Servian reforms are much disputed because the accounts are clearly influenced by events from later periods,[48] but the reforms regarding the tribal system and the army fit the necessities of the sixth century, with the development of Rome as an urban centre, and the expansion of Rome's territory, as a result of the successes which culminated in the proud formula of the Rome–Carthage treaty. Therefore I have discussed both the internal reforms of Rome and the transformation of relations between Rome and Latium in this section, for they are intimately connected.

The Servian Reforms and the Organization of Roman Territory

There is a strong tradition in the sources which attributes a major reorganization of society to the king Servius Tullius. He was thought to have reorganized the army into a new system of centuries, and also to have reformed the tribal organization of Rome, instituting four urban tribes in place of the previous three, reflecting the growth in the city and new rural tribes in Rome's territory. When one examines the nature of these reforms, one is

---

[47] Pol. 3. 22 f.; Ar. *Pol.* 1280a 36 ff.; Walbank 1957: 337 ff. (sceptical), cf. Cornell in *CAH* vii (2), 255–7, Scullard, ibid. 517 ff. On Lake Regillus see Cornell in *CAH* vii (2), 262, 274 ff.   [48] Thomsen 1980 discusses all aspects of this.

reminded at several points of Athenian reformers like Solon and Cleisthenes, and no doubt the tradition has been affected by such considerations. Nevertheless, the reforms are at least consonant with a society which was growing in size and power. In so far as the political history of the period can be understood, we seem to have strong monarchies, whose strength derived in part from the ability to command a large army. We may begin with the reorganization of territory.

The earliest division of the Ager Romanus seems to have been by *pagi*. By chance we know the name of one *pagus*, the Lemonius, and this is also the name of a tribe just to the south-east of Rome.[49] Oxyrhynchus Papyrus 2088 has the tantalizing words *pagosque in tribu*, possibly referring to a Servian reorganization of the *pagi* into the *tribus*. Capogrossi Colognesi[50] sees the *pagi* as early divisions of the Ager Romanus, dominated by the *gentes*, or in other words, the élite. The *pagi* were replaced by the *tribus* which retained connections with the *gentes* as shown by their names.

The connection between the *pagi* and the tribes was a geographical one, and although a reorganization would not have been neat, one may assume that the *pagi* gave the geographical basis for the larger tribes. The *pagi* may well have continued as rural centres within the tribes; this can be suggested for Tor de Cenci.[51] Some of the tribes have the names of *gentes* who were clearly important in the fifth century and presumably before, and one would suppose therefore that these represented the power bases of the *gens*, with their *clientes* working the land.

If this is close to the truth, we can add something to our understanding of the most important *gentes*. Originally based on the *pagi*, many must represent strong agrarian interests in what became the suburbs of Rome. Some may have been drawn into the widening Roman influence; others may have moved out from Rome to colonize these areas.

It is unlikely that such processes were confined to Rome, because the gentilitial system seems to be spread throughout Latium, and there was clearly an aristocracy which needed to

---

[49] Festus p102L.
[50] Capogrossi Colognesi in Momigliano and Schiavone 1988: 275 ff.
[51] Drummond op. cit. 146 n. 81 for caution; Bedini 1988–9, 1990 for Tor de Cenci.

be supported in its expenditure. It is interesting therefore that the intensive surveys of Antemnae, Fidenae, and Crustumerium show that, in the seventh century, settlement began to move out along the roads, but use of territory dramatically increased in the sixth century. At Fidenae, every attempt seems to have been made to fulfil completely the agricultural potential of the area, and the presence of roof-tiles may indicate permanent dwellings. The greater part of the settlements are groupings of a larger or smaller number of dwelling-places, and inhabitants seem to have been buried in the area in which they worked. At Crustumerium, as at Fidenae, settlement follows the road pattern; in the former, the renowned agricultural land was improved at this time by *cunicoli* or drains for water.[52]

This sixth-century expansion and exploitation of territory may be suggested for Rome as well, being a simultaneous process with the establishment of a more stable aristocracy, a stronger army, and a vigorous development of Rome itself, and probably also a contributory factor to those developments. It must also have led to conflict with the Latins.

There is considerable evidence which indicates the importance of military activity in Rome in the sixth century, and which encourages faith in a reorganization of the military at about this time, a reorganization which took on an increasingly political aspect, as the centuriate organization, which could absorb more people, replaced the narrower and more inflexible curiate system.

In the early sixth-century tombs weapons were still being deposited in quantity, and fortifications were clearly in place in most Latin centres, including Rome itself. Terracotta friezes from the Palatine show warriors in chariots and on horseback.[53] The cult of Mars at the Regia cannot be divorced from its military connotations, and at least two Roman festivals of some antiquity are concerned with the return of an army, the Roman Triumph, which was heavily influenced by Etruscan ceremony, and the Ludi Romani.

Indeed Rome in the sixth century was already developing the large and effective army which was always the key to its power. It is reckoned, on the basis of the details of the Servian centuries,

[52] Quilici and Quilici Gigli 1986: 378 ff.
[53] *GRT* 92 ff.

that Rome could field an army of several thousand men by the battle of Lake Regillus, far surpassing the army of any other Latin state acting on its own.[54] In the context of this strong military commitment, it is worth reconsidering the purpose of the Servian reforms, and the development of the tribal system in particular.

The size of this army is a matter of some dispute. The evidence we have is essentially the accounts of Livy and Dionysius, which are demonstrably affected by later military reforms, and antiquarian evidence from Varro and the author of POxy 2088 regarding Servius' reform of the centuries and the tribes. Fraccaro proposed an army of 6,000 infantry on the basis of a careful reading of this evidence; Thomsen and Richard preferred a figure of 4,000. Either way, this is a formidable force, and shows the plausibility of the claims of Rome's territorial expansion in the sixth century, especially if we remember that this is only the *classis* of fully armed troops, and the majority fell outside this group.

It is possible that the tribal and military reforms should be taken together. Siewert has suggested that, when Cleisthenes reformed the political geography of Attica, he may also have had in mind facilitating the call-up of soldiers to the centre of Athens in time of war.[55] The evidence for the connection of the tribes and warfare is limited, but it is interesting that the Fabian *gens* was prepared to operate as a military unit by itself in defence of its own tribal area, as well as the city of Rome. The Agrimensores preserve a mention of *ager arcefinius*, near the borders of territory seized from the enemy, which the farmers both cultivated and defended; the Claudia, Clustumina, and Fabia tribes would all be candidates for containing such land, and thus encouraging military activity by the inhabitants of the tribe.[56]

However, just as the *trittyes* of Attica seem aligned on roads to Athens, so the organization of the rural tribes may have assisted

[54] Thomsen 1980: 144 ff.   [55] Siewert 1982.
[56] Frontin *de agr. qual.* p2, 18 ff. (ed. Thüln): *Ager est arcefinius, qui nulla mensura continetur. finitur secundum antiquam observationem fluminibus, fossis, montibus, viis, arboribus ante missis, aquarum divergiis et si qua loca ante a possessore potuerunt optineri. nam ager arcefinius, sicut ait Varro, ab arcendis hostibus est appellatus: qui postea interventu litium per ea loca quibus finit terminos accipere coepit. in his agris nullum ius subsicivorum intervenit* ('Land is *arcefinius* which is not enclosed by any measure. According to the old rule, it was bounded by rivers, ditches, mountains,

the levy of the general army. Servius' division of the city into four urban tribes, as opposed to the three Romulean ones, seems to be based on the new topography of an expanded city. If Humbert is correct in seeing a gradual expansion of the rural tribes, eventually reaching seventeen around the time of the battle of Lake Regillus, there is also a gradual incorporation of larger areas of territory. The reorganization of the scattered *pagi* into tribes, apparently centred on these *pagi* and dominated by *gentes*, may represent a gradual strengthening of the ties between the immediate vicinity of Rome and the city, and may have had the effect of improving the speed of the levy of the general army, as well as its completeness in times of emergency. If some responsibility for the levy rested on the *gentes*, one must note that many of the family heads within *gentes* were part of the Roman political system, certainly under the Republic and probably before, and consequently made the decisions concerning war. Some of these men together with their sons would have been front-line fighters or cavalry, and their dependants and *clientes* must have been the backbone of the army. In fact, it is hard to see how the tribal system could not have been used in levying the army, though it was not related to the organization of the full army in the field.

The history of Rome's organization of its territory is in part the history of the expansion of Roman domination over Latium. The earliest organization of Rome into the three 'Romulean' tribes, if true, represents the community as a single entity with little influence on the surrounding area. The tribes are doubled under Tarquinius Priscus. Servius Tullius' four urban tribes seem to represent a major reordering of Roman society consequent on its expansion. By 495 BC Livy tells us that the number of tribes was raised to twenty-one (2. 21), the four urban tribes and the seventeen rural tribes. This information is a crucial indication of the extent and nature of Roman expansion around the beginning of the fifth century.

The Servian organization was expressly territorial, and the four urban tribes, the Suburana, Esquilina, Collina and Palatina,

roads, established trees, watersheds, and whatever other places the possessor had been able to get hold of. For *ager arcefinius*, as Varro tells us, is so called from warding off enemies: later, through arbitration, there began to be an acceptance of where the boundaries ran in those areas. In these lands there is no law concerning land left over after boundaries have been drawn').

remained the basis for the division of Rome into regions.[57] Perhaps it is the origin of the phrase *Roma quadrata*, which occurs in POxy 2088, together with the information that Servius somehow connected the *pagi* with the tribes.

In this account, the extent of the twenty-one tribes by 495 is very significant; the Romilia, and later the Galeria and Fabia, represent the extent of Rome's possessions across the Tiber, though these are the tribes which may have spread the most in the course of the fifth and early fourth centuries before the decisive conquest of Veii. The Clustumina stretches furthest to the north. The rest describe a semicircle of land which reaches out to some of the most important Latin settlements, Gabii, Tusculum, Aricia, Lavinium. Within its arc we may reckon Castel di Decima and Ficana, Antemnae, Fidenae, and Crustumerium, and possibly Ficulea and Collatia in the troubled northern region, though both may in fact have been outside the original extent of the tribes. According to the sources, Fidenae resisted Rome for some time; Crustumerium was uneasy under Rome's domination. Of Antemnae, we know only enough to suggest that it did valuable garrison duty for Rome then, as in more modern times. The implication that all other settlements within the circle of Rome's domination were either put out of existence or subordinated to Roman power is clear.

We may return to specific instances, in an attempt to show the effects of the Roman expansion. In the case of a relatively wealthy community, such as Castel di Decima had been, one assumes that, if the absorption into the tribal system occurred before Lake Regillus and before the beginning of the Republic, then the leaders of that society, possibly already related by marriage to Roman aristocrats, may have taken up some kind of high position in the Roman state, if they were not annihilated.

Something of the sort seems to have happened in the case of the communities to the north of Rome, which became part of the tribal system early in the Republic. So L. Sergius Fidenas is found as consul for 437 and 429, investigating collusion between Fidenae and Veii; his *gens* may have owned land around Fidenae and possibly also defended that land for Rome. Whether the land was granted to the Sergii, or was always theirs, we do not know,

[57] See Thomsen 1980: 115 ff. for a lucid discussion.

but we do know that the Claudii were granted land around Crustumerium, and may again have acted as defenders. Their chiefs were also admitted to the patriciate.[58] One may also consider Tor de Cenci and its burials in this light.[59]

In short, in a number of instances, the expansion of Rome's territory affected areas which may have been occupied by people of some rank and already in some way connected with Roman aristocracy, perhaps by marriage or by religious alliance. (Antemnae, for instance, on the borders of Rome's five-mile boundary, may have shared in boundary festivals like the Ambarvalia; other individuals may well have gathered at their nearest main temples, which may have been in Rome.) Some parts may even have been colonized or occupied by Romans from the city, as suggested above. The Ager Romanus was closely bound in to the Roman political and military system through the tribes, and it is unlikely that they had much independent political life, though Fidenae, the largest settlement within the territory, was recalcitrant. The absorption of so much land, and the inhabitants, was a crucial step for Rome, for it undoubtedly increased the size of an already large and victorious army; some *gentes* may have benefited, and some families in particular, as expansion increased the opportunities for exploitation.

One indication of an alternative to absorption is the treaty with Gabii which seems to have predated the battle of Lake Regillus and is attributed to Tarquinius Superbus.[60] Gabii, having resisted Rome's forcible attempts to incorporate it, joined in a treaty or *foedus* of its own free will, and that this was the first such treaty might be indicated by the unique consequences which it brought. Dionysius, who claimed that he saw the treaty preserved on a leather shield in the temple of Semo Sancus, characterized it as an *isopoliteia* (4. 58 f.), which Humbert suggests is his indication of the Latin *jura*. More significant is the fact that Roman magistrates wore the *cinctus Gabinus* as a sacred vestment for certain solemnities, and Ager Gabinus was juridically distinct from both Ager Romanus and Ager Peregrinus (foreign land). Rome was recognized by the Foedus Gabinum as the foremost

---

[58] Quilici and Quilici Gigli 1980: 378 ff. with references.
[59] Bedini 1988–9, 1990.
[60] Sherwin-White 1971: 19 f.; Humbert 1978: 86 ff.

power in Latium, and this may have been an incentive for the unrest among the other communities.

Gabii, close to the borders of the Ager Romanus, had a large sixth-century temple on an earlier votive deposit, and the burial evidence from Osteria dell'Osa indicates at least one sixth-century chamber tomb. Presumably such a site would have had its own aristocracy, with religious and military duties, just like the Roman *gentes*. The power of Rome was so great, however, that by the fifth century, Gabii's best hope was alliance rather than resistance, and all the Latin settlements relied on the might of Rome during the troubled century or so that followed Lake Regillus. The future lay not in alliance, but in a closer and closer identification with Rome, and a subordination of independence to the demands of an ever-increasing centre.

Relations between Latium and Rome

Our evidence for the relations between Rome and her neighbours in the sixth century and at the beginning of the fifth is extremely patchy and unreliable, often contaminated by the situation in the fourth century and always seen from the Roman point of view, either directly or through the distorting vision of Greek writers. Nevertheless, it is possible to make some approach to the subject of relations in the region.

The evidence of inscriptions and the openness of Latin religion indicate that Latin communities were not closed to each other or to influences from Etruria, and perhaps further afield.[61] In particular, the inscriptions attest the movement of people from community to community, and one suspects that some represent a permanent change of abode.[62] This is attested in the sources, with the move of Demaratus from Corinth to Tarquinia, and then of his son Lucumo to Rome; later on Tarquinius Superbus, of the same dynasty, was forced to move a number of times after his expulsion from Rome. Deliberate choice and desperation are both effective motives for a change of abode, and the instance of the Claudii who migrated as a group into Latin territory shows that movement was not confined to individuals.

[61] Ampolo 1970/1; 1976/7.
[62] See Appendix 1 for inscriptions.

We should beware of assuming that this apparent openness indicates a primitive or only partially defined social organization, as Sherwin-White suggested, and others after him; but Humbert may be exaggerating when he claims that 'dès l'époque royale, la notion de citoyonneté et de cité politique est déjà parfaitement formée à Rome et dans le Latium'.[63] The evidence is partly archaeological; as shown above, by the beginning of the fifth century many communities of the region possessed effective defences, public religious buildings (some inside and some perhaps deliberately outside the settlement), and monumental private architecture. This sense of communal identity can probably be assigned to synoecism in the sixth century.

Whether notions of citizenship found any written or legal form before the beginning of the sixth century may be doubted. The First Carthaginian Treaty gives an important indication of self-conscious settlements. For Rome itself, we may point to the tribal system which represents a deliberate organization of territory, and to the Twelve Tables, in particular the provision that no one could be sold into slavery except *trans Tiberim peregre* (abroad across the Tiber, i.e. outside this territory) (III.5). For the rest of Latium, we may think of the Foedus Cassianum after the battle of Lake Regillus, and the *jura* which the Latins had with respect to Rome, of *commercium* and *conubium*, and also a complex entitlement to the citizenship of another community by simple *migratio*; this may have included the right to vote where appropriate. The organization of the Latin League around various religious festivals and the participation of Latin settlements in the military operations of the League may also be adduced.

It is extremely difficult to pin these aspects down in time. It is generally supposed that the Latin League must have been in existence by the late sixth century, in order to permit the battle of Lake Regillus; it is possible that the dedication at the Grove of Aricia was the charter for this anti-Roman organization. The rights of the Latins, described by Cornell as characteristic of a society in which the idea of the state was not strongly developed, are thought by Humbert to be the product of the formal diplomatic agreements of the early fifth century.[64] Humbert is more

---

[63] Humbert 1978: 83 and n. 110. Sherwin-White does see the treaty with Gabii as important (1971: 20).
[64] Humbert 1978: 81–4; Cornell in *CAH* vii (2), 270.

confident than Cornell that early Latin communities had a clear legal and political status, but in fact both scholars describe an essentially similar process of the hardening of practice into law. It is possible that the Foedus Cassianum, and the need to make a clear statement about the relative status of Rome and the Latin settlements, accelerated this.

Livy and Dionysius give us details of the treaty which was supposed to have been struck by Sp. Cassius after the battle had been won. Cicero claimed to have seen the bronze tablet with the treaty terms in the Forum; Festus reports two phrases 'in the Latin treaty', and Dionysius gives the terms, while Livy implies his belief in the treaty by mentioning its renewal in 358, and proceeding with assumptions concerning restrictions upon the Latins which on his account can only have come from the treaty.

The terms in Dionysius are as follows (6. 95. 2):

Let there be peace among the Romans and all the Latin cities as long as the heavens and the earth shall remain where they are. Let them neither make war upon one another themselves, nor bring in foreign enemies nor grant a safe passage to those who shall make war upon either. Let them assist one another when warred upon, with all their forces, and let each have an equal share of the spoils and booty taken in their common wars. Let suits relating to private contracts be determined within ten days, and in the nation where the contract was made. And let it not be permitted to add anything to, or take anything away from these treaties except by the consent both of the Romans and of all the Latins.

Dionysius' treaty does not contain the quotes found in Festus in any form,[65] so we must assume that either the two treaties referred to are not the same, or else that Dionysius is giving a summary of a text which he was barely able to understand. If he is giving a summary, one is inclined to wonder if he has transferred the terms into quite different language, or even if he was reporting the treaties of the fourth century.

The right to contract a legal marriage with a partner from another Latin community (*conubium*), and to deal with persons from other Latin communities and to make legally binding contracts (*commercium*; in particular, to own real property in the territory of another Latin state) are crucial to the existence of an

[65] Festus 166L.

economic community in Latium. These rights also represent an economy not based simply on gift-exchange, and may presuppose much more complicated processes of building up and using capital. No doubt the rights came to cover more advanced transactions in time, but they could not have had this flexibility if they had not begun as respected institutions. The marriage rights may also have incorporated important provisions concerning inheritance, and Franciosi has shown that one could not marry within one's own *gens*, which might have encouraged some individuals to look outside their own community.[66]

The right of *migratio* is perhaps more complex. It would appear that Latins had the right to seek exile in another settlement in order to escape persecution. It would also appear that at some stage, Latins possessed the right to change their abode and become citizens of another settlement. The incorporation went so far as to include voting rights. It would appear that it was not necessary to take up permanent residence in Rome to exercise this vote, and it may be that a Roman could cast a vote in the Latin settlements.

The right seems particularly appropriate as the demands made on the Latins to contribute towards the military activity of the area grew. It remains possible that it was introduced later than the Foedus Cassianum, and this view is strengthened by the fact that the right is usually mentioned in connection with agrarian unrest, an issue of the late Republic (but also of the early Republic, according to all our sources).[67]

It does seem that the rights which have been discussed have a particular relevance to the aristocracy. That is not to say that laws did not in theory apply equally to all members of Latin society, but intermarriage, commercial transactions, especially concerning real estate, and political activity were surely the province of the privileged classes at the beginning of the fifth century. We do not often hear of the immigration of poor people; artisans are

[66] On the Latin *jura* see Alföldi 1965: 36 ff.: Humbert 1978: 85 ff.; Brunt 1988 511; Cornell in *CAH* vii (2), (n. 18) 269. Some oblique support for Humbert's position might be found in a recent inscription, SEG XXXVI 982A, in which the word *isoteleia* is used in a proxeny decree for a Carian found at Iasus from between 500 and 450 BC, its earliest use; Humbert rightly sees a comparison between the Latin rights and the Greek concepts of *isopoliteia* and *isoteleia*. On gentilitial exogamy, see Franciosi (ed.) 1988 27 ff. [67] Humbert 1978: 98 f.

likely to have moved around a good deal without settling, and were not necessarily particularly poor. The *clientes* of Attus Clausus came to Rome under his protection; others may have found themselves forcibly incorporated into Rome. On the whole, however, the rights of Latins subsequent to the Foedus Cassianum seem most appropriate to the nobility, who almost certainly did involve themselves in the affairs of their neighbours, and often their kinsfolk. The tradition concerning Octavius Mamilius as son-in-law and supporter of Tarquinius Superbus may be a later fiction, but possibly quite close to the sorts of relationships that did exist.

A deeper consideration of the concept of *exilium* is revealing. Although the early Latin communities may have been somewhat amorphous, the fortifications which begin in the eighth century at a number of sites appear to represent a sense of community, as suggested above. Much of the evidence discussed in this chapter has shown the importance of the aristocracy, and in particular, of the institution of the *gentes*, and it may be suggested that, even in the sixth century, the community was closely identified with its leading members.[68]

Exilium was the right to move from one community to another, if one was in some trouble in the first. Crifò insists against Mommsen that this did not automatically mean loss of citizenship in the first community; it was joining another community's citizenship which had this effect. He suggests that such moves came through the spread of *gentes* through Latium, indicating that a *gens* may have had branches in different settlements, or that there were *adgnati* in different Latin cities.[69]

The ability to enter another community's citizenship, which is indicated in *exilium* and in *migratio*, indicates the sense of a

[68] The importance of the *curiae* as a body of citizens and the curious feature of Roman private law, that a magistrate does not judge a case himself, but appoints another, may both in different ways indicate the importance of the gentilitial associations which may have originally defined the citizen body. The *curiae* were dominated by the *gentes* it seems, and even a king had to have their approval; and in the field of law, the state was not given unlimited authority over the citizens. From a slightly different angle, Betteridge (1989) suggests that the development of the 'public domain' was necessary to control self-destructive competition consequent upon the 6th-century influx of wealth and opportunity into Latium.

[69] Crifò 1961, and a different view from L. Monaco in Franciosi 1988: 91 ff.

community which has been deduced from the archaeological evidence. It also indicates that one could not be a citizen in two places; this may have some religious reason, given the tutelary nature of gods in Latium, but it is also tied to the concern of the membership of a citizenry which is attested by the Comitia Calata's supervision of moves between the *plebs* and the patriciate. On the other hand, there is also a sense of 'openness' which Ampolo referred to, in that one was able to join another community, possibly through one's gentilitial connections. To begin with, there may be similarities with Greek *xenia*. The Foedus Cassianum probably granted a *ius exilii*, though there is nothing about *exilium* which is directly related to the Foedus. This is a stronger expression of the state's concern alongside the gentilitial aspects of the previous practices; there could be a public side now to becoming part of another community's citizenship as well. Thus, from a sort of *xenia* one moves to the concept of *hospitum publicum*;[70] one has the concept of *migratio*, with a possible formal right to vote; and one has the *interdictio aquae et ignis*, which prevents the return of an unwanted person, by and for the benefit of the community.

It has been suggested that in the sixth century there is a dramatic change in Latin society, centred on the development of an 'urban' society; public buildings replace private funerals, public cults join gentilitial religion, public space develops in the centre of major settlements. The legal changes discussed above, although only sketchily understood, form part of this development, as the customs of an aristocratic archaic society become the rights which communities must respect and from which individuals may profit. The 'openness' of Latin society, by which Ampolo indicated the possibilities of gentilitial ties crossing communities, and individuals following them, still exists after the Foedus Cassianum, but the rights are now enshrined at the level of the community.

THE RELIGIOUS ORGANIZATIONS OF LATIUM

The presence of a number of temples in major Latin settlements has been stressed repeatedly. To move beyond this it is necessary

[70] Humbert 1978: 135 ff.

to turn to the literary sources, and consider the religious leagues which they allege to have existed in Latium at least at the end of the sixth century, and from then onwards. A current definition of a Greek amphictyony may serve as a basis for this discussion:

an amphictyony was an association of communities, ethnic or national, grouped around a common religious sanctuary; its purpose the administration of the sanctuary and to some extent the management of relations between its members or even of its members as a whole and outsiders. The two functions are not wholly separable and will have developed together, but it is more likely that in origin common cult led to communal arrangement than that community of interest created a religious focus.[71]

One assumes that religious associations in Latium worked in a similar manner, though we are less well-informed about them. It seems very plausible that, at the great religious festivals, much business was conducted other than the purely sacred, and much news was passed. This would be especially true if the representatives of the Latins at the priestly level were from the aristocracy, which had interacted throughout the region for many years already. It also seems likely that the religious association of certain peoples or settlements could also form the basis for military alliance, and it has been assumed that we can work from the 'thirty Alban peoples' who shared meat on the Alban Hill to the Latin League itself.[72] However, the two lists we have, one in Pliny, which contains *populi* extinct at the time of writing, and another in Dionysius of twenty-nine settlements which conspired against Rome at the beginning of the fifth century,[73] are not the same, and are of doubtful origin and reference. A third list comes from Cato's *Origines* and is quoted in Priscian; it may derive ultimately from a lost inscription.[74] Priscian was interested in the verbal form of one member of the list, the last he quotes, and we cannot tell whether he has given us the whole list, or just those up to the one he was interested in, but it was different from Pliny's and Dionysius'. Cato includes Pometia; Dionysius has Satricum; the two may in fact have been the same, but Dionysius

[71] Forrest in *CAH* iii (3), 312.
[72] Alföldi 1965: 10 ff.; Pliny *HN* 3. 5. 68–70.
[73] Dion. Hal. 5. 61. 3.   [74] Cato fr.58P.

used the later name, and possibly therefore a different source.[75] The possibility of invention in these lists seems quite high. In particular, the attempt to name twenty-nine cities other than Rome for Lake Regillus, to make up the number thirty, appears contrived, and one cannot equate Dionysius' list of the anti-Roman league with the Catonian list of those at Aricia, if that is complete, unless we assume that Cato gives us only the core of participants.

The completeness of the Catonian list is an important question, since it represents those peoples present when Egerius Baebius (or Laevius), the Latin *dicator* from Tusculum, dedicated the grove of Diana in the wood at Aricia. The account is to some extent supported by Festus who says *Manius Egeri[us lucum] Nemorensem Dianae consecravit* ('Manius Egerius consecrated the grove at Nemi to Diana').

Alföldi[76] held that the temple at Aricia cannot predate 500 BC by much, if at all, though his evidence for this was based on his beliefs about the purpose of the sanctuary. He was convinced that it predated the temple of Diana on the Aventine at Rome, which ancient sources dated to the reign of Servius Tullius, and which he regarded as one of the products of Rome's defeat of the Latins at Regillus. The point is crucial; either the Latins set up a shrine in opposition to an already dominant Rome, or Rome had to wait until after its victory over the Latins to claim its religious superiority.

Both Livy and Dionysius claim that Servius' temple of Diana was inspired by the temple of Artemis at Ephesos and the league of Ionian cities which were gathered around it. This might well be a later identification, inspired not least by the role which the temple played in Latin affairs; indeed, there is no other evidence for a league of Ionian cities around the temple at Artemis. Dionysius (Dion. Hal 4. 26. 5) speaks of a bronze stele with the *nomoi* of the Latin League written in old Greek characters, which still stood in his own day, but Dionysius may not have dated it correctly and may have been mistaken about its authenticity. The tradition suggested that Rome won the hegemony of the Latin League from Alba in the time of Tullus Hostilius, and this

[75] Maaskant-Kleibrink 1987: 13 ff.
[76] Alföldi 1965: 47 ff., 85 ff.; cf. Thomsen 1980: 292 ff.

hegemony was simply renewed repeatedly. Mommsen and Cornell have not accepted this as an accurate historical picture,[77] though it presumably reflects a Roman belief, perhaps of some antiquity. Now the dedication reported by Cato, which has no date, ought to represent a new departure, at the very least a reconsecration of a shrine which we know already had a votive deposit from the seventh century; it is entirely plausible that the shrine at Aricia preceded the Servian shrine on the Aventine, but was rededicated for a particular purpose at the beginning of the fifth century.[78]

Yet there are further complications. From a coin of 43 BC we have a representation of the cult statue of Aricia as *triformis*, i.e. Hecate, Trivia, and Diana. Alföldi insists that on artistic grounds the statue must be from *c*.500, but this is not an absolute certainty. The Diana on the Aventine had a *xoanon* or wooden cult statue similar to that of Artemis and was single in form. The statue apparently came from the Phocaeans at Massalia (Strabo 4. 1. 5), but not necessarily in the sixth century; though it is interesting that in the Massalian Ephesion there was a copy of the cult statue of the temple of Artemis at Ephesos. The difference in cult statue may be important, but its significance is unknown.

The 'political' interpretation of the evidence for the two temples of Diana is that Servius' temple was a bid for supremacy at a federal level in Latium, and that the grove at Aricia represented resistance; or, on Alföldi's dating or the hypothesis that the dedication was a reconsecration of an old cult, that the Arician dedication came first, and that the cult could be transferred to Rome only after Lake Regillus. It is also possible that the cult was part of Rome's claims to have won the battle of Lake Regillus.

The temples at Aricia and on the Aventine have received most attention, but there are a number of other temples which may also have had a federal significance. It is certainly quite likely that there were many overlapping leagues in Latium.[79]

If we conceive of a somewhat amorphous and ill-defined sense

[77] Cornell in *CAH* vii (2), 265 and n. 22.
[78] Thomsen 1980: 300.
[79] Cornell in *CAH* vii (2), 268.

of community in the ninth and eighth centuries, giving way to more defined concepts of the state in the seventh and sixth, which archaeology indicates, and which might also be inferred from studies of legal development and the creation of territories, the points where the leagues intersect might well be regarded as of special importance; hence the predominance of places like Gabii, Lavinium, Fidenae, and Rome. The idea of stacked leagues would explain the number of common cults which appear to exist in quite a small area.

It may be significant that many temples which might have a federal significance are outside the settlement itself. Such temples in Greece are regarded by de Polignac as particularly important for the definition of a community, and may have been equally so in Latium.[80] Both temples to Diana discussed above were outside their respective city limits. So were the temples or sanctuaries to Aphrodite or Venus at Lavinium and Ardea,[81] the shrine to Juno at Gabii, and the temple of Diana at Tusculum which Pliny says was *sacratus a Latio* ('hallowed by Latium').[82] Moreover, there are a number of temples to Juno, whom Palmer regards as a particularly important deity in the federal life of Latium. Juno was worshipped by all the *curiae* at Rome, and there was a Juno Curitis at Falerii, according to Varro; Palmer suspects a wider presence throughout the region.[83] The Mater Matuta worshipped at Satricum and the Forum Boarium in Rome were presumably one and the same.

There is a large question about the nature of the leagues. Some religious sites in antiquity were managed by one settlement, but open to all. Delphi and Delos might be examples, though an amphictyony underlies Delphi at least. Other leagues were strictly exclusive. The Panionium was exclusive, and so was the Hexapolis which became a Pentapolis after the expulsion of Halicarnassus.[84]

The meeting of the Latins at the Feriae Latinae to worship Jupiter Latiaris was surely, as its name suggests, a strictly Latin gathering, in which Rome was represented in later centuries by

---

[80] De Polignac 1984: 85 ff. Lavinium has both urban and rural sanctuaries, and others may emerge. Neat 'bipolarity' can seldom be shown in Latium, but the principle may be the same, defining the boundaries of a community.
[81] Strabo 5. 3. 5. [82] Pliny *HN* 16. 242. [83] Palmer 1974: 3–56.
[84] Hdt. 1. 142 (Panionium); 1. 144 (Hexapolis).

its magistrates.[85] The magistrates of Rome should probably be regarded in this instance in particular as descendants of the sixth-century aristocracy and inheritors of the sort of religious prerogatives which that aristocracy claimed. The three sixth-century altars at Lavinium in the archaic period may represent sacrifice to a triad or an exclusive ritual (or both). We do not know how archaic the procession of Roman magistrates to worship at Lavinium was, but it has been suggested that it did not predate the fourth century and the incorporation of Lavinium into Roman territory.[86] On the other hand, some Central Italian shrines were undoubtedly visited by outsiders, as the Greek dedications in the temple of Aphrodite at Gravisca amply attest. Perhaps the shrine to the Dioscuri at Lavinium, or the Forum Boarium temples in Rome, particularly the Ara Maxima, if it is so ancient, which was outside the Pomerium, were also open in the same way.

Without forcing the evidence too much, one may conclude that there were some exclusive and some overlapping leagues and festivals in Latium, and some temples which may have been less exclusive. It is possible to connect the leagues with the aristocratic basis of Latin society. The interaction of aristocrats throughout Latium and beyond, and the religious privileges of that aristocracy, have been repeatedly attested and discussed. It is not surprising therefore that leagues should have existed, at least one attesting the communal culture of the region, others perhaps expressing more limited interaction. By the sixth century, the survey around Fidenae would indicate a spread of habitation; Fidenae would represent the focus for nearby small communities, inasmuch as they were separate. By the fourth century Praeneste and Tivoli have *oppida* which are under their control, and for which they would presumably be the religious focus.[87] Nor would it be surprising, given the military duties of the aristocracy, if some of the leagues lay beneath military organizations like the Latin League, which met at the Lucus Feroniae near Aricia.

One may be able to go further. Forrest has suggested that, around 700, the religious leagues of Greece may have undergone

[85] Alföldi 1965: 19 ff.; Scullard 1981: 111 ff.
[86] Dubourdieu 1989: 150–1; Macr. 3. 4. 11; Serv. *ad Aen.* 2. 296.
[87] Livy 6. 29. 6; 7. 18. 2; 7. 19. 1.

Rome and Latium 221

some kind of crisis or transformation. This is the period of the transformation of the Hexapolis, and perhaps the war declared by the Panionium against Melite.[88] In the Kalourian amphictyony, Sparta may have taken over Prasiae and Argos Nauplion.[89] Orchomenos may have defected from an Athenian to an Aeginetan alliance, and prompted the long-standing disaffection between the two.[90] In Euboea, the Lelantine War may also have taken place within the context of the disintegration of a league as Eretria, the more prosperous site, distanced itself from Chalcis.

A religious league is something that might threaten to override a member state, but which could also be dominated by one of its members. The problems around 700 might be connected with the internal transformation of the polis at roughly the same time, with greater self-definition, the development of the religious *genê* which Bourriot discusses, and the increased building of temples.[91]

A bold interpretation of this complex network of facts, assumptions, and guesses might well connect the difficulties in the religious leagues with the development of the polis as a community not to be overridden by the larger interests of its league; or the attempt by one polis, or by a league as a whole, to give a political function to a religious foundation, which failed because of the 'growing particularism of the Greek polis'.[92]

From the Greek situation we may return to sixth-century Latium. This was also a period in which large temples were built, and in which the sense of a local, urban identity is advancing. It also seems that the aristocracy was defining its duties and its privileges more and more sharply, perhaps because these were clearer and more manifold in an urban context than before. The leagues were, in Cornell's words, 'part of the residue of pre-urban or "pre-political" institutions' onto which the city-states were superimposed.[93] By the later sixth century there may have been some attempt to use the leagues, and certainly to use religion, as an expression of a political hegemony.

---

[88] Huxley 1966: 47–8; Vitr. 4. 13–5.   [89] Strabo 8. 6. 14.
[90] Coldstream 1977: 38–9 for early Athenian connections; Kraay 1976: 110 for Aeginetan coinage c.525 (but denying federal significance); Hdt. 5. 80. 1 for the supposed mythical connection between Thebes and Aegina against Athens c.500.
[91] Morris 1987: 190; cf. Snodgrass 1980: 58 ff.
[92] Davies in *CAH* iv (2), 380.   [93] Cornell in *CAH* vii (2), 269.

Examples of this would be the Roman domination of the Latin League, which may have been transmitted to the Feriae Latinae and was commemorated in the Ludi Romani. The conflict between the temples of Diana at Aricia and on the Aventine, the erection of a temple to Castor and Pollux in connection with Lake Regillus, when we know of worship of the same deities at Lavinium, and possibly Tusculum, and the possible *evocatio* of Juno from Gabii[94] are further indications. Finally, two priesthoods of communities reputedly destroyed in the regal period, and located outside the expanded Ager Romanus of the early fifth century, were kept alive at Rome; they are the Sacerdos Caeninensis and Cabensis.[95] No doubt there were priesthoods of Latin communities inside the Ager Romanus which were also transferred to Rome or were absorbed into already existing Roman cults.

Both in Greece and in Latium, then, we may see religious leagues as indications of a communal identity which preceded the polis or city-state. When these institutions were strengthened, conflict within (and between) the leagues was likely, and since representation at religious festivals was probably an aristocratic affair, when aristocracies within urban settlements began to adopt a 'political' aspect the leagues were bound to reflect this. They might remain as symbols of some memory of an earlier unity, or as a political body, but they could not survive unchanged the transformation of their constituent members.

Much of the preceding chapter has been highly speculative and has avoided some of the more intractable problems of the archaic period, such as the reasons for the expulsion of Tarquinius Superbus; the nature of the new Republican government and the chronology of the change; the precise definition of the patriciate; and the veracity of the early Fasti.

On such issues, archaeology has nothing to tell us; but it has added depth to our understanding of Latin society. For instance, we know more about the material expression of superiority used by the élite. We are gaining more knowledge about the settlement patterns of individual centres, and of the region as a whole, and how these reflect what we can understand about the evolution of

[94] Palmer 1970: 181.
[95] Palmer 1970: 134 n. 4.

legal relationships between states. Finally, although most of the details of archaic Latin religion are obscure to us, the discovery of temples and votive deposits has emphasized the significance of this aspect of Latin life. This chapter should have indicated some of the ways in which the material record and the literary tradition can be used together to develop an understanding of archaic Latium.

12
General Conclusions

The aim of this book has been to present the available archaeological evidence for Rome and Latium Vetus from $c.1000$ to $c.500$ BC and to proceed from the evidence to some conclusions concerning the economy and society of the region. The archaeological discoveries of the past twenty or so years have allowed us radically to improve our understanding of the region, and at the same time to be more precise about its place in Central Italian and Mediterranean culture, as this too has become better known. The development of theoretical approaches in the study of ancient history and material culture usefully underpins our knowledge of both.

The book should have indicated the generally homogeneous nature of Latium, from the early burial material to later urban development. It would not be right to suggest that one could define the boundaries of Latium at any time with accuracy, but the region does hold together as a cultural entity. Roughly speaking, the area is bounded by the Tiber in the north, the Monti Lepini to the east, and the Pomptine marshes in the south, and covers roughly 2,500 km^2; it is comparable in size to Attica or the Argolid.

The first 'urban' or proto-urban settlements in Italy seem to have grown up in the late second millennium on the southern coasts, at a time from which Cypriot and Mycenaean objects have been found in the region. It has been argued that there is a direct relationship between the presence of external trading movements, flowing westwards as far as Sardinia at least, in search of raw materials, and the development of these stable, organized communities. The emergence of 'urban' communities in Italy and of a trading route from the east along its coast seems to have been of tremendous importance in spurring economic and social development.

We cannot assume that the absence of 'luxury' goods in the

archaeological record implies the absence of social and economic differentiation, since at some periods we may not be able to identify such goods or recover the means of differentiation. This may be the case for the early Latin communities, which are sometimes thought to have been roughly egalitarian. The presence of imported goods later on allows us to see 'luxuries' and social differentiation more clearly.

To become involved in a trading process and hence to import goods from outside requires the production of some form of surplus for exchange; to create a surplus, in particular in agriculture, requires an intensification which is not to be found in the simplest peasant communities, and which is often also the product of population growth. The control of a surplus implies some form of aristocratic or oligarchic organization, which is itself stabilized by the arrival of new and luxury items which permit clear differentiation between social groups. Such developments may spread as more communities choose to take part in trading networks, or as they are required to emulate neighbours with whom they are in some way bound by reciprocal ties.

This very basic model or framework seems to work well for the development of Central Italy. Some Mycenaean goods have been found in Etruria, and Sardinia clearly played a full and important role in the trading network. The falling away of Mycenaean civilization may not have entirely stopped a trade in which Cyprus played a crucial part. The existence of such contacts, and internal developments like population growth, may have led to the abandonment around 900 of small settlements in Etruria in favour of the larger centres which then dominated the region. One would expect these larger communities to have a more highly developed society and economy, and, in time, a larger surplus production, and it is also interesting that Etruscan mineral exploitation seems to have begun in earnest after 900.

The Etruscan participation in the earlier trading activities was probably limited because of the absence of settled proto-urban communities and the low degree of mineral exploitation. The region participated more extensively in the trade of the orientalizing period, which is related to the presence of Greeks and Phoenicians in Campania and southern Italy from the eighth century, by which time it had both the economic and social maturity to benefit from the advantages of external trade.

There are no reliable traces of Mycenaean culture in Latium, and the development of proto-urban settlements in the area came much later than in Etruria. Latium also has less wealth potential, in mineral and agricultural terms, than Etruria, and was therefore not in a good position to take part in trade. Latium may have acted as a land route between Etruria and the south, and this was probably significant in her development, but it may not have enriched the region to a great degree.

It is important to distinguish wherever possible between direct trade between Greeks and Phoenicians and a particular area, and the movement of Greek or Phoenician goods into an area via the mediation of other Italians. It is possible that all or most of the Graeco-Phoenician goods in Latium were brought by Etruscans or native Campanians. The Etruscan element is particularly crucial, because the aristocratic nature of society from at least the eighth century allows one to suppose that many goods were exchanged as part of aristocratic gift-giving. The Praenestine tombs are a significant example; the goods are identical with others found at Cerveteri, and we may suspect an alliance of marriage, kinship, or friendship which brought these foreign exotica from Etruria to Latium without assuming the presence of foreign (non-Italian) traders at Rome or Praeneste.

The 'princely' tombs at Praeneste and elsewhere are presumably indications of an aristocracy clearly and perhaps competitively differentiating itself from the rest of society, and also developing links outside the community. The possibilities for conspicuous display afforded by imports would have encouraged the development of an aristocratic society, with attendant practices such as gift-giving.

In the sixth century conspicuous consumption seems to have been directed in a different direction, towards major buildings. Palaces and temples (which must have required considerable control of labour) are lasting indications of an individual and his family's wealth and status, and a continuum of economic transactions may develop around them more easily than around tombs. Examples would be the attendance of *clientes* at the palaces, and deposition of expensive gifts in temples, where they might be seen, rather than underground.

The importance of Greek culture in Central Italian society is marked in the sixth century. While in the seventh century the rarity of Greek objects may have given them extra value, by the sixth century they seem to have had favoured cultural status. Greek pottery is found in large quantities from the mid-sixth century in Etruscan burials, and to a lesser degree in some Latin stratigraphy, and Greek models were copied extensively. Architectural terracottas, apparently developed in Greek centres of southern Italy and Campania, were widely exported, and some scholars have sought Greek originals in religious and social developments, such as the cult of Ceres at Rome and the development of 'hoplite' warfare in Central Italy.

The influence is most marked in Campania, where Greeks were resident, and in Etruria. In the sixth century, Etruria seems to retain a general economic superiority over Latium, and the greater concentration of Greek objects in that region is probably one consequence of this.

Greek inscriptions, especially at Gravisca, indicate that there must have been direct contact between Greeks and Etruscans. Such inscriptions have not been found in Latium, and unless we find a hitherto unexcavated sixth-century port at Ostia, we must assume that Rome was not connected to a coastal port as Tarquinia and Cerveteri were; it operated as a port itself, however. Etruscan inscriptions are common at Rome and elsewhere, together with considerable amounts of bucchero pottery; all the evidence points to a deep penetration of Latium by Etruscan culture.

It is therefore at least a possibility that direct contact between Greeks and Latins was still limited in the sixth century, and that the strong links with Etruria provided much of the imported material found in Latium. This would raise doubts about the extent to which Greek culture influenced Latin religion and society, but it would be unreasonable not to assume some degree of contact at least at Rome, and maybe at the port of Lavinium too. Whether or not these contacts can be traced to Rome's position as an adjunct of Etruria, it is quite possible that the growing size and impressiveness of Latin sites in general, and Rome in particular, may have attracted more external interest in the area, as may have been intended. The development of a more stable and defined aristocracy in sixth-century Latium may be in part a move towards developing greater trade links, as well as being encouraged by the trade already existing.

One further indication of Rome's participation in foreign affairs might be the treaty with Carthage, whose terms are given by Polybius, but whose authenticity has not been accepted by all scholars. Sardinia, with its large Punic element, had continued to trade with Etruria, and Rome may have benefited from that.

There is a hiatus in the import of Greek goods in the fifth century in both Latium and Etruria. The reasons for this may well lie in the local areas as much as in Campania and Greece; both Etruria and Latium were engaged in military activity (the Latins extensively, it seems), and the Etruscans had turned their attention to southern Gaul. Both regions may have ceased to try to be a part of trading networks which were quite effective without them. The position of Latium recovered in the fourth century, when the expansion of Rome could not fail to attract Greek attention.

Latin economy was based on agriculture. From 1000 onwards, there was a move to differentiate social groups through increasingly elaborate burials. This ceased at a time when Latin society was undergoing other changes too, and although the demand for imported goods does not seem to have been reduced immediately, the income from the control of labour and resources was turned towards more lasting and evident symbols of aristocratic power.

With regard to the social development of Latium, we have already suggested that the apparent egalitarianism of the earliest graves may be a function of the low economic development of Latium, and may also be imposed by the nature of the material record. By 900 it is clear that some form of hierarchy was operating, and it is quite possible that it had existed before; it was the development of economic and social ties with other communities, the drive towards surplus production, and the influx of imported luxury items which made an aristocracy visible in their burials.

One might argue that earlier it was possible to honour the leaders of tenth-century society with communally offered goods of low intrinsic value but high honorific status. One might also suggest that the act of public burial within a necropolis was limited to the leaders of society from a very early period and throughout Latin civilization. Such an argument would lead one to suppose not an undifferentiated society but an undifferentiated aristocracy, whose position was defined in traditional ways. Particular shapes and forms of pottery then assume ritual status beyond their intrinsic value. The kinds of objects buried (weapons, vessels, jewellery, spindle-whorls, etc.) remained in use into the sixth century, becoming increasingly elaborate in form and perhaps less constrained by tight ritual considerations.

The coherence of Latin burial around 1000 may indicate a sort of tribal unity. The discovery of important sites on the coast predating 1000 indicates that, although the Alban Hills communities were notable for their strictly similar burial practices and their interlinked fortunes, they were probably not the first founders of Latin civilization. Perhaps individual communities did not exceed 100 people, and they were often organized in clusters which were later to form unified settlements, but perhaps they began as autonomous. It is not possible to be precise about the organization of the society; it has been suggested that the family became the significant element of Latin society over time, and that early on the community or groups within it but larger than the family unit retained a pre-eminent position. If honour was granted by the community, it would make sense for land to be public and not private property.

The development of differentiation in burials is a process, one aspect of which might be the change from honour granted by a community to honour demanded by individuals from the community, but that must remain a hypothesis, given our evidence. Also important was the change from cremation to inhumation, which took place around 900, and which at Osteria dell'Osa at least can be identified in a few comparatively wealthy cremations surrounded by some contemporary inhumations, which suggests that, for a time, the form of burial was a sign of status.

From 900 on, differences in the wealth of burials grow, culminating in the major seventh-century princely tombs; as much as a century before this, one can cite major warrior burials throughout Central Italy. The late seventh- and sixth-century burials in Latium are so few in number that one can only suppose that burial in the traditional necropolis was an increasingly restricted privilege. It is possible that even in the ninth and eighth centuries, well represented in the necropoleis, burial was in some way limited, perhaps to those belonging to an appropriate social group, which some would define as the *gens*. Low-wealth burials might represent *clientes*. The late seventh-century burials, including the chamber tomb at Osteria dell'Osa, can be seen as the emergence of a familial system from within the gentilitial structures, but the *gens* was still strong in the sixth century, as far as we can tell, and it is interesting that the chamber tombs which hold a family group, and are so typical of Etruscan burials, were not widely used in Latium.

Those excluded from burial in the ninth and eighth centuries might include criminals and social outcasts, and those unable to afford armour, together with their dependants, or those classed as poor by some other criterion. Exclusion may not have been as widespread in this period as in the seventh and early sixth centuries, when poverty, dependence, and failure to find access to a *clientela* may have been factors, together with the separation of an aristocracy enabled by the wealth differentials encouraged by a developing economy. It may be that the openness of Latin society, and the contacts between aristocrats of different places, which encouraged self-definition and competition, also led to a more radical class division in this period than before.

One indication of the changing nature of society can also be found in the number of communal building works in Latin communities from the late eighth century on. Some of these are fortifications, which tends to indicate that the separation of communities within a small area was becoming more difficult to maintain, perhaps because of population pressure, and synoecism was beginning to occur. Fortifications indicate a sense of community within the settlement, allowing cooperative activity, but also a sense of identity distinct from that of one's neighbours, and they also indicate contacts between communities which were evidently not always friendly. The massive landfill operation in Rome in the late seventh century also indicates a developed sense of community.

The nature of these building works implies a clear organization of labour. This probably also extended to agriculture. We cannot tell if the two were separate, specialized activities, or when slavery began in Latium. It cannot make much sense to separate the emergence of a defined aristocracy from the growth in communal building work, since they are contemporary. The aristocracy should be assumed to be the organizing group, and their status may well have rested on their ability to command the labour resources of others.

General Conclusions 231

It is quite likely that in the seventh century in Latium, and Central Italy generally, there were similar moves to *nexum* and debt-bondage as are attested in Solonian Attica; once again, this is not to be distinguished from the increasing wealth of some burials. The possibilities for expenditure encourage desire; both entail the need for surplus and the drive towards exploitation. If the possibilities increase, as they seem to have done throughout the seventh and sixth centuries, the need for a surplus and exploitation to attain it will also increase.

We may suggest that there were small communities in the tenth century, perhaps with some rudimentary social differentiation (on grounds of military prowess, charisma, etc.) acknowledged by the community. The communities grew, and gradually, social and economic differentiation increased, and perhaps also the exploitation of the less privileged members of society to sustain the status of the more privileged.

In the seventh century, the increased economic possibilities and the effects of aristocratic interaction bring a clearer differentiation of the upper class, and the emergence of powerful families within it. The control of labour resources was increasingly in the hands of these few. The development of this more sophisticated aristocracy runs parallel with the development of large stable settlements of a recognizably urban nature.

It may be suggested that it was links between these powerful families through common interests or marriage or both that formed the social groups which at Rome are known as *gentes*. Some may also have been deliberately created; the patriciate at Rome was not the sudden creation of either the kings or the Republic, but part of a continuing process of defining (and closing) the aristocracy with regard to outsiders. Whether any of the Republican *gentes* had predecessors in late seventh- or sixth-century tombs or palaces is not recoverable, but it is important that one need not see the aristocratic structure of Rome as an entirely artificial construct without early predecessors, as Bourriot and Roussel suggested for Greek institutions.

A fundamental aspect of this archaic Latin society was religion. Temple-building became widespread in the sixth century, and one can perhaps assume that the major priestly offices were held by aristocrats. Religious leagues were also important, and it is possible that the politicization of these leagues attested in the sixth century reflects the conflict which dominant aristocracies, and the growing size of Rome, brought to Latium in the period. This conflict is also to be traced in the development of formal *jura* between Latin communities in the sixth century; some may well have existed before Lake Regillus, but it was the Roman victory there which led to a treaty enshrining and limiting the openness of Latin society, and which permitted the expansion of Rome.

The expansion itself was organized through the tribal system of the city and its *ager*, which was a reform of a previous, less centralized system of the *pagi*. The expansion of Roman territory, itself connected with the establishment of the Republican *gentes*, as the tribal names suggest, also led to the expansion of the army through the *centuriae*.

All the institutional details which we have from literary sources coincide with the archaeological evidence, in that both indicate a continuing prosperity at Rome (and, from the material remains, at the major Latin sites through the sixth century), which worked mainly to the benefit of a small proportion of society. Generally similar patterns of urbanization, and also details such as the style of temples and of decoration, suggest a largely homogeneous culture.

The book ends at a crucial point. The Romans, victorious over the Latins at Lake Regillus, but still somewhat overshadowed by their Etruscan neighbours, and endeavouring to maintain an unjustly exclusive political system in a period of relative material prosperity, spent the next century or so in almost continuous warfare against invasions from the inland tribes, and in civil unrest. The material and literary evidence from the archaic period indicates the unspectacular but steady development of a society sufficiently stable to survive this difficult time, and then able to expand and dominate Italy as it had dominated Latium.

APPENDIX 1
Inscriptions in Latium

The following Appendix gives an account of the epigraphic evidence from Latium, and other inscriptions relevant to the area. Some of the inscriptions have been cited in the text. Cornell rightly points out that we should not regard the sample as representative, or argue from the paucity of finds, and we cannot guess how many inscriptions have been lost.[1]

The earliest Latin inscription has been found at Osteria dell'Osa. In a late IIB burial a kantharos vase was found with some letters, which have been read as *EUOIN* or *EULIN*. The inscription has defied interpretation, though the Greek εὔοινος has been suggested, and also Eulius (an Etruscan name) and εὔλινος, a cult epithet of Eileithyia, the Greek goddess whom Coarelli identified with Uni and Mater Matuta in the Forum Boarium complex. What is most striking about the inscription, however, regardless of its meaning, is the fact that it attests some kind of literacy a generation before the first inscription in Greece.[2]

Another early inscription is the single word *Vetusia* on bronze bowl at Praeneste. This is generally believed to be a name, possibly of a woman, and has been compared with the tribal name Voturia. It should be dated around 630 BC.[3]

Slightly later comes an inscription on a fragment of a bucchero kylix at Satricum, which reads: *mi mu[lu larisal]e velxainasi*. This has been interpreted as 'I have been given by Laris Velchaina,' a name which has also been documented at Caere.[4]

---

[1] Collections of relevant inscriptions include *TLE*; *CLP* 372 ff.; *GRT* 16 ff.; Colonna 1980: 53 f.; Colonna 1987: 55 ff. On Etruscan see Pallottino, 'I documenti scritti e la lingua' in *Rasenna* 309-67 with references. On the sorts of objects discussed here, with the names of their 'owners', see the large collection in Agostiniani 1982. On literacy see Harris 1989: 149 ff., Stoddart and Whitley 1988; Cornell 1991.
[2] See Bietti-Sestieri, De Santis and La Regina 1988-9: 83 ff.; Holloway 1994: 112 f. For Coarelli's identifications see Coarelli 1988: 328 ff.
[3] *CLP* 374; Prosdocimi 1979: 379 ff.; Cornell 1991: 16 ff. I have again refrained from using the evidence of the controversial Manios fibula, on which see most recently Holloway 1994: 161 ff.
[4] *CLP* 374 f.

234   *Appendix* 1

An Italo-Geometric plate from the Esquiline necropolis bears the letters *snu[—]*, a combination which is more common in Etruscan.[5]

From the same burial ground comes a fragment of a Corinthian olpa with a Greek inscription which has been variously transcribed as *KTEKTOU* and *KLEIKLOU*, but in both forms is thought to represent the name of a Greek in the genitive case.[6]

From S. Omobono, there is an impasto vase fragment with the letters *uqnus[—?]*, which is also usually thought to be Etruscan.[7] All these inscriptions are dated to the late seventh century.

The Lapis Niger, discussed above, cannot be dated except by its context on a pavement of the first half of the sixth century.[8] Near the Lapis Niger were found nine fragments of bucchero vases, with odd letters, and another fragment was found by the temple of Vesta with the word *vis*. The letters *ana* were found on an impasto olla in the Cloaca Maxima; this may represent a connection with Anna Perennna, who had a sanctuary on the banks of the Tiber. All these fragments come from the second half of the sixth century.[9]

The obscure inscription on a three-cupped dedication from Rome which appears to mention an owner named Duenos belongs to the first half of the sixth century, though it has also been suggested that the words refer to a *vir bonus*, which might be taken as indicating an aristocrat. The vase certainly seems by its type and its context on the slope of the Quirinal to be part of a votive deposit, to which the inscription, apparently asking for the love of a young girl or virgin, would be appropriate.[10]

From the sixth century, and also from S. Omobono, there is the inscription on the back of a lion modelled in ivory which reads: *araz silqetenas spurianas*. The first word has been taken as an Etruscan name, the second as a gentilitial derived from the name of the Phoenician coastal town of Sulcis in Sardinia, and the third as a further title, a patronymic, or the name of another gentilitial group with whom Araz Silqetanas had a connection; the name is found in this form in Tarquinia in around 530 BC.[11]

From the same place comes a bucchero ciotola with the letters *ououios* which is likely to represent a name; and a bucchero coppetta with the letters *ua[—]*. Both belong to the second half of the sixth century, and the former is probably the earlier.[12]

At the foot of the Capitol, near the altar of Saturn, was found a bucchero cup with an Etruscan inscription indicating possession: *ni araziia laraniia*.[13]

[5] Colonna 1987: 58.   [6] *CLP* 375; cf. Colonna 1987: 57 f.
[7] *CLP* 375; *GRT* 21.   [8] On the Lapis Niger, see *GRT* 58 ff.; Wilkins 1990.
[9] Colonna 1980: 53 ff.   [10] *GRT* 20 ff.; Prosdocimi 1979: 173 ff.
[11] *GRT* 21.   [12] Colonna 1980: 57.   [13] Colonna 1987: 58.

Inscriptions

In a different deposition but not far away was found a bucchero fragment with the letters: *[—] + enteisiua[—]*, which has been interpreted as a dedication to the deity Carmenta, a nymph whose cult was connected with the Capitoline hill. This must remain an intriguing possibility, but no more.[14]

Finally there is the grey bucchero cup found near the Regia, with the word *REX* inscribed on the inside.[15] These three instances are all dated to the second half of the sixth century.

There are also inscriptions found in other Latin sites. At Lavinium, there is a mid-sixth-century Attic black-figure kylix which bears a fragmentary Greek inscription: χαιρε και πιει ευ, a formulaic phrase quite common on such vessels. It is interesting to speculate on whether the owner of the kylix understood the Greek or simply regarded it as a mysterious adjunct to the value of his possession.[16]

Also from Lavinium comes the bronze strip bearing a dedication to the Dioscuri: *CASTOREI:PODLOUQUEIQUE|QUROIS*. The names are Latin transcriptions of the Greek, and the inscription probably belongs to the late sixth century, just before the battle of Lake Regillus, in which, according to a tradition which may be *post eventum*, the Dioscuri played an important role on the Romans' side.[17]

At Satricum, in addition to the fragment mentioned above, there is of course the famous inscription from the temple of Mater Matuta:[18]

[———?]
[—]iei steterai Popliosio Valesiosio
suodales Mamertei.

The inscription was on a block of dark grey tufa, 87 cm across the inscribed face by 63 cm by 15–16 cm high. It had been carefully worked with chisel and saw to present smooth surfaces. It was found between two other blocks of the same material of approximately the same height, which had received the same careful workmanship, but do not appear to have been inscribed. All three blocks were placed in the foundations of the second major temple at Satricum, built after the first had been destroyed by fire. The inscription block was placed so that the inscription was upside down, and the three stones closely abutted another layer of tufa blocks, with a filling of earth in between. They seem to have been at least two blocks beneath floor level. In other words, at the time that they were placed in the second temple the inscription was no longer intended to be read; yet it seems to have been treated with some care. It is worth noting that a large round block of stone was placed in the north-

---

[14] *GRT* 22.   [15] *GRT* 22 f.   [16] *GRT* 190.   [17] *GRT* 190 f.
[18] Stibbe *et al*. 1980; Versnel 1982; Ferenczy 1987; *GRT* 23 f.

west corner of the temple, and it has been suggested that this was the altar of the previous building.

The letters run from left to right, and are clearly and neatly carved. The stone has been damaged at the left-hand side so that we suspect there are letters missing at the beginning of the first line; it is impossible to tell whether the second line is complete or not.

Inevitably, in the first line one identifies two names in the genitive case, Poplios Valesios, or Publius Valerius in later Latin. The preceding letters may be taken as a single word *steterai* meaning to have set up. This seems the most favoured interpretation, but it is worth bearing in mind an alternative division to leave a word *eterai*, perhaps comparable to the Greek ἑταῖροι. Approximately four or five letters could precede the first letter of the inscription as we have it.

In the second line, *suodales* has been taken as a nominative, and must be either the subject or in apposition to a subject expressed in the lost part of the inscription, and perhaps at the very beginning. *Mamartei* is presumed to be the dative of Mamars or Mars. Guarducci[19] took these two words together, and this use of the dative can be found, though with religious groups, a formulation such as *suodales Martiales* might be expected. If this is not correct, we should have to take Mars as the recipient of the dedication, though the temple belongs to Mater Matuta. This conjunction might be compared to the adjacent cellae of Ops and Mars in the Regia.[20]

The most plausible context for this inscription seems to be as the base of a sculpture, like the base at Tivoli and at Lavinium. The absence of metal or holes for fastening a metal sculpture may suggest that the monument was all of stone, and perhaps even a lion of the Etruscan type. This dedication was perhaps destroyed at the same time as the first temple, and the dedication stones used in the refounding of the temple, with a due regard to their significance.

Dating the inscription is not particularly easy. The archaeological evidence for the second temple, largely architectural terracotta antefixes which have been put into a rough sequence, would suggest that it was rebuilt around the beginning of the fifth century,[21] and the style of lettering would fit reasonably well in this context, with parallels then to the Lapis Niger, dated to the sixth century by context, and the ciotola at Acqua Acetosa Laurentina; the Tivoli dedication would be slightly later. All this of course can only be tentatively suggested, since local variants in writing and the care with which the inscriptions are made can have a significant impact quite apart from chronology; but on the whole

[19] Guarducci in Versnel 1982.
[20] On Mars see Scholz 1970.
[21] Chiarucci and Gizzi 1985: 50 ff.

Inscriptions

there seems no reason to believe that an early fifth century *terminus ante quem* is wildly wrong. Problems are caused if one tries to push the original dedication too far back into the sixth century; it is already our earliest Latin example of the use of two names. Ferenczy's suggestion that the inscription belongs to the fourth century BC does not seem to have much merit, and his dismissal of the archaeological evidence, uncertain though it may be, is cavalier.

Equally fascinating is the later fifth century inscription found on a miniature axe blade in the Volscian cemetery at Satricum; the inscription, *iúkús⁺:ko:efiei*, is not open to interpretation until more of the Volscian language has been discovered, but its existence is evidence for a degree of literacy in the Volscian peoples in the fifth century, at the time when they were coming into conflict with the Latins.[22]

Near Tivoli was recovered a tufa base for an unknown object bearing the words:

*Hoi m/ed mitat Kavio/s [—] + /onios
Qetios d/[o]no/m pro fileo/d.*

Near the base was a votive deposit, and this object may have supported a bronze statue at some time. One suggestion as to its meaning is that it is a dedication by *Kavios [—]onios Qetios* to an unmentioned deity on behalf of his son. The language is probably Latin, though Sabine has been suggested. The three names for one person at the time can be paralleled in the Faliscan area; the second is likely to be a gentilitial name, and the third a patronymic. It has been dated to the late sixth century.[23]

Three inscriptions may be mentioned at Acqua Acetosa Laurentina. A tile from the early sixth-century buildings bears the letters *[—]tartispo[—]*. From late sixth- or early fifth-century contexts, there is a brocchetta of argilla clay wih the name *Manias* (a genitive of possession) on its neck, and a bucchero scodella with the Latin name *KAPKAFAIOS*.[24] Both of these are fragmentary vessels, so it is not absolutely certain that there was not a second name.

At Ficana there is a painted Italo-Geometric olla from the late seventh century with what appears to be a numerical inscription, *XXXXXIIII*. There is a sixth-century piece of bucchero with the letters *eco f[—]*.[25]

Of uncertain provenance are a fifth-century plate with *eqo fulfios* on the inside and *pias* on the outside, and a fifth-century Attic vase with the words *palps blaisios*; a number of other inscriptions, some quite complete, some only a single letter, have been found in other parts of Latium.[26]

It is worth mentioning one or two relevant inscriptions from Etruria.

---

[22] *GRT* 25.   [23] *GRT* 24; Prosdocimi 1979: 370 ff.
[24] Colonna 1980: 65; the name may be of a divinity.   [25] Colonna 1980: 65.
[26] Ibid. 67 f.

238   *Appendix* 1

From Caere in the seventh century comes the inscription: *kalaturus φapenas cenecuheθie*, possibly a Latin Kalator Fabius.[27] (From the same time and place come recognizably Italic or Faliscan names *ate peticina* [Atto Peticio], and Tita Vendia).[28] A sixth-century inscription reads *mi hulus larziia*, which is comparable to the inscriptions in Rome with the same name.[29]

From Tarquinia in the late seventh century comes an inscription painted on the bottom of an argilla oinochoe found in a funerary corredo which reads: *aχapri rutile hipukrates*. The first word is unknown; the second is a Latin praenomen; the third is an Etruscan translation of a Greek aristocratic name. Ampolo has suggested that the inscription is proof of a Greek aristocrat comfortably resident in Etruscan society.[30]

At Veii in the late seventh-century tomb was found a bucchero anfora with the inscription: *mi tites latines*; one may compare a late archaic inscription at Orvieto which reads: *mi latin[e]s kailes*.[31] The last name of this inscription is also found at Aleria at Corsica, together with the suggestive fifth-century name Klavtie, which may represent the Claudian name, on an Attic red-figure kylix *c*.425 BC. The Claudii are also found in a fourth-century chamber tomb in Caere, and we know of a close connection between Caere and Corsica, though there are other explanations for these appearances.[32] To complete the neat circle of evidence, the name *Kailes* may indicate Caelius; this name is known from the François tomb painting of Caelius and Aulus Vibenna; Caelius is being liberated by Macstrna, who has been identified as Servius Tullius the king of Rome. There is a late archaic inscription on a bucchero vase in the sanctuary of Portonaccio at Veii with the words: *mine muluv[an]ece a.vile vipien.nas*.[33]

---

[27] *TLE* 65b; the inscription, with the words *cena* and *ze* on the edges, is found on an Italo-Geometric skyphos. Ampolo 1976: 341.
 [28] *Ate Peticina*: *TLE* 865, a late 7th-century impasto oinochoe, with *mi ates qutum peticinas* on the neck, *aθineθiaptala* in a different hand on the body and two crosses under the foot (SE 31 1963 206.3; SE 35 1968 563 f.). *Tita Vendia*: on a late 7th-century red impasto pithos (SE 21 1950/51 397 ff.); this is sometimes thought to have been Faliscan. Ampolo 1976: 341.
 [29] SE 33 1965 502.11, an Attic kylix from the second half of the 6th century. *Hulus* is probably to be equated with Folnius, and, according to Rix (1963: 191) is securely Roman; Colonna 1987: 58.
 [30] *TLE* 155, *NSc* 1932: 110.
 [31] For the Veii inscription see *CLP* 376; for that from Orvieto, see Colonna 1987 61 n. 45.
 [32] Heurgon in Jehasse 1973: 551; Fraschetti 1977; on the chamber tomb see M. Pallottino 1969.
 [33] For the Tomba François see *GRT* 18 f.; for the Veientine inscription with Vibenna, *TLE* 35, *GRT* 19.

APPENDIX 2
Latin Sites

This appendix is a brief survey of the major Latin sites which have been discussed above. A brief bibliography is appended to each site. This gazetteer is not intended as a complete account of any site, but merely for quick reference.

ACQUA ACETOSA LAURENTINA

Acqua Acetosa Laurentina to the south of Rome shows both burial and habitation evidence; there is a cluster of excavated settlement nearby, in an area which was part of the Ager Romanus from the early fifth century on.

There are forty or so tombs from the eighth to the fourth centuries, at least fifteen of which belonged to IVA. One contained a chariot, and evidence of sacrifices and libations has been found. The later tombs were grandly built, but had limited corredi, although an early fifth-century deposition shows a silver ring.

Of the three houses discovered, one has a cistern, kiln, and associated child burials. Bucchero and argilla have been found in the tombs and the habitation. Interestingly, the houses seem to have been superseded, since one of them was destroyed to make way for a chamber tomb.

See *GRT* 171 ff., 255 ff.; Bedini 1980, 1981; Holloway 1994: 120 f.

ALBAN HILLS

The majority of the evidence which we have from the Alban Hills comes from the burials published by Gierow, one or two other burials discovered more recently, and some scatters of pottery which indicate that settlement continued into Period IIB. The area was culturally conservative, retaining incineration after other areas had turned to inhumation. The general abandonment of the area after around 850 is undeniable, notwithstanding the continued religious significance of the area as the place of the Feriae Latinae.

See *CLP* 68 ff.; Gierow 1964–6; Chiarucci 1978, 1987.

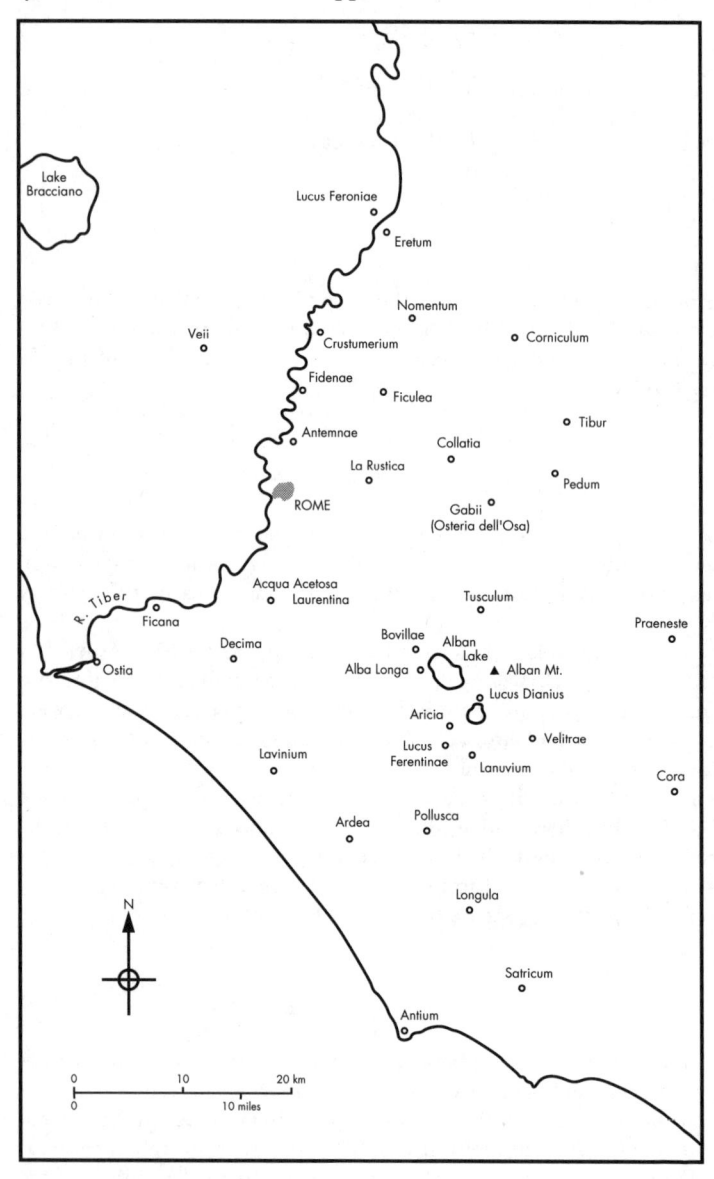

MAP 1. *Archaic Latium*

ANAGNIA

The site of Anagnia was to be the central site of the Hernici. It is most interesting for the votive deposit at S. Cecilia from the sixth century on, and the inscriptions that have been found there.

On the whole, the votive vases are wheel-turned miniatures, from a wide variety of cultures, Latin, Etruscan, and Greek; there are a handful of fragments of Attic black-figure. There is also a large number of personal ornaments in bronze, iron, and other materials, especially of fibulae. The fibulae with *arco a bozze* show a clear connection with Campania. The site is towards the southern limit of Latium, and seems to have participated in trade with Campania, an indication of the increasing cultural connections of the late sixth century.

Of the inscriptions discovered at the site, the majority show a clear Etruscan influence.

See *GRT* 223 ff.; Gatti 1990, 1993.

ANTEMNAE

The site is known largely through survey. There is a small amount of material from Antemnae from the second half of the eighth century, but in the seventh the evidence is much more satisfactory. Hut foundations and associated child burials have been found, and also typical Latin pottery, a piece of painted Italo-Geometric ware, and some bronze jewellery. Bucchero formed a very high percentage of the pottery on the site.

Intense occupation of the site in the sixth century is indicated by clusters of roof-tiles, and large amounts of ceramic, bronze, and copper. There were urban buildings, and cisterns and wells formed a drainage system. A wall and ditch defended the site, and from the early fifth century at least there is indication of a sanctuary of Juno Lanuvina in the form of terracotta decoration.

See *CLP* 147; *GRT* 152 f.; Quilici and Quilici Gigli 1978.

ARDEA

Ardea does not show much burial evidence; the necropolis has not been uncovered. The two central aspects of the archaeology are the two bronze hoards, one from Phase I and one from Phase III, and the development of the urban space, with houses, temples, and fortifications coming in the seventh and sixth centuries.

The earliest hoard contains about 1.5 kg of bronze axes and fibulae, some broken, some not. The eighth-century hoard (*CLP* pp. 312 ff.)

contained 293 pieces, again axes and fibulae. Either may indicate pre-monetal currency, perhaps the latter with more likelihood; they may also indicate reworking of bronze in Ardea.

With regard to the urban development, the first fortifications date from the seventh century. The site shows quite a complex fortification pattern, with an agger defending the acropolis, and another defending the area of Civitavecchia; the south-western approach is less easy because of natural contours. There were at least three temples on the site; one (the earliest, from a fragment of Velletri-style terracotta) to Juno on the acropolis, one to Hercules at Civitavecchia, and a third to the Dioscuri on the Colle della Noce. There was also the federal sanctuary, the Aphrodisium, attested by literary evidence to be near Ardea, and an

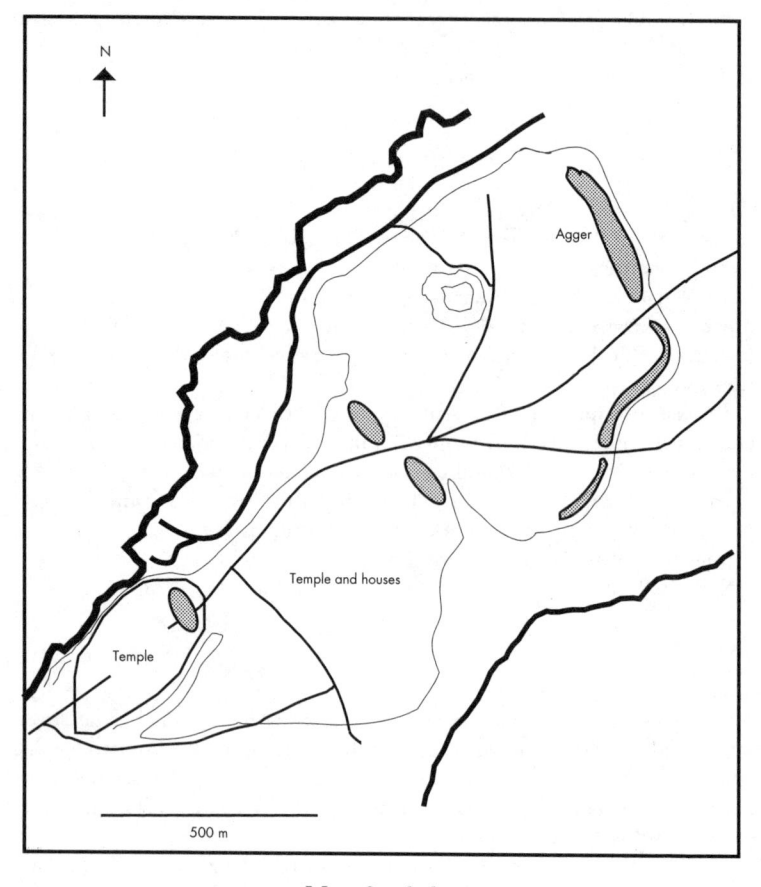

MAP 2. *Ardea*

Latin Sites 243

altar with a rather Greek form has been found on the Colle della Banditella.
From the seventh century there are at least four dwellings; details are scarce.
See *CLP* 312 ff.; *GRT* 192 ff.; Andrén 1961; Morselli and Tortorici 1982; Crescenzi and Tortorici 1984; Melis and Rathje 1984: 389 ff.; Colonna 1984: 409 f.

CASTEL DI DECIMA

The necropolis at Castel di Decima began in Phase II and flourished in IVA, after which it faded away, and was much reduced by the fifth century. The site may owe its prosperity to the trade route between Etruria and Campania along the Fossa di Malafede. The necropolis is one of the more wealthy in Latium, and contains prestige items for both men and women.
See *CLP* 252 ff.; Guaitoli et al. 1974; Bedini and Cordano 1977; Zevi 1977; Holloway 1994: 114 ff.

CASTIGLIONE

Castiglione is another of the sites around the Castiglione crater, roughly opposite to Osteria dell'Osa. The excavation carried out was limited, but there are indications of habitation from ceramic scatters, and also a necropolis, which contained at least twenty tombs from IIA and possibly IIB. The grave goods are similar in style to those at Osteria dell'Osa, but slightly less wealthy.
See Bietti-Sestieri in Bietti-Sestieri (ed.) 1984: 160–70.

CRUSTUMERIUM

Crustumerium shows evidence of Phase I habitation with ceramic scatters, and there may have been a necropolis at Site Z where IIA dolia have been found. The site seems to have been occupied by a number of small villages.
There is a marked consolidation in the eighth century, and some weapons have been found in a burial. The amount of iron in the burials is quite striking; a lance point is among the male armour, and an iron fibula *a sanguisuga* is found in a female tomb. There are clear indications of Etruscan and Faliscan influence.
By the later seventh century, the site covered 40 ha and was thus one of the larger sites in Latium. Tumuli are found along the roads, and

there is a certain amount of deliberate superimposition, as was found at Osteria dell'Osa in the eighth century. The tumuli may in a way represent boundaries.

One particular site (Site U) appears to develop its own fortifications, and covers some 4 or 5 ha. Similar situations occur near Tivoli, Gabii, Praeneste, and Ardea, and possibly with the Aventine Hill at Rome.

Settlement was dense in the sixth century, and follows the complex road pattern. The agricultural potential of the land was improved by the installation of cuniculi. A major wall was constructed for defence.

See *CLP* 151; Quilici and Quilici Gigli 1980; di Gennaro 1988 for eighth-century tombs.

FICANA

The most important discovery at Ficana, about five or ten kilometres upstream from Ostia, is a complete banqueting service from outside a house; the finds date from Phase IVA. It appears that a fire destroyed the house and the service at the same time, and the pottery was deposited in a rubbish-pit.

The deposit appears to represent a full banqueting service, and the house may therefore have been used as a banqueting hall. The deposit is significant as a control for burial goods and as an indication of the spread of symposiastic customs in the seventh century.

There is also evidence for a house to the south-west of M. Cugno, which has an unusual rectangular shape and internal structure; it dates from the early sixth century. From IIB onwards, there are infant tombs which are associated with settlement; the corredi have typical Latin pottery.

See *CLP* 250 f.; *GRT* 178 ff.; Rathje 1983 for full publication of the banqueting service; Rathje in Murray (ed.) 1990 for further speculation; Pavolini 1981 for the other house; Jarva 1981 for infant tombs. Holloway 1994: 123 f.

FIDENAE

There is some evidence of Phase I settlement from ceramic scatters around the hill of Villa Spada; there were at least two separate settlements. The evidence improves in IIA, perhaps after the absorption of settlers in the Fosso di Settebagni.

In IIB and III Fidenae continued to increase in size, and to make inroads into the surrounding territory. A hut of 6.2 m by 5.2 m has been discovered to the north of the settlement around this period, with pottery inside, and the first evidence for the domestic cat in Latium; it was destroyed by fire. By the seventh century bucchero was arriving in large quantities across the river Tiber. There is some seventh-century evidence from the necropolis on site 61, which has unfortunately been almost completely destroyed.

In the sixth century prosperity was high, with settlement focused on two hills, which now appear to be closely linked. Miniature vases and a fifth-century antefix representing Juno Lanuvina seem to indicate a sanctuary on the main hill.

All roads seem to have led to this main hill, which was fortified with gates on every road. One road runs straight in front of a foundation wall of a major building; perhaps a sign of regular planning. There are some small burial sites outside the city.

The territory of the settlement seems to have increased greatly, with every effort being made to fulfil the area's agricultural potential. There are dwelling-places and burials out in the country.

There was also one very wealthy late sixth- or early fifth-century burial of a woman just within the settlement. The corpse was placed in a sarcophagus (a similar development was occurring at Rome, where a sarcophagus has been found on the Esquiline). The corredo contains gold and silver jewellery, some of which appears to come from Vulci, or at least shows clear similarities with jewellery from that area.

See *CLP* 148 f.; *GRT* 155 ff., 260 f. for tomb; Quilici and Quilici Gigli 1986; Bietti-Sestieri, Grossi Mazzorin and De Santis 1990 for hut.

GABII

In the seventh century or thereabouts, the scattered communities on the Castiglione crater seem to have unified, in a process which occurred throughout Latium. Gabii became the site of the unified community, and in the second quarter of the sixth century came the first phases of a temple just outside the city, on the road to Tibur. There may have been some sort of sanctuary here in the seventh century. The temple had one cella and was about 5.5 m wide by 8.4 m long, and was probably dedicated to Juno. Architectural terracottas were found, similar to those at the Regia at Rome.

A considerable number of bronze kouroi and korai have been found on the site; similar examples can be cited from the Lapis Niger, Satricum, and Lavinium.

See *CLP* 186; *GRT* 159 ff.; Colonna 1984: 401 ff.

LANUVIUM

The Colle S. Lorenzo appears to have been inhabited from the ninth century onwards, though we have fairly limited evidence concerning it.

The first fortifications were built in the sixth century, at roughly the same time as the podium to the first temple to Juno Sospita, an edifice with three cellae measuring 15.4 m by 23.8 m in all.

The site has also produced one extraordinary burial from the late sixth or early fifth century; a male burial from a chamber tomb. The corredo is striking and shows contacts with Etruria, and thence to the Greek world of athletics and war, with a bronze disc, on one side of which is engraved a young man with a discus, and on the other a man on horseback, dressed for combat or display, and a remarkable set of highly decorated armour.

See *GRT* 196 ff., 265 ff.; Chiarucci 1983.

LAVINIUM

Lavinium is one of the most important of Latin sites. Situated on the coast, it seems as open to foreign influence as any Latin site after Rome. Its history seems to date back to the early tenth century, and to continue uninterrupted. The early evidence is from burials, some of which, like the Tomb of the Warrior, are unusually wealthy.

From the eighth century on, we have evidence of three huts A, C, and E, with associated tombs, and the first of the pottery kilns, and possibly the first fortifications. The evidence for the huts has now increased; some thirty huts are now known. There were about twenty-nine children's burials associated. In the same urban area, there was a votive deposit with no less than 30,000 miniature vases from 650–600, which were reused in third-century BC terracing; this is the first urban cult attested in Lavinium.

About 100 m away from the shrine of the thirteen altars one wealthy IVA tomb under a tumulus appears to have received continued veneration into the fourth century, and has been identified as the heroon of Aeneas. The body, probably male, was put in a box, and buried with rather a large corredo, including one piece of imported pottery. See *CLP* 305 ff.

In the seventh to sixth centuries, the first deposits were made at the eastern sanctuary, the north-eastern sanctuary, and the Thirteen Altars sanctuary. The pottery includes bucchero and Italo-Geometric ware. Fortification and habitation continued into the sixth century, when the site appears fully urbanized. There were major houses built in the centre at this time which remained in use, with refurbishments, into the early third century BC.

See *CLP* 291 ff.; *GRT* 182 ff.; *Lavinium* I, II; Guaitoli 1984; Fenelli and Guaitoli 1990.

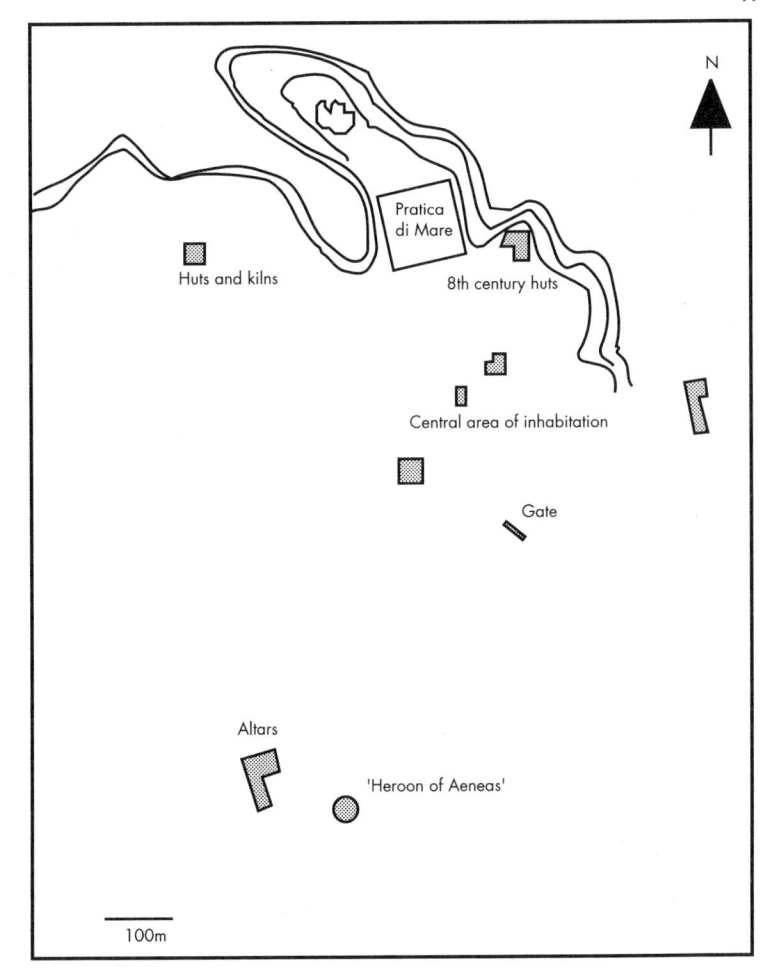

MAP 3. *Lavinium*

OSTERIA DELL'OSA

Osteria dell'Osa is situated on the Castiglione crater; there was a necropolis there from which 600 tombs have now been uncovered. The necropolis begins in Period I. There are some major incinerations around 900 which form the centre of the inhumations in Period II. The burials decrease in Period III, but there appears to be a new, central, coherent group, and there is a chamber tomb in Period IVB.

Although the burials are not outstandingly wealthy, they are particularly important because this is the only largely complete necropolis in Latium yet known. The evidence shows distinct groups within society, which are identified in the funerary ritual, and different treatment being given to men and women and different age groups.

The site has also yielded the earliest inscription in Italy.

See *CLP* 166 ff.; Ricerca 1979; Bietti-Sestieri 1984; idem. in Bietti-Sestieri (ed.) 1985; Bietti-Sestieri 1993a, 1993b; Holloway 1994: 103 ff.

PRAENESTE

The site of Praeneste is best known in the archaic period for the uniquely wealthy burials discovered in the nineteenth century. The Tomba Bernardini is the wealthiest of the tombs, with well over a hundred items. Some indication of the identity of the deceased is given by an inscription

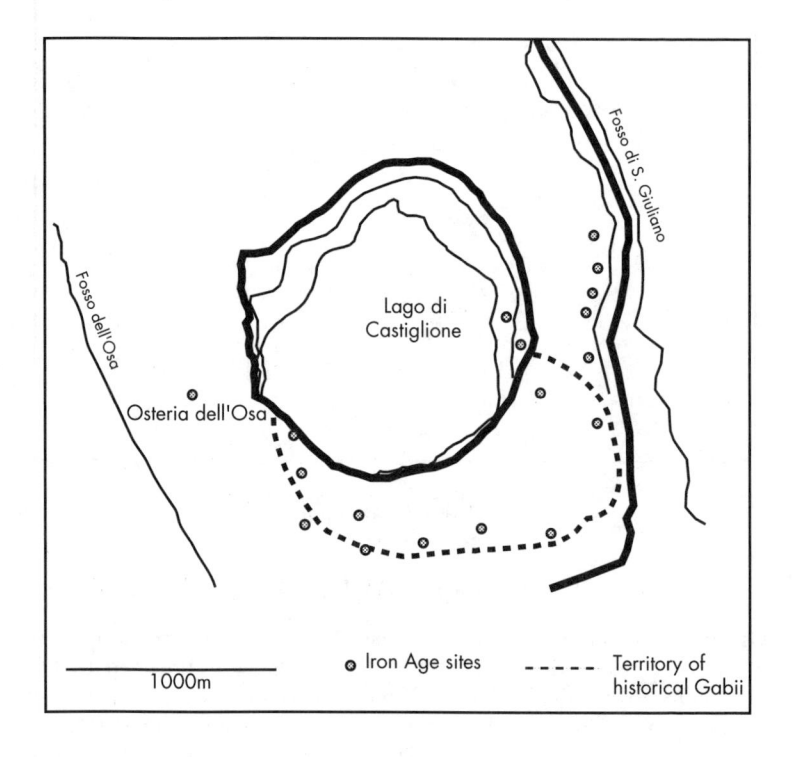

MAP 4. *Osteria Dell'Osa*

on a silver cup, written from right to left, which reads Vetusia. This has been interpreted as a feminine name, which would correspond to the Latin *nomen* Veturius, taken by one of the tribes south of Rome along the important routes between Etruria and Campania. This may form part of the explanation for the close link between these tombs at Praeneste and the Tomba Regolini-Galassi at Caere.

See *CLP* 213 ff. for all the tombs; Canciani and von Hase 1979 for the Tomba Bernardini and full bibliography; *GRT* 143, 164 ff., 262 ff.; Holloway 1994: 156 ff.

ROME

The earliest evidence from Rome is in the form of burials in the Forum and on the Esquiline Hill. The burials increase in wealth over time. By the eighth century we see huts on the Palatine, and there may be some early fortifications. The seventh century brings massive earthworks to secure the Forum area for further settlement. Towards the end of the period the first pavement of the Forum itself was constructed.

In Period IVB there was a major development of the central area of Rome, with the second pavement of the Forum area, the first stone structure at the Regia, and the beginning of votive deposits at the Lapis Niger and S. Omobono.

The major evidence from the sixth century is as follows:

Forum: Establishment of the Lapis Niger inscription and votive deposit.
Regia: At the beginning of the seventh century the area was apparently occupied by animal pens or sheds. Some of these were destroyed in the late seventh century to make way for the first stone structure, which was built over child burials; a cippus stood roughly above one of them. The building was rebuilt four times in the sixth century.
Private housing: Sixth-century houses have been found alongside earlier walls around the Palatine and the Sacred Way. They appear to have been luxurious, and were occupied for several centuries.
Temples and Sanctuaries: Forum Boarium.

There was a votive deposit of the seventh century with associated huts, similar to that at Satricum, and a sacred area with a ditch for sacrifices remaining in use into the sixth century, then at least one stone building in the early sixth century. Later in this century, probably between 540 and 530, this older temple, having been destroyed by fire, was rebuilt on a slightly larger scale. In the third century two much larger temples, on a different orientation, were built, and these were dedicated to Fortuna and Mater Matuta. There are some fragments of Greek pottery, making up the deposit of around a hundred such fragments from the late seventh century on. The sixth-century fragments amount to only a handful.

The temple of Jupiter Optimus Maximus is dated by literary evidence to the end of the sixth century; the temple of the Dioscuri now appears to be early fifth-century from the evidence of architectural terracottas.

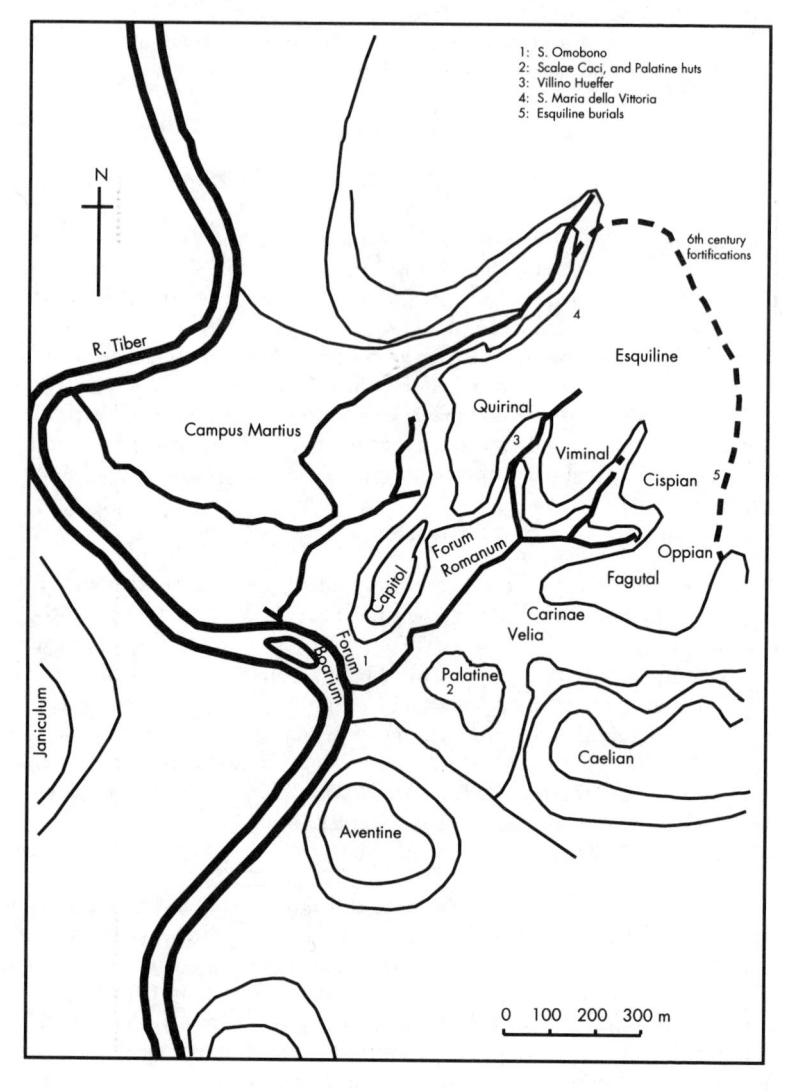

MAP 5. *Early Rome*

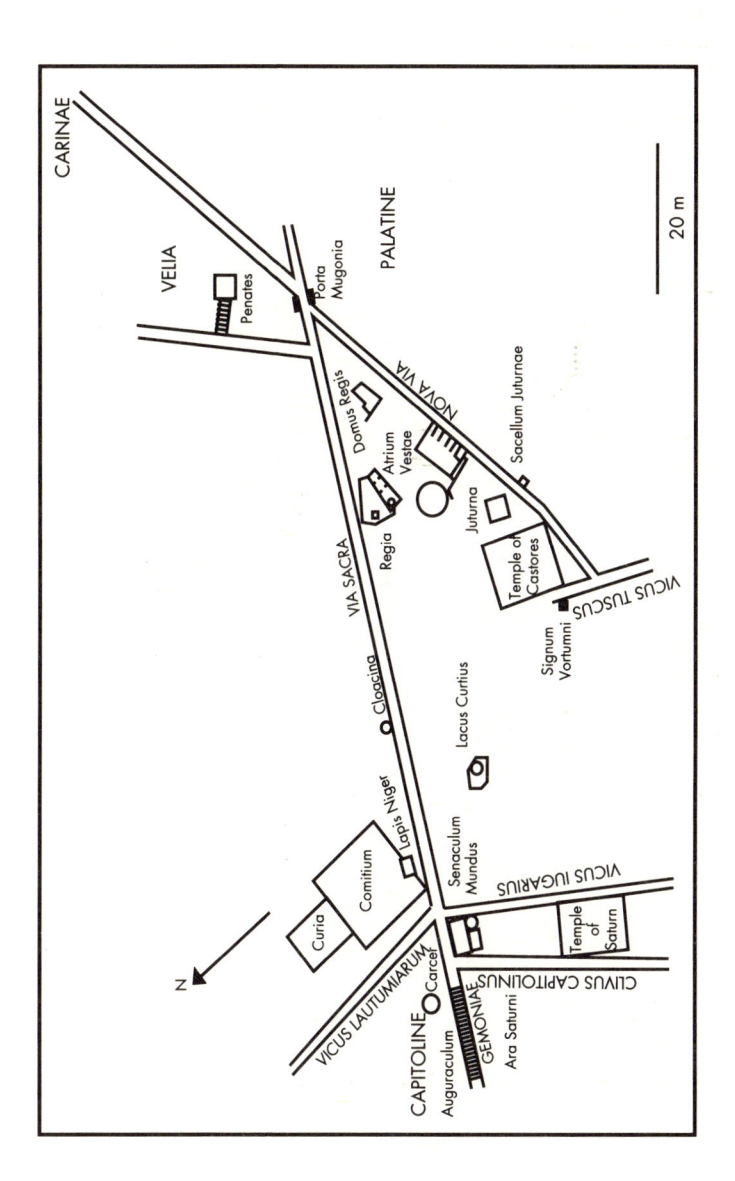

MAP 6. *The Roman Forum*

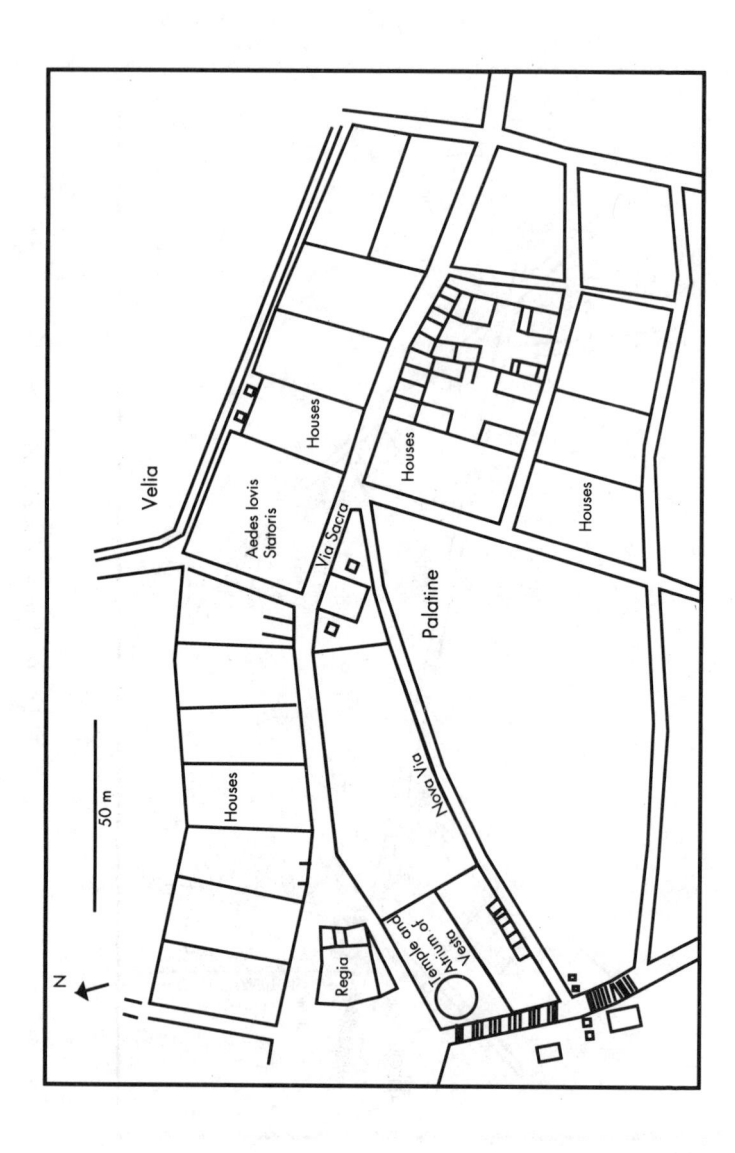

MAP 7. *Sixth-century Rome: temples and houses along the Via Sacra*

See *CLP* 99 ff.; *GRT* passim; Gjerstad, *Early Rome*, i–vi; Coarelli 1986, 1988; Holloway 1994: ch. 2, 4, 5, 6.

SATRICUM

Excavation at Satricum has focused on the temple area on the acropolis, and the houses nearby, as well as a necropolis including the fifth-century burials which have been attributed to a phase of Volscian occupation.
I give here a rough chronology of the developments on the site.
Period IIB/III: Early huts and associated material, including some burials.
Seventh century: The first votive deposit, on the site of the later temple to Mater Matuta. Some increase in the size of huts.
Seventh to sixth centuries: First stone-built houses (including building A); continuation of the votive deposit in the sacellum. Some luxury goods in the votive deposit and the tombs, including silver and imported Greek pottery (Proto-Corinthian). Also the rubbish pits, possibly associated with ritual cooking for burials
550–500: Complete reconstruction of the habitation, with larger and grander stone-built houses. The votive deposit ends with the construction of the first stone-built temple.
500: Construction of the second temple.
Building A:
620/10–550 (Third phase of the building).
Foundations of new stone building, also roof-tiles, portico, courtyard, cistern, and storeroom. This building destroyed by fire.
550–510/490 (Fourth phase of building).
Walls and post-holes for portico survive; the rebuilding is roughly contemporary with the first temple.
510/490–400/350 (fifth phase of building).

The site may have been taken over by the Volscians late in the sixth century, and there is a cemetery from this period.
See *CLP* 323 ff.; *GRT* 230 ff.; Maaskant-Kleibrink 1988; Gnade 1992; Holloway 1994: 142 ff.

TIBUR

The necropolis at Tibur contains almost 100 tombs from Phase I through to the early sixth century. It is interesting that there are a number of different centres, especially in the later periods, which may indicate territoriality, and the density of finds in the area suggests the consider-

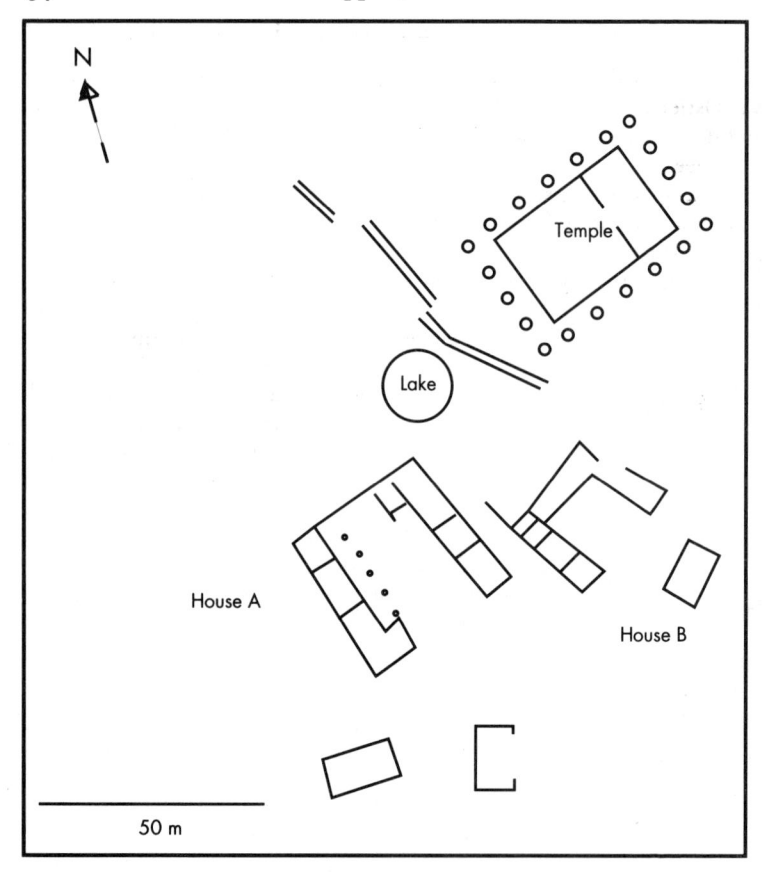

MAP 8. *Satricum: mid-sixth century*

able power and influence of Tibur, which continued into the fourth century, when *oppida* under the city's control are mentioned.

Most important, the inhumations at Tivoli, although their corredi are much the same as those of other Latin centres, are marked out by circles and not rectangles. The circles, roughly between 3 m and 5 m in diameter, are marked out with tufa stones. This burial practice is also found in the Osco-Umbrian area in the interior of Italy, and is a striking indication of a different set of cultural affiliations.

See *CLP* 188 ff.

TOR DE CENCI

A recently discovered site on an ancient crossroads. One road leads to the Via Ostiense and the Via Laurentina; the other to the Fossa di Malafede and down to Castel Porziano. A number of archaic fragments of pottery have been found in the area, and Tor de Cenci has been interpreted as the *compitum* or crossroads of a *pagus*. Interestingly, the roads are not incompatible with the dimensions of the chariots which have been found at various places.

There are twenty or so tombs from the seventh and sixth centuries, many of them chamber tombs; there were another thirty or so tombs from a later period. The earlier tombs have impasto and argilla pottery; by the later sixth century the corredi have disappeared. Perhaps significantly, one tomb (T21) appears to have had a seventh-century phase, then a chamber tomb, and possibly a fifth-century reuse. There is one piece of Attic black glaze.

See Bedini 1988–9; 1990.

TORRINO

Torrino, near Acqua Acetosa Laurentina, Castel di Decima, and Tor de Cenci has yielded two chamber tombs from the late seventh century. There were fourteen burials in all, and a generous spread of quality bucchero and argilla pottery, with thirty-nine vases in T2. The tombs appear to have been used into the sixth century, and some structural changes were made over time.

See Bedini and Ruffo 1981.

VALVISCIOLO

The site of Valvisciolo is remarkable for an extraordinary series of terraces, built down the hillside in the late seventh and early sixth centuries, which represent perhaps the most advanced fortification work in the region. The site was abandoned in the later sixth century, perhaps for the site of Norba nearby, which was also well-defended. The area must have been very open to the threat of Volscian hostility throughout the fifth century.

At the same time as the walls were built, a votive deposit began at the site, which contains metalwork and pottery, some miniature, mostly of Latin production, but perhaps with some Etruscan influence.

See *GRT* 209 ff.

List of References

Periodicals abbreviated according to *L'Année Philologique*.

Acanfora, M. O. (ed.) (1976), 'Gli scavi della necropoli dell'Osa: Relazione preliminare per le campagne 1971–2', *BPI*, 23 (1972–4): 259–75.

Acquaro, E., Godart, L., Mazza, F., and Musti, D. (1988), *Momenti precoloniali nel Mediterraneo antico* (Rome).

Agostiniani, L. (1982), *Le 'Iscrizioni Parlanti' dell'Italia antica* (Florence).

Åkerstrom, A. (1954), 'Untersuchungen über die figurlichen Terakottafriese aus Etrurien und Latium', *Opusc. Rom.*, 1: 191–231.

Alföldi, A. (1962), 'Ager Romanus Antiquus', *Hermes* 90: 187–94.

—— (1964), *Early Rome and the Latins* (Ann Arbor, Mich.).

Almagro-Gorbea, M. (1981), 'L'Area del tempio di Giunone Gabina nel VI–V sec a.C.', *AL*, 4: 297–304.

—— (1982), *El Santuario del Juno en Gabii* (Rome).

Altheim, F. (1938), *A History of Roman Religion* (London).

Ammanato, F., Di Gennaro, F., and Pulimanti, A. M. (1985), 'Prospezioni nell'area del piano di zona "Fidene 27"', *Bull.Com.*, 89: 136–8.

Ammerman, A. (1990), 'On the Origins of the Forum Romanum', *AJA* 94: 627–45.

Ampolo, C. (1970–71), 'Su alcuni mutamenti sociali nel Lazio tra l'VIII sec e il IV sec.' *Dd'A*, 37–99.

—— (1976/7), 'Demarato. Osservazioni sulla mobilità sociale arcaica.' *Dd'A*, 333–45.

—— (1980), 'Le condizione materiali della produzione. Agricultura e paessagio agrario', in *Atti*, 15–46.

—— (1980–2). 'Le origini di Roma e la "Cité Antique"', *MEFRA*, 92: 567–76.

—— (1981a), 'I gruppi etnici in Roma arcaica: posizione del problema e fonti', in *Gli Etruschi in Roma*, 45–70.

—— (1981b), 'La città arcaica e le sue feste: due ricerche sul Septimontium e sull'Equus October', *AL*, 4: 233–40.

—— (1981c), 'Il gruppo acroteriale di S. Omobono', *PP*, 36: 32–5.

—— (1984a), 'Il lusso nelle società arcaiche', *Opus*, 3(2), 469–76.

—— (1984b), 'Il lusso funerario e la città arcaica', *AION ArchStAnt*, 6: 71–102.

—— (1986), 'Roma ed il Latium Vetus nel VI e V sec. a.C.', *PCIA*, 8: 391–467.

Andrén, A. (1940), *Architectural Terracottas from Etrusco-Italic Temples* (Lund).

—— (1961), 'Scavi e scoperte sull'Acropoli di Ardea', *Opusc. Rom.* 3: 1–68.

Angle, M., and Gianni, A. (1985), 'An application of quantitive methods for a socio-economic analysis of an Iron Age necropolis', in Malone and Stoddart (eds.) 1985 iii 145–63.

Anzidei, A. P., Bietti-Sestieri, A. M. and De Santis, A. (1985), *Roma e il Lazio dall'età della pietra alla formazione della città* (Roma).

Appaduri, A. (1986) (ed.), *The Social Life of Things: Commodities in Cultural Perspective* (Cambridge).

Ashby, T. (1927), *The Roman Campagna in Classical Times* (London).

—— (1986), *Un archeologo fotografa la campagna Romana tra '800 e '900* (Rome).

Åström, P. (1986), 'Hala Sultan Tekke—An International Harbour Town of the late Cypriot Bronze Age', *Opusc. Ath.*, 16: 7–17.

Balmuth, M. S. (1987) (ed.), *Studies in Sardinian Archaeology III: Nuragic Sardinia and the Mycenaean World* (Oxford).

Balsdon, J. P. V. D. (1971), 'Dionysius on Romulus: A political pamphlet?' *JRS* 61: 18–27.

Barber, E. J. W. (1991), *Prehistoric Textiles: The Development of Cloth in the Neolithic and Bronze Ages with Special Reference to the Aegean* (Princeton, NJ).

Barker, G. (1981), *Landscape and Society: Prehistoric Central Italy* (London).

—— (1989), 'The archaeology of the Italian shepherd.' *PCPS*, 35: 1–19.

—— and Hodges, R. (1981) (eds.), *Archaeology and Italian Society: Prehistoric, Roman and Medieval Studies* (Oxford).

—— and Rasmussen, T. (1988), 'The archaeology of an Etruscan polis: a preliminary report on the Tuscania project (1986 and 1987 seasons)', *PBSR*, 25–42.

Barreca, F. (ed.) (1985), *Civiltà Nuragica* (Milan).

Bartoloni, G. (1984), 'Riti funerari dell'aristocrazia in Etruria e nel Lazio. L'esempio di Veio.' *Opus*, 3(1): 13–30.

—— (1985), 'Le urne a capanna: ancora sulle prime scoperte nei Colli Albani', in Swaddling (ed.), 235–48.

—— (1987), 'Esibizione di richezza a Roma nel VI e V secolo: Doni votivi e corredi funerari', *Sc. Ant.*, 1: 143–59.

—— (1989–90), 'I depositivi votivi di Roma arcaica: Alcune considerazioni', *Sc. Ant.*, 3–4: 747–59.

Bartoloni, G., Burerelli, F., D'Atri, V., and De Santis, A. (1987), *Le urne a capanne rinvenuti in Italia* (Rome).
Bartoloni, G., Cataldi Dini, M., and Zevi, F. (1982), 'Aspetti dell'ideologia funeraria nella necropoli di Castel di Decima', in Gnoli and Vernant (1982) (eds.), 257–73.
Bass, G. F. (1967), 'Cape Gelidonyia: A Bronze Age Shipwreck', *TAPhS*, 57(8).
Bayet, J. (1926), *Les origines de l'Hercule romain* (Paris).
Beard, M. and North J. (1990) (eds.), *Pagan Priests: Religion and Power in the Ancient World* (London).
Bedini, A. (1980), 'Abitato protostorico in località Acqua Acetosa Laurentina', *AL*, 3: 58–64.
—— (1981), 'Edifici di abitazione di epoca arcaica in località Acqua Acetosa Laurentina', *AL*, 3: 253–7.
—— (1983), 'Due nuove tombe a camera presso l'abitato della Laurentina: Nota su alcuni tipi di sepolture nel VI e V sec. a.C.', *AL*, 5: 28–37.
—— (1984), 'Struttura ed organizzazione delle tombe "principesche" nel Lazio. Acqua Acetosa Laurentina: un esempio', *Opus*, 3(2), 377–82.
—— (1985), 'Tre corredi protostorici dal Torrino: Osservazioni sull'affermarsi e la funzione delle aristocrazie terriere nell'VIII secolo a.C. nel Lazio', *AL*, 7: 44–64.
—— (1988–9), 'Tor de' Cenci (Roma)—Tombe protostoriche', *NSc*, 42–43, 221–82.
—— (1990), 'Un compitum de origine protostorica a Tor de Cenci', *AL*, 10: 121–33.
—— and Cordano, F. (1975), 'Castel Di Decima (Roma). La Necropoli Arcaica', *NSc* 369–408.
—— (1977), 'L'ottavo secolo nel Lazio e l'inizio dell'orientalizzante antico alla luce di recenti scoperte nella necropoli di Castel di Decima', *PdP*, 32: 274–311.
—— and Ruffo M. (1981), 'Contributo alla conoscenza del territorio a sud di Roma in epoca protostorica', *AL*, 4: 57–68.
Beijer, A. J. (1991), 'Un centro di produzione di vasi d'impasto a Borgo le Ferriere ("Satricum") nel periodo dell'orientalizzante', *MedNed InstRom* 50: 63–86.
Beloch, K. J. (1886), *Die Bevölkerung der griechisch-römischen Welt* (Leipzig).
Berggren, E. and Berggren K. (1980), *The Iron Age Test Square in the N-E part of Area D* (Stockholm).
—— and Bergonzi, G. (1979), 'La fase piu antica della cultura laziale', in *Il Bronzo Finale*, 399–423.
Bernal, M. (1987), *Black Athena: The Afroasiatic Roots of Classical*

Civilisation, vol. 1: *The Fabrication of Ancient Greece 1785–1985* (London).

Bernard Knapp, A. (1990), 'Copper Production and Mediterranean Trade: The view from Cyprus', *Opusc. Ath.*, 18: 109–16.

—— (1993), 'Thalassocracies in Bronze Age eastern Mediterranean Trade: making and breaking a myth', *World Archaeology*, 24(3): 332–47.

Bernardi, A. (1973), *Nomen Latinum* (Pavia).

Betteridge, J. (1989), 'Urbanisation in Rome and Latium Vetus', unpublished Ph.D. thesis (London).

Bianco Peroni, V. (1979), *I rasoi nell'Italia continentale* (Prähistorische Bronzefunde VIII.2) (Munich).

Bickerman, E. J. (1952), 'Origines Gentium.' *CP*, 47: 65–81.

—— (1969), 'Some reflections on early Roman history', *RFIC*, 97: 393–408.

Bidditu, I. and Bruni, L. (1985), 'Stipe votiva del VI-V sec. a.C. ad Anagnia', *AL*, 7: 106–8.

Bietti-Sestieri, A. M. (1973), 'Central and Southern Italy in the Late Bronze Age', in Hackens, Holloway, and Holloway (eds.), 55–122.

—— (1976/7), 'Contributo allo studio delle forme di scambio della tarda età del bronzo nell'Italia continentale', *Dd'A*, 201–41.

—— (1981), 'Produzione e scambio nell'Italia protostorico: alcune ipotesi sul ruolo dell'industria metallurgica nell'Etruria mineraria alla fine dell'età del bronzo', in *L'Etruria Mineraria*, 223–64.

—— (1979) (ed.), *Ricerca su una comunità del Lazio protostorico* (Rome).

—— (1984) (ed.), *Preistoria e protostoria nel territorio di Roma* (Rome).

—— (1985a), 'The Iron Age necropolis of Osteria dell'Osa, Rome', in Malone and Stoddart, iii. 111–44.

—— (1985b), 'Contact, exchange and conflict in the Italian Bronze Age: The Mycenaeans on the Tyrrhenian coasts and islands,' in Malone and Stoddart (eds.), 305–53.

—— (1992a), *The Iron Age Community of Osteria dell'Osa: A study of socio-political development on central Tyrrhenian Italy* (Cambridge).

—— (1992b) (ed.), *La necropoli laziale di Osteria dell'Osa* (Rome).

—— and De Santis, A. (1985), 'Indicatori archeologici di cambiamento nella struttura delle comunità laziali nell'VIII secolo a.C.', *Dd'A*, 34–45.

—— De Santis, A., and La Regina, A. (1989–90), 'Elementi di tipo cultuale e doni personali nella necropoli laziale di Osteria dell'Osa', *Sc. Ant.*, 3–4: 65–88.

—— Grossi Mazzorin, J., and De Santis A. (1990), 'Fidene: La struttura dell'età del ferro', *AL*, 10: 115–20.

Bietti Sestieri, A. M., Pontrandolfo, A. G., and Parise, N. (1987) (eds.), *Archeologia e antropologia: Contibuti di preistoria e archeologia classica* (Rome).

Binford, L. R. (1972), *An Archaeological Perspective* (New York).

—— (1983), *Working at Archaeology* (London).

Bisi, A. M. (1986), 'Le role de Chypre dans la Civilisation Phénicienne d'Occident: Etat de la question et éssai de synthèse', in Karageorghis (ed.), 341–50.

Blake, H. McK., Potter, T. W., and Whitehouse, D. B. (1978) (eds.), *Papers in Italian Archaeology 1: The Lancaster Seminar. Recent research in prehistoric, classical and medieval archaeology* (Oxford).

Blake, M. E. (1947), *Ancient Roman Construction in Italy from the Prehistoric Period to Augustus* (Washington).

Blanck, H., and Weber-Lehmann, C. (1987) (eds.), *Malerei der Etrusker in Zeichnungen des 19 Jahrhunderts* (Mainz).

Boardman, J. (1972), 'Herakles, Peisistratos and sons', *RA*, 57–72.

—— (1978), 'Herakles, Delphi and Kleisthenes of Sicyon', *RA*, 227–34.

—— (1980), *The Greeks Overseas* (London).

Boddington, A., Garland, A. N., and Janaway, R. C. (1987) (eds.), *Death, Decay and Reconstruction: Approaches to Archaeology and Forensic Science* (Manchester).

Bonfante L. (1986) (ed.), *Etruscan Life and Afterlife: A Handbook of Etruscan Studies* (Warminster).

—— and von Heintze, H. (1976) (eds.), *Essays in Archaeology and the Humanities, In Memoriam Otto G. Brendel* (Mainz).

Bonfante Warren, L. (1970), 'Roman Triumphs and Etruscan Kings: The changing face of the triumph', *JRS*, 60: 49–66.

Bonghi Jovino, M., and Chiaramonte Treré, C. (1987) (eds.), *Tarquinia: Ricerche, Scavi e Prospettive* (Rome).

Bonnet, C. (1988), *Melqart: Cultes et mythes de l'Héraclès tyrien en Mediterranée*. (Leuven).

Bordenache, G. and Bartolini, G. (1975), 'La collezione Castellani di oreficerie', in *Nuove scoperte e acquisizioni nell'Etruria meridionale* (Rome), 77–82.

Boserup, E. (1965), *The Conditions of Agricultural Growth* (Chicago).

Botsford, G. W. (1909), *The Roman Assemblies from their Origin to the End of the Republic* (London).

Bound, M. and Vallintine, R., (1983), 'A wreck of possible Etruscan origin off Giglio island', *IJNA*, 12: 113–22.

Bourriot, F. (1976), *Recherches sur la nature du genos: Etudes d'histoire sociale Athénienne—périodes archaïque et classique* (Paris).

Bouzek J. (1985), *The Aegean, Anatolia and Europe: Cultural interrela-*

tions in the second millennium BC (Studies in Mediterranean Archaeology 29, Prague).
Bradley, R. (1985), 'Consumption, Change and the Archaeological Record: The archaeology of monuments and the archaeology of deliberate deposits', *Univ. of Edinburgh Dept. of Archaeology Occasional Papers* 13.
Braudel, F. (1984), *Civilisation and Capitalism 15th to 18th Century*, trans. S. Reynolds, 3 vols. (London).
Brelich, A. (1976), *Tre variazioni romane sul tema delle origini*, 2nd edn. (Rome).
Bremmer, J., Horsfall, N. (1987), *Roman Myth and Mythography* (London).
Brendel, O. (1978), *Etruscan Art* (London).
Briquel, D. (1972), 'Sur les faits d'écriture en Sabine et dans l'ager Capenas', *MEFRA*, 84: 789–845.
Il Bronzo Finale (1979), *Atti della XXI Riunione Scientifica, Istituto Italiano di Preistoria e Protostoria* (Florence).
Brown, F. E. (1967), 'New Soundings in the Regia: the evidence for the early Republic', in *Origines*, 45–64.
——— (1974–5), 'La Protostoria della Regia', *RendPontAcc* 47: 15–36.
——— (1976), 'Of Huts and Houses', in Bonfante and von Heintze (eds.) 5–12.
Brunt, P. A. (1988), *The Fall of the Roman Republic and Related Essays* (Oxford).
Campanile, E. (1991) (ed.), *Rapporti linguistici e culturali tra i popoli dell'Italia antica* (Pisa).
Canciani, F. and von Hase, F.-W. (1979), *La Tomba Bernardini di Palestrina* (Rome).
Carancini, G. L., Massetti, S. and Posi, F. (1985), 'L'area tra Umbria meridionale e Sabina alla fine della protostoria', *Dd'A*, ser. 3, 3(2), 37–65.
Cardarelli, A. (1979), 'Siti del passaggio alla media età del Bronzo nel Lazio', *AL*, 2: 139–47.
Castagnoli, F. (1972), *Orthogonal Planning in Antiquity* (Cambridge, Mass.).
——— (1972) (ed.), *Lavinium I: Topographia generale fonti e storia delle ricerche* (Rome).
——— (1975) (ed.), *Lavinium II: Le tredici are* (Rome).
——— (1978), 'Testudo, tegula deliciaria e il tempio di Giove Capitolino', *MEFRA*, 37–45.
——— (1988), '"Ibam forte Via Sacra" (Hor. Sat. 1.9.1)', *QITA*, 10: 99–114.
Catalano, P. (1965), *Linee del sistema sovrannazionale romano I* (Turin).
Cataldi, M. (1981), 'Ficana: Saggio di scavo sullo pendici sud-occidentali di Monte Cugno, nelle vicinanze del moderno casale', *AL*, 4: 274–86.

Cataldi, M. (1984), 'Ficana: campagne di scavo 1980–83', *AL*, 6: 91–97.
Cels-Saint-Hilaire, J. and Feuvrier-Prevotat, C. (1979), 'Guerres, échanges, pouvoir à Rome à l'époque archaique', *DHA*, 103–44.
Champeaux, J. (1982), *Fortuna: Le culte de la Fortune à Rome et dans le monde romain. I. Des origines à la mort de César* (Rome).
Champion, T. C. (1989) (ed.), *Centre and Periphery: Comparative Studies* (London).
Chapman, R., Kinnes, I. and Randsborg, K. (1981) (eds.), *The Archaeology of Death* (Cambridge).
Chiarucci, P. (1978), *Colli Albani. Preistoria e Protostoria*. (DocAlb 5).
—— (1983), *Lanuvium* (Rome).
—— (1987), 'Nuovi materiali e recenti scoperte della civiltà laziale nell'area Albana', *AL*, 8: 203–7.
—— Gizzi, T. (1985), *Area Sacra di Satricum: Tra scavo e restituzione* (Rome).
Childe, V. (1950), 'The urban revolution', *Town Planning Review*, 21(1): 1–17.
Civiltà arcaica del Sabini mella valle del Tevere (1973–7), 3 vols. (Rome).
Civiltà del ferro (1959), (Bologna).
Claessen, H. J. M. and Skalnik, P. (1978) (eds.), *The Early State* (The Hague).
Clarke, D. L. (1978), *Analytical Archaeology* (London).
—— (1979), *Analytical Archaeologist, Collected Papers* (London).
Close-Brooks, J. and Ridgway, D. (1979), 'Veii in the Iron Age', in Ridgway and Ridgway, 95–127.
Coarelli, F. (1986), *Il Foro Romano: Periodo arcaico* (Rome).
—— (1988), *Il Foro Boario* (Rome).
Cohen, R. and Service, E.R. (1978) (eds.), *Origins of the State: The Anthropology of Political Evolution* (Philadelphia).
Coldstream, J. N. (1977), *Geometric Greece* (London).
Colonna, G. (1967), 'L'Etruria meridionale interna dal Villanoviana alle tombe rupestri', *StEtr*, 35: 3–30.
—— (1973), 'Ricerche sull'Etruria interna Volsiniense', *StEtr*, 41: 45–72.
—— (1974), 'Preistoria e protostoria di Roma e del Lazio', *PCIA*, 2: 283–346.
—— (1976), '"Scriba cum rege sedens"', *Mélanges à J. Heurgon* (Rome), i. 187–95.
—— (1977), 'Un aspetto oscuro del Lazio antico: Le tombe del VI-V sc. a.C.', *PP*, 32: 131–65.
—— (1980a), 'Le iscrizioni strumentali latine del VI e V secolo a.C.', in C. M. Stibbe *et al.*, *Lapis Satricarus*, 53–69.
—— (1981a), 'Quali Etruschi a Roma', in *Gli Etruschi e Roma*, 159–72.

References

—— (1981b), 'L'ideologia e il conflitto delle culture', *AL*, 4: 229–32.
—— (1984), 'I templi del Lazio fino al V secolo compreso', *AL*, 6: 396–411.
—— (1985) (ed.), *Santuari d'Etruria* (Milan).
—— (1987), 'Etruria e Lazio nell'età dei Tarquini', in *Etruria e Lazio Arcaico*, 55–66.
Cook, R. M. (1989), 'The Francis-Vickers Chronology', *JHS*, 109: 164–70.
Cook, V. (1988), 'Cyprus and the outside world during the transition from the Bronze Age to the Iron Age', *Opusc. Ath.*, 17: 13–32.
Cornell, T. (1975), 'Aeneas and the twins', *PCPS*, 1–32.
—— (1977), 'Aeneas' arrival in Italy', *LCM*, 77–8.
—— (1979–80), 'Rome and Latium Vetus 1974–79', in *Archaeological Reports*, 71–89.
—— (1985–86), 'Rome and Latium Vetus 1980–85', in *Archaeological Reports*, 123–33.
—— (1991), 'The tyranny of the evidence: a discussion of the possible uses of literacy in Etruria and Latium in the archaic age', in J. H. Humphrey (ed.), *Literacy in the Roman World* (*Journal of Roman Archaeology, Supplementary Series 3*) 7–34.
Crescenzi, L. (1981), *Velletri: Archeologia, Territorio, Museo* (Velletri).
—— and Tortorici, E. (1984), 'Il caso di Ardea', *AL*, 6: 345–50.
Crifò, G. (1961), *Ricerche sull'exilium: I: L'origine dell'Istituto e gli elementi della sua evoluzione* (Milano).
Cristofani, M. (1978), *L'arte degli Etruschi, Produzione e Comrumo* (Turin).
—— (1985) (ed.), *Civiltà degli Etruschi* (Milan).
—— (1987) (ed.), *Etruria e Lazio arcaico* (Rome).
—— (1990), 'Osservazioni sulle decorazioni fittili arcaiche del santuario di Sant'Omobono', *AL*, 10: 31–7.
Cunliffe, B. W. (1988), *Greeks, Romans and Barbarians* (London).
Curti, S. (1987), 'Note di metodologia interpretativa dei dati funerari. Una necropoli dell'età del ferro laziale ed il metodo simbolico-contestuale', *Sc. Ant.*, 1: 121–42.
D'Agostino, B. (1977), *Tombe 'principesche' dell'orientalizzante antico da Pontecagnano. MonAnt SerMisc* II.1 (Rome).
—— (1979), 'Le necropoli protostoriche della Valle del Sarno: La ceramica di tipo greco', *AION ArchStAnt* 1: 59–75.
—— (1982), 'L'ideologia funeraria nell'età del ferro in Campania: Pontecagnano, nascita di un potere di funzione stabile', in Gnoli and Vernant (eds.), 202–21.
—— (1987), 'Società dei vivi, comunità dei morti: un rapporto difficile', in Bietti-Sestieri, Pontrandolfo, and Parise (eds.) 47–58.

D'Agostino, B. (1989), 'Image and Society in archaic Etruria', *JRS*, 79: 1–10.

—— (1990), 'Military Organization and Social Structure in archaic Etruria', in Murray and Price (eds.), 59–82.

—— and Gastaldi, P. (1988) (eds.), *Pontecaganao II: La necropoli del Picentino. I: Le tombe della prima età del ferro* (Naples).

Dalley, S. (1987), 'Near Eastern patron deities of mining and smelting in the late Bronze Age and early Iron Age', *Report of the Department of Antiquities of Cyprus*, 61–6.

Davico, A. (1951), 'Ricostruzione probabile dell'abitazione laziale del primo periodo del ferro secondo le testimonianze dello scavo su Germalo', *MonAnt.*, 41: coll. 125 ff.

Davison, J. M. (1972), *Seven Italic Tomb-Groups from Narce* (Istituto di Studi Etruschi ed Italici I, Florence).

De Francisci, P. (1959), *Primordia Civitatis* (Rome).

Degrassi, A. (1949), Epigraphia Romana. *Doxa*, 2: 47–135.

—— (1963), *Fasti Ammi Numani et Juliani* (*Inscriptioner Italiacae XIII Fasti et Elogia*, Fasc. 2) (Rome).

De la Genière, J. (1979), 'The Iron Age in Southern Italy', in Ridgway and Ridgway (eds.), 59–93.

Delpino, F. and Fugazzola Delpino, M. A. (1979), 'Il Ripostiglio di Rimessone', in *Il Bronzo Finale*, 425–52.

De Marchi, A. (1896–1903), *Il Culto Privato di Roma Antica* (Milan).

De Martino, E. (1958), *Morte e pianto rituale nel mondo antico: Dal lamento pagano al pianto di Maria* (Turin).

Denismore Curtis, C. (1925), 'The Barberini Tomb', *MAAR*, 5: 9–52.

De Polignac, F. (1984), *La Naissance de la Cité grecque: Cultes, espace et société VIIIe–VIIe siècles avant J.C.* (Paris).

Deriu, A., Buchner, G. and Ridgway, D. (1986), 'Provenance and firing techniques of Geometric pottery from Veii: A Mossbauer Investigation', *AION ArchStAnt* 8: 99–116.

De Salvia, F. (1978), 'Un ruolo apotropaico dello scarabeo egizio nel contesto culturale greco-arcaico di Pithekoussai (Ischia)', in *Hommages à Maarten J. Vermaseren* (Leiden), iii. 1003–61.

Descoeudres, J.-P. and Kearsley, R. (1983), 'Greek pottery at Veii: another look', *ABSA*, 78: 9–53.

Devereux, G. (1970), 'The equus October reconsidered', *Mnemosyne*, 23: 297–301.

De Waele, J. (1981), 'Satricum nel VI e V sec. a.C.: L'Architettura templare', *AL*, 4: 310–16.

Di Gennaro, F. (1979), 'Topografia dell'insediamento della media età del bronzo nel Lazio', *AL*, 2: 148–56.

—— (1986), *Forme di insediamento tra Tevere e Fiora dal Bronzo Finale al principio dell'età del Ferro* (Florence).

—— (1988), 'Primi resultati degli scavi nella necropoli di Crustumerium: tre complessi funerari della fase IVA', *AL*, 9: 113–23.

—— and Messineo, G. (1985), 'Sepoltura femminile presso il margine della città antica', *BullCom* 89: 138–46.

—— and Stoddart, S. (1982), 'A review of the evidence for prehistoric activity in part of S. Etruria', *PBSR*, 50: 1–21.

Diósdi, G. (1970), *Ownership in Ancient and Preclassical Law* (Budapest).

Domenico, L. and Miari, M. (1991), 'La distribuzione dei siti di necropoli in Etruria meridionale nel Bronzo Finale: documentazione ed elaborazione dei dati', in Herring, Whitehouse, and Wilkins (eds.), i. 61–82.

Douglas, M. and Isherwood, B. (1979), *The World of Things: Towards an Anthropology of Consumption* (London)

Douglas Van Buren, E. (1921), *Figurative Terra-cotta Revetments in Etruria and Latium in the 6th and 5th centuries BC* (London).

—— (1923), *Archaic Fictile Revetments in Sicily and Magna Graecia* (London).

—— (1926), *Greek Fictile Revetments in the Archaic Period* (London).

Drerup, H. (1969), *Griechische Baukunst in geometrischer Zeit* (Göttingen).

Drews, R. (1981), 'The Coming of the City to Central Italy', *AJAH*, 6: 133–65.

Dubourdieu, A. (1989), *Les origines et le développement du culte des Pénates à Rome* (Rome).

Dulière, C. (1979), *Lupa Romana: Recherches d'iconographie et essai d'interpretation* (Brussels and Rome).

Dumézil, G. (1964), 'Remarques sur la stèle archaïque du Forum', *CollLat* 70 (*Hommages à J. Bayet*) 172–79.

—— (1970a), *Archaic Roman Religion* (London).

—— (1970b), 'A propos de l'inscription du Lapis Niger', *Latomus*, 29: 1038–45.

—— (1975), *Fêtes romaines d'automne et d'été* (Paris).

—— (1979), *Mariages Indo-Européens* (Paris).

Dury-Moyaeres, G. (1981), *Enée et Lavinium: à propos des découvertes archéologiques récentes* (Brussels).

Edlund, I. E. M. (1987), *The Gods and the Place: Location and Function of Sanctuaries in the Countryside of Etruria and Magna Graecia (700–400 BC)* (Stockholm).

Emiliozzi, A. (1988), 'Nuovi documenti d'archivio per la Tomba Bernardini di Palestrina', *AL*, 9: 301–11.

Enea e Lazio: Archeologia e mito (1981), (Rome).

Etruria e Lazio arcaico: Atti dell'incontro di studio (1987), (Quaderni di archeologia Etrusco-Italica 15) (Rome).

Fenelli, M. (1984), 'Lavinium', *AL*, 6: 325–44.
―― and Guaitoli, M. (1990), 'Nuovi dati degli scavi di Lavinium', *AL*, 10: 182–93.
Ferenczy, E. (1987), 'Uber das Problem des Inschrift von Satricum', *Gymnasium* 94: 97–108.
Filippi, G. (1979), 'Primo contributo alla conoscenza del territorio Sabino nell'età preistorica e protostorica', *AL*, 2: 111–15.
Firmani, M. A. S. (1979), 'Ricerche nella Sabina Velina e Tiberina', *AL*, 2: 116–21.
Forrest, W. G. (1978), *The Emergence of Greek Democracy* (London).
Forsberg, S. and Thomasson, B.E. (1984) (eds.), *San Giovenale: Materiali e problemi* (Stockholm).
Fowler, W. W. (1899), *The Roman Festivals of the Republic* (London).
―― (1911), *The Religious Experience of the Roman People* (London).
Foxhall, L. and Davies, J. K. (1984), *The Trojan War: Its Historicity and Context* (Bristol).
Franciosi, G. (1984–88), *Ricerche sulla organizzazione gentilizia romana I, II* (Naples).
―― (1989), *Famiglia e persone in Roma antica dall'età arcaica al principato* (Turin).
Francis, E. D. (1990), *Image and Idea in Fifth Century Greece: Art and Literature after the Persian Wars* (London).
Frank, T. (1924), *Roman Buildings of the Republic. An attempt to date them from their materials* (Papers and Monographs of the American Academy in Rome III).
Frankenstein, S. (1979), 'The Phoenicians in the far-west: a function of Neo-Assyrian Imperialism', in Larsen (ed.), 263–94.
Fraschetti, A. (1977), 'A proposito dei Clautie ceretani', *QUCC*, 157–62.
―― (1984), 'Feste dei monti, festa della città', *Studi Storici: Rivista trimestrale dell'Istituto Gramsci*, 25: 35–54.
Frederiksen, M. (1976–7), 'Archaeology in South Italy and Sicily', *Archaeological Reports*, 43–76.
―― (1984), *Campania* (London).
Frier, B. W. (1979), *Libri Annales Pontificorum Maximorum: The origins of the annalistic tradition.* (American Academy at Rome, Papers and Monographs 27, Rome).
Fugazzola Delpino, M. A. (1979), 'The Proto-Villanovan: a survey', in Ridgway and Ridgway, 31–57.
Funaioli, H. (1907), *Grammaticae Romanae Fragmente* (Leipzig).
Fustel De Coulanges, N. D. (1980), *The Ancient City* (London) .
Gabba, E. (1960), 'Studi su Dionigi d'Alicarnasso, I: La costituzione di Romolo', *Athenaeum*, NS 38: 175–252.
Gale, N. H. and Stos-Gale, Z. A. (1987), 'Oxhide Ingots from Sardinia,

References 267

Crete and Cyprus and the Bronze Age copper trade: New scientific evidence', in Balmuth (ed.), 135–78.
Galeotti, L. (1988), 'Considerazioni sul carro a due ruote nell'Etruria e nel Latium Vetus', *AC*, 38–40: 94–104.
Galinsky, G. K. (1969), *Aeneas, Sicily and Rome* (Princeton, NJ).
Garbini, G. (1985), 'Scrittura fenicia nell'età del bronzo dell'Italia centrale', *PP* 446–51.
Garnsey, P. (1988), *Famine and Food Supply in the Graeco-Roman World* (Cambridge).
Gatti, S. (1986), 'Anagnia', *StEtr*, 54: 345–47.
—— (1987), 'Anagni: Rinvenimento di un deposito votivo', *AL*, 8: 253–8.
—— (1988), 'Anagni, S. Cecilia: Seconda e terza campagna di scavo', *AL*, 9: 218–27.
—— (1990), 'Graffiti arcaici dai santuari degli Etruschi', *AL*, 10: 241–7.
—— (1993), *Dives Anagnia: Archeologia nella valle del Sacco* (Rome).
Gelsomino, R. (1975), *Varrone e i sette colli di Roma* (Rome).
—— (1976), 'Varrone e i sette colli di Roma', in *Atti del Congresso internazionale di Studi Varroniani* (Rieti), ii. 379–89.
Gianni A. and Guidi, A. (1985), 'Un modello di ricerca sulle strategie insediamentali delle communità protostoriche laziali', *Riv di Arch* 9: 30–5.
Gierow, P. G. (1964–6), *The Iron Age Culture of Latium*, 2 vols. (Lund).
—— (1983), 'I Colli Albani nel quadro archeologico della civiltà laziale', *Op. Rom.*, 14: 7–18.
Gill, C. and Wiseman T. P. (1993), *Lies and Fiction in the Ancient World* (Exeter).
Ginge, B. (1990), 'Oriental influences on Etruscan polychrome ceramics: the evidence from Satricum', *AnalRomInstDan.*, 19: 7–24.
Giovannini, A. (1985), 'Le sel et la fortune de Rome', *Athenaeum*, 63: 373–86.
Giuliani, C. F. and Verduchi, P. (1987), *L'Area centrale del Foro Romano* (Florence).
Gjerstad, E. (1953–73), *Early Rome*, (6 vols.) (Lund).
—— (1951), 'The Agger of Servius Tullius', *Studies presented to D. M. Robinson* (Saint Louis), i. 413–22.
—— (1954a), 'The Fortifications of early Rome', *Opusc. Rom.*, i. 56 ff.
—— (1954b), 'Sugrundaria. Neue Beitrage zur klassischen Altertumswissenschaft', *Festschrift zum 60 Geburtstag von B. Schweitzer* (Stuttgart), 291–6.
—— (1962), *Legends and Facts of Early Roman History* (Lund).
Gli Etruschi e Roma (1981),

Gnade, M. and Van Barken, E. J. M. (1992), *The South-West Necropolis of Satricum: Excavations 1981–1986*, (Amsterdam).

Gnoli, G. and Vernant, J.-P. (1982) (eds.), *Le Mort, les Morts dans les sociétés anciennes*. (Cambridge).

Gras, M. (1981), 'L'Etrurie minière et la reprise des échanges entre l'Orient et l'Occident: quelques observations', in *L'Etruria Mineraria*, 315–322.

——— (1985), *Trafics Tyrrhéniens Archaïques* (Rome).

——— Rouillard, P., and Teixidor, J. (1989), *L'Univers Phénicien* (Paris).

Greci e Latini nel Lazio antico (1982), Atti del Convegno della Società Italiana per lo Studio dell'Antichità Classica *(SISAC)* (Rome).

Grottanelli, C. (1987), 'Servio Tullio, Fortuna e L'Oriente', *Dd'A*, 71–110.

Guaitoli, M. (1977), 'Considerazioni su alcune città ed insediamenti del Lazio in età protostorica ed arcaica', *MDAI(R)*, 84: 5–25.

——— (1979), 'L'abitato di Castel di Decima', *AL*, 2: 37–40.

——— (1981a), 'Gabii', *PP*, 36 152–73.

——— (1981b), 'Gabii: Osservazioni sulle fasi di sviluppo dell'abitato', *QITA*, 9: 23–54.

——— (1981c), 'Lavinium', *AL*, iv. 287–92.

——— (1984), 'Urbanistica', *AL*, vi. 364–81.

——— Piciarreta, F., and Sommella, P. (1974), 'Contributi per una carta archeologica del territorio di Castel di Decima', *QITA*, 6: 43–130.

Guarducci, M. (1980), 'La cosidetta Fibula Prenestina: Antiquari, Eruditi e Falsari nella Roma dell'Ottocento', *Atti dell'Accademia Nazionale dei Lincei*, Mem. Ser.VIII, xxiv (4), 415–574.

Guidi, A. (1982), 'Sulle prime fasi dell'urbanizzazione nel Lazio protostorico', *Opus*, 1/2: 279–90.

——— (1982a), 'Alcune osservazione sul popolamento dei Colli Albani in età protostorica', *Riv di Arch*, 6: 31–4.

——— (1985), 'An application of the rank-size rule to protostoric settlements in the middle Tyrrhenian area', in Malone and Stoddart (eds.), iii. 217–42.

Hackens, T., Holloway, N. D., and Holloway, R. R. (1983) (eds.), *Crossroads of the Mediterranean* (Louvain).

Harding, A. F. (1984), *The Mycenaeans and Europe* (London).

Harris, W. V. (1989), *Ancient Literacy* (Cambridge, Mass.).

Hedeager, L. (1992), *Iron-Age Societies: From Tribe to State in Northern Europe, 500 BC to AD 700* (Oxford).

Heldring, B. (1984), 'La sesta e la settima campagna di scavo dell'Istituto Olandese di Roma a Satricum', *AL*, 6: 98–103.

——— and Gnade, M. (1987), 'La nona campagna dell'Istituto Olandese di Roma a Satricum', *AL*, 8: 285–93.

Hellström, P. (1975), *Luni sul Mignone* 2.2: *The Zone of the Large Iron Age Building* (Stockholm).
Heltzer, M. and Lipiński, E. (1988) (eds.), *Society and Economy in the Eastern Mediterranean c1500 to c1000 BC* (London).
Hencken, H. (1956), 'Carp's tongue swords in Spain, France and Italy', *Zephyrus*: 7: 125–78.
—— 1968, *Tarquinia, Villanovans and Early Etruscans* (American School of Prehistoric Research, vol. 23).
Herring, E., Whitehouse, R., and Wilkins, J. (1991) (eds.), *Papers of the Fourth Conference of Italian Archaeology* (London).
Heurgon, J. (1969), 'La Magna Graecia e i santuari del Lazio', in *Atti del ottavo convegno di studi sulla Magna Graecia* (Taranto), 9–31.
—— (1977), 'Onomastique étrusque: La denomination gentilice', in N. Duval (ed.), *L'Onomastique Latine* (Paris), 25–32.
Hodder, I. (1982), *Symbols in Action: Ethnoarchaeological Studies of Material Culture* (Cambridge).
—— (1989 (ed.), *The Meaning of Things: Material Culture and Symbolic Expression* (London).
Hölbl, G. (1979), *Beziehungen der ägyptischen Kultur zu Altitalien* (Leiden).
Holland, L. A. (1925), 'The Faliscans in Prehistoric Times' (American Academy in Rome, Papers and Monographs V).
—— (1953), 'Septimontium or Saeptimontium?' *TAPA*, 84: 16–34.
—— (1961), *Janus and the Bridge* (American Academy at Rome, Papers and Monographs XXI).
—— (1962), 'The attribute of Portunus and the Verona Scholion on Aeneid 5.241', in *Hommages à A. Grenier* (Coll. Lat. 58), 817–23.
Holloway, R. R. (1991), *The Archaeology of Ancient Sicily* (London).
—— (1994), *The Archaeology of Early Rome and Latium* (London).
Hooker, J. T. (1976), *Mycenaean Greece* (London)
Humbert, M. (1978), *Municipium et Civitas Sine Suffragio: L'Organisation de la conquête jusqu'à la guerre sociale* (Rome).
Humphreys, S. C. (1978), *Anthropology and the Greeks* (London).
—— (1983), *The Family, Women and Death* (London).
——(1990), Review of I. Morris (1987). *Helios*, 17: 263–8.
—— and King, H. (1981) (eds.), *Mortality and Immortality: The Anthropology and Archaeology of Death* (London).
Haxley, G. L. (1966), *The Early Ionians* (London).
Ichnussa: La Sardegna delle origini all'età classica (1981), (Milan).
Isler, H. P. (1983), 'Ceramisti greci in Etruria in epoca tardogeometrica', *Quaderni ticinesi: Numismatica e antichità classiche*, 12: 9–48.
James, P., Thorpe, I. J., Kokkinos, N., Morkot, R., and Frankish, J.

(1991), *Centuries of Darkness: A Challenge to the Conventional Chronology of Old World Archaeology* (London).

Jannot, J.-R. (1984), *Les Reliefs archaïques de Chiusi* (Rome).

Jarva, E. (1981), 'Area di tombe infantili a Ficana', *AL*, 4: 269–73.

Jehasse, J. L. (1973), *Le nécropole préromaine d'Aléria* (1960–68). (Suppl. Gallia, 15).

Johannowsky, W. (1969), 'Scambi tra ambiente greco e ambiente italico nel periodo precoloniale e protocoloniale e loro conseguenze', *Dd'A*, 31–43, 213–19.

Johnston, A. W. (1979), *Trademarks on Greek Vases* (Warminster).

────── (1985), 'Etruscans in the Greek vase trade', in *Il Commercio Etrusco arcaico*, 249–55.

Jones, G. D. B. (1962–3), 'Capena and the Ager Capenas', *PBSR*, 30: 116–207, 31, 100–58.

Jordan, H. and Hülsen, C. (1878–1907), *Topografie der Stadt Rom im Altertum*, 2 vols. (Berlin).

Kahane, A., Threipland, L. M., and Ward-Perkins, J. B. (1968), 'The Ager Veientanus north and east of Rome', *PBSR*, 36: 1–218.

Karageorghis, V. (1976), *Kition: Mycenaean and Phoenician Discoveries in Cyprus* (London).

────── (1986) (ed.), *Acts of the International Symposium 'Cyprus between the Orient and the Occident'* (Nicosia).

────── (1989) (ed.), *Proceedings of an International Symposium on the Civilisations of the Aegean and their Diffusion in Cyprus and the eastern Mediterranean 2000–600 BC* (Larnaca).

Karo, G. (1898), 'Cenni sulla cronologia preclassica nell'Italia centrale.' *BPI*, 24: 117–61.

────── (1920), 'Orient und Hellas in archaïsche Zeit', *AthMitt* 45: 106–62.

Kearns, E. (1985), 'Change and Continuity in Religious Structures after Cleisthenes', in Cartledge and Harvey (eds.), *Crux: Essays presented to G.E.M. de Ste. Croix* (Exeter), 189–207.

Kilgour, A. (1938), 'The Ambarvalia and the Sacrificium Deae Diae', *Mnemosyne* III. 6: 225–40.

Knoop, R. R. (1987), *Antefixa Satricana: Sixth-Century Architectural Terracottas from the sanctuary of Mater Matuta at Satricum (Le Ferriere)* (Assen and Maastricht).

Kraay, C. M. (1976), *Archaic and Classical Greek Coins* (London).

Lambert, S. D. (1976), 'The Ionian Phyle and Phratry in Archaic and Classical Athens', (unpubl. D.Phil. thesis, Oxford).

────── (1993), *The Phratries of Attica* (Ann Arbor, Mich.).

La Rocca, E. (1974–5), 'Due tombe dell'Esquilino: Alcune novità sul

commercio euboico in Italia centrale nell'VIII sec. a.C.', *Dd'A*, 8: 86–103.
—— (1977), 'Note sulle importazioni greche in territorie laziale nell'VIII sec a.c.', *PP,* 32: 375–97.
—— (1978), 'Crateri in argilla figulina del Geometrico Recente a Vulci: Aspetti della produzione ceramica d'imitazione euboica nel Villanoviano avanzato', *MEFRA*, 90: 465–514.
Larsen, M. T. (1979) (ed.), *Power and Propaganda: A Symposium on Ancient Empires* (Mesopotamia, Copenhagen Studies in Assyriology, vol. 7).
Last, H. (1945), 'The Servian reforms', *JRS*, 35: 30–48.
Le Gall, J. (1953), *Le Tibre, fleuve de Rome dans l'Antiquité* (Paris).
Lenaghan, J. O. (1969), *A Commentary on Cicero's Oration 'De Haruspicum responso'* (Paris).
Lilliu, G. (1986), *Società e cultura in Sardegna nei periodi orientalizzante ed arcaico (fine VIII sec. a.c.–480 a.C.)*: Rapporti fra Sardegna, Fenicii, Etruschi e Greci (Cagliari).
Lo Schiavo, F. (1981), 'Osservazioni sul problema dei rapporti fra Sardegna ed Etruria in età Nuragica', in *L'Etruria Mineraria*, 299–314.
—— (1985), 'Nuragic Sardinia in its Mediterranean Setting: Some recent advances', *Univ. of Edinburgh Dept. of Archaeology Occasional Papers* 12.
—— Macnamara, E., and Vagnetti, L. (1985), 'Late Cypriot imports to Italy and their influence on local bronzework', *PBSR*, 53: 1–71.
Lugli, G. (1930–8), *I monumenti antichi di Roma e suburbio* (Rome).
—— (1933), 'Le mura di Servio Tullio e le cosi dette mura serviane', *Historia: Studi per l'antichità classica*, 7: 3–45.
—— (1952–69), *Fontes ad topographiam veteris urbis Romae pertinentes* (Rome).
—— (1957), *La tecnica edilizia romana* (Rome).
Lulof, P. S. (1991), 'Un gruppo di statue fittili tardo-arcaiche da Satricum (Le Ferriere)', *MedNedInstRom*, 50: 87–101.
Maaskant-Kleibrink, M. and Olde Dubbelink, R. (1985), 'Stepping over and over-stepping thresholds: on the identification of hut-floors, cooking areas and rubbish pits at the site of Satricum', in Malone and Stoddart (eds.), iii. 203–16.
—— (1987) (ed.), *Excavations at Borgo Le Ferriere* (Groningen).
Macnamara, E. (1984), 'A note on the background of some Sardinian bronze typologies, and the exchange of some bronze types between Sardinia and her neighbours during the Italian Late Bronze and Early Iron Ages', *Opus*, iii. (2), 421–7.

Magdelain, A. (1990), *Jus Imperium Auctoritas: études de droit romain*. (Rome).

Malkin, I. (1987), *Religion and Colonization in Ancient Greece* (Leiden).

Malone, C. and Stoddart, S. (1985) (eds.), *Papers in Italian Archaeology IV: The Cambridge Conference* (Oxford).

Mancini, G. (1915), 'Saggio di scavo intorno e solto la chiesa di S. Maria delle Neve e delle SS. Stimmate e scoperta di un tempio volsco', *NSc*, 68–88.

Mangani, E. (1988), 'Recenti indagine ad Antemnae', *AL*, 9: 124–31.

Marazzi, M. and Tusa, S. (1979), 'Die mykenische Penetration im westlichen Mittelmeerraum', *Klio*, 61: 309–51.

Marazzi, M., Tusa, S., and Vagnetti, L. (1986) (eds.), *Traffici micenei nel mediterraneo: Problemi storici e documentazione archeologica* (Taranto).

Markoe, G. (1985), *Phoenician Bronze and Silver Bowls from Cyprus and the Mediterranean* (Univ. of California Publications, Classical Studies).

Marshall, F.H. (1911), *Catalogue of the Jewellery, Greek, Etruscan and Roman in the British Museum* (London).

Martinori, E. (1931), *Via Salaria* (Rome).

Matthäus, H. (1989), 'Cypern und Sardinien im frühen 1. Jahrtausend v. Chr.', in Peltenburg (ed.), 244–55.

Mauss, M. (1954), *The Gift (London)*

Mazzolani, M. (1969), *Anagnia* (Rome).

Meiggs, R. (1973), *Roman Ostia* (Oxford).

Mele, A. (1979), *Il commercio greco arcaico: Prexis ed emporie*. (Cahiers du Centre Jean Bérard IV, Naples).

Melis, F. and Rathje, A. (1984), 'Considerazioni sullo studio dell'architettura domestica arcaica', *AL*, 6: 382–95.

Mengarelli, R. and Paribeni, R. (1909), 'Norma: Scavi sulle terrazze sostenute da mura poligonali presso l'abbazia di Valvisciolo', *NSc*, 241–60.

Meyer, J. C. (1980), 'Roman history in the light of the import of Attic vases to Rome and Etruria in the 6th and 5th centuries BC', *Analecta Romana Instituti Danici*, 9: 47–67.

—— (1983), *Pre-Republican Rome (Analecta Romana Instituti Danici*, Suppl. XI).

Michels, A. K. (1953), 'The Topography and Interpretation of the Lupercalia', *TAPA*, 84: 35–59.

Millett, M. (1990), *The Romanization of Britain: An Essay in Archaeological Interpretation* (Cambridge).

Mitchell, R. E. (1980), *Patricians and Plebeians: The Origins of the Roman State* (Ithaca, NY).

Modes du contact et processus de transformation dans les sociétés antiques (1983), Actes du Colloque du Cortone (24–30 mai 1981) organisé par *la*

Scuola Normale superiore et l'École Française de Rome, avec la collaboration de la Centre de Recherches d'Histoire Ancienne de l'Université de Besançon (Collection de l'École Française de Rome 67) (Pisa and Rome).
Momigliano, A. (1963), 'An Interim Report on the origins of Rome', *JRS*, 53: 95–121.
——— and Schiavone, A. (1988), *Storia di Roma*, vol. 1 (Rome).
Mommsen, T. (1859), *Die römische Chronologie bis auf Caesar*, 2nd edn. (Berlin).
——— (1864–79), *Römische Forschungen* (Berlin).
Montelius, O. (1885–1910), *La Civilisation primitive en Italie depuis l'introduction des metaux I, II* (Stockholm).
——— (1903), *Die typologische Methode* (Stockholm).
——— (1912), *Die vorklassische Chronologie Italiens* (Stockholm).
Moretti, L. (1984), 'Epigraphia 26: Sulle iscrizioni greche di Gravisca', *RFIC*, 112 (314–18).
Morris, I. (1986), 'Gift and Commodity in Archaic Greece', *Man, NS* 21: 1–17.
——— (1987), *Burial and the Ancient Society: The Rise of the Greek City-State* (Cambridge).
——— (1992), *Death Ritual and Social Structure in Classical Antiquity* (Cambridge).
Morselli, E. and Tortorici, F. (1982), *Ardea* (Florence).
Müller-Karpe, H. (1959a), *Beitrage zur Chronologie der Urnenfelderzeit nördlich und sudlich der Alpen* (Berlin).
——— (1959b), *Vom Anfang Roms* (Heidelberg).
——— (1962), *Zur Stadtwerdung Roms* (Heidelberg).
Murray, O. (1990) (ed.), *Sympotica: A Symposium on the Symposion* (Oxford).
——— (1990) (eds.), *The Greek City from Homer to Alexander* (Oxford).
Murray Threipland, L. and Torelli, M. (1970), 'A semi-subterranean Etruscan building in the Casale Pian Roseto (Veio) area', *PBSR*, 38: 62–123.
Musti, D. (1970), *Tendenze nella storiografia romana e greca su Roma arcaica: Studi su Livio e Dionigi d'Alicarnasso* (Rome).
——— (1981), 'Etruschi e Greci nella rappresentazione dionisiana delle origine di Roma', in *Gli Etruschi a Roma*, 23–44.
Nielsen, I. and Zahle, J. (1985), 'The Temple of Castor and Pollux on the Forum Romanum. A preliminary report on the Scandinavian excavations 1983–85 (I)', *Acta Arch*, 56 [1987]: 1–29.
Nilsson, M. P. (1955–61), *Geschichte der griechischen Religion* (Munich).
Olshausen, E. (1978), '"Uber die römischen Ackerbruder". Geschichte eines Kultes', *ANRW* 2.16.1: 820–32.

Les Origines de la république romaine (1967), (Entretiens Foundation Hardt XIII) (Geneva).

O'Shea, J. M. (1984), *Mortuary Variability: An Archaeological Investigation* (London).

Osborne, R. (1987), *Classical Landscape with Figures: The Ancient Greek City and its Countryside* (London).

Østenberg, C. F. (1967), *Luni sul Mignone e problemi della preistoria d'Italia* (Lund).

———— (1975), *Case Etrusche di Acquarossa* (Rome).

Otto, W. F. (1909), 'Römische Sondergötter', *RM*, 64: 449–68.

Pacciarelli, M. (1979), 'Topografia dell'insediamento dell'età del bronzo recente nel Lazio', *AL*, 2: 161–70.

Pallottino, M. (1939), 'Sulle facies culturali arcaiche dell'Etruria', *StEtr*, 13: 85–129.

———— (1940), 'Appunti di protostoria Etrusca e Latina', *StEtr*, 14: 27–32.

———— (1955), 'Le origini storiche dei popoli italici', in *Relazioni del X Congresso Internazionale di Scienze Storiche*, ii. 3–60.

———— (1960), 'Le origini di Roma', *Arch. Class.*, 12: 1–50.

———— (1969), 'Caere. L'Ermeneutica tra due documenti-chiave', *StEtr*, 37: 79–91.

———— (1977), 'Servius Tullius à la lumiére des nouvelles découvertes archéologiques et épigraphiques', *CRAI*, 216–35.

———— Colonna, G., Vlad Borelli, L., and Garbini, G. (1964), 'Scavi nel santuario etrusco di Pyrgi. Relazione preliminare della settima campagna 1964 e scoperte di tre lamine d'oro inscritte in etrusco e in punico', *Arch. Class.*, 16: 49–117.

———— Colonna, G., Prayon, F., Cristofani, M., De Simone, C., Rix, H., Tovar, A., Bloch, R., Krauskopf, I., and Von Vacano, O.-W. (1981), *Die Göttin von Pyrgi: Akten des Colloquiums zum Thema. Archäologische, Linguistiche, und religiongeschichtliche Aspeckte, Tübingen 1979* (Florence).

Palmer, R. E. A. (1969), *The King and the Comitium* (Historia Einzelschriften 11).

———— (1970), *The Archaic Community of the Romans* (Cambridge).

———— (1974), *Roman Religion and Roman Empire: Five Essays* (Philadelphia).

———— (1990), 'Cults of Hercules, Apollo Caelispex and Fortuna in and around the Roman Cattle-Market', *JRA*, 3: 234–44.

Pareti, L. (1947), *La Tomba Regolini-Galassi del Museo Gregoriano Etrusco e la Civiltà dell'Italia Centrale nel sec. VII a.C.* (Rome).

Park Poe, J. (1978), 'The Septimontium and Subura', *TAPA*, 108: 147–54.

References

Pavolini, C. (1981), 'Ficana: Edificio sulle pendici sud-occidentali di Monte Cugno', *AL*, 4: 258–68.

Peltenburg, E. (1989) (ed.), *Early Society in Cyprus* (Edinburgh).

Peroni, R. (1979a), 'L'insediamento subappeninico della Valle del Foro e il problema della continuità di insediamento tra l'età del Bronzo Recente e quella Finale nel Lazio', *AL*, 2: 171–6.

────── (1979b), 'Le ultime pagine di Ferrante Rittatore Vonwiller sul "Protovillanoviano"', in *Il Bronzo Finale*, 32–46.

────── (1979c), 'From Bronze Age to Iron Age: Economic, historical and social considerations', in Ridgway and Ridgway, 7–30.

────── (1980) (ed.), *Il Bronzo Finale in Italia: Studi a cura di Renato Peroni, con gli Atti del Centro Studi di Protostoria 1978–9* (Bari).

────── (1981) (ed.), *Necropoli e usi funerari nell'età del ferro* (Bari).

────── (1988), 'Comunità e insediamento in Italia fra Età del bronzo e prima Età del ferro', in Momigliano and Schiavone, 7–37.

Perret, J. (1942), *Les Origines de la légende troyenne de Rome* (Paris).

Peruzzi, E. (1980), *Mycenaeans in Early Latium* (Rome).

Pesce, G. (1961), *Sardegna Punica* (Cagliari).

Pini, E. and Seripi, A. (1986), 'Per un tentativo di ricostruzione dei territori dei centri protostorici laziali', *Riv di Arch.*, 10: 15–21.

Pinza, G. (1905), *Monumenti primitivi di Roma a del Lazio antico* (MonAnt 15).

Platner, S. B. and Ashby, T. (1929), *A Topographical Dictionary of Ancient Rome* (London).

Pohl, I. (1972), *The Iron Age Necropolis of Sorbo at Cerveteri* (Stockholm).

────── (1977), *The Iron Age Habitation in Area E (San Giovenale)* (Stockholm).

────── (1980), 'San Giovenale da villaggio protovillanoviano a città etrusca: Due sopravvivenze tipologiche ed il loro significato per la cronologia delle fasi culturali', *PP*, 35: 131–42.

Popoli e Civiltà dell' Italia Antica (1974–1992).

Postgate, J. N. (1979), 'The economic structure of the Assyrian empire', in Larsen (ed.), 193–221.

Pot, T. (1987), 'Two Etruscan gold dental appliances found in 19th century excavations at Satricum and Praeneste', *Mededelingen van het Nederlands Instituut te Rome*, 12: 35–40.

Potter, T. (1976), *A Faliscan Town in South Etruria: Excavations at Narce 1966–71* (London).

────── (1979), *The Changing Landscape of S. Etruria* (London).

Poucet, J. (1960), 'Le Septimontium et la Succusa chez Festus et Varron', *BullInstBelge*, 32: 25–73.

Poucet, J. (1967a), *Recherches sur la legende sabine des origines de Rome* (Louvain).
—— (1967b), 'L'importance du terme "colli" pour l'étude du développement de la Rome archaïque', *AC*, 36: 99–115.
—— (1985), *Les origines de Rome* (Brussels).
Pouthier, P. (1981), *Ops et la conception de l'abondance dans la religion romaine jusqu'à la mort d'Auguste* (Rome).
Preller, R. (1858), *Römische Mythologie* (Berlin).
Prosdocimi, A. L. (1979), 'Studi sul Latino arcaico', *StEtr.* 47: 173–221.
Purcell, N. (1989), 'Rediscovering the Roman Forum', *JRA*, 2: 156–66.
Quilici, L. (1979), *Roma primitiva e le origini della civiltà laziale* (Rome).
Quilici, L. and Quilici Gigli, S. (1978), *Antemnae* (Rome).
—— (1980), *Crustumerium* (Rome).
—— (1986), *Fidenae* (Rome).
—— (1987), 'L'Abitato di Monte Carbolino', *AL*, 8: 259–77.
—— (1988), 'Ricerche su Norba', *AL*, 9: 233–56.
Raaflaub, K. (1986) (ed.), *Social Struggles in Archaic Rome: Perspectives on the Roman Conflict of the Orders* (Berkeley and Los Angeles, Calif.).
Radke, G. (1972), 'Acca Laurentina und die Fratres Arvales: Ein Stück römisch-sabinischer Frühgeschichte', *ANRW*, 1(2): 421–41.
—— (1973), 'Viae Publicae Romanae', R. E. Pauly-Wissowa, *Real-Encyclopaedie*, Suppl. XIII (Munich) cc164457.
Rallo, A. (1989) (ed.), *Le Donne in Etruria* (Rome).
Rasenna: Storia e Civiltà degli Etruschi (1986), (Milan).
Rasmussen, T. (1979), *Bucchero Pottery from Southern Etruria* (Cambridge).
Rathje, A. (1979), 'Oriental Imports in Etruria in the 8th and 7th centuries B.C.: Their origins and implications', in Ridgway and Ridgway, 145–83.
—— (1983) 'A banquet service from the Latin city of Ficana', *Analecta Romana Instituti Danici*, 12: 7–29.
—— (1990), 'The adoption of the Homeric banquet in Central Italy in the orientalizing period', in O. Murray (ed.), 279–88.
Rendeli, M. (1989), '"Muratori, ho fretta di erigere questa casa" (Ant. Pal. 14.136): Concorrenza fra formazioni urbane dell'Italia centrale tirrenica nella costruzione di edifici di culto arcaico', *RIASA*, 49–68.
—— (1991), 'Sulla nascita delle comunità urbane in Etruria meridionale', *AION ArchStAnt*, 13: 9–45.
Renfrew, C. (1977) (ed.), *The Explanation of Cultural Change: Models in Prehistory* (London).
Renfrew, C. and Cherry, J. F. (1986) (eds.), *Peer-Polity Interaction and Socio-political Change* (Cambridge).

Richard, J.-C. (1976), 'Le Culte du "Sol" et les "Aurelii": A propos de Paul Fest. p22L', in *Mélanges à J. Heurgon* (Rome), ii. 915–25.
Ridgway, D. (1969), 'Il contesto indigeno in Etruria prima e dopo l'arrivo dei Greci', *Dd'A*, 3: 23–30.
────── (1988), 'Italy from the Bronze Age to the Iron Age' and 'The Etruscans', *CAH* iv. 623–33 and 634–75.
────── (1991), 'Understanding Oxhides', *Antiquity*, 65: 420–2.
────── (1992), *The First Western Greeks* (Cambridge).
────── and Ridgway, F. R. (1979), *Italy before the Romans* (London).
────── Deriu, A., and Boitani, F. (1985), 'Provenance and firing techniques of Geometric pottery from Veii: A Mossbauer Investigation', *ABSA*, 80: 139–50.
Rittatore Vonwiller, F. (1975), 'La Cultura Protovillanoviana with Ripostigli "Protovillanoviani" dell'Italia Peninsulare (M.A. Fugazzola Delpino)', *PCIA*, IV, 11–41.
Rix, H. (1963), *Das etruskische Cognomen: Untersuchungen zu System, Morphologie und Verwendung der Personennamen auf des jüngeren Inschriften Nordetruriens* (Wiesbaden).
────── (1972), 'Zum Ursprung des römisch-mittelitalischen Gentilnamensystem', *ANRW*, 1 (2): 700–58.
Robertson, N. (1975) (ed.), *The Archaeology of Cyprus: Recent Developments* (Park Ridge, NJ).
Roma arcaica e le recente scoperte archeologiche (1980), Giornale di studio in orore di U. Coli (Milan).
Roussel, D. (1976), *Tribu et Cité: Etudes sur les groupes sociaux dans les cités grecques aux époques archaïque et classique* (Paris).
Rowlands, M., Larsen, M., and Kristiansen, K. (1987) (eds.), *Centre and Periphery in the Ancient World* (Cambridge).
Ruggiero, I. (1990), 'La cinta muraria presso il Foro Boario in età arcaica e medio Repubblicana', *AL*, 10: 23–30.
Rykwert, J. (1988), *The Idea of a Town: The Anthropology of Urban Form in Rome, Italy and the Ancient World* (Cambridge Mass.).
Säflund, G. (1932), *Le Mura di Roma Repubblicana* (Acta Inst. Rom. Regni Sueciae I, Lund).
Salmon, E. T. (1953), 'Rome and the Latins', *Phoenix*, 93–104 and 123–35.
Santoro, P. (1985), 'Le necropli della Sabina Tiberina da Colle del Forno a Otricoli', *Dd'A*, 67–76.
Saulnier, C. (1980), *L'Armée et la Guerre dans le monde Etrusco-Romain (VIIIe-IVe sec)* (Paris).
Scholz, U. (1970), *Studien zum altitalische und altrömischen Marskult und Marsmythos* (Heidelberg).
Schulze, W. (1904), *Zur Geschichte lateinischer Eigennamen* (Berlin).

Sciortino, I. and Segala, E. (1990), 'Rinvenimento di un deposito votivo presso il clivo Capitolino', *AL*, 10: 17–22.

Scott-Ryberg, I. (1940), *An Archaeological Record of Rome from the 7th to the 2nd centuries BC* (London).

Scullard, H. H. (1981), *Festivals and Ceremonies of the Roman Republic* (London).

Serra Ridgway, F. (1991), 'Etruscan art and culture: a bibliography 1978–1990', *JRA*, 4: 5–27.

Shanks, M. and Tilley, C. (1987), *Re-Constructing Archaeology: Theory and Practice* (Cambridge).

Sherratt, A. (forthcoming), 'The origins of commerce: A perspective on ancient trade'.

Sherratt. S. and Sherratt, A. (1993), 'The Growth of the Mediterranean Economy in the early first millennium BC', *World Archaeology*, 24 (3): 361–78.

Sherwin-White, A. N. (1971), *The Roman Citizenship*, 2nd edn. (Oxford).

Shipp, G. P. (1951), 'Two notes on Latin vocabulary', *Glotta*, 31: 244–6.

Siewert, P. (1982), *Die Trittyen Attikas und die Heeresreform des Kleisthenes* (Munich).

Silver, M. (1985), *Economic Structures of the Ancient Near East* (London).

Smith, T. R. (1987), *Mycenaean Trade and Interaction in the West Central Mediterranean 1600–1000 BC* (Oxford).

Snodgrass, A. (1980), *Archaic Greece* (London).

Sommella Mura, A. (1977), 'La decorazione del tempio arcaico', *PP*, 32: 62–128.

—— (1981), 'Il gruppo di Eracle e Atena', *PP*, 36: 59–64.

Sourvinou-Inwood, C. (1983), 'A trauma in flux: death in the 8th century and after', in R. Hägg (ed.), *The Greek Renaissance of the 8th Century BC: Tradition and Innovation* (Stockholm), 33–49.

Spivey, N. (1987), *The Micali Painter and his Followers* (Oxford).

—— and Stoddart, S. (1990), *Etruscan Italy* (London).

Staccioli, R. (1976), 'Considerazioni sui complessi monumentali di Murlo e di Acquarossa', in *Mélanges à J. Heurgon* (Rome), ii. 961–72.

Stara-Tedde, G. (1905), 'I boschi sacri dell'antica Roma', *BullCom*, 3: 189–232.

Steinby, E. M. (1989) (ed.), *Lacus Juturnae* I (Rome).

Steingräber, S. (1986) (ed.), *Etruscan Paintings: Catalogue raisonée of Etruscan Wall-painting* (New York).

Stibbe, C. M. (1984–5), 'Satricum: Sporadic finds from the excavations 1977–80.' *NSc*, 221–52.

—— (1987), 'Satricum e Pometia: Due nome per la stessa città', *MedNedInstRom* 47 NS 12: 7–16.

—— Colonna, G., De Simone, C., and Versnel, H. S. (1980), *Lapis*

References 279

Satricanus: Archaeological, Linguistic and Historical Aspects of the new inscription from Satricum (The Hague).
Stoddart, S. and Whitley, J. (1988), 'The social context of literacy in archaic Greece and Etruria,' *Antiquity*, 62: 761–72.
Stopponi, S. (1985) (ed.), *Case e Palazzi d'Etruria* (Milan).
Ström, I (1983), Review of Rasmussen 1979, *Gnomon*, 53: 789–92.
Swaddling, J. (1985) (ed.), *Italian Iron Age Artefacts in the British Museum* (London).
Syme, R. (1980), *Some Arval Brethren* (Oxford).
Tatton-Brown, V. (1989) (ed.), *Cyprus and the East Mediterranean in the Iron Age* (London).
Taylor, L. R. (1960), *The Voting Districts of the Roman Republic: The Thirty-Five Urban and Rural Tribes* (American Academy at Rome Papers and Monographs XX).
—— (1966) *Roman Voting Assemblies* (Ann Arbor, Mich.).
Il Tevere e le altri vie d'acque nel Lazio antico (1986), *AL* 7 (2).
Thomas, R. (1992), *Literacy and Orality in Ancient Greece* (Cambridge).
Thomasson, B. E. (ed.) (1967–72), *San Giovenale*, vol. 1. (Stockholm).
Thomsen, R. (1980), *King Servius Tullius: A Historical Synthesis* (Copenhagen).
Todd, M. (1978), *The Walls of Rome* (London).
Toms, J. (1986), 'The relative chronology of the Villanovan cemetery of Quattro Fontanili at Veii', AION ArchStAnt 8: 41–97.
Torelli, M. (1971), 'Il santuario di Hera a Gravisca', *PP*, 26: 44–67.
—— (1974–5), 'Tre studi di storia etrusca', *Dd'A*, 8: 3–78.
—— (1977), 'Il santuario greco a Gravisca', *PP*, 32: 398–458.
—— (1979), 'Rome et l'Etrurie archaique', in *Terre et paysans dépendants dans les sociétés antiques* (Toulouse), 251–312.
—— (1982), 'Per la definizione del commercio greco-orientale: il caso di Gravisca', *PP*, 37: 304–25.
—— (1983), 'Polis e Palazzo: Architettura, ideologia e artigianato greco in Etruria tra VII e VI sec. a.C.', in *Architecture et Société de l'archaisme grec à la fin de la république romaine* (Rome), 471–500.
—— (1984), *Lavinio e Roma: Riti iniziatici e matrimonio tra archeologia e storia* (Rome).
—— (1985), *Storia degli Etruschi* (Rome).
—— (1987), *La Società Etrusca: L'Età arcaica, l'età classica* (Rome).
Toubert, P. (1973), *Les Structures du Latium médiéval: Le Latium méridional et la Sabine du IXe siècle à la fin du XIIe siècle* (Rome).
Treuil, R., Darcque, P., Poursat, J.-C., and Touchais, G. (1989), *Les Civilisations égéennes du Néolithique et de l'age du Bronze* (Paris).
Tronchetti, C. (1973), 'Contributo al problema delle rotte commerciale arcaiche', *Dd'A*, 7: 5–16.

Trümpy, C. (1983), 'La fibule de Préneste: Document inestimable ou falsification?' *MH*, XL: 65–74.

Ucko, P. J. (1969–70), 'Ethnography and archaeological interpretation of funerary remains', *World Archaeology*, 1: 262–80.

────── Tringham, R., and Dimbleby, G. W. (1972) (eds.), *Man, Settlement and Urbanism* (London).

Ulf, C. (1982), *Das römische Lupercalienfest: Ein Modellfall für Methodenprobleme in der Altertumwissenschaft* (Darmstadt).

Vagnetti, L. (1970), 'I Micenei in Italia', *PP*, 359–80.

────── (1982) (ed.), *XXII Convegno di studi sulla Magna Graecia 'Magna Graecia e mondo Miceneo: nuovi documenti'* (Taranto).

────── (1983), 'I Micenei in Occidente: Dati acquisiti e prospettive future', in *Modes du contacts*, 165–85.

Valditara, G. (1986), 'Aspetti religiosi del regno di Servio Tullio', *Studia et Documenta Historiae et Juris*, 52: 395–434.

Vallet, G. (1982) (ed.), *La céramique grecque ou de tradition grecque au VIIIe siècle en Italie Centrale* (Naples).

Van Berchem, D. (1959/60), 'Hercule Melqart à l'Ara Maxima', *RendPontAcc*, 32: 61–8.

────── (1960), 'Trois cas d'asylie archaique', *MH*, 17: 21–33.

────── (1967), 'Sanctuaires d'Hercule Melqart: Contributions à l'étude de l'expansion phénicienne en Méditerranée', *Syria*, 44: 73–109, 307–38.

Versnel, H. S. (1970), *Triumphus: An Inquiry into the Origin, Development and Meaning of the Roman Triumph* (Leiden).

────── (1982), 'Die neue Inschrift von Satricum in historischer Sicht', *Gymnasium*, 89: 193–235.

Verzar, M. (1980), 'Pyrgi e l'Afrodite di Cipro: Considerazioni sul programma decorativo del Tempio B', *MEFRA*, 92: 35–86.

Walbank, F. W. (1957), *A Historical Commentary on Polybius* (Oxford).

Warden, P. G. (1973), 'The "Colline Metallifere": Prolegomena to the study of mineral exploitation in Central Italy', in Hackens, Holloway, and Holloway (eds.), 349–64.

Ward-Perkins, J. B. (1961), 'Veii: The historical topography of the ancient city', *PBSR*, 29: 1–123.

Watson, A. (1971), *The Law of Succession in the later Roman Republic* (Oxford).

────── (1972), 'Roman private law and the Leges Regiae', *JRS*, 62: 100–5.

────── (1975), *Rome of the XII Tables: Persons and Property* (Princeton, NJ).

Weinstock, S. (1971), *Divus Julius* (Oxford).

Wertime, T. A. and Muhly, J. D. (1980) (eds.), *The Coming of the Age of Iron* (London).

References

Westrup, C. W. (1954), 'Sur les gentes et les curiae de la royauté primitive', *RIDA*, 3 ser. 1: 43–73.
Whitehouse, R. (1973), 'The earliest towns in peninsular Italy', in Renfrew (ed.), 617–24.
Whitley, J. (1988), 'Early States and Hero-Cults: a re-appraisal', *JHS*, 108: 173–82.
Whittaker, C. R. (1974), 'The Western Phoenicians: Colonization and Assimilation', *PCPS*, 20: 58–79.
—— (1988) (ed.), *Pastoral Economies in Classical Antiquity* (Cambridge).
Wieacker, F. (1988), *Römische Rechtsgeschichte: Quellenkunde, Rechtsbildung, Jurisprudenz und Rechtsliteratur. I: Einleitung; Quellenkunde; Frühzeit und Republik* (Munich).
Wieselgren, T. (1969), *Luni sul Mignone 2.1: The Iron Age Settlement on the Acropolis* (Lund).
Wikander, C. (1986), *Sicilian Architectural Terracottas: A Reappraisal* (Stockholm).
—— and Wikander, O. (1990), 'The early monumental complex at Acquarossa: a preliminary report', *Opusc.Rom.*, 18: 189–205.
Wikander, O. (1988), 'Ancient Roof-Tiles: Use and Function.' *Opusc. Ath.*, 17: 203–16.
Wikander, O. and Roos, P. (1986), *Architettura Etrusca nel Viterbese: Ricerche svedesi a San Giovenale e Acquarossa 1956–86* (Rome).
Wilkins, J. (1990), 'Nation and Language in Ancient Italy: problems of the linguistic evidence', *Accordia Research Papers*, 1: 53–72.
Wissowa, G. (1904), 'Septimontium e Subura', in *Gesammelte Abhandlungen zur römischen Religions- und Stadtgeschichte* (Munich), 230–52.
—— (1912), *Religion und Kultus der Romer* (Munich).
Worsaae, J. J. A. (1849), *The Primeval Antiquities of Denmark* (London).
York, M. (1986), *The Festival Calendar of Numa Pompilius* (New York).
Zevi, F. (1977), 'Alcuni aspetti della necropoli di Castel di Decima', *PP*, 32: 241–73.

INDEX

Roman numerals in the index refer to periods in Latial chronology; see Chronology p. xii.

Acqua Acetosa Laurentina 239
  III 78, 81
  IVA 90, 91
  IVB 99
  6th century 132–3, 195
Acquarossa 143–4, 149, 159, 175
Aegina 145
ager arcefinius 206
Ager Gabinus 209–10
Ager Peregrinus 209
agriculture 32, 88–9, 114–22, 141, 158, 162, 189, 225
Alalia, battle of 149
Alba Longa (Alban Hills) 53, 173
Alban Hills 239
  I 30, 37–40, 122–3
  II 46, 49–54
  III 77
  IVA 90
  6th century 164–72, 216
Alföldi, A. 217–18
Ambarvalia 157, 209
amber:
  Late Bronze Age 26, 28
  I 43
  III 79
  IVA 95
Amburbium 157
Ammerman, A. 101
amphictyony 216
Ampolo, A. 153, 215
Anagnia 138, 241
Ancus Marcius 133, 173, 180
Antemnae 241
  I 36
  III 83
  6th century 129–30, 205, 208–9
Antium (Anzio) 81
Aphrodite 146

Appaduri, A. 18
Appius Claudius 191, 214
Aprilia 38, 122
Ardea 241–3
  Sub-Apennine 34, 122
  I 34–5, 45
  II 55, 56
  III 79, 81, 120
  IVA 86
  6th century 135–6, 152, 219
  Rimessone hoard 38, 40–1
Argeorum Sacraria 156, 164
Argos, Argolid 195, 224
Aricia 208, 211, 217–18, 220
army 111, 144, 198, 205–7
artisans 33, 40, 41–2, 47, 65–6, 103, 118
  bronzesmiths 29, 30, 42, 65
  potters 18, 40, 41–2, 65, 78
Astarte 146, 160–2
Athens, Attica 108, 113, 145, 147, 160, 190, 195, 206–7, 224
Attus Clausus, *see* Appius Claudius
augurs 202
A. Gell. 5. 12. 1: 201

barley 54
beans 54, 116
Bedini, A. 78, 99
Beloch, J. 155
Bietti-Sestieri, A. M. 26 n., 33–4, 47–8, 57–71, 78, 82–3
Binford, L. 10–12, 58
bone:
  Late Bronze Age 26
  III 79
  IVA 95
  6th century 138
Boni, G. 153
Bovillae (Alban Hills) 202

bronze:
  Late Bronze Age 26, 28, 30–1, 32, 47, 123
  I 49
  II 50–1
  III 78–9
  IVA 90, 95
  6th century 132, 135, 137, 138, 144–5
  Rimessone hoard, see Ardea
bronze figurines 132, 135, 137

Cacus 116
Caere Cerveteri 17, 24, 38, 46, 47, 51, 55, 90, 94–5, 120, 144, 145–6, 148, 226
  Sorbo necropolis 45
Calatia 76
calendar 97, 171
Campania 55, 56, 75–7, 84, 85, 88, 91, 108, 135, 147, 149, 188, 225
Campo del Fico 77
Campo di S. Susanna (Rieti) 27
Capua 76
Caracupa 61
Carandini, A. 153, 155
Carthage 26, 149, 161–2, 202, 228
Cassius Hemina fr. 19P 200
Castel di Decima 243
  II 56, 60
  III 77, 78, 81, 83, 123
  IVA 85, 90, 91–2
  IVB 99
  6th century 208
Castiglione (Gabii) 54, 61, 62, 64, 243
cattle 117, 182
Ceres Liber Liberaque 188–9
  see also Rome, temples
Cerveteri, see Caere
chariots 80, 91, 92, 95, 110
Chiarucci, P. 51
chronology 21–3
Cicero:
  De Div. 2. 36. 77: 168
  De Domo sua 13. 34, 14. 36, 14. 37: 200
  De Har. resp. 15. 32: 199
  De Leg. 2. 22: 202
Circeii 138
Clarke, D. 10–12
Cleisthenes 204, 206
clientes 190–1, 207, 214, 226
Coarelli, F. 102, 150–84
coinage, currency 20, 79, 144–5
Collatia 208

Colle della Mola (Doganella di Rocca Priora) 34
Collegia 198
Colle Ripoli 34, 37
Colle S. Magno (Frosinone) 34
Colonna, G. 21–2, 42, 51
Comitia Calata 169–71, 183, 197, 200
Comitia Centuriata 111, 205
Comitia Curiata 169–71
commercium 211–13
compitum 194
conubium 211–13
copper 28
Cordano, F. 78
Corinth 108, 145, 147, 160, 186, 210
Cornell, T. 203, 211, 221
Crichi 75
Crifò, G. 214
Crustumerium 243–4
  I 36
  II 53, 56–7, 64
  III 77
  IVA 86
  6th century 131–2, 188, 192, 205, 208
Cumae 55, 75–6, 80, 94
Cures Sabina 57
Curia Calabra 169–71, 197
curiae 169–71, 176–7
Cyprus 25, 26, 27, 74, 225

Dea Dia 168, 180
Delos 219
Delphi 94, 149, 219
Demaratus 210
dental fittings 103–4
De Vir. Ill. II. 2: 171
Dion. Hal.:
  2. 7. 4: 197
  3. 38: 133
  4. 14. 3: 195
  4. 26. 5: 217
  4. 63: 138
  5. 25. 2: 171
  5. 40: 131 n.
  6. 95. 2: 212
  8. 14: 138
Dioscuri 135, 165
Diósdi, G. 192
Douglas, M. 19
drainage 115, 131, 158, 205
Duenos vase 103, 159, 234
duoviri sacris faciundis 202

Index

Egeria 158
Egerius Baebius/Egerius Laevius 217
Egyptian faience 28, 76, 90, 92, 95
Elba 31, 49, 75, 148
Ephesos, temple of Artemis 163, 217
Equus October 156, 172, 175–8
ercto non cito 192
Eretria 195
Etruria 24, 29–31, 44–9, 75–7, 93–7, 108, 111, 118–20, 122, 143–9, 151, 160, 175, 178, 183–4, 188
Euboea 80, 92, 120, 221
exilium 214–15

Falerii 132
Faunus 201
Feriae Latinae 110, 219–20
Festus:
  78L 200
  274L 200
  284L 199
fetials 202
fibulae 26, 107, 109
  I 38, 39, 41
  II 50–1, 55, 62
  III 79
  IVA 90, 91, 93–5
Ficana 244
  I 38, 122
  II 56
  IVA 86–8, 90, 110, 111, 120, 124
  6th century 133–4, 144, 159, 208
Ficulea 208
Fidenae 244–5
  Middle Bronze Age 36, 54, 61
  I 36, 54, 123
  II 53, 56–7, 64
  III 77, 83
  IVA 86
  IVB 104
  6th century 130–1, 154, 186, 188, 192, 205, 208–9, 220
fish 54, 117, 158
flamen Dialis 169
flamen Martialis 169
flamen Quirinalis 169
Foedus Cassianum 211–15
Forrest, G. 190, 220
fortifications 56, 81, 86, 110, 113, 137, 140–1, 152–5, 230
Fortuna 146, 151, 160–2, 173
  see also Servius Tullius; Rome, Forum Boarium, S. Omobono

Fossa di Settebagni 36
Francavilla Marittima 75
Franciosi, G. 194, 213
Fratres Arvales 157, 168
Frattesina 26, 29

Gabii 131, 132, 208, 209–10, 245
Gaius *Inst.* 3. 154: 192
Gaul 147, 228
Gelon of Syracuse 151
Gennaro, F. di 48
genos 193, 221
gens, gentilitial society 33–4, 63–4, 82–3, 123–5, 189–210, 213–15
  Aurelia 202
  Calpurnia 199
  Claudia 199–200, 209, 210; see also Appius Claudius
  Fabia 193, 200–1
  Julia 201–2
  Pinaria 199
  Potitia 199
  Quintilia 200
  Sergia 208–9
  Valeria 174; see also Publius Valerius Publicola
Gierow, P. 22, 45, 52
gift-giving 20–1, 33, 43, 85, 93–7, 114, 120–1
Gjerstad, E. 22, 45, 52, 153–4
glass, glass paste 26, 138
goats, see sheep
gold:
  I 39
  II 60
  III 79
  IVA 85, 92, 93–5
  IVB 103, 106
Gras, M. 146–7
Gravisca 145–7, 184, 220, 227
Grottaferrata (Alban Hills) 52
Guaitoli, M. 54–6
Guidi, A. 48–9

hektemorage 113, 191
Hephaestus 171
Heracles/Hercules 116, 161–2, 164, 182, 183–4, 199, 201
Hexapolis 219–21
Hodder, I. 12–13, 18
Homer *Od.*:
  9. 116 ff.: 88
  19. 225 ff.: 94

houses (stone-built):
  IVA 86
  IVB 100–1, 111
  6th century 85, 133–4, 138–40, 141, 144
Humbert, M. 211
huts:
  I 35–6
  II 55
  III 77–8, 81
  IVA 86–7
  IVB 100–1
hut-urns 25, 35, 38–9, 42, 62

Ilithyia, see Leucothea
infant burials 19, 61, 63, 78, 89, 101, 124, 133
iron 119
  Late Bronze Age 30–1
  I 49
  III 75, 79
  IVA 90, 95
  6th century 138
ivory 26

jewellery:
  I 34
  III 80, 106
  6th century 130
Johnston, A. 184
Juno 164
Jupiter 164
  Jupiter Latiaris 219–20
  see also Rome, temples: Jupiter Optimus Maximus, Jupiter Stator

kalator 169–71
king, kingship 168–70, 173–8, 185–6

Lake Regillus, battle of 157, 203, 206–7, 210, 211, 218
land tenure 191–2, 196
Lanuvium 111, 136–7, 188, 197, 245–6
Lars Porsenna 165
La Rustica 57, 78
Latinienses 36
Latin League 216–23
Lavinium (Pratica di Mare) 246
  Middle Bronze Age 34
  I 35, 43, 45
  II 55

III 77, 81
IVA 86, 90–1
6th century 132, 134–5, 208, 219–20
'Heroon of Aeneas' 195
Lelantine war 120, 221
Lemnos 149
Leucothea 145, 160–2
Livy:
  1. 56. 3: 138
  2. 10: 171
  2. 16. 4: 131 n.
  2. 20: 203
  2. 21: 207
  2. 39: 138
  5. 46: 200
  22. 18: 201
  41. 16: 132
Lucania 149
Lucumo 210
Ludi Romani 205, 222
Luni sul Mignone 27, 45–7
Lupercalia 116, 155, 172, 200
Luperci 202
Lydia 94

Macr. *Sat*. 1. 16. 7: 194
Magna Graecia 24, 28, 122, 147, 161, 164, 174, 188, 225
maiores flamines 202
Malagrotta 123
Marino (Alban Hills) 52
Mars 131, 175–8, 205
Massalia 163, 218
Mater Matuta 160–2, 219
  see also Rome, Forum Boarium, S. Omobono; Satricum
Melqart 161–2, 183
Meyer, J. 21–2
Micali painter 148
migratio 211, 214
millet 54
Minerva 164
Mitchell, R. 193
Momigliano, A. 154, 191
Mommsen, T. 192, 214
Montelius, O. 21
Monte Rovello 27
Monte S. Angelo (Arcese) 34
Morris, I. 11, 41 n., 58
Müller-Karpe, H. 21, 25, 49
Murlo 148, 159, 175
Mycenaeans, Mycenaean culture 24–9, 72, 122, 225–6

Index 287

names 192–3
Narce 45
Naucratis (Egypt) 145, 147
necropoleis 9–16, 19–20, 40, 113, 140, 145
  transition from cremation to
    inhumation 22, 37, 46, 50, 107–8,
    113, 229–30
nexum 189
Norba 137–8
Numa 158, 159, 173, 198

Octavius Mamilius 214
olives, olive oil 104, 182
Olympia 94, 149
Ops Consiva 177–8
O'Shea, J. M. 13–14
Osteria del Curato (Rome) 34
Osteria dell'Osa 247–8
  I 35, 39, 41
  II 51, 53, 54, 56, 57–71, 107–8, 123
  III 82–3
  IVA 92
  IVB 98, 195
Ostia 34, 179–81, 227
ostrich eggs 26

pagus 194, 204, 207
Palmer, R. 219
Palombara Sabina 57
Panionium 219–21
Parilia 116
patricians 170, 189–202
Paulus 226L 169
Pentapolis, *see* Hexapolis
Peroni, R. 21, 32–3
Peschiera 26
Phocaeans 163
Phoenicia, Phoenicians 72–7, 94–5, 108–9, 118, 119–20, 142, 146, 161–2, 183–4
Piediluco (Umbria) 27
pigeons 54
pigs 54, 117
Pinza, G. 52
Pithecusa 21, 74–7, 80
plebeians 165, 170, 191
Pliny *HN*:
  7. 187: 202
  16. 69. 216: 201
Plut:
  Cor. 28: 138
  Fab. Max. 1: 201
  Popl. 21: 131 n.
  Pol.:

3. 22: 184
3. 94: 201
Pontecagnano 65, 95
Pontifex Maximus 169–70
pontifices 202
population 32, 35, 41, 47, 84, 99–100, 113
Populi Albenses 36, 216–17
Porto Cesareo 75
Portunus 180–2
Potter, T. 45
pottery:
  argilla figulina 78, 122
  bucchero 17, 60, 92, 93, 104, 109, 130, 132, 138, 140, 148, 227
  chevron skyphoi 76, 109
  Etrusco-Corinthian 140, 106, 122, 132, 138, 148, 159
  Greek imported pottery 17, 19, 106, 140, 148, 149, 153, 159–60, 188;
    Attic 137, 138, 146, 171, 181, 184;
    Corinthian 132, 134–5, 159, 166;
    8th century 75–6, 80–1; proto-Corinthian 91, 92, 93;
    Spartan 135, 137, 159
  Latin impasto 18; I 38, 40–1; II 62–3;
    III 77–8; IVA 90, 93; 6th
    century 135, 138, 140
  use of wheel 78, 109
Po Valley 24, 25, 26
POxy 2088: 154 n., 206, 208
Praeneste (Palestrina) 248–9
  Late Bronze Age 34
  II 56
  7th century graves 17, 20, 21, 85, 93–7, 120, 124, 195, 226
  4th century 220
prestige goods 14–15, 19–20, 75, 85–6, 89, 93–7, 106–14, 119, 225
Privernum 132
Proto-Villanovan culture 12, 22, 29, 33, 42, 45–6
Publius Valerius Publicola 173–4, 236–7
  see also Satricum, inscription
Purcell, N. 117
Pyrgi 145–7, 160–2

rex, *see* king
rex sacrorum 169, 174, 202
Richard, J-C. 191
Ridgway, D. 12, 30, 76
Rieti 57
Riserva del Truglio (Alban Hills) 90–1

Index

Rome 249–52
 Middle Bronze Age 34
 I 34, 45, 122–3
 II 49–54, 56
 III 79–81, 83
 IVA 85
 IVB 100
 Aedes Larum 173
 Ara Maxima 161, 164, 182, 199, 220
 Arch of Augustus 35
 Arx 171, 172
 Carinae 171
 Cloaca Maxima 101, 158
 Domus Aurea 162
 Esquiline 159
 Esquiline necropolis: II 52–3, 63;
    III 80; IVA 89
 Fagutal 172
 Ficus Ruminalis 177
 Forum 101–3, 158, 166–78; Ara
    Saturni 102, 165, 166–78;
    Comitium 102, 158, 166–78;
    Curia Hostilia 102, 166–78;
    Graecostasis 167; Lapis
    Niger 102, 131, 132, 167–71, 185;
    necropolis 35, 50–4, 101, 174;
    Volcanal 102, 165, 166–78
 Forum of Augustus 35
 Forum Boarium 179–83;
    S. Omobono 79–80, 102, 144,
    159–62, 219; walls 155, 181–2
 Lacus Curtius 158
 Lacus Juturnae 158, 165
 Lucus Streniae 172
 Lupercal 158; see also Lupercalia
 Mundus 177
 murus terreus 81, 152, 154
 Palatine: Domus Augustana 81, 101;
    House of Livia 35; huts 81, 101
 Pomerium 154–5, 181–2, 220
 Pons Sublicius 180
 Porta Mugonia 172
 Quirinal: necropolis 53, 80; votive
    deposits 158
 Regia: I 35; II 52 n.; IVB 102; 6th
    century 144, 172, 173–8, 205
 roads: Clivus Capitolinus 172; Via
    Appia 179; Via Campana 180;
    Via Nova 171–8; Via
    Praenestina 179; Via Sacra
    III 80; Via Sacra IVA 89; Via
    Sacra 6th century 85, 155, 171–8;
    Via Salaria 179–80; Vicus
 Cuprius 172; Vicus
    Iugarius 172; Vicus Orbius 172;
    Vicus Sceleratus 172; Vicus
    Tuscus 172
 Tabernae Veteres 178
 temples: Ceres Liber Liberaque 165;
    Diana (Aventine) 163, 173,
    217–18; Dioscuri (Temple of
    Castor) 165, 222; Fides
    (Capitol) 163; Fors Fortuna
    (Porta Portese) 162, 180; Juno
    (Arx) 163; Juno Lucina
    (Cispian) 163; Juno Sospita
    (Palatine) 163; Jupiter Optimus
    Maximus (Capitoline) 164;
    Jupiter Stator (Forum) 173;
    Mercury (Aventine) 165;
    Quirinus (Quirinal) 163; Semo
    Sancus (Quirinal) 163; Vesta
    (Forum) 102, 159, 172
 Tigillum Sororium 81
 Tullianum 158
 Turris Mamilia 178
 Velia 81, 155, 173
Romulus 173, 192, 197
Rosella 178

Sabina, Sabines 34, 37, 40 n., 56, 131,
    145, 163
Sacerdos Cabensis 222
Sacerdos Caenensis 222
Sacravienses 176
Säflund, G. 153
Salii 202
salt 179–80
San Giovenale 27, 45–7
sanctuaries, *see* temples
Santis, A. de 78
Sardinia 24, 25–6, 28, 74, 123, 224, 228
Sasso di Furbara 39
Satricum 253
 II 54, 55
 III 77, 81, 83
 IVA 86, 87–8, 90
 IVB 100, 103, 111, 124
 6th century 132, 138–40, 144, 186, 187,
    219
 inscription 192, 198, 235–7
Satyrion 75
Scoglio del Tonno 75
Septimontium 155
Sergius Fidenas, L. 208
Servius Ad *Aen.* 10. 316: 201

Index

Servius Tullius 81, 146, 150–1, 159–62, 172–3, 183, 198, 203–9
sheep 54, 62, 117, 182
Sherratt, A. 118–20
shipwrecks 25, 74
　Cape Gelidonyia 28
　Giglio 145
Sicily 24, 28, 29, 47, 147, 149, 164
Siewert, P. 206
Signia 138
silver 79, 85, 92, 95
Smith, T. R. 73, 121–2
Sol 202
Solinus 1. 21. 6: 173
Solon 187, 190–1, 204
South Italy, *see* Magna Graecia
spindle-whorls 39, 41, 63, 91
spinning 41, 63
Spurius Cassius 165
Stoddart, S. 48
Suburanenses 176
suodales 198
Suovetaurilia 116
Symmachus (330.10 Seeck) 201

Tabulae Iguvinae 197
Tac. *Ann*. 2. 41, 15. 23: 202.
Tarquinia 24, 46–8, 53, 55, 120, 145–8, 210
Tarquinius Priscus 150–1, 173, 178, 186
Tarquinius Superbus 101, 150–1, 164, 173, 186, 210
temples 141–2, 158–65, 186–8, 215–23
　Ardea 136, 219
　Circeii 138
　Gabii 87, 132, 219, 222
　Graviscia 146–7
　Lanuvium 87
　Lavinium 134–5, 219
　Norba 138
　Pyrgi 145–7
　Satricum 87, 101, 138–40, 219
　Signia 138
　Tusculum 219
　Velletri 87
　see also Rome, temples
Terni-Acciaierie 38, 40, 42
terracotta decoration 129–30, 132, 135, 136–7, 139–40, 144, 147, 159, 174, 205
Thefarie Velianas 146
Theseus 174
Thuc. 1. 6: 94
Tibur (Tivoli) 253–4

Middle Bronze Age 34
　I 34
　II 54, 56–7
　III 77, 78
4th century 220
tin 26, 28
Tolfa-Allumiere 31, 38, 39, 42, 46, 49, 90, 120
Toms, J. 22
Tor de Cenci 99, 123, 194–5, 204, 209, 255
Torelli, M. 144, 147
Torre del Michelicchio 75
Torre Galli 75
Torre S. Anastasio (Lavinium) 55
Torrino 77, 255
town planning 130, 141, 143
transhumance 116–17
tribes:
　Aemilia 194
　Claudia 131, 206
　Clustumina 131, 206, 208
　Fabia 206, 208
　Galeria 208
　Romilia 208
　Romulean 196
　Servian 203–10
　Veturia 94
trittyes 207
triumph 102, 205
Tullia 172
Tullus Hostilius 173, 217
Turan 146
turtles 54
Tuscania 48, 143
Tusculum 56, 176, 208, 217, 219
　see also Octavius Mamilius; Rome, Turris Mamilia
Tutienses 36
Twelve Tables 110, 187, 192, 211

Uni 146, 149, 160–2

Valvisciolo 137, 255
Vediovis 201–2
Veii 47, 51, 53, 56, 76, 80–1, 131, 143, 152, 154, 179–80, 182, 188
Velitrae (Velletri) 56, 137, 159
Vestal Virgins 159
　see also Rome, temples, Vesta
Vetulonia 95
Villa Cavaletti (Alban Hills) 35, 39–40

Villanovan culture 11, 12, 22, 29–30, 44, 45–6
Volaterra 148
Volscians 140
votive deposits 102, 121, 131
   Gabii 132
   Lavinium 134–5
   Rome 158–60
   Satricum 139
   Valvisciolo 137
   Velitrae 137
Vulci 48, 55

Ward-Perkins, J. 47–8
warfare, *see* army
weapons:
   I 34, 39
   II 56, 62, 64
   III 80, 83
   IVA 91, 92
   6th century 136
   in graves 14, 43, 107, 110–11
   in hoards 38
wheat 54
Whitley, J. 195
wills 169–71
   see also Comitia Calata; *commercium*
wine, wine-drinking 74, 87–9, 90, 95, 104, 109–10, 182, 198
Worsaae, J. 21
writing, literacy 27, 76, 103, 233–8

xenia 215